GOOGLE CLOUD PROFESSIONAL CLOUD NETWORK ENGINEER

MASTER THE EXAM: 10 PRACTICE TESTS, 500 RIGOROUS QUESTIONS, SOLID FOUNDATION, GAIN WEALTH OF INSIGHTS, EXPERT EXPLANATIONS AND ONE ULTIMATE GOAL

ANAND M
AMEENA PUBLICATIONS

DEDICATION

To the Visionaries in My Professional Odyssey

This book is dedicated to the mentors and leaders who guided me through triumph and adversity in my professional universe. Your guidance has illuminated the path to success and taught me to seize opportunities and surmount obstacles. Thank you for imparting the advice to those who taught me the value of strategic thinking and the significance of innovation to transform obstacles into stepping stones. Your visionary leadership has inspired my creativity and motivated me to forge new paths.

Thank you for sharing the best and worst of your experiences with me, kind and severe employers. As I present this book to the world, I am aware that you have been my inspiration. All of your roles as mentors, advisors, and even occasional adversaries have helped me become a better professional and storyteller.

This dedication is a tribute to your impact on my journey, a narrative woven with threads of gratitude, introspection, and profound gratitude for the lessons you've inscribed into my story.

With deep gratitude and enduring respect,
Anand M

FROM TECH TO LIFE SKILLS – MY EBOOKS COLLECTION

Dive into my rich collection of eBooks, curated meticulously across diverse and essential domains.

Pro Tips and Tricks Series: Empower yourself with life-enhancing skills and professional essentials with our well-crafted guides.

Hot IT Certifications and Tech Series: Stay ahead in the tech game. Whether you're eyeing certifications in AWS, PMP, or prompt engineering, harnessing the power of ChatGPT with tools like Excel, PowerPoint, Word, and more!, we've got you covered!

Essential Life Skills: Embark on a journey within. From yoga to holistic well-being, Master the art of culinary, baking, and more delve deep and rediscover yourself.

Stay Updated & Engaged
For an entire world of my knowledge, tips, and treasures, follow me on Amazon
https://www.amazon.com/author/anandm

Your Feedback Matters!
Your support, feedback, and ratings are the wind beneath my wings. It drives me to curate content that brings immense value to every aspect of life. Please take a moment to share your thoughts and rate the books. Together, let's keep the flame of knowledge burning bright!

★★★★½

Best Regards,

ANAND M

INTRODUCTION

Embark on your transformative journey to mastering the **Google Cloud Professional Cloud Network Engineer exam** with our essential guide, *"GOOGLE CLOUD PROFESSIONAL CLOUD NETWORK ENGINEER - MASTER THE EXAM."* This indispensable resource is designed to be your ultimate companion in achieving success, offering an extensive array of tools including **10 meticulously crafted practice tests, encompassing a total of 500 challenging and insightful questions**. Each question is carefully constructed to not only challenge your understanding but also to deepen your knowledge and insight into the complex world of Google Cloud Networking.

In the ever-evolving realm of cloud technology, obtaining a Google Cloud certification isn't just an achievement; it's a clear demonstration of your expertise and proficiency in the field. Securing the title of a Google Cloud Certified Professional Cloud Network Engineer marks you as an expert, proficient in the critical and intricate aspects of networking within the Google Cloud environment. Whether you are an experienced professional seeking to validate your skills or a newcomer embarking on a journey into the world of cloud networking, this book lays a comprehensive and robust foundation.

Each question in our guide is accompanied by detailed expert explanations, clarifying complex concepts and providing valuable strategies and insights for your exam preparation. These explanations ensure that your understanding of Google Cloud Networking is not only thorough but also nuanced, helping you navigate the subtleties of this challenging field.

In today's digitally driven world, where cloud computing is at the forefront of innovation and business efficiency, holding a Google Cloud Professional Cloud Network Engineer certification distinguishes you in the competitive realm of cloud computing. Whether your goal is to excel as a Cloud Network Engineer, a Google Cloud Architect, or to deepen your expertise in Google Cloud's networking solutions, this book is a crucial stepping stone on your path to becoming a certified expert.

Key Exam Details:

Duration: The exam is structured to be completed in two hours, testing your knowledge and skills effectively.

Registration Fee: A registration fee of $200 (plus applicable taxes) is required to sit for the exam.

Language: The exam is conducted exclusively in English, ensuring a consistent testing standard.

Exam Format: Comprising 50-60 questions, the exam utilizes multiple-choice and multiple-select formats, meticulously designed to evaluate both your practical skills and theoretical understanding. The exam is proctored and adheres to Google's rigorous standards.

Start your journey towards mastering the Google Cloud Professional Cloud Network Engineer certification with this guide as your comprehensive resource, lighting your path to success in the exam. Your pursuit of becoming a certified expert in Google Cloud Networking begins here.

ADVANTAGES OF CERTIFICATION

Before delving into the complexities of the **Google Cloud Professional Cloud Network Engineer** exam, it's crucial to understand the significant benefits that come with this prestigious certification. As you embark on your journey to earn the Google Cloud Professional Cloud Network Engineer credential, consider these compelling advantages:

Enhanced Professional Recognition: In the dynamic and rapidly advancing field of cloud technology, Google Cloud is a leading player. Obtaining the Google Cloud Professional Cloud Network Engineer certification places you in an elite group of cloud network professionals. It not only validates your skills and expertise in a critical area of cloud technology but also acts as a testament to your extensive understanding of Google Cloud's networking tools and practices. This certification distinguishes you in the industry, boosting your professional recognition.

Career Advancement and Opportunities: This certification is more than a testament to your proficiency; it is a reflection of your commitment and depth of knowledge in cloud networking within the Google Cloud environment. It acts as a springboard for professional development, often leading to more challenging roles and senior positions in cloud networking and computing.

Financial Benefits: Specialized certifications typically lead to increased earning potential. The Google Cloud Professional Cloud Network Engineer certification is associated with higher salary prospects, offering significant returns on your investment of time and effort.

Competitive Edge in the Job Market: In the highly competitive IT and cloud computing landscape, this certification sets you apart. It strategically positions you for roles that match your expertise and career goals, making you an attractive candidate for top-tier positions.

In-Depth Knowledge and Practical Experience: Beyond theoretical knowledge, this certification emphasizes practical skills in designing, implementing, and managing networks within the Google Cloud ecosystem. As a certified professional, you will excel in creating efficient, secure, and scalable network solutions, demonstrating an expertise that goes beyond basic understanding.

Networking and Community Engagement: Earning this certification connects you with a global community of professionals in the same field. This network acts as a valuable platform for collaboration, sharing knowledge, and exploring new career opportunities, greatly enhancing your professional development.

In summary, the Google Cloud Professional Cloud Network Engineer certification is a transformative step in your career. It not only elevates your status in the realm of cloud networking but also equips you with the skills, knowledge, and network necessary to confidently face the ever-changing landscape of cloud computing and networking.

CONTENTS

PRACTICE TEST 1 - QUESTIONS ONLY

QUESTION 1

You are responsible for setting up a global load balancer in Google Cloud to distribute traffic to multiple regions. Which GCP service should you use for this purpose, considering both performance and availability?

A) Google Cloud CDN
B) Google Cloud DNS
C) Google Cloud Storage
D) Google Cloud Load Balancing
E) Google Cloud Identity and Access Management (IAM)

QUESTION 2

Your organization has multiple projects in Google Cloud, and you need to establish secure and controlled communication between them. What should you set up to achieve this while ensuring isolation and maintaining control over traffic flow?

A) VPC Peering between projects
B) VPN tunnels between projects
C) Shared VPC with Host Projects
D) VPC Network Peering between projects
E) Google Cloud Interconnect between projects.

QUESTION 3

Your organization is planning to set up a hybrid cloud architecture, with some applications running in Google Cloud and others on-premises. Security and data privacy are top priorities. What GCP service should you use to establish a secure and private connection between your on-premises data center and Google Cloud while ensuring minimal latency?

A) Google Cloud VPN
B) Google Cloud Dedicated Interconnect
C) Google Cloud Interconnect
D) Google Cloud VPC Peering
E) Google Cloud CDN

QUESTION 4

Your company has recently implemented Identity-Aware Proxy (IAP) for secure access to Google Cloud resources. You want to grant external contractors access to specific Compute Engine instances without exposing them to unnecessary resources. What is the most efficient and secure way to achieve this?

A) Add external contractors to a Google Group, then create IAM roles to allow access to specific

Compute Engine instances based on membership in the group.

 B) Share individual SSH keys with external contractors and add their SSH keys to the Compute Engine instances' metadata.

 C) Grant the external contractors the Compute Engine Admin role to manage their own access.

 D) Enable the "Allow HTTP traffic" and "Allow HTTPS traffic" options on the Compute Engine instances to allow external access.

 E) Create separate VPCs for external contractors and use VPC Network Peering to connect them to the internal network.

QUESTION 5

Your organization requires a cost-effective solution for secure connectivity to Google Cloud over the RFC 1918 address space. You also anticipate data processing workloads spiking to 2 Gbps during heavy analytics operations. Which option should you consider?

A) Set up a Cloud VPN with multiple redundant tunnels.
B) Use Google Cloud Dedicated Interconnect for primary connectivity and VPN as a backup.
C) Deploy a dedicated fiber optic link for maximum bandwidth.
D) Opt for a Direct Peering connection with Google Cloud.
E) Utilize a Content Delivery Network (CDN) for data transfer.

QUESTION 6

Your organization is planning to migrate a legacy on-premises application to Google Cloud, and you need to ensure seamless connectivity between the on-premises data center and Google Cloud resources. What networking approach should you consider?

A) Deploy multiple Cloud VPNs with IPsec encryption for secure connectivity.
B) Utilize Google Cloud Dedicated Interconnect for dedicated, high-speed connectivity.
C) Implement hybrid DNS solutions to route traffic between on-premises and Google Cloud resources.
D) Set up Direct Peering between the on-premises data center and Google Cloud.
E) Establish private fiber optic links for point-to-point connectivity.

QUESTION 7

In a multi-regional GCP setup, you need to ensure low latency and high availability for your services. Your application is hosted in us-east1 and europe-west1. How should you configure your network for optimal performance?

A) Use a single VPC with subnets in both regions.
B) Deploy dedicated Interconnects in each region.
C) Implement Cloud CDN for content distribution.
D) Use Cloud Load Balancing with a multi-regional backend service.
E) Set up VPC Peering between the two regions.

QUESTION 8

Your company's global IT infrastructure spans multiple Google Cloud projects and VPCs. To simplify network management, you want to establish centralized control over routing and traffic between these projects and VPCs. What Google Cloud networking solution should you implement?

A) Create a Cloud VPN tunnel between all projects and VPCs to establish private communication channels.
B) Set up Shared VPC to centrally manage routing and traffic across all projects and VPCs.
C) Implement Cloud Interconnect to connect all projects and VPCs via dedicated and high-speed connections.
D) Configure a Google Cloud NAT gateway in each project and VPC to manage traffic routing.
E) Utilize VPC Network Peering to establish direct connections between projects and VPCs for simplified routing.

QUESTION 9

Your organization is expanding its presence on Google Cloud, and you need to ensure that your applications can seamlessly scale while maintaining high availability. Which architectural approach should you consider for your Google Cloud deployment?

A) Deploy all services in a single Google Cloud region to minimize latency.
B) Utilize multiple Google Cloud projects for isolation and security.
C) Implement microservices architecture to decouple components.
D) Use Google Kubernetes Engine (GKE) for container orchestration.
E) Set up a global load balancer with multi-region backend services.

QUESTION 10

Your organization manages several VPC networks on Google Cloud, each dedicated to different projects. You need to establish private connectivity between these VPCs while ensuring internet access and connecting to an external data center. What is the most suitable approach?

A) Create a VPC Peering connection between each VPC.
B) Set up a central hub VPC and configure VPC Peering connections from all project VPCs to the hub VPC.
C) Use Cloud Interconnect Dedicated for private connectivity.
D) Deploy Cloud VPN for secure connectivity between projects.
E) Merge all VPCs into a single VPC architecture.

QUESTION 11

Your organization is migrating a complex, multi-tier application to Google Cloud. The application consists of web servers, application servers, and a database server. To ensure high availability and scalability, you need to architect a solution that distributes workloads across multiple instances and can automatically recover from instance failures. What Google Cloud service or feature should you consider for this complex application architecture, and what advantages does it offer?

A) Google Cloud Kubernetes Engine (GKE) for containerized application deployment.
B) Google Cloud Compute Engine with auto-scaling managed instance groups.
C) Google Cloud App Engine for platform-managed application deployment.
D) Google Cloud Load Balancing with health checks and auto-healing capabilities.
E) Google Cloud Endpoints for API management and load balancing.

QUESTION 12

You are tasked with designing a network architecture for a data analytics platform in GCP that must ensure data isolation and high throughput between computational resources and databases. The platform will be deployed across multiple projects within the same organization. What is the most effective network design for this scenario?

A) Implement Shared VPC for centralized management across projects.
B) Use VPC Peering between each project's network.
C) Set up dedicated VPCs for each project with Cloud VPN for interconnectivity.
D) Deploy a Dedicated Interconnect for each project.
E) Create a single VPC with separate subnets for each project.

QUESTION 13

For a global e-commerce platform running on GKE, you need to set up a reliable and efficient content delivery mechanism. The platform is heavily accessed from various geographical locations. Which combination of GCP services and configurations should you use?

A) Implement multi-regional GKE clusters and use Cloud CDN.
B) Set up a single regional GKE cluster and configure Cloud CDN with Cloud Load Balancing.
C) Deploy global GKE clusters and utilize Cloud Armor for content delivery.
D) Use regional GKE clusters with dedicated Interconnects for each region.
E) Create a multi-regional GKE cluster and implement Global Load Balancing with Cloud Armor.

QUESTION 14

You are responsible for securing a Google Cloud project that processes sensitive customer data. The project involves multiple virtual machines in a VPC. To enhance security, you want to isolate workloads within the VPC and prevent unauthorized communication between instances. Which GCP networking feature should you recommend?

A) Google Cloud Firewall Rules
B) Google Cloud VPN with dedicated tunnels
C) Google Cloud VPC Service Controls
D) Google Cloud Network Peering
E) Google Cloud Shared VPC

QUESTION 15

For a GCP-hosted web application, you need to configure the firewall to ensure only HTTPS traffic reaches your front-end servers, while allowing unrestricted access from a set of internal IP addresses for administration. What is the best firewall configuration for this setup?

A) Allow ingress on port 443 from any source and all traffic from internal IPs.
B) Deny all ingress except on port 443 and allow all egress.
C) Allow ingress on ports 80 and 443, and all traffic from internal IPs.
D) Implement stateful inspection for all ingress and egress traffic.
E) Deny all egress and allow ingress on port 443 and from internal IPs.

QUESTION 16

Your organization is planning to expand its Google Cloud infrastructure globally to accommodate increased demand. You want to ensure low-latency access for users across the world. What GCP networking strategy should you recommend for this expansion?

A) Establish a single global VPC to centralize resources.
B) Deploy multiple regional VPCs in key geographical locations.
C) Utilize Google Cloud Load Balancers for global traffic distribution.
D) Implement Google Cloud VPN for secure connections.
E) Use Google Cloud CDN for content delivery.

QUESTION 17

Your organization is planning to deploy a web application that requires global low-latency access and high availability. What GCP networking solution should you recommend for optimizing user experience and minimizing downtime?

A) Use a single regional VPC for resource deployment.
B) Implement Google Cloud CDN for content delivery.
C) Utilize Google Cloud VPN for secure access.
D) Set up Google Cloud Load Balancing with global anycast IP addresses.
E) Create multiple independent VPCs in different regions.

QUESTION 18

You are responsible for optimizing your organization's Google Cloud costs. One of your strategies is to analyze and optimize the usage of Google Kubernetes Engine (GKE) clusters. What should you consider when implementing an autoscaling policy for GKE nodes?

A) Autoscale based solely on CPU utilization.
B) Autoscale based on both CPU and memory utilization.
C) Implement a fixed-size node pool to minimize costs.
D) Use custom metrics from Stackdriver Monitoring for autoscaling.
E) Disable autoscaling to maintain cost predictability.

QUESTION 19

As the Organization Admin for a multinational corporation, an engineer in your team is tasked with deploying several main storage buckets across different departments and enabling uniform access to service accounts. You need to configure the Identity and Access Management (IAM) settings for the engineer so they can accomplish this with minimal effort. What action should you take?

A) Provide the engineer with the Storage Admin IAM role and Project IAM Admin role at the organization level.
B) Assign the engineer the Storage Admin IAM role at the department level.
C) Grant the engineer both the Storage Admin IAM role and Project IAM Admin role at the department level.
D) Assign the engineer the Storage Admin IAM role at the organization level.
E) Create a custom IAM role with the required permissions for the engineer.

QUESTION 20

As the Organization Admin for a multinational corporation, an engineer in your team is tasked with deploying several main storage buckets across different departments and enabling uniform access to service accounts. You need to configure the Identity and Access Management (IAM) settings for the engineer so they can accomplish this with minimal effort. What action should you take?

A) Provide the engineer with the Storage Admin IAM role and Project IAM Admin role at the organization level.
B) Assign the engineer the Storage Admin IAM role at the department level.
C) Grant the engineer both the Storage Admin IAM role and Project IAM Admin role at the department level.
D) Assign the engineer the Storage Admin IAM role at the organization level.
E) Create a custom IAM role for the engineer with specific permissions.

QUESTION 21

You want to set up a high-bandwidth link to Google Cloud that can reach Cloud Storage with a private IP address and that does not require an intermediary vendor. Which connection method should you select?

A) Carrier Peering
B) Partner Interconnect
C) Dedicated Interconnect
D) Direct Peering

QUESTION 22

As the Organization Admin for a multinational corporation, an engineer in your team is tasked with deploying several main storage buckets across different departments and enabling uniform access to service accounts. You need to configure the Identity and Access Management (IAM) settings for the engineer so they can accomplish this with minimal effort. What action should you take?

A) Provide the engineer with the Storage Admin IAM role and Project IAM Admin role at the organization level.
B) Assign the engineer the Storage Admin IAM role at the department level.
C) Grant the engineer both the Storage Admin IAM role and Project IAM Admin role at the department level.
D) Assign the engineer the Storage Admin IAM role at the organization level.
E) Create a custom IAM role with the necessary permissions.

QUESTION 23

You are deploying a multi-tier web application in GCP and need to ensure that only legitimate web traffic reaches your backend services. The application requires protection against DDoS attacks and web-based exploits. What configuration should you use to achieve these security objectives?

A) Set up Cloud Armor with a security policy targeting an external HTTP(S) load balancer.
B) Implement a series of VPC firewall rules to filter traffic based on source IPs and protocols.
C) Configure a Cloud VPN to create an encrypted tunnel for web traffic.
D) Use Private Google Access to restrict web traffic to authorized sources only.

E) Create a custom routing policy in your VPC to direct web traffic through a security inspection service.

QUESTION 24

Your company is planning to set up a hybrid cloud environment with Google Cloud Platform (GCP) and an on-premises data center. The goal is to establish secure and high-speed connectivity between GCP and the data center. What two solutions should you recommend for achieving this objective?

A) Use Cloud VPN to create a site-to-site VPN connection.
B) Implement Dedicated Interconnect for a dedicated, high-bandwidth connection.
C) Deploy an additional layer of security by setting up a Bastion Host in the data center.
D) Utilize Google Cloud CDN for data caching between GCP and the data center.
E) Set up Google Cloud Router for dynamic routing between the two environments.

QUESTION 25

Your organization is using Google Cloud's Identity and Access Management (IAM) to manage permissions for Google Cloud resources. You want to grant a group of users the ability to create and manage virtual machine instances in a specific project, but you want to restrict them from making changes to IAM roles and permissions. Which IAM role should you assign to this group to meet these requirements?

A) Compute Admin
B) Security Admin
C) Compute Instance Admin (v1)
D) IAM Role Viewer
E) Project Editor

QUESTION 26

You're implementing a secure connection between GCP and multiple external cloud providers. The goal is to facilitate secure and efficient communication between services hosted on GCP and those on other cloud platforms. What approach should you adopt for this setup?

A) Use Dedicated Interconnect for each connection to external cloud providers.
B) Set up Cloud VPN tunnels from GCP to each external cloud provider.
C) Implement VPC Network Peering with each external cloud provider.
D) Configure Private Google Access for secure communication with external services.
E) Establish a series of Cloud Routers with custom routes for each external cloud provider.

QUESTION 27

As part of your infrastructure expansion to Google Cloud, you need to ensure that on-premises data centers in Germany and Japan with Dedicated Interconnects are linked to Google Cloud regions europe-west3 and asia-northeast1. What should be your approach?

A) Configure Dedicated Interconnects directly to VPCs in the respective regions.
B) Establish Dedicated Interconnects in the central hub region (europe-west3) and leverage Interconnect attachments.
C) Deploy a separate VPN connection for each data center.

D) Use Cloud Interconnect for cost-effective connectivity.
E) None of the above.

QUESTION 28

In a GCP environment, you need to set up a high-performance connection between your Compute Engine instances and a BigQuery dataset for real-time analytics. The Compute Engine instances and the BigQuery dataset are in different regions. What is the most effective setup for this requirement?

A) Utilize Dedicated Interconnect for low-latency inter-region communication.
B) Set up VPC Peering between the regions hosting the Compute Engine instances and BigQuery.
C) Configure each Compute Engine instance with Premium Network Tier for optimized network performance.
D) Implement a Global Load Balancer to route traffic efficiently between Compute Engine and BigQuery.
E) Use Cloud VPN with dynamic routing for secure and efficient data transfer.

QUESTION 29

Your organization is responsible for a Google Cloud project containing numerous App Engine applications. You must secure API access to Memorystore instances and Spanner databases, allowing traffic only from your organization's head office networks. What is the most suitable approach for achieving this goal?

A) Formulate an access context policy for each individual App Engine application, specifying head office network IP ranges, and apply these policies to Memorystore and Spanner.
B) Establish a VPC Service Controls perimeter for your project with an access context policy encompassing your organization's head office network IP ranges.
C) Create separate VPC Service Controls perimeters for each App Engine application, each with access context policies defining your organization's head office network IP ranges.
D) Define a series of firewall rules to block API access to Memorystore and Spanner from networks not recognized as part of your head office.
E) None of the above.

QUESTION 30

Your enterprise manages a single Google Cloud project with a multitude of App Engine applications. You are tasked with safeguarding API access to your Memorystore instances and Spanner databases to ensure that only API traffic from your organization's head office networks is permitted. How should you proceed?

A) Establish an access context policy that includes your App Engine applications and head office network IP ranges, and then implement the policy for Memorystore and Spanner.
B) Create a VPC Service Controls perimeter for your project with an access context policy that includes your organization's head office network IP ranges.
C) Generate a VPC Service Controls perimeter for each App Engine application with an access context policy that includes your organization's head office network IP ranges.
D) Configure a firewall rule to reject API access to Memorystore and Spanner from all networks not recognized as part of your head office.
E) None of the above.

QUESTION 31

You manage a series of IoT devices within a secure network in an existing Google Cloud Virtual Private Cloud (VPC). You're tasked with integrating additional data processing components using Cloud Run and Cloud Functions to process information from the IoT devices. The network traffic load between your serverless data processors and the IoT devices is minimal. Each serverless component must ensure seamless communication with any of the IoT devices. Your goal is to deploy a solution that minimizes costs. What should you do?

A) Deploy your serverless data processing components directly into the secure network of the existing VPC. Create firewall rules to allow traffic from Cloud Run and Cloud Functions to the IoT devices.
B) Generate a dedicated VPC for each serverless component and set up VPC peering between them and the existing VPC. Implement routing and firewall rules to control communication.
C) Create a VPN connection between the serverless data processing components and the IoT devices to ensure secure communication. Set up custom routes to optimize traffic.
D) Implement a Global Load Balancer to distribute traffic efficiently between the serverless data processing components and the IoT devices.
E) None of the above.

QUESTION 32

You are tasked with enhancing the security of a GCP environment that hosts several web applications. These applications are exposed to the internet and need protection against common web exploits and DDoS attacks. What combination of GCP services should you use to secure these applications?

A) Implement Cloud Armor with security policies attached to Global HTTP(S) Load Balancers.
B) Use Cloud VPN with strong encryption for all incoming traffic to the applications.
C) Configure VPC Service Controls around the applications for isolation.
D) Set up Network Load Balancers with Cloud IDS for each application.
E) Utilize Cloud Endpoints with security policies for API-based applications.

QUESTION 33

You are designing a network architecture for a financial institution that requires strict compliance and security measures. The organization operates multiple VPCs, each dedicated to different business units. What network architecture should you implement to ensure secure and compliant communication between these VPCs while minimizing exposure to external threats?

A) Use Shared VPC with custom routing and firewall rules to control traffic between VPCs.
B) Deploy a separate VPN tunnel between each VPC to isolate communication.
C) Establish VPC Peering connections between all VPCs to enable secure communication.
D) Create a single VPC for all business units to centralize network security and compliance measures.
E) None of the above.

QUESTION 34

Your organization is planning to establish a hybrid cloud setup, with some workloads hosted in Google Cloud and others on-premises. You need a secure and reliable connection between the two environments. What complex networking solution should you design to achieve this goal?

A) Cloud VPN with BGP
B) Dedicated Interconnect with VPC Peering
C) Cloud Interconnect with Direct Peering
D) Transit Gateway with VPN Gateway
E) VPC Peering with Cloud Router

QUESTION 35

Your organization is managing a complex multi-tier application architecture that spans multiple subnets, and you need to ensure precise traffic routing for specific components. What is the most appropriate approach to achieve this complex network configuration?

A) Set up custom routes with more precision than the default network routes, specifying the next hops for each component without network tags.
B) Reconfigure the application architecture to consolidate all components within a single subnet, simplifying the routing requirements.
C) Delete all default network routes and establish distinct custom routes for each component with network tags to differentiate traffic.
D) Create more specific custom routes than the default network routes, designating next hops for each component, and assign network tags for precise routing.
E) Implement a Cloud Router to dynamically manage routing between components and subnets.

QUESTION 36

You need to design a network for a set of applications in GCP that require low-latency communication with each other but must be isolated from the internet. Additionally, these applications need to access Google Cloud services such as BigQuery and Cloud Storage. What network configuration should you implement?

A) Use Private Google Access with VPC firewall rules to restrict internet access and enable internal communication.
B) Configure VPC Service Controls to isolate applications and Google Cloud services within a secure perimeter.
C) Set up Internal TCP/UDP Load Balancer for inter-application communication and Private Google Access for Cloud services.
D) Implement Shared VPC for the applications with custom routes for inter-service communication and Private Google Access.
E) Create separate subnets for each application, configure VPC peering for inter-service communication, and use Cloud VPN for Cloud services access.

QUESTION 37

You are configuring a network for a set of applications in GCP that require secure, low-latency access to Cloud Spanner databases across multiple regions. What network configuration best supports low-latency and secure database access?

A) Use Cloud VPN for secure, encrypted connections to Cloud Spanner.

B) Configure Cloud Interconnect for direct, low-latency access to Cloud Spanner.
C) Enable Private Google Access on the subnetworks for secure, internal access to Cloud Spanner.
D) Implement VPC Peering with the Cloud Spanner network for optimal connectivity.
E) Set up dedicated VPCs for each application with custom routes to Cloud Spanner.

QUESTION 38

You are responsible for setting up a secure, private network connection between two Google Cloud Virtual Private Clouds (VPCs) located in different regions. Your goal is to minimize latency while maintaining encryption and isolation. Which Google Cloud networking solution should you implement to achieve these objectives?

A) Google Cloud VPN with VPC peering
B) Cloud Interconnect with Google Cloud Router
C) VPC peering with Cloud VPN
D) Cloud DNS with Cloud CDN
E) Google Cloud Load Balancing with VPC Service Controls

QUESTION 39

You are managing a Google Cloud project with multiple VPCs, and you need to ensure secure communication between them. Additionally, you want to control routing between VPCs for specific services. Which Google Cloud networking feature should you implement to achieve these objectives effectively?

A) Google Cloud VPN with VPC peering
B) VPC Service Controls with Cloud NAT
C) Google Cloud VPN with Cloud Identity-Aware Proxy (IAP)
D) Shared VPC with VPC peering
E) Google Cloud Load Balancing with VPC Service Controls

QUESTION 40

You are tasked with designing a highly available architecture for your organization's mission-critical application on Google Cloud. The application must withstand regional failures and maintain low latency. Which combination of Google Cloud services or features should you incorporate into your design to achieve these objectives effectively?

A) Google Cloud VPN and Google Cloud Storage
B) Google Cloud Load Balancing and Google Cloud Pub/Sub
C) Google Cloud Spanner and Google Cloud CDN
D) Google Cloud Interconnect and Google Cloud Armor
E) Google Cloud VPC Peering and Google Cloud Bigtable

QUESTION 41

Your organization operates a multi-tier application on Google Cloud that requires horizontal scaling and load balancing to handle variable workloads. You want to ensure efficient resource utilization and low-latency access for end users. Which combination of Google Cloud services or features should you implement to achieve these objectives effectively?

A) Google Cloud Dataprep and Google Cloud Filestore
B) Google Cloud Spanner and Google Cloud Identity-Aware Proxy (IAP)
C) Google Cloud CDN and Google Cloud Compute Engine Autoscaler
D) Google Cloud Spanner and Google Cloud Load Balancing
E) Google Cloud Spanner and Google Cloud VPC Peering

QUESTION 42

Your organization is planning to implement a disaster recovery solution for your critical applications on Google Cloud. You need to ensure data replication and failover capabilities between regions. Which combination of Google Cloud services or features should you incorporate into your disaster recovery strategy to achieve these objectives effectively?

A) Google Cloud VPN and Google Cloud Bigtable
B) Google Cloud CDN and Google Cloud Compute Engine Autoscaler
C) Google Cloud Spanner and Google Cloud Interconnect
D) Google Cloud Storage and Google Cloud DNS
E) Google Cloud Load Balancing and Google Cloud VPC Peering

QUESTION 43

You have implemented a pilot project on Compute Engine with instances manually configured in one zone of the finance sector. As the project transitions to a fully operational production stage, you aim to enhance the reliability of your application and provide scaling capabilities based on demand. What is the best approach to set up your instances for this purpose?

A) Configure an unmanaged instance group in a solitary zone and proceed to deploy an HTTP load balancer targeting this instance group.
B) Establish individual managed instance groups for each sector, opt for a Single zone setting, and evenly distribute your instances across various zones within the same sector.
C) Set up a regional managed instance group, designate the preferred region, and pick the option for distributing instances across multiple zones.
D) Put together separate unmanaged instance groups for every zone needed and allocate the instances among the zones on your own discretion.
E) Configure a global managed instance group across multiple zones within the finance sector.

QUESTION 44

Your organization operates a high-traffic online video streaming service. Your servers are configured with private IP addresses, and users connect through a regional load balancer. To enhance security, you've enlisted a DDoS protection service and need to limit your backend servers to accept connections solely from this DDoS mitigation provider. How should you proceed?

A) Create a VPC Service Controls Perimeter that blocks all traffic except for the DDoS protection service.
B) Create a Cloud Armor Security Policy that blocks all traffic except for the DDoS protection service.
C) Create a VPC Firewall rule that blocks all traffic except for the DDoS protection service.
D) Create a Cloud Identity-Aware Proxy (IAP) to manage backend server access for the DDoS protection

service.
E) Create a VPC Flow Log to monitor and filter traffic from the DDoS protection service.

QUESTION 45

You are managing a complex Google Cloud project with multiple VPCs connected through Cloud VPN tunnels. Recently, you have experienced intermittent connectivity issues between certain VPCs. You suspect that the Cloud VPN tunnels may be the cause. What actions should you take to troubleshoot and resolve this issue effectively?

A) Review the VPC firewall rules for each VPC.
B) Check the on-premises VPN devices for potential misconfigurations.
C) Create custom routes in each VPC to explicitly specify the routes for the remote VPCs.
D) Increase the VPN tunnel bandwidth to improve connectivity.
E) Re-create the VPN tunnels for the affected VPCs.

QUESTION 46

Your organization is considering using Google Kubernetes Engine (GKE) for container orchestration. You want to ensure high availability and minimal downtime during updates. What GKE feature or approach should you prioritize for this purpose?

A) Use Regional Clusters for automatic failover.
B) Implement Node Pools with different instance types for redundancy.
C) Employ Rolling Updates to minimize downtime during application updates.
D) Use Horizontal Pod Autoscaling to adjust the number of replicas based on traffic.
E) Set up GKE Multi-Zone Clusters for fault tolerance.

QUESTION 47

Your organization needs to establish a highly available and geographically distributed architecture for a critical application on Google Cloud. You want to ensure that the architecture can handle region-wide outages without service disruption. What Google Cloud service or feature should you leverage to achieve this level of geographical redundancy?

A) Google Cloud DNS.
B) Google Cloud Spanner.
C) Google Cloud CDN.
D) Google Cloud Pub/Sub.
E) Google Cloud Bigtable.

QUESTION 48

In a GCP environment with a complex application landscape, you need to design a network that enables secure communication between microservices deployed in multiple Kubernetes Engine clusters. The microservices require low-latency communication and should be isolated from external access. What network setup should be implemented for secure and efficient inter-microservice communication?

A) Use VPC Network Peering between the Kubernetes Engine clusters' networks.

B) Configure Internal Load Balancers in each cluster for microservices communication.

C) Implement Shared VPC across all Kubernetes Engine clusters with network policies based on labels.

D) Establish Cloud VPN tunnels between clusters for encrypted communication.

E) Set up a Global VPC with optimized routes for inter-cluster microservices communication.

QUESTION 49

For a global online application in GCP that requires low-latency database access across multiple regions, which configuration ensures optimal database performance?

A) Use Cloud Spanner for a globally distributed database.

B) Configure regional instances of Cloud SQL and route traffic based on the user's location.

C) Implement Cloud Bigtable with multi-regional setup.

D) Set up regional Cloud Memorystore instances for low-latency access.

E) Deploy Cloud Firestore in Datastore mode for global database access.

QUESTION 50

For a global online retail platform on GCP, which network configuration is most suitable to manage varying traffic loads, optimize content delivery, and provide security against web attacks, while distributing traffic efficiently to worldwide data centers?

A) Global HTTP(S) Load Balancer with Cloud Armor and Cloud CDN.

B) Regional Network Load Balancers with Cloud IDS for traffic analysis and DDoS protection.

C) TCP/SSL Proxy Load Balancers in each region with VPC Service Controls for security.

D) Internal Load Balancers in each region with Cloud VPN for global traffic management.

E) Cloud Run instances globally with Cloud Endpoints for security and traffic distribution.

PRACTICE TEST 1 - ANSWERS ONLY

QUESTION 1

Answer – D) Google Cloud Load Balancing

Option D - Using Google Cloud Load Balancing is correct because it's designed for global load balancing, ensuring both performance and availability.
Option A - Google Cloud CDN is not used for load balancing but for content delivery.
Option B - Google Cloud DNS is used for DNS resolution, not load balancing.
Option C - Google Cloud Storage is for object storage, not load balancing.
Option E - Google Cloud IAM is for access management, not load balancing.

QUESTION 2

Answer – C) Shared VPC with Host Projects

Option C - Implementing Shared VPC with Host Projects allows secure and controlled communication between projects while maintaining isolation and control over traffic flow.
Option A - VPC Peering may not provide sufficient isolation between projects.
Option B - VPN tunnels between projects can be complex to manage.
Option D - VPC Network Peering is for VPCs, not projects.
Option E - Google Cloud Interconnect is typically used for external connectivity, not inter-project communication.

QUESTION 3

Answer – B) Google Cloud Dedicated Interconnect

Option B - Using Google Cloud Dedicated Interconnect provides a secure and private connection between on-premises data centers and Google Cloud with minimal latency.
Option A - Google Cloud VPN may introduce latency and is not as dedicated as Interconnect.
Option C - Google Cloud Interconnect is related to connectivity but may not provide the same level of privacy as Dedicated Interconnect.
Option D - VPC Peering is for connecting VPCs, not on-premises data centers.
Option E - CDN is for content delivery and not suitable for direct data center connectivity.

QUESTION 4

Answer – A) Add external contractors to a Google Group, then create IAM roles to allow access to specific Compute Engine instances based on membership in the group.

Option A - Adding external contractors to a Google Group and assigning IAM roles based on group membership is the most efficient and secure way to control access to specific instances.
Option B - Sharing individual SSH keys is not scalable or secure for managing access.
Option C - Granting Compute Engine Admin roles provides excessive permissions.
Option D - Enabling HTTP/HTTPS traffic does not address secure access to instances.

Option E - Creating separate VPCs and using VPC Network Peering may be overly complex for this requirement.

QUESTION 5

Answer - B) Use Google Cloud Dedicated Interconnect for primary connectivity and VPN as a backup.

Option B is a cost-effective solution that provides the required high-speed connectivity with Google Cloud while using VPN as a backup for redundancy.
Option A may not handle the anticipated workload and lacks redundancy.
Option C is costly and may not be necessary for the given requirements.
Option D does not offer the same level of performance as Dedicated Interconnect.
Option E is more suitable for content delivery, not primary connectivity.

QUESTION 6

Answer - B) Utilize Google Cloud Dedicated Interconnect for dedicated, high-speed connectivity.

Option B provides the most appropriate networking approach to ensure seamless connectivity between on-premises data centers and Google Cloud resources, especially for high-speed, dedicated connections.
Option A mentions VPNs but does not focus on high-speed or dedicated connections.
Option C mentions DNS but doesn't provide the connectivity itself.
Option D focuses on peering, which may not guarantee the same level of performance.
Option E introduces complexity and may not be cost-effective.

QUESTION 7

Answer – D) Use Cloud Load Balancing with a multi-regional backend service.

A) Incorrect. A single VPC can lead to latency due to distance.
B) Incorrect. While Interconnects provide reliable connections, they don't address latency for distributed services.
C) Incorrect. Cloud CDN is beneficial for static content, not dynamic application traffic.
D) Correct. This ensures traffic is served from the nearest region, reducing latency.
E) Incorrect. VPC Peering does not inherently reduce latency or increase availability.

QUESTION 8

Answer - B) Set up Shared VPC to centrally manage routing and traffic across all projects and VPCs.

Option B is the correct choice as it enables centralized control over routing and traffic management across multiple projects and VPCs using Shared VPC.
Option A suggests VPN tunnels, which may not provide the level of centralization desired.
Option C talks about Cloud Interconnect, which focuses on connectivity but doesn't centralize routing control.
Option D mentions NAT gateways, which are used for address translation, not centralized routing.
Option E discusses VPC Network Peering, which creates direct connections but doesn't provide centralized routing control.

QUESTION 9

Answer - E) Set up a global load balancer with multi-region backend services.

Option E (global load balancer with multi-region backend services) is the recommended approach to ensure high availability and scalability by distributing traffic across multiple regions.
Option A (single region) may lead to latency issues.
Option B (multiple projects) can provide isolation but doesn't inherently guarantee high availability.
Option C (microservices) and Option D (GKE) are important components but do not address the overall architecture for high availability and scalability.

QUESTION 10

Answer - B) Set up a central hub VPC and configure VPC Peering connections from all project VPCs to the hub VPC.

Option A would create a complex and inefficient mesh of connections.
Option C refers to a different Google Cloud service.
Option D provides secure connectivity but doesn't address the central hub requirement.
Option B is the correct choice as it aligns with the requirements, providing a central hub for private connectivity while maintaining separate VPCs for different projects.

QUESTION 11

Answer - D) Google Cloud Load Balancing with health checks and auto-healing capabilities.

Option A is suitable for containerized applications but may require more manual configuration for auto-recovery.
Option B provides auto-scaling managed instance groups but doesn't offer native load balancing.
Option C is a platform-managed service but doesn't focus on auto-recovery.
Option E is for API management and load balancing but doesn't address auto-recovery for multi-tier applications.
Option D is the correct choice as Google Cloud Load Balancing provides health checks and auto-healing capabilities, distributing workloads and automatically recovering from instance failures, making it suitable for complex multi-tier applications.

QUESTION 12

Answer – A) Implement Shared VPC for centralized management across projects.

A) Correct. Ensures data isolation and high throughput within an organization.
B) Incorrect. VPC Peering can become complex with multiple projects.
C) Incorrect. VPNs may not provide the necessary throughput.
D) Incorrect. Overly costly and complex for intra-organizational connectivity.
E) Incorrect. Lacks the necessary data isolation between projects.

QUESTION 13

Answer – B) Set up a single regional GKE cluster and configure Cloud CDN with Cloud Load Balancing.

A) Incorrect. Multi-regional clusters are not necessary for content delivery.
B) Correct. Cloud CDN with Cloud Load Balancing optimizes global content delivery.
C) Incorrect. Cloud Armor is for security, not content delivery.
D) Incorrect. Dedicated Interconnects are for network connections, not content delivery.
E) Incorrect. Cloud Armor does not aid in content delivery.

QUESTION 14

Answer - C) Google Cloud VPC Service Controls

C) Google Cloud VPC Service Controls - VPC Service Controls provide granular access controls and isolation within a VPC, enhancing security by preventing unauthorized communication between instances.
 A) Google Cloud Firewall Rules - Firewall rules control traffic but may not provide the level of isolation needed.
 B) Google Cloud VPN with dedicated tunnels - VPNs are for secure access, not necessarily for workload isolation.
 D) Google Cloud Network Peering - Network Peering is for communication between VPCs, not specifically for isolating workloads within a VPC.
 E) Google Cloud Shared VPC - Shared VPC allows shared resources but does not directly address workload isolation for security.

QUESTION 15

Answer – A) Allow ingress on port 443 from any source and all traffic from internal IPs.

A) Correct. Secures web traffic and allows necessary internal access.
B) Incorrect. This configuration does not allow for internal unrestricted access.
C) Incorrect. Port 80 (HTTP) should not be open for a HTTPS-only setup.
D) Incorrect. Stateful inspection does not specify port or IP-based rules.
E) Incorrect. Denying all egress can disrupt necessary outbound communication.

QUESTION 16

Answer - B) Deploy multiple regional VPCs in key geographical locations.

B) Deploy multiple regional VPCs in key geographical locations - This strategy allows you to distribute resources closer to users, ensuring low-latency access as you expand globally.
 A) Establish a single global VPC to centralize resources - Centralizing resources may introduce latency for users in distant regions.
 C) Utilize Google Cloud Load Balancers for global traffic distribution - Load balancers distribute traffic but do not necessarily address resource placement.
 D) Implement Google Cloud VPN for secure connections - VPNs focus on secure access, not resource placement for low-latency access.
 E) Use Google Cloud CDN for content delivery - CDN is for content caching and may not directly address resource placement for low-latency access.

QUESTION 17

Answer - D) Set up Google Cloud Load Balancing with global anycast IP addresses.

D) Set up Google Cloud Load Balancing with global anycast IP addresses - This solution ensures low-latency access, high availability, and optimal user experience for a global web application.
 A) Using a single regional VPC may introduce latency for users in distant regions and does not provide high availability across regions.
 B) Google Cloud CDN is for content delivery and may not directly address application deployment and high availability.
 C) Google Cloud VPN is for secure access but does not optimize user experience or minimize downtime for web applications.
 E) Creating multiple independent VPCs can introduce complexity and does not inherently provide global low-latency access and high availability.

QUESTION 18

Answer - B) Autoscale based on both CPU and memory utilization.

B) Autoscaling based on both CPU and memory utilization is a more comprehensive approach as it considers both resource consumption factors.
 A) Autoscaling based solely on CPU may not account for memory-related performance issues.
 C) Implementing a fixed-size node pool may not be cost-efficient, as it may lead to underutilized resources.
 D) Using custom metrics for autoscaling can be beneficial but is not specified as the primary consideration.
 E) Disabling autoscaling may lead to resource inefficiency and missed cost-saving opportunities.

QUESTION 19

Answer - E) Create a custom IAM role with the required permissions for the engineer.

E) Creating a custom IAM role with the specific permissions needed for the engineer is the most efficient way to configure IAM settings for minimal effort while maintaining security and control.
 A) Providing both Storage Admin and Project IAM Admin roles at the organization level may grant excessive permissions.
 B) Assigning the Storage Admin IAM role at the department level may not provide the necessary permissions for other required actions.
 C) Granting both roles at the department level may overcomplicate permissions.
 D) Assigning the Storage Admin IAM role at the organization level may grant more permissions than needed.

QUESTION 20

Answer - B) Assign the engineer the Storage Admin IAM role at the department level.

B) To enable the engineer to manage storage buckets across different departments with minimal effort, you should assign them the Storage Admin IAM role at the department level, ensuring they have the necessary permissions.
 A) Providing both the Storage Admin and Project IAM Admin roles at the organization level may grant

excessive permissions.

C) Granting both roles at the department level may lead to over-entitlement.

D) Assigning the Storage Admin role at the organization level may be too broad.

E) Creating a custom IAM role could be more complex and less efficient.

QUESTION 21

Answer - C) Dedicated Interconnect

C) To set up a high-bandwidth link to Google Cloud with a private IP address for Cloud Storage and without the need for an intermediary vendor, you should select Dedicated Interconnect. This option provides a direct, private connection to Google's network.

A) Carrier Peering does not provide a private connection to Cloud Storage.

B) Partner Interconnect typically requires a partner to establish the connection.

D) Direct Peering is used for peering with Google's public IP space, not for Cloud Storage access with a private IP.

QUESTION 22

Answer - C) Grant the engineer both the Storage Admin IAM role and Project IAM Admin role at the department level.

C) To enable the engineer to deploy storage buckets across different departments and manage service accounts with minimal effort, it's best to grant them both the Storage Admin IAM role and Project IAM Admin role at the department level, providing granular control.

A) Providing both roles at the organization level might grant excessive permissions.

B) Assigning the Storage Admin IAM role at the department level alone might not cover all necessary permissions.

D) Assigning the Storage Admin IAM role at the organization level might grant too many permissions globally.

E) Creating a custom IAM role is an option but may not be as efficient as using existing roles for this scenario.

QUESTION 23

Answer – A) Set up Cloud Armor with a security policy targeting an external HTTP(S) load balancer.

A) Correct. Cloud Armor provides DDoS protection and can filter web exploits when linked to a load balancer.

B) Incorrect. VPC firewall rules alone are insufficient for complex web security needs.

C) Incorrect. Cloud VPN is not designed for filtering web traffic or protecting against DDoS.

D) Incorrect. Private Google Access is for accessing Google services, not for general web traffic security.

E) Incorrect. Custom routing doesn't provide the necessary security controls for web exploits and DDoS attacks.

QUESTION 24

Answer - A) Use Cloud VPN to create a site-to-site VPN connection.

B) Implement Dedicated Interconnect for a dedicated, high-bandwidth connection.

Option C - Deploying a Bastion Host is more related to security access than network connectivity.
Option D - Google Cloud CDN is not typically used for connecting GCP and on-premises data centers.
Option E - Google Cloud Router is for dynamic routing within Google Cloud, not between on-premises and GCP. Choice A (Use Cloud VPN to create a site-to-site VPN connection) - Creating a site-to-site VPN connection using Cloud VPN is an effective way to establish a secure and high-speed connection between GCP and an on-premises data center. It ensures encrypted communication and can provide low-latency connectivity.
Choice B (Implement Dedicated Interconnect for a dedicated, high-bandwidth connection) - Implementing Dedicated Interconnect offers a dedicated, high-bandwidth connection between GCP and the data center, ensuring fast and reliable network connectivity. This is particularly suitable for enterprises with high traffic requirements.

QUESTION 25

Answer - C) Compute Instance Admin (v1)

Option A - Compute Admin grants permissions to manage IAM roles and permissions, which is not desired.
Option B - Security Admin provides permissions related to security but may also allow changes to IAM roles and permissions.
Option D - IAM Role Viewer only allows viewing roles, not creating or managing virtual machine instances.
Option E - Project Editor provides broad permissions, including IAM management, which is not desired.
Choice C - The Compute Instance Admin (v1) role provides the necessary permissions to create and manage virtual machine instances in a specific project while restricting changes to IAM roles and permissions, aligning with the requirements.

QUESTION 26

Answer – B) Set up Cloud VPN tunnels from GCP to each external cloud provider.

A) Incorrect. Dedicated Interconnect is not typically used for connections to other cloud providers.
B) Correct. Cloud VPN tunnels provide secure, efficient communication between clouds.
C) Incorrect. VPC Network Peering is not feasible with external cloud providers.
D) Incorrect. Private Google Access is for Google services, not external cloud connectivity.
E) Incorrect. Cloud Routers alone do not establish secure connections to external clouds.

QUESTION 27

Answer - B) Establish Dedicated Interconnects in the central hub region (europe-west3) and leverage Interconnect attachments.

Option A - Configuring Dedicated Interconnects directly to VPCs may limit flexibility and scalability.
Option C - Deploying separate VPN connections for each data center may not utilize Dedicated Interconnects effectively.
Option D - Cloud Interconnect is not the best choice for Dedicated Interconnects. Choice B - Establishing Dedicated Interconnects in the central hub region (europe-west3) and using Interconnect attachments allows for centralized and efficient connectivity to both Germany and Japan data centers, simplifying management and routing.

QUESTION 28

Answer – C) Configure each Compute Engine instance with Premium Network Tier for optimized network performance.

A) Incorrect. Dedicated Interconnect is for on-premises to GCP connections, not inter-region in GCP.
B) Incorrect. VPC Peering is not used for BigQuery access.
C) Correct. Premium Network Tier provides optimized performance for inter-region traffic.
D) Incorrect. Global Load Balancer is not used for this type of backend communication.
E) Incorrect. Cloud VPN is not optimal for high-performance, real-time analytics data transfer.

QUESTION 29

Answer - B) Establish a VPC Service Controls perimeter for your project with an access context policy that encompasses your organization's head office network IP ranges.

Option A - Creating individual access context policies for each application may lead to administrative complexity.
Option C - Creating separate VPC Service Controls perimeters for each application may result in management overhead.
Option D - While firewall rules are an option, VPC Service Controls offer a more comprehensive security approach. Choice B - Setting up a VPC Service Controls perimeter for your project with a comprehensive access context policy that covers head office network IP ranges provides centralized and efficient API access control for Memorystore and Spanner across all applications in the project.

QUESTION 30

Answer - C) Generate a VPC Service Controls perimeter for each App Engine application with an access context policy that includes your organization's head office network IP ranges.

Option A - Establishing an access context policy for individual applications may not be the most efficient approach.
Option B - Creating a VPC Service Controls perimeter for the entire project may not provide fine-grained control over individual App Engine applications.
Option D - Configuring a firewall rule is not the most suitable method for enforcing access control to Memorystore and Spanner. Choice C - Creating a VPC Service Controls perimeter for each App Engine application with an access context policy offers precise control over API access from head office networks, ensuring security.

QUESTION 31

Answer - A) Deploy your serverless data processing components directly into the secure network of the existing VPC. Create firewall rules to allow traffic from Cloud Run and Cloud Functions to the IoT devices.

Option B - While creating dedicated VPCs is an option, it adds unnecessary complexity for minimal network traffic.
Option C - Creating a VPN connection is not the most efficient approach for minimizing costs in this scenario.
Option D - Using a Global Load Balancer is not directly related to minimizing costs in this context. Choice A - Deploying serverless components within the existing secure network and configuring firewall rules is

a cost-effective solution to ensure communication while minimizing costs.

QUESTION 32

Answer – A) Implement Cloud Armor with security policies attached to Global HTTP(S) Load Balancers.

A) Correct. Cloud Armor provides protection against web exploits and DDoS, and Global Load Balancers distribute traffic.
B) Incorrect. VPN is not designed for protecting web applications from internet threats.
C) Incorrect. VPC Service Controls are for securing data, not for mitigating web attacks.
D) Incorrect. Network Load Balancers and Cloud IDS don't provide the specific protections needed for web applications.
E) Incorrect. While Cloud Endpoints secure APIs, they do not offer comprehensive DDoS protection.

QUESTION 33

Answer - A) Use Shared VPC with custom routing and firewall rules to control traffic between VPCs.

Option B - Deploying separate VPN tunnels between each VPC can introduce complexity and overhead.
Option C - VPC Peering connections may not provide the required level of security and compliance control.
Option D - Creating a single VPC for all business units may not align with the organization's structure and compliance requirements. Choice A - Using Shared VPC with custom routing and firewall rules allows for centralized control over traffic between VPCs, ensuring secure and compliant communication while minimizing exposure to external threats.

QUESTION 34

Answer - B) Dedicated Interconnect with VPC Peering

A) Cloud VPN with BGP - Explanation: Cloud VPN provides secure connections, but it may not offer the same level of reliability and dedicated bandwidth as Dedicated Interconnect. BGP is useful for dynamic routing but may not replace Dedicated Interconnect.
C) Cloud Interconnect with Direct Peering - Explanation: Cloud Interconnect connects to Google Cloud, but it may not provide the same dedicated connectivity as Dedicated Interconnect. Direct Peering focuses on Google's network.
D) Transit Gateway with VPN Gateway - Explanation: Transit Gateway can connect multiple VPCs, but it may not provide the dedicated connectivity required for hybrid setups. VPN Gateway is useful for secure connections but may not replace Dedicated Interconnect.
E) VPC Peering with Cloud Router - Explanation: VPC Peering connects VPCs within Google Cloud and may not directly address hybrid cloud connectivity. Cloud Router is used for dynamic BGP routing within VPCs.
B) Dedicated Interconnect with VPC Peering - Explanation: This combination provides dedicated, reliable connectivity to connect Google Cloud with on-premises environments effectively.

QUESTION 35

Answer - D) Create more specific custom routes than the default network routes, designating next hops for each component, and assign network tags for precise routing.

D) Create more specific custom routes than the default network routes, designating next hops for each component, and assign network tags for precise routing - Explanation: Creating more specific custom routes and using network tags allows for precise traffic routing for each component in the complex multi-tier application architecture.

A) Set up custom routes with more precision than the default network routes - Explanation: While custom routes are useful, this option does not consider the use of network tags for differentiation.

B) Reconfigure the application architecture to consolidate all components within a single subnet - Explanation: Consolidating all components into a single subnet may not be practical or efficient for complex multi-tier applications.

C) Delete all default network routes and establish distinct custom routes for each component with network tags - Explanation: Deleting default routes introduces complexity, and this option may not be necessary for precise routing.

E) Implement a Cloud Router to dynamically manage routing between components and subnets - Explanation: Cloud Router is used for dynamic BGP routing within VPCs and may not provide the level of precision required for complex multi-tier applications with multiple subnets.

QUESTION 36

Answer – A) Use Private Google Access with VPC firewall rules to restrict internet access and enable internal communication.

A) Correct. Private Google Access allows access to Google services without internet exposure, and firewall rules manage internal communication.
B) Incorrect. VPC Service Controls are for data access control, not for network traffic management.
C) Incorrect. Internal Load Balancer is not necessary for basic inter-application communication.
D) Incorrect. Shared VPC is more for resource sharing across projects, not for internal communication isolation.
E) Incorrect. Separate subnets and VPC peering are complex and Cloud VPN is not required for accessing Google Cloud services internally.

QUESTION 37

Answer – C) Enable Private Google Access on the subnetworks for secure, internal access to Cloud Spanner.

A) Incorrect. VPN may introduce additional latency.
B) Incorrect. Interconnect is typically for on-premises to GCP connections, not for intra-GCP services.
C) Correct. Private Google Access provides secure, internal, and low-latency access to Cloud Spanner.
D) Incorrect. VPC Peering is not used for accessing managed services like Cloud Spanner.
E) Incorrect. Separate VPCs with custom routes add complexity without improving latency or security.

QUESTION 38

Answer - B) Cloud Interconnect with Google Cloud Router

A) Google Cloud VPN with VPC peering - VPN and VPC peering provide encrypted connections, but Interconnect with Router offers lower-latency dedicated connectivity.
B) Cloud Interconnect with Google Cloud Router - Correct answer. Cloud Interconnect provides low-latency, private connectivity between regions, and Router handles dynamic routing.

C) VPC peering with Cloud VPN - This combination focuses on encrypted connections and VPC connectivity but does not offer low-latency dedicated connections.
D) Cloud DNS with Cloud CDN - DNS and CDN provide DNS resolution and content delivery but not private connectivity.
E) Google Cloud Load Balancing with VPC Service Controls - Load balancing and Service Controls focus on traffic distribution and access control but not dedicated private connections.

QUESTION 39

Answer - D) Shared VPC with VPC peering

A) Google Cloud VPN with VPC peering - VPN and VPC peering provide connectivity but do not offer fine-grained routing control between VPCs.
B) VPC Service Controls with Cloud NAT - These services enhance access control but do not control routing between VPCs.
C) Google Cloud VPN with Cloud Identity-Aware Proxy (IAP) - While VPN offers connectivity, IAP is about identity-based access control, not VPC routing.
D) Correct answer. Shared VPC with VPC peering allows you to control routing and secure communication between multiple VPCs effectively.
E) Google Cloud Load Balancing with VPC Service Controls - These services focus on traffic distribution and access control, not routing between VPCs.

QUESTION 40

Answer - C) Google Cloud Spanner and Google Cloud CDN

A) Google Cloud VPN and Google Cloud Storage provide secure connectivity and storage but may not inherently address high availability and low latency in the event of regional failures.
B) Google Cloud Load Balancing and Google Cloud Pub/Sub offer load distribution and messaging capabilities but may not directly address high availability and low latency requirements.
C) Correct answer. Google Cloud Spanner is a globally distributed, horizontally scalable database, and Google Cloud CDN focuses on content delivery, making them suitable for achieving high availability and low latency even in the face of regional failures.
D) Google Cloud Interconnect and Google Cloud Armor provide dedicated connections and security but may not inherently address regional failure tolerance and latency.
E) Google Cloud VPC Peering connects VPCs, and Google Cloud Bigtable is a NoSQL database, but they may not directly address the specified high availability and low latency requirements.

QUESTION 41

Answer - D) Google Cloud Spanner and Google Cloud Load Balancing

A) Google Cloud Dataprep and Google Cloud Filestore are not primarily related to load balancing and resource utilization for multi-tier applications.
B) Google Cloud Spanner is a database, and Google Cloud Identity-Aware Proxy (IAP) focuses on identity management; they are not primarily load balancing solutions.
C) Google Cloud CDN and Google Cloud Compute Engine Autoscaler offer content delivery and scaling capabilities, but they may not provide the same level of load balancing and low-latency access as Google Cloud Load Balancing.

D) Correct answer. Google Cloud Spanner is a globally distributed, horizontally scalable database, and Google Cloud Load Balancing ensures efficient resource utilization and low-latency access for end users by distributing traffic across instances.
E) Google Cloud Spanner and Google Cloud VPC Peering may not be the primary components for load balancing and resource utilization.

QUESTION 42

Answer - D) Google Cloud Storage and Google Cloud DNS

A) Google Cloud VPN and Google Cloud Bigtable may not be the primary components for disaster recovery and data replication between regions.
B) Google Cloud CDN and Google Cloud Compute Engine Autoscaler are not primarily designed for disaster recovery and data replication.
C) Google Cloud Spanner and Google Cloud Interconnect focus on database and connectivity but may not be the primary components for disaster recovery.
D) Correct answer. Google Cloud Storage offers data replication between regions, and Google Cloud DNS provides domain name resolution for disaster recovery scenarios.
E) Google Cloud Load Balancing and Google Cloud VPC Peering may not be the primary components for data replication and failover between regions.

QUESTION 43

Answer - C) Set up a regional managed instance group, designate the preferred region, and pick the option for distributing instances across multiple zones.

A) Configuring an unmanaged instance group in a solitary zone may not provide the desired reliability and scalability for a production application.
B) Creating individual managed instance groups for each sector within a single zone doesn't fully utilize Google Cloud's multi-zone capabilities for reliability.
C) Correct answer. Setting up a regional managed instance group with distribution across multiple zones within a preferred region offers both reliability and scalability based on demand.
D) Creating separate unmanaged instance groups for each zone lacks the automation and management capabilities that managed instance groups provide.
E) A global managed instance group is typically used for distributing instances worldwide, which may not be necessary for a finance sector project focused on reliability and scaling within a region.

QUESTION 44

Answer - C) Create a VPC Firewall rule that blocks all traffic except for the DDoS protection service.

A) VPC Service Controls Perimeter is more about data protection than restricting traffic sources.
B) Cloud Armor Security Policy is focused on web application firewall (WAF) rules, not for restricting backend server access.
C) Correct answer. Creating a VPC Firewall rule allows you to precisely control incoming traffic and restrict it to the DDoS protection service.
D) Cloud Identity-Aware Proxy (IAP) is used for identity-based access to applications, not for restricting traffic sources.
E) VPC Flow Log is for monitoring and analyzing network traffic but doesn't directly restrict traffic

sources.

QUESTION 45

Answer - B) Check the on-premises VPN devices for potential misconfigurations.

A) Reviewing VPC firewall rules may be necessary but is unlikely to resolve connectivity issues stemming from on-premises VPN device misconfigurations.
C) Creating custom routes may not be needed if the VPN tunnels are correctly configured.
D) Increasing tunnel bandwidth may not address misconfigurations.
E) Re-creating tunnels should be a last resort after checking for misconfigurations.
B) Checking the on-premises VPN devices is crucial because intermittent connectivity issues often result from misconfigured VPN devices or network settings on the on-premises side.

QUESTION 46

Answer - C) Employ Rolling Updates to minimize downtime during application updates.

A) Regional Clusters provide failover but do not address update downtime directly.
B) Node Pools with different instance types improve resource utilization but are not primarily for high availability.
C) Rolling Updates in GKE minimize downtime during application updates by gradually replacing Pods.
D) Horizontal Pod Autoscaling adjusts the number of replicas but is unrelated to update downtime.
E) Multi-Zone Clusters offer fault tolerance but do not specifically target update downtime.

QUESTION 47

Answer - B) Google Cloud Spanner.

A) Google Cloud DNS provides domain name resolution but does not inherently provide geographical redundancy.
B) Google Cloud Spanner is a globally distributed, horizontally scalable database that ensures high availability and geographical redundancy.
C) Google Cloud CDN accelerates content delivery but does not inherently provide geographical redundancy.
D) Google Cloud Pub/Sub is a messaging service but does not inherently provide geographical redundancy.
E) Google Cloud Bigtable is a NoSQL database but does not inherently provide geographical redundancy.

QUESTION 48

Answer – C) Implement Shared VPC across all Kubernetes Engine clusters with network policies based on labels.

A) Incorrect. Network Peering is not the most efficient for low-latency communication between clusters.
B) Incorrect. Internal Load Balancers are for traffic distribution within a cluster, not between clusters.
C) Correct. Shared VPC with network policies provides secure, efficient, and isolated communication

between microservices in different clusters.
D) Incorrect. VPN tunnels are not required for communication within GCP and may add latency.
E) Incorrect. A Global VPC does not inherently provide the necessary isolation and security for microservices communication.

QUESTION 49

Answer – A) Use Cloud Spanner for a globally distributed database.

A) Correct. Cloud Spanner provides a globally distributed database solution, ideal for low-latency access across regions.
B) Incorrect. Regional Cloud SQL instances would not provide the same level of global performance as Cloud Spanner.
C) Incorrect. Cloud Bigtable is suitable for high-volume data but may not provide the best latency for global access.
D) Incorrect. Cloud Memorystore is region-specific and not ideal for global low-latency access.
E) Incorrect. Firestore in Datastore mode is not primarily designed for global low-latency scenarios.

QUESTION 50

Answer – A) Global HTTP(S) Load Balancer with Cloud Armor and Cloud CDN.

A) Correct. Global HTTP(S) Load Balancing, Cloud Armor, and Cloud CDN provide the necessary dynamic scaling, security, and efficient content delivery for a global online platform.
B) Incorrect. Network Load Balancers are not ideal for global traffic distribution and advanced security needs.
C) Incorrect. TCP/SSL Proxy Load Balancers are not the best choice for global traffic distribution and security.
D) Incorrect. Internal Load Balancers and VPNs are not suitable for high-traffic, global online platforms.
E) Incorrect. Cloud Run and Endpoints do not provide the necessary scaling and advanced security for a global retail platform.

PRACTICE TEST 2 - QUESTIONS ONLY

QUESTION 1

You are configuring a VPC (Virtual Private Cloud) network in Google Cloud. You need to ensure that instances within the VPC can communicate with each other using private IPs. Which firewall rule should you create to achieve this while adhering to the principle of least privilege?

A) Allow all internal traffic within the VPC.
B) Allow all external traffic to the VPC.
C) Allow ICMP traffic within the VPC.
D) Allow SSH traffic within the VPC.
E) Deny all traffic within the VPC.

QUESTION 2

You are tasked with designing a highly available network architecture in Google Cloud for your e-commerce application. What network load balancing solution should you consider to distribute traffic across multiple regions while ensuring minimal downtime?

A) Google Cloud Global Load Balancing
B) Google Cloud HTTP(S) Load Balancing
C) Google Cloud Internal TCP/UDP Load Balancing
D) Google Cloud Regional Load Balancing
E) Google Cloud Traffic Director with Service Directory.

QUESTION 3

Your company has recently initiated a new streaming service. Upon deploying the service for high availability utilizing managed instance groups, autoscaling, and a network load balancer at the front, you observe intermittent but intense traffic spikes causing autoscaling to hit its peak capacity, leading to streaming disruptions for users. After reviewing the situation, you suspect a DDoS attack. You want to swiftly re-establish service for users and ensure continuous streaming while keeping costs down. What two actions should you perform? (Select two.)

A) Expand the maximum capacity of the autoscaling mechanism of the backend
B) Temporarily take down the streaming platform from Google Cloud for several hours to deter the ongoing attack
C) Implement Cloud Armor to block the IP addresses linked to the attacking source
D) Switch to a global HTTP(s) load balancer and redirect your streaming service backend onto this load balancer
E) Directly access the backend Compute Engine instances via SSH to check the authentication and system logs for deeper insights into the attack

QUESTION 4

Your company has deployed a Google Kubernetes Engine (GKE) cluster for a highly available microservices application. You want to ensure that the GKE nodes can securely access a specific Google Cloud Storage bucket without exposing the data publicly. What should you do to achieve this while following the principle of least privilege?

A) Use a Service Account with Storage Object Viewer role attached to the GKE nodes.
B) Configure the Google Cloud Storage bucket to be publicly accessible and allow anonymous access.
C) Enable Private Google Access on the GKE cluster.
D) Use the GKE nodes' default service account to access the Google Cloud Storage bucket.
E) Create a VPC Service Controls perimeter around the GKE cluster.

QUESTION 5

Your organization operates in multiple regions, and you need a cost-effective, global solution for connecting to Google Cloud. What approach should you consider?

A) Establish separate Direct Interconnects in each region for optimal performance.
B) Set up a Cloud VPN with redundant tunnels between regions.
C) Implement a Google Cloud Partner Interconnect for centralized connectivity.
D) Utilize Google's Global Load Balancer for routing traffic.
E) Deploy a private fiber network connecting all regions.

QUESTION 6

Your organization has implemented a multi-region architecture in Google Cloud, and you need to ensure high availability and disaster recovery for your applications. What networking strategies should you prioritize?

A) Deploy dedicated interconnects in each region for low-latency communication.
B) Set up Cloud VPNs with multiple redundant tunnels for robust connectivity.
C) Implement Global Load Balancing to distribute traffic across regions.
D) Use VPC Peering extensively to connect VPC networks in different regions.
E) Utilize Google Cloud CDN to optimize content delivery across regions.

QUESTION 7

You are configuring a hybrid cloud network between a GCP VPC and an on-premises network. The GCP VPC uses the range 172.16.0.0/12 and the on-premises network uses 10.0.0.0/8. You must ensure optimal routing and redundancy. Which of the following configurations should you use for the Cloud Router and VPN setup?

A) Use dynamic routing with BGP, set local ASN to 64512, and peer ASN to 64513.
B) Establish a static VPN with no BGP, manually configure routes in VPC.
C) Use dynamic routing with BGP, set local ASN to 65000, and peer ASN to the same value.
D) Establish two VPNs, one with dynamic routing (BGP) and the other with static routing.
E) Use dynamic routing with BGP, set both Cloud Routers to different local ASNs but the same peer ASN.

QUESTION 8

Your organization needs to ensure that data stored in Google Cloud Storage buckets within a specific project is encrypted at rest using customer-managed encryption keys (CMEK). What should you do to achieve this?

A) Enable Cloud Storage default encryption for the project and select Google-managed keys for encryption.
B) Create a Cloud Storage custom encryption policy that enforces the use of CMEK for all buckets in the project.
C) Set up a Google Cloud Key Management Service (KMS) key ring and grant permissions to the project for using customer-managed keys.
D) Configure a Cloud Identity and Access Management (IAM) policy that restricts access to buckets in the project, ensuring data encryption.
E) Utilize the Cloud Storage Uniform Bucket-level Access feature to enforce CMEK for all objects in the project's buckets.

QUESTION 9

Your organization is migrating its on-premises data warehouse to Google Cloud, and you need to ensure secure communication between your on-premises network and Google Cloud VPC. Which Google Cloud networking solution should you implement to meet this requirement while maintaining high availability and low latency?

A) Set up a VPN tunnel between your on-premises network and Google Cloud using Cloud VPN.
B) Establish a Dedicated Interconnect connection between your on-premises network and Google Cloud.
C) Deploy an External Load Balancer to route traffic between your on-premises network and Google Cloud VPC.
D) Use a Direct Peering connection to connect your on-premises network and Google Cloud.
E) Configure a Cloud Router for routing between your on-premises network and Google Cloud VPC.

QUESTION 10

In a multi-project Google Cloud environment, you need to ensure secure and private connectivity between Virtual Private Cloud (VPC) networks across different projects, while also allowing internet access and connecting to an external data center. Which architectural approach should you consider?

A) Implementing a standalone VPC for each project with individual VPN tunnels.
B) Creating a central hub VPC with VPC Peering to connect to other VPCs.
C) Using Cloud Interconnect Dedicated for private connectivity.
D) Utilizing Cloud VPN for secure connectivity between projects.
E) Merging all VPCs into a single VPC network.

QUESTION 11

Your organization is planning to deploy a machine learning model on Google Cloud to process large datasets and generate real-time predictions. The model needs to scale dynamically with varying workloads and leverage specialized hardware for enhanced performance. What Google Cloud service should you recommend for this complex machine learning deployment, and what key advantages does it offer?

A) Google Cloud AutoML for automated machine learning model creation.
B) Google Cloud AI Platform for building, training, and deploying machine learning models.
C) Google Cloud Dataflow for real-time data processing.
D) Google Cloud Dataprep for data preparation and transformation.
E) Google Cloud TPU (Tensor Processing Unit) for high-performance machine learning.

QUESTION 12

For a company expanding its operations globally, you need to set up a secure, high-bandwidth connection between your GCP VPC in asia-southeast1 and multiple on-premises sites in Europe and Asia. Considering scalability and redundancy, which configuration should you choose?

A) Utilize multiple Cloud VPNs with dynamic routing for each site.
B) Deploy Dedicated Interconnects at each on-premises site.
C) Establish a single Partner Interconnect with regional redundancy.
D) Create multiple Partner Interconnects with a global routing setup.
E) Set up a hybrid approach with both Dedicated and Partner Interconnects.

QUESTION 13

You are tasked with enhancing the network security of a multi-tier application running on GKE. The application requires both internal and external communication controls. How should you configure network policies and firewalls in GKE for optimal security and functionality?

A) Apply network policies at the Pod level and configure GCP firewalls for external traffic.
B) Implement network policies at the Node level and use Cloud Armor for all traffic.
C) Use GKE Ingress for internal traffic and GCP firewalls for external traffic.
D) Configure network policies for each GKE Service and employ Cloud Armor for external threats.
E) Rely solely on GCP firewalls for both internal and external traffic control.

QUESTION 14

You are managing a Google Cloud project that requires cost optimization while ensuring optimal network performance. The project involves multiple virtual machine instances in different regions. What GCP networking solution should you recommend to balance cost and performance effectively?

A) Utilize Google Cloud VPN for secure inter-region communication.
B) Implement Google Cloud Interconnect for dedicated high-speed connections between regions.
C) Set up a global load balancer to distribute traffic across regions.
D) Use Google Cloud CDN for content caching in each region.
E) Deploy Google Cloud Router with BGP for dynamic routing across regions.

QUESTION 15

In a GCP environment, you need to configure firewalls for a set of VMs running critical business applications. These VMs should only be accessible by specific corporate office networks. Which firewall rule configuration would be most effective?

A) Allow ingress from specific corporate network IPs on required application ports.
B) Deny all ingress and egress, except from VPN-connected IPs.
C) Set up a firewall rule to allow all ingress traffic from the internet.
D) Implement firewall rules to allow ingress on all ports from specific regions.
E) Create rules to allow all egress and deny ingress except on port 80 (HTTP).

QUESTION 16

Your organization needs to ensure data sovereignty and compliance for a Google Cloud project that involves sensitive customer data. The project spans multiple regions and requires strict control over where data is stored. What GCP networking solution should you recommend to meet these requirements?

A) Google Cloud CDN for content caching.
B) Google Cloud Storage for data storage.
C) Google Cloud Dedicated Interconnect for direct connections.
D) Google Cloud Regional Persistent Disks for data storage.
E) Google Cloud Network Peering for data transfer.

QUESTION 17

Your organization is planning to implement a disaster recovery (DR) strategy for critical applications in Google Cloud. You want to ensure minimal data loss and fast recovery in case of a disaster. What GCP networking feature should you recommend for achieving these objectives?

A) Google Cloud Load Balancing for traffic distribution.
B) Google Cloud VPN for secure access.
C) Google Cloud Interconnect for dedicated connections.
D) Google Cloud Dedicated Interconnect with multiple redundant connections.
E) Google Cloud Cloud Storage for data replication and backup.

QUESTION 18

Your organization's media processing system is transitioning its compute-heavy video rendering servers from an on-site data center to Google Cloud. The video rendering servers vary significantly in terms of their libraries and setups. This transition to Google Cloud will be a straightforward rehosting, and a unified network load balancer will cater to all incoming rendering requests. You are inclined to utilize Google Cloud-native solutions when applicable. What is the appropriate method to accomplish this deployment on Google Cloud?

A) Leverage the Equal Cost Multipath (ECMP) routing feature of Google Cloud to evenly distribute the traffic to your rendering servers by setting up several static routes with identical priority directed to the rendering server instances.
B) Implement a third-party front-end solution tailored to handle the diversity in configuration of your rendering servers, setting this up in front of the servers.
C) Set up a managed instance group using one of the virtual machine images from your in-house rendering servers, and associate this managed instance group with a target pool that is connected to your network load balancer.
D) Establish a target pool, incorporate all the rendering instances within this pool, and configure this

pool to work in conjunction with your network load balancer.
 E) Utilize Google Kubernetes Engine (GKE) to containerize your rendering servers and manage them using Kubernetes.

QUESTION 19

In setting up a disaster recovery plan, you configured Cloud NAT for your virtual machines in Google Cloud. You notice that a particular VM isn't using Cloud NAT when connecting to external services. What is the primary reason for this behavior?

A) There are custom-defined routes directing traffic to private IP ranges.
 B) The VM has been assigned a publicly routable IP address.
 C) The VM is deployed with several network interfaces.
 D) The VM is reachable through an external IP address provided by a Google Cloud load balancer.
 E) The VM is using a VPN tunnel for external connections.

QUESTION 20

In setting up a disaster recovery plan, you configured Cloud NAT for your virtual machines in Google Cloud. You notice that a particular VM isn't using Cloud NAT when connecting to external services. What is the primary reason for this behavior?

A) There are custom-defined routes directing traffic to private IP ranges.
 B) The VM has been assigned a publicly routable IP address.
 C) The VM is deployed with several network interfaces.
 D) The VM is reachable through an external IP address provided by a Google Cloud load balancer.
 E) There is a firewall rule blocking the VM's outgoing traffic.

QUESTION 21

Your organization's media processing system is transitioning its compute-heavy video rendering servers from an on-site data center to Google Cloud. The video rendering servers vary significantly in terms of their libraries and setups. This transition to Google Cloud will be a straightforward rehosting, and a unified network load balancer will cater to all incoming rendering requests. You are inclined to utilize Google Cloud-native solutions when applicable. What is the appropriate method to accomplish this deployment on Google Cloud?

A) Leverage the Equal Cost Multipath (ECMP) routing feature of Google Cloud to evenly distribute the traffic to your rendering servers by setting up several static routes with identical priority directed to the rendering server instances.
 B) Implement a third-party front-end solution tailored to handle the diversity in configuration of your rendering servers, setting this up in front of the servers.
 C) Set up a managed instance group using one of the virtual machine images from your in-house rendering servers, and associate this managed instance group with a target pool that is connected to your network load balancer.
 D) Establish a target pool, incorporate all the rendering instances within this pool, and configure this pool to work in conjunction with your network load balancer.
 E) Use Google Kubernetes Engine (GKE) to containerize your video rendering servers and deploy them with Kubernetes for efficient management and scaling.

QUESTION 22

In setting up a disaster recovery plan, you configured Cloud NAT for your virtual machines in Google Cloud. You notice that a particular VM isn't using Cloud NAT when connecting to external services. What is the primary reason for this behavior?

A) There are custom-defined routes directing traffic to private IP ranges.
B) The VM has been assigned a publicly routable IP address.
C) The VM is deployed with several network interfaces.
D) The VM is reachable through an external IP address provided by a Google Cloud load balancer.
E) Cloud NAT is not properly configured.

QUESTION 23

In a GCP environment, your e-commerce platform needs to securely handle API traffic, which includes sensitive payment information. The APIs are hosted on VMs in your VPC. How should you configure network security to safeguard this data while ensuring high availability?

A) Set up an internal HTTP(S) load balancer with a backend service linked to Google Cloud Armor.
B) Implement a Cloud VPN to encrypt API traffic between your VPC and clients.
C) Use VPC Service Controls to isolate the API services within your VPC.
D) Configure SSL policies on an external HTTP(S) load balancer combined with Cloud Armor.
E) Create a Private Google Access setup for VMs in the VPC to handle API traffic securely.

QUESTION 24

You are tasked with optimizing network performance for a Google Kubernetes Engine (GKE) cluster. The cluster is running microservices that communicate frequently with each other. Which two strategies should you implement to improve network performance?

A) Increase the number of nodes in the GKE cluster.
B) Enable VPC Flow Logs to monitor network traffic.
C) Implement IP masquerading for outbound connections.
D) Use Google Cloud CDN for caching microservices data.
E) Configure Container-Optimized OS for GKE nodes.

QUESTION 25

Your organization is planning to set up a disaster recovery (DR) solution in Google Cloud. The DR plan requires near real-time data replication to a secondary region for failover. What two Google Cloud services or features should you recommend to achieve this data replication and failover capability?

A) Use Google Cloud Spanner for real-time data replication.
B) Set up Google Cloud Storage for object-level replication.
C) Implement Google Cloud Pub/Sub for event-driven data synchronization.
D) Utilize Google Cloud Dataprep for data transformation.
E) Configure Google Cloud Storage Coldline for data archiving.

QUESTION 26

In a multi-cloud architecture with GCP and an external corporate data center connected via HA VPN, you need to configure DNS so that Compute Engine instances can resolve both internal corporate and Google Cloud hostnames. How should you proceed according to Google's best practices?

A) Set up a private forwarding zone in Cloud DNS for "hq.example.net", direct it to the corporate DNS server, and link it with the central networking VPC.
B) Create a private Cloud DNS zone for "hq.example.net" and manually configure each Compute Engine instance to use this DNS.
C) Implement a Cloud DNS peering zone for "hq.example.net", targeting the central networking VPC, and configure the corporate DNS server to resolve Google Cloud hostnames.
D) Configure each VPC's Cloud DNS to forward requests for "hq.example.net" to the corporate DNS server directly.
E) Establish a DNS policy in Cloud DNS to forward "hq.example.net" queries to the corporate DNS server and use Google's public DNS for other queries.

QUESTION 27

You are tasked with implementing a virtual inline security appliance in Google Cloud to perform deep packet inspection and intrusion prevention. The appliance needs to be placed in europe-west3. Which architectural approach should you choose?

A) Formulate a single VPC in a Shared VPC Host Project.
B) Establish one VPC within a Shared VPC Service Project.
C) Create 2 VPCs in a Shared VPC Host Project.
D) Establish 2 VPCs in a Shared VPC Host Project.
E) None of the above.

QUESTION 28

You have a private GKE cluster in the europe-west4-a region and a VM in the same VPC but different subnetwork. You need to configure kubectl on the VM to interact with the GKE cluster. How should you proceed?

A) Add the VM's subnet 10.142.80.0/24 to masterAuthorizedNetworksConfig and use the privateEndpoint 10.142.64.2 for kubectl.
B) Assign an external IP to the VM, add it to masterAuthorizedNetworksConfig, and use the publicEndpoint 34.89.72.19 for kubectl.
C) Include the cluster's subnet 10.142.0.0/20 in masterAuthorizedNetworksConfig and set kubectl to the publicEndpoint 34.89.72.19.
D) Add the master's subnet 10.142.64.0/28 to masterAuthorizedNetworksConfig and configure kubectl to connect to 10.142.64.2.
E) Configure kubectl to use the privateEndpoint 10.142.64.2 without modifying the masterAuthorizedNetworksConfig, as they are in the same VPC.

QUESTION 29

Your organization manages a Google Cloud project with multiple App Engine applications. You need to implement strict API access controls for Memorystore instances and Spanner databases to permit traffic exclusively from your head office networks. What should be your recommended approach?

A) Establish an access context policy for each App Engine application separately, including head office network IP ranges, and implement these policies for Memorystore and Spanner.
B) Create a VPC Service Controls perimeter for your project with an access context policy that encompasses your organization's head office network IP ranges.
C) Generate separate VPC Service Controls perimeters for each App Engine application, each with access context policies specifying your organization's head office network IP ranges.
D) Configure a set of firewall rules to deny API access to Memorystore and Spanner from networks not recognized as part of your head office.
E) None of the above.

QUESTION 30

You manage a series of IoT devices within a secure network in an existing Google Cloud Virtual Private Cloud (VPC). You're tasked with integrating additional data processing components using Cloud Run and Cloud Functions to process information from the IoT devices. The network traffic load between your serverless data processors and the IoT devices is minimal. Each serverless component must ensure seamless communication with any of the IoT devices. Your goal is to deploy a solution that minimizes costs. What should you do?

A) Generate an individual serverless VPC access connector for each Cloud Run and Cloud Function. Tailor the connectors to provide connectivity pathways between the serverless components and the IoT devices.
B) Deploy your serverless data processing components directly into the secure network of the existing VPC. Adjust firewall rules to facilitate communication paths between the serverless components and the IoT devices.
C) Set up your serverless components within a new serverless-dedicated VPC. Establish VPC peering between this new VPC and your current VPC, and update firewall rules to permit communication between the serverless components and the IoT devices.
D) Create a single serverless VPC access connector. Configure the serverless components to leverage the connector to interface with the IoT devices.
E) None of the above.

QUESTION 31

Your enterprise manages a single Google Cloud project with a multitude of App Engine applications. You are tasked with safeguarding API access to your Memorystore instances and Spanner databases to ensure that only API traffic from your organization's head office networks is permitted. How should you proceed?

A) Create a VPC Service Controls perimeter for your project with an access context policy that includes your organization's head office network IP ranges, and then implement the policy for Memorystore and Spanner.
B) Configure a custom firewall rule that explicitly allows API traffic from your organization's head office

networks to access Memorystore and Spanner.

C) Generate a VPC Service Controls perimeter for each App Engine application with an access context policy that includes your organization's head office network IP ranges.

D) Set up a dedicated VPN tunnel from your head office to Google Cloud and configure the necessary routing to restrict API access to Memorystore and Spanner from your head office.

E) None of the above.

QUESTION 32

In a GCP environment, you need to configure secure communication between services running in Kubernetes Engine in Project A and managed databases in Project B. Both projects are under the same organization. What is the most secure and efficient way to enable this communication?

A) Use VPC Peering between the two projects.

B) Configure Shared VPC across both projects.

C) Implement Cloud VPN for inter-project communication.

D) Set up a dedicated Interconnect for the services and databases.

E) Utilize Private Google Access in both projects for internal communication.

QUESTION 33

Your company is launching a new web application and needs to distribute content globally with low latency. Which Google Cloud service should you use to achieve this goal, considering both static and dynamic content?

A) Use Google Cloud Storage to host static content and Cloud CDN for caching and delivering it globally.

B) Deploy multiple virtual machines across regions and use a load balancer for distributing the content.

C) Set up a Cloud SQL database in each region to serve dynamic content.

D) Use Google Kubernetes Engine (GKE) with global load balancing for both static and dynamic content.

E) None of the above.

QUESTION 34

Your organization is running a highly regulated healthcare application in Google Cloud, and it requires strict encryption and access control measures. Which combination of Google Cloud networking services and features should you implement to meet these complex security requirements effectively?

A) VPC Service Controls with Google Cloud Armor

B) Private Google Access with Identity-Aware Proxy

C) VPN Gateway with SSL Proxy Load Balancer

D) Cloud NAT with Global Load Balancer

E) Anycast IP Routing with Firewall Rules

QUESTION 35

Your organization is expanding its network architecture and needs to ensure efficient traffic routing and low-latency access between virtual_machine-1 and virtual_machine-2, which are in different subnets. What complex networking solution should you implement to achieve this goal effectively?

A) Set up a custom route with more precision than the default network route, directing traffic from virtual_machine-1 to virtual_machine-2 without network tags.
B) Migrate virtual_machine-2 to a separate Virtual Private Cloud (VPC) and establish VPC Peering with virtual_machine-1's VPC, optimizing routing for low-latency access.
C) Delete the default network route and create a distinct custom route with a network tag assigned to virtual_machine-1 for precise traffic routing to virtual_machine-2.
D) Create a more specific custom route than the default network route, designating virtual_machine-2 as the next hop and assigning a network tag to virtual_machine-1.
E) Implement an SSL VPN gateway to establish a secure connection between virtual_machine-1 and virtual_machine-2 while optimizing traffic routing.

QUESTION 36

For a GKE cluster setup within an existing network infrastructure that requires secure access from a corporate network and efficient IP allocation, what configuration should you choose?

A) VPC-native GKE cluster with Google-managed IP ranges, /21 pod CIDR, /24 service CIDR, and a network proxy for control plane access.
B) Private GKE cluster with VPC advanced routing, /24 CIDR blocks for pods and services, and a network proxy for control plane.
C) GKE cluster with VPC-native custom IP ranges, privateEndpoint for control plane, /24 CIDR for pods and services, network proxy, and master authorized networks enabled.
D) VPC-native GKE cluster with user-defined IP ranges, GKE network policy, /24 CIDR for pods and services, network proxy, and master authorized networks.
E) Standard GKE cluster with separate subnets for pods and services, private nodes, and VPN setup for kubectl access to the control plane.

QUESTION 37

For a global online retail platform requiring external load balancing while preserving the client's IP address, which GCP load balancer should you use?

A) Internal Load Balancer
B) Network Load Balancer
C) HTTP(S) Load Balancer
D) TCP/SSL Proxy Load Balancer
E) Global Load Balancer with Client IP header preservation

QUESTION 38

You are designing a network architecture for a global e-commerce platform that requires low-latency access to product images and videos. Your goal is to distribute these assets efficiently across Google Cloud regions. Which Google Cloud service should you use to achieve this goal, ensuring content is cached closer to end-users while minimizing latency?

A) Google Cloud CDN with Google Cloud Armor
B) Traffic Director with Cloud Spanner
C) Google Cloud Storage with VPC peering

D) Google Cloud Pub/Sub with Google Cloud Load Balancing

E) Google Cloud Dataflow with Google Cloud Storage

QUESTION 39

You are transitioning your healthcare organization's VMs to use Google Cloud DNS. You need to transfer your existing BIND zone file to the new service. What is the appropriate command to execute this action?

A) gcloud dns record-sets import ZONE_FILE --zone-file-format --zone MANAGED_ZONE

B) gcloud dns record-sets import ZONE_FILE --replace-origin-ns --zone MANAGED_ZONE

C) gcloud dns record-sets import ZONE_FILE --zone MANAGED_ZONE

D) gcloud dns record-sets import ZONE_FILE --delete-all-existing --zone MANAGED_ZONE

E) gcloud dns record-sets export ZONE_FILE --zone-file-format --zone MANAGED_ZONE

QUESTION 40

Your organization is planning to deploy a machine learning model for image recognition on Google Cloud. The model will process large volumes of image data and requires high compute resources. Which Google Cloud compute service or feature should you choose to ensure that your machine learning model can efficiently process image data and scale as needed?

A) Google Compute Engine

B) Google Kubernetes Engine (GKE)

C) Google Cloud Functions

D) Google Cloud Run

E) Google AI Platform

QUESTION 41

Your organization is migrating its on-premises servers to Google Cloud, and data security is a top concern. You want to ensure data encryption at rest and in transit. Which combination of Google Cloud services or features should you implement to achieve these objectives effectively?

A) Google Cloud VPN and Google Cloud DNS

B) Google Cloud Identity-Aware Proxy (IAP) and Google Cloud CDN

C) Google Cloud Storage and Google Cloud KMS

D) Google Cloud Spanner and Google Cloud Load Balancing

E) Google Cloud Compute Engine Autoscaler and Google Cloud Pub/Sub

QUESTION 42

You are tasked with designing a network architecture for a global e-commerce platform on Google Cloud. The platform needs to ensure low-latency access for customers worldwide. Which Google Cloud service or feature should you use to optimize latency and improve global access?

A) Google Cloud VPN and Google Cloud DNS

B) Google Cloud CDN and Google Cloud Compute Engine Autoscaler

C) Google Cloud Spanner and Google Cloud Load Balancing

D) Google Cloud Storage and Google Cloud DNS
E) Google Cloud Load Balancing and Google Cloud VPC Peering

QUESTION 43

Your organization has a cybersecurity division that administers network safeguards and digital certificates. An infrastructure division is in charge of handling network configurations. The infrastructure division requires the capability to view firewall configurations but should not have permissions to create, amend, or remove them. How would you configure the access rights for the infrastructure division in Google Cloud?

A) Assign members of the infrastructure team the roles/compute.networkViewer role.
B) Assign members of the infrastructure team a custom role with permissions including compute.subnetworks.get and compute.firewalls.get.
C) Assign members of the infrastructure team the roles/compute.networkUser role.
D) Assign members of the infrastructure team the roles/compute.networkViewer role and grant them the compute.subnetworks.useExternal permission.
E) Assign members of the infrastructure team the roles/owner role.

QUESTION 44

You are transitioning your healthcare organization's VMs to use Google Cloud DNS. You need to transfer your existing BIND zone file to the new service. What is the appropriate command to execute this action?

A) gcloud dns record-sets import ZONE_FILE --zone-file-format --zone MANAGED_ZONE
B) gcloud dns record-sets import ZONE_FILE --replace-origin-ns --zone MANAGED_ZONE
C) gcloud dns record-sets import ZONE_FILE --zone MANAGED_ZONE
D) gcloud dns record-sets import ZONE_FILE --delete-all-existing --zone MANAGED_ZONE

QUESTION 45

Your organization is deploying a globally distributed application on Google Cloud. High availability and low-latency access are critical. You have decided to use Google Cloud's global load balancer. Which routing mode should you choose to optimize traffic for your scenario?

A) Single-region routing mode.
B) Failover routing mode.
C) Multicast routing mode.
D) Anycast routing mode.
E) Multi-region routing mode.

QUESTION 46

Your organization wants to set up an efficient, automated backup and recovery solution for Google Cloud resources. What is the recommended approach to achieve this?

A) Manually create snapshots of virtual machines on a daily basis.
B) Use Cloud Storage buckets to store regular backups of data.

C) Implement automated backups using Cloud Pub/Sub and Cloud Functions.
D) Rely on the built-in backup features of Google Cloud services like Cloud SQL and Compute Engine.
E) Schedule periodic exports of data to an external backup solution.

QUESTION 47

You are responsible for securing access to your organization's Google Cloud resources. You want to implement multi-factor authentication (MFA) for enhanced security. Which two MFA methods are supported by Google Cloud Identity Platform? (Choose two.)

A) SMS authentication.
B) Fingerprint recognition.
C) Time-based one-time password (TOTP) authentication.
D) Smart card authentication.
E) Voice recognition.

QUESTION 48

You are configuring a GCP network for a series of Compute Engine instances that process sensitive data. To ensure data security, you need to log all outbound connections from these instances to external IP addresses for audit and compliance purposes. What configuration should you implement for comprehensive logging?

A) Enable VPC Flow Logs for the subnetworks hosting the Compute Engine instances.
B) Set up individual logging for each Compute Engine instance using Cloud Monitoring.
C) Implement Cloud IDS for detailed logging and analysis of outbound connections.
D) Use egress firewall rules with logging enabled to capture all outbound traffic from the instances.
E) Establish Cloud NAT with logging for all outbound connections from the instances.

QUESTION 49

You are tasked with optimizing network performance for a set of Compute Engine instances that heavily interact with Cloud Storage. The setup should minimize latency and maximize throughput for data transfers. What network configuration should you implement?

A) Enable Private Google Access for the Compute Engine instances.
B) Configure each instance with Premium Network Tier.
C) Use Dedicated Interconnect for direct connectivity to Cloud Storage.
D) Set up VPC Peering between the Compute Engine network and Cloud Storage.
E) Implement Cloud VPN for secure and efficient data transfer to Cloud Storage.

QUESTION 50

In a GCP environment, you are configuring a network for a set of applications that require frequent data exchanges with an external, non-Google cloud service. The setup requires high throughput and low latency for these data exchanges. What network configuration optimizes performance for this requirement?

A) Use Cloud VPN with high-throughput tunnels for the data exchanges.
B) Configure Dedicated Interconnect for a direct, high-speed connection to the external service.
C) Implement Private Google Access for secure, high-speed access to external services.
D) Enable Premium Network Tier on the Compute Engine instances hosting the applications.
E) Set up Cloud Interconnect with a custom routing configuration to optimize data transfer.

PRACTICE TEST 2 - ANSWERS ONLY

QUESTION 1

Answer – A) Allow all internal traffic within the VPC.

Option A - Allowing all internal traffic within the VPC is correct because it allows instances to communicate using private IPs while adhering to the principle of least privilege.
Option B - Allowing all external traffic to the VPC is not suitable for this scenario as it would expose the VPC to the public internet.
Option C - Allowing ICMP traffic within the VPC is too permissive and may not be necessary for all communication.
Option D - Allowing SSH traffic within the VPC is specific and doesn't cover all internal traffic.
Option E - Denying all traffic within the VPC would block all communication, which is not the desired outcome.

QUESTION 2

Answer – A) Google Cloud Global Load Balancing

Option A - Google Cloud Global Load Balancing provides high availability and minimal downtime by distributing traffic across multiple regions.
Option B - HTTP(S) Load Balancing is regional, not global.
Option C - Internal TCP/UDP Load Balancing is for internal traffic.
Option D - Regional Load Balancing is not global.
Option E - Traffic Director is not a global load balancer but a traffic management solution.

QUESTION 3

Answer – A) Expand the maximum capacity of the autoscaling mechanism of the backend
Answer – C) Implement Cloud Armor

Option A - Expanding the maximum capacity of the autoscaling mechanism allows your backend to handle unexpected traffic surges and mitigate the effects of the DDoS attack.
Option C - Implementing Cloud Armor to block attacking IP addresses helps in reducing the impact of the ongoing DDoS attack.
Option B - Temporarily taking down the streaming platform is not a recommended action as it disrupts service for legitimate users.
Option D - Switching to a global HTTP(s) load balancer may not directly mitigate the DDoS attack.
Option E - Accessing backend Compute Engine instances via SSH for logs can be useful but does not address immediate service recovery.

QUESTION 4

Answer – A) Use a Service Account with Storage Object Viewer role attached to the GKE nodes.

Option A - Using a Service Account with the Storage Object Viewer role attached to the GKE nodes

provides secure access to the specific bucket without exposing data publicly.
 Option B - Configuring the bucket to be publicly accessible is not in line with the principle of least privilege and is a security risk.
 Option C - Enabling Private Google Access on the GKE cluster allows outbound internet access but doesn't address the bucket access issue.
 Option D - Using the default service account may not have the necessary permissions and is not recommended for security reasons.
 Option E - Creating a VPC Service Controls perimeter may not be necessary for this specific requirement and could be complex.

QUESTION 5

Answer - C) Implement a Google Cloud Partner Interconnect for centralized connectivity.

Option C provides a cost-effective, centralized solution that allows your organization to connect to Google Cloud from multiple regions with efficient data transfer.
Option A introduces complexity and may not be cost-effective.
Option B offers redundancy but may not provide optimal performance globally.
Option D is more focused on load balancing and doesn't address connectivity directly.
Option E is costly and may not be feasible for global connectivity.

QUESTION 6

Answer - C) Implement Global Load Balancing to distribute traffic across regions.
Answer - D) Use VPC Peering extensively to connect VPC networks in different regions.

Option C and D are the networking strategies that prioritize high availability and disaster recovery in a multi-region architecture.
Option C uses Global Load Balancing for traffic distribution, and Option D connects VPC networks across regions.
Option A with dedicated interconnects might be costly and may not address disaster recovery.
Option B mentions VPNs but does not specifically address multi-region strategies.
Option E focuses on content delivery but not application high availability.

QUESTION 7

Answer – A) Use dynamic routing with BGP, set local ASN to 64512, and peer ASN to 64513.

A) Correct. Using BGP with different ASNs ensures optimal routing and redundancy.
B) Incorrect. Static VPNs do not dynamically update routes, leading to potential routing issues.
C) Incorrect. Using the same ASN for local and peer can cause routing conflicts.
D) Incorrect. Mixing dynamic and static VPNs adds unnecessary complexity without benefits.
E) Incorrect. Having different local ASNs but the same peer ASN can lead to routing loops.

QUESTION 8

Answer - B) Create a Cloud Storage custom encryption policy that enforces the use of CMEK for all buckets in the project.

Option B is the correct approach as it involves creating a custom encryption policy to enforce CMEK usage for all buckets in the project, ensuring data is encrypted at rest using customer-managed keys.
Option A discusses default encryption but relies on Google-managed keys, not CMEK.
Option C mentions Google Cloud KMS but doesn't specify how to enforce CMEK for all buckets.
Option D talks about IAM policies for access control, not encryption.
Option E refers to Uniform Bucket-level Access but doesn't address CMEK enforcement.

QUESTION 9

Answer - B) Establish a Dedicated Interconnect connection between your on-premises network and Google Cloud.
Answer - D) Use a Direct Peering connection to connect your on-premises network and Google Cloud.

Option B (Dedicated Interconnect) is the recommended solution as it provides a dedicated and highly available connection between your on-premises network and Google Cloud, ensuring low latency and high reliability.
Option D (Direct Peering) can be used in conjunction with Dedicated Interconnect for additional redundancy.
Option A (Cloud VPN) is a less performant option for large-scale data transfers, and option C (External Load Balancer) is not a suitable choice for connecting on-premises networks.
Option E (Cloud Router) is used for routing within Google Cloud VPCs and is not designed for connecting on-premises networks.

QUESTION 10

Answer - B) Creating a central hub VPC with VPC Peering to connect to other VPCs.

Option A is not efficient for managing multiple projects.
Option C refers to a different Google Cloud service.
Option D provides secure connectivity but doesn't address the central hub requirement.
Option B is the correct choice as it aligns with the requirements, providing a central hub for secure and private connectivity while maintaining separate VPCs for different projects.

QUESTION 11

Answer - B) Google Cloud AI Platform for building, training, and deploying machine learning models.

Option A is for automated machine learning but may not cover custom model deployment.
Option C is for real-time data processing but not specifically for machine learning model deployment.
Option D is for data preparation and transformation but doesn't focus on model deployment.
Option E is for specialized hardware but doesn't address the full machine learning model lifecycle.
Option B is the correct choice as Google Cloud AI Platform provides end-to-end capabilities for building, training, and deploying machine learning models, including dynamic scaling and specialized hardware support, making it suitable for complex machine learning deployments.

QUESTION 12

Answer – D) Create multiple Partner Interconnects with a global routing setup.

A) Incorrect. VPNs may not provide the required bandwidth.
B) Incorrect. Dedicated Interconnects at each site are costly and complex.
C) Incorrect. A single Interconnect lacks redundancy.
D) Correct. Provides scalability and redundancy across regions.
E) Incorrect. Hybrid approach adds unnecessary complexity.

QUESTION 13

Answer – A) Apply network policies at the Pod level and configure GCP firewalls for external traffic.

A) Correct. Network policies at the Pod level and GCP firewalls for external traffic provide comprehensive security.
B) Incorrect. Nodes are not the ideal granularity for network policies in GKE.
C) Incorrect. GKE Ingress does not manage internal traffic between pods.
D) Incorrect. Network policies are not configured at the GKE Service level.
E) Incorrect. GCP firewalls alone are not sufficient for internal GKE traffic control.

QUESTION 14

Answer - C) Set up a global load balancer to distribute traffic across regions.

C) Set up a global load balancer to distribute traffic across regions - A global load balancer can balance traffic efficiently across regions while optimizing cost and performance.
A) Utilize Google Cloud VPN for secure inter-region communication - VPNs are for secure access, not load balancing or cost optimization.
B) Implement Google Cloud Interconnect for dedicated high-speed connections - Interconnect may be costly and is not typically used for balancing traffic between regions.
D) Use Google Cloud CDN for content caching in each region - CDN focuses on content delivery and may not directly address inter-region traffic balancing.
E) Deploy Google Cloud Router with BGP for dynamic routing - Router with BGP is used for routing within GCP but does not specifically optimize cost and performance for inter-region communication.

QUESTION 15

Answer – A) Allow ingress from specific corporate network IPs on required application ports.

A) Correct. Ensures access is limited to authorized networks.
B) Incorrect. Too restrictive and may not cover all necessary corporate networks.
C) Incorrect. Allowing all ingress from the internet is insecure.
D) Incorrect. Allowing all ports from specific regions is too permissive.
E) Incorrect. Allowing all egress and restricting ingress to HTTP does not match the requirement.

QUESTION 16

Answer - D) Google Cloud Regional Persistent Disks for data storage.

D) Google Cloud Regional Persistent Disks for data storage - Regional Persistent Disks allow you to store data in specific regions, ensuring data sovereignty and compliance by controlling where data is stored.
A) Google Cloud CDN for content caching - CDN is for caching content and may not directly address data

sovereignty and compliance requirements.

B) Google Cloud Storage for data storage - While Google Cloud Storage is versatile, it may not provide the same level of control over data placement as Regional Persistent Disks.

C) Google Cloud Dedicated Interconnect for direct connections - Interconnect is for connectivity, not data storage.

E) Google Cloud Network Peering for data transfer - Network Peering is for communication between networks, not data storage control.

QUESTION 17

Answer - D) Google Cloud Dedicated Interconnect with multiple redundant connections.

D) Google Cloud Dedicated Interconnect with multiple redundant connections - This option ensures high availability and minimal data loss for critical applications in a disaster recovery scenario.

A) Google Cloud Load Balancing focuses on traffic distribution but does not specifically address disaster recovery.

B) Google Cloud VPN provides secure access but may not offer the same level of redundancy and data loss prevention as Dedicated Interconnect.

C) Google Cloud Interconnect provides dedicated connections but may not emphasize redundancy as much as Dedicated Interconnect with multiple connections.

E) Google Cloud Cloud Storage is for data replication and backup, which is important for disaster recovery but not the primary focus of this question.

QUESTION 18

Answer - C) Set up a managed instance group using one of the virtual machine images from your in-house rendering servers, and associate this managed instance group with a target pool that is connected to your network load balancer.

C) Set up a managed instance group using virtual machine images from your in-house rendering servers and associate it with a target pool connected to the network load balancer. This approach allows for easy management, scaling, and Google Cloud-native load balancing while preserving your unique server configurations.

A) Leveraging ECMP routing with static routes is not the typical approach for managing rendering server instances on Google Cloud.

B) Implementing a third-party front-end solution may add complexity and is not necessarily Google Cloud-native.

D) Establishing a target pool for rendering instances is a step in the right direction, but setting up a managed instance group provides additional benefits for managing and scaling the instances.

E) Utilizing Google Kubernetes Engine (GKE) for containerization may not align with the straightforward rehosting approach mentioned in the scenario.

QUESTION 19

Answer - B) The VM has been assigned a publicly routable IP address.

B) The VM not using Cloud NAT when connecting to external services is likely because it has been assigned a publicly routable IP address, bypassing the need for NAT.

A) Custom-defined routes directing traffic to private IP ranges wouldn't affect Cloud NAT configuration.

C) The number of network interfaces on the VM is generally unrelated to Cloud NAT usage.
D) A Google Cloud load balancer typically doesn't impact Cloud NAT configuration.
E) Using a VPN tunnel doesn't directly influence Cloud NAT behavior.

QUESTION 20

Answer - A) There are custom-defined routes directing traffic to private IP ranges.

A) The primary reason for the VM not using Cloud NAT could be custom-defined routes directing traffic to private IP ranges, bypassing Cloud NAT.
B) Assigning a publicly routable IP address to the VM wouldn't affect Cloud NAT usage.
C) The number of network interfaces typically doesn't impact Cloud NAT usage.
D) VMs reachable through external IP addresses wouldn't necessarily avoid Cloud NAT.
E) Firewall rules might affect traffic, but they are not the primary reason in this context.

QUESTION 21

Answer - C) Set up a managed instance group using one of the virtual machine images from your in-house rendering servers, and associate this managed instance group with a target pool that is connected to your network load balancer.

C) To accomplish this deployment on Google Cloud while leveraging Google Cloud-native solutions, you can set up a managed instance group using one of the virtual machine images from your in-house rendering servers. Associate this managed instance group with a target pool that is connected to your network load balancer for efficient traffic distribution.
A) Leveraging ECMP routing for this scenario may not be the most straightforward approach.
B) Implementing a third-party front-end solution introduces unnecessary complexity.
D) Establishing a target pool is part of the recommended approach but does not cover the complete deployment method.
E) While GKE is a viable option, it may introduce additional complexity and overhead if not necessary.

QUESTION 22

Answer - B) The VM has been assigned a publicly routable IP address.

B) The VM has been assigned a publicly routable IP address, which bypasses the need for Cloud NAT when connecting to external services.
A) Custom-defined routes directing traffic to private IP ranges might affect internal routing but wouldn't impact Cloud NAT behavior.
C) The number of network interfaces on the VM doesn't directly relate to Cloud NAT usage.
D) The use of an external IP address provided by a Google Cloud load balancer is unrelated to Cloud NAT.
E) Cloud NAT configuration issues would likely affect all VMs, not just a particular one.

QUESTION 23

Answer – D) Configure SSL policies on an external HTTP(S) load balancer combined with Cloud Armor.

A) Incorrect. Internal load balancer is for intra-VPC traffic, not external API traffic.

B) Incorrect. Cloud VPN is not typically used for client-API interactions.

C) Incorrect. VPC Service Controls are more for data within GCP services, not API traffic security.

D) Correct. SSL policies on an external load balancer with Cloud Armor provide security and availability for API traffic.

E) Incorrect. Private Google Access is for accessing Google services from your VPC, not for securing API traffic.

QUESTION 24

Answer - C) Implement IP masquerading for outbound connections.

E) Configure Container-Optimized OS for GKE nodes.

Option A - Increasing the number of nodes may not directly improve network performance and could lead to higher costs.

Option B - Enabling VPC Flow Logs is useful for monitoring but doesn't directly improve network performance.

Option D - Using Google Cloud CDN is more focused on content caching, not microservices communication. Choice C (Implement IP masquerading for outbound connections) - Implementing IP masquerading for outbound connections can help in optimizing network performance by allowing multiple internal IP addresses to share a single external IP address when communicating with external services. This can reduce the number of external IP addresses needed and improve network efficiency.

Choice E (Configure Container-Optimized OS for GKE nodes) - Configuring Container-Optimized OS for GKE nodes can improve network performance as it is designed for running containers efficiently. This optimized OS can enhance the overall performance of microservices running on GKE nodes.

QUESTION 25

Answer - A) Use Google Cloud Spanner for real-time data replication.

C) Implement Google Cloud Pub/Sub for event-driven data synchronization.

Option B - While Google Cloud Storage can replicate data, it may not provide near real-time replication suitable for disaster recovery.

Option D - Google Cloud Dataprep is for data transformation and not real-time replication or failover.

Option E - Google Cloud Storage Coldline is for data archiving and not suitable for real-time replication.

Choice A - Google Cloud Spanner supports real-time, globally distributed database replication, making it suitable for near real-time data replication and failover in disaster recovery scenarios.

Choice C - Implementing Google Cloud Pub/Sub allows for event-driven data synchronization, which can be used for near real-time data replication and failover in disaster recovery scenarios.

QUESTION 26

Answer – A) Set up a private forwarding zone in Cloud DNS for "hq.example.net", direct it to the corporate DNS server, and link it with the central networking VPC.

A) Correct. This setup integrates corporate and Google Cloud DNS resolution efficiently.

B) Incorrect. Manual configuration of each instance is not scalable.

C) Incorrect. DNS peering does not facilitate integration with an external corporate DNS.

D) Incorrect. Direct forwarding from each VPC is less efficient than centralizing in the networking VPC.

E) Incorrect. DNS policies are not the recommended method for integrating with external corporate DNS servers.

QUESTION 27

Answer - A) Formulate a single VPC in a Shared VPC Host Project.

Option B - Configuring a 2-NIC VM in the Service Project is not recommended for deep packet inspection.
Option C - Creating 2 VPCs in the Host Project may complicate routing and firewall configuration.
Option D - Setting up a 2-NIC instance is not mentioned in the requirements. Choice A - Formulating a single VPC in a Shared VPC Host Project with a dual-NIC VM in europe-west3 allows for effective placement of the security appliance, simplifying routing and firewall setup.

QUESTION 28

Answer – A) Add the VM's subnet 10.142.80.0/24 to masterAuthorizedNetworksConfig and use the privateEndpoint 10.142.64.2 for kubectl.

A) Correct. This configuration ensures secure internal communication from the VM to the GKE cluster.
B) Incorrect. Adding an external IP is unnecessary and less secure for internal communication.
C) Incorrect. Using the public endpoint is not recommended for a VM within the same VPC.
D) Incorrect. The master's subnet is not relevant for the VM's network configuration.
E) Incorrect. The masterAuthorizedNetworksConfig needs to include the VM's subnet for secure access.

QUESTION 29

Answer - B) Create a VPC Service Controls perimeter for your project with an access context policy that encompasses your organization's head office network IP ranges.

Option A - Establishing separate access context policies for each application may result in administrative complexity.
Option C - Creating individual VPC Service Controls perimeters for each application may lead to management overhead.
Option D - While firewall rules can provide protection, VPC Service Controls offer a more comprehensive solution. Choice B - Establishing a VPC Service Controls perimeter for your project with a comprehensive access context policy that covers head office network IP ranges provides centralized and efficient API access control for Memorystore and Spanner across all applications in the project.

QUESTION 30

Answer - B) Deploy your serverless data processing components directly into the secure network of the existing VPC. Adjust firewall rules to facilitate communication paths between the serverless components and the IoT devices.

Option A - Generating individual VPC access connectors for each component may lead to increased complexity and costs.
Option C - Setting up a new serverless-dedicated VPC with peering may not be the most cost-effective solution for minimal network traffic.
Option D - Creating a single VPC access connector might not be the most efficient approach for minimizing costs. Choice B - Deploying serverless components directly into the existing VPC and adjusting

firewall rules offers a cost-effective solution for minimal network traffic and ensures seamless communication with IoT devices.

QUESTION 31

Answer - A) Create a VPC Service Controls perimeter for your project with an access context policy that includes your organization's head office network IP ranges, and then implement the policy for Memorystore and Spanner.

Option B - While configuring a custom firewall rule is an option, using VPC Service Controls provides a more comprehensive solution.
Option D - Setting up a VPN tunnel is a valid approach but may not be the most efficient way to control API access. Choice A - Creating a VPC Service Controls perimeter for the project with the right access context policy ensures that only traffic from the head office networks is permitted, meeting the security requirements.

QUESTION 32

Answer – B) Configure Shared VPC across both projects.

A) Incorrect. VPC Peering is less efficient for this scenario.
B) Correct. Shared VPC allows secure and efficient inter-project communication.
C) Incorrect. Cloud VPN is not necessary within the same organization.
D) Incorrect. Dedicated Interconnect is for connecting external networks, not for inter-project GCP communication.
E) Incorrect. Private Google Access is for accessing Google services, not for communication between GCP resources in different projects.

QUESTION 33

Answer - A) Use Google Cloud Storage to host static content and Cloud CDN for caching and delivering it globally.

Option B - Deploying multiple virtual machines may not be the most cost-effective and efficient solution for content distribution.
Option C - Setting up a Cloud SQL database in each region for dynamic content may introduce complexity and synchronization challenges.
Option D - While GKE with global load balancing can be used for dynamic content, it may be overkill for serving static content. Choice A - Using Google Cloud Storage to host static content and Cloud CDN for caching and delivering it globally is a cost-effective and efficient way to achieve low-latency content distribution.

QUESTION 34

Answer - A) VPC Service Controls with Google Cloud Armor

A) VPC Service Controls with Google Cloud Armor - Explanation: This combination provides strict access controls and security features for healthcare applications in Google Cloud.
B) Private Google Access with Identity-Aware Proxy - Explanation: This combination focuses on access

control but may not provide the same level of security features as VPC Service Controls and Google Cloud Armor.

C) VPN Gateway with SSL Proxy Load Balancer - Explanation: VPN Gateway and SSL Proxy Load Balancer focus on secure connections and load balancing but may not provide the same security measures as VPC Service Controls and Google Cloud Armor.

D) Cloud NAT with Global Load Balancer - Explanation: Cloud NAT and Global Load Balancer are useful but may not directly address strict encryption and access control measures required for highly regulated healthcare applications.

E) Anycast IP Routing with Firewall Rules - Explanation: Anycast IP routing can improve routing efficiency, but Firewall Rules alone may not provide the required security features. This combination may not meet the complex security requirements effectively.

QUESTION 35

Answer - B) Migrate virtual_machine-2 to a separate Virtual Private Cloud (VPC) and establish VPC Peering with virtual_machine-1's VPC, optimizing routing for low-latency access.

B) Migrate virtual_machine-2 to a separate Virtual Private Cloud (VPC) and establish VPC Peering with virtual_machine-1's VPC, optimizing routing for low-latency access - Explanation: Migrating virtual_machine-2 to a separate VPC and establishing VPC Peering with virtual_machine-1's VPC is the most effective solution to ensure low-latency access and efficient traffic routing between the two machines.

A) Set up a custom route with more precision than the default network route - Explanation: While creating a custom route is useful, it may not directly address the requirement for low-latency access and optimizing traffic routing.

C) Delete the default network route and create a distinct custom route with a network tag - Explanation: Deleting the default route and using network tags introduces complexity that may not be necessary for optimizing routing.

D) Create a more specific custom route with a network tag - Explanation: This option introduces network tags, which may not be needed for efficient traffic routing.

E) Implement an SSL VPN gateway - Explanation: Implementing an SSL VPN gateway focuses on secure connections and may not directly optimize traffic routing and low-latency access between the two virtual machines.

QUESTION 36

Answer – C) GKE cluster with VPC-native custom IP ranges, privateEndpoint for control plane, /24 CIDR for pods and services, network proxy, and master authorized networks enabled.

A) Incorrect. Google-managed IP ranges may not meet the requirement to minimize IP allocations.
B) Incorrect. This setup doesn't specify the privateEndpoint, which is crucial for not exposing nodes to the internet.
C) Correct. This setup aligns with all requirements: efficient IP allocation, no public exposure, and secure kubectl access.
D) Incorrect. The choice does not explicitly mention the privateEndpoint for the control plane.
E) Incorrect. Standard clusters do not offer the same level of control over IP allocation and exposure as VPC-native configurations.

QUESTION 37

Answer – B) Network Load Balancer

A) Incorrect. Internal Load Balancer is for internal network traffic, not global external traffic.
B) Correct. Network Load Balancer preserves the client's IP address in incoming traffic.
C) Incorrect. HTTP(S) Load Balancer typically modifies the client IP address.
D) Incorrect. TCP/SSL Proxy Load Balancer does not preserve the original client IP address.
E) Incorrect. Even with IP header preservation, Global Load Balancers other than Network Load Balancer may modify the client IP.

QUESTION 38

Answer - A) Google Cloud CDN with Google Cloud Armor

A) Google Cloud CDN with Google Cloud Armor - Correct answer. CDN with Armor provides content delivery and security features, caching content closer to end-users.
B) Traffic Director with Cloud Spanner - These services are for traffic management and database operations, not content caching.
C) Google Cloud Storage with VPC peering - While Storage is for data storage, it does not inherently offer content caching.
D) Google Cloud Pub/Sub with Google Cloud Load Balancing - Pub/Sub and Load Balancing are used for messaging and traffic distribution but not content caching.
E) Google Cloud Dataflow with Google Cloud Storage - Dataflow and Storage are used for data processing and storage, not content caching.

QUESTION 39

Answer - C) gcloud dns record-sets import ZONE_FILE --zone MANAGED_ZONE

A) gcloud dns record-sets import ZONE_FILE --zone-file-format --zone MANAGED_ZONE - While this option is close, it contains unnecessary flags and options.
B) gcloud dns record-sets import ZONE_FILE --replace-origin-ns --zone MANAGED_ZONE - This option includes an unnecessary flag for replacing origin NS records.
C) gcloud dns record-sets import ZONE_FILE --zone MANAGED_ZONE - Correct answer. This command imports the BIND zone file to Google Cloud DNS for the specified managed zone.
D) gcloud dns record-sets import ZONE_FILE --delete-all-existing --zone MANAGED_ZONE - This option unnecessarily includes a flag to delete all existing records.
E) gcloud dns record-sets export ZONE_FILE --zone-file-format --zone MANAGED_ZONE - This command is for exporting records, not importing them into Google Cloud DNS.

QUESTION 40

Answer - B) Google Kubernetes Engine (GKE)

A) Google Compute Engine - While it offers compute resources, GKE provides container orchestration and scalability advantages for machine learning workloads.
B) Correct answer. GKE is well-suited for deploying machine learning models, as it offers efficient resource allocation, scalability, and containerized deployment for image recognition tasks.
C) Google Cloud Functions - Functions are designed for event-driven, serverless computing and may not

be the best choice for resource-intensive machine learning tasks.

D) Google Cloud Run - Run is designed for containerized applications but may not provide the same level of control and scalability as GKE for machine learning workloads.

E) Google AI Platform - While it offers machine learning services, GKE provides more flexibility and control for deploying custom machine learning models at scale.

QUESTION 41

Answer - C) Google Cloud Storage and Google Cloud KMS

A) Google Cloud VPN and Google Cloud DNS provide secure connectivity and DNS services but may not inherently provide data encryption at rest or in transit for other Google Cloud services.

B) Google Cloud Identity-Aware Proxy (IAP) and Google Cloud CDN focus on identity management and content delivery but may not directly address data encryption requirements.

C) Correct answer. Google Cloud Storage offers data replication between regions, and Google Cloud DNS provides domain name resolution for disaster recovery scenarios.

D) Google Cloud Spanner is a database, and Google Cloud Load Balancing focuses on traffic distribution; they may not be primarily related to data encryption.

E) Google Cloud Compute Engine Autoscaler and Google Cloud Pub/Sub are not directly related to data encryption at rest and in transit.

QUESTION 42

Answer - B) Google Cloud CDN and Google Cloud Compute Engine Autoscaler

A) Google Cloud VPN and Google Cloud DNS provide secure connectivity and DNS services but may not inherently provide data encryption at rest and in transit without additional configurations.

B) Correct answer. Google Cloud CDN and Google Cloud Compute Engine Autoscaler focus on content delivery and scaling, optimizing latency and improving global access for customers.

C) Google Cloud Spanner is a database, and Google Cloud Load Balancing focuses on traffic distribution; they may not be the primary solutions for latency optimization.

D) Google Cloud Storage and Google Cloud DNS offer storage and DNS services but may not be the primary choices for optimizing latency.

E) Google Cloud Load Balancing and Google Cloud VPC Peering may not be the primary components for latency optimization and global access improvement.

QUESTION 43

Answer - B) Assign members of the infrastructure team a custom role with permissions including compute.subnetworks.get and compute.firewalls.get.

A) The compute.networkViewer role provides read-only access to network resources but does not specifically grant access to firewall configurations.

B) Correct answer. Assigning a custom role with specific permissions for viewing subnetworks and firewalls while preventing modifications is the most suitable option.

C) The compute.networkUser role allows users to use network resources but doesn't grant the necessary read access to firewall configurations.

D) Granting the compute.subnetworks.useExternal permission is not required to view firewall configurations and may not be sufficient.

E) Assigning the roles/owner role provides full control over resources, which is not suitable for the infrastructure team's requirement of view-only access to firewalls.

QUESTION 44

Answer - C) gcloud dns record-sets import ZONE_FILE --zone MANAGED_ZONE

A) Incorrect syntax. The correct command does not include "--zone-file-format."
B) Incorrect syntax. The correct command does not include "--replace-origin-ns."
C) Correct answer. The appropriate command to import a BIND zone file to Google Cloud DNS is "gcloud dns record-sets import ZONE_FILE --zone MANAGED_ZONE."
D) Incorrect syntax. The correct command does not include "--delete-all-existing."

QUESTION 45

Answer - E) Multi-region routing mode.

A) Single-region routing mode would not optimize traffic for a globally distributed application.
B) Failover routing mode is not focused on optimizing traffic but on providing failover capabilities.
C) Multicast routing mode is not typically used in Google Cloud for this purpose.
D) Anycast routing mode is not a routing mode offered by Google Cloud.
E) Multi-region routing mode is designed for globally distributed applications, providing low-latency access and high availability by directing traffic to the nearest location.

QUESTION 46

Answer - D) Rely on the built-in backup features of Google Cloud services like Cloud SQL and Compute Engine.

A) Manual snapshots are not automated and may lead to human errors.
B) While Cloud Storage can store backups, it doesn't automate the backup process.
C) Implementing automated backups using Cloud Pub/Sub and Cloud Functions can be complex and may not cover all resources.
D) Google Cloud services often offer built-in backup features that are efficient and automated.
E) Scheduling periodic exports to an external solution may not be as efficient as using native Google Cloud backup features.

QUESTION 47

Answer - A) SMS authentication and C) Time-based one-time password (TOTP) authentication.

A) SMS authentication sends one-time codes via SMS for MFA.
B) Fingerprint recognition and voice recognition are not standard MFA methods offered by Google Cloud Identity Platform.
C) Time-based one-time password (TOTP) authentication generates one-time codes through a mobile app or hardware token for MFA.
D) Smart card authentication is not a standard MFA method offered by Google Cloud Identity Platform.
E) Voice recognition is not a standard MFA method offered by Google Cloud Identity Platform.

QUESTION 48

Answer – A) Enable VPC Flow Logs for the subnetworks hosting the Compute Engine instances.

A) Correct. VPC Flow Logs capture detailed information about network traffic, including outbound connections, which is essential for security audits.
B) Incorrect. Cloud Monitoring provides performance metrics but not detailed logging of network connections.
C) Incorrect. Cloud IDS is focused on intrusion detection, not specifically on logging outbound connections.
D) Incorrect. While egress firewall rules can restrict traffic, they do not provide comprehensive logging.
E) Incorrect. Cloud NAT manages outbound connections but does not provide detailed logging for compliance purposes.

QUESTION 49

Answer – B) Configure each instance with Premium Network Tier.

A) Incorrect. Private Google Access is for accessing Google services, not specifically for optimizing performance to Cloud Storage.
B) Correct. Premium Network Tier offers improved throughput and lower latency for cloud services like Cloud Storage.
C) Incorrect. Dedicated Interconnect is typically for on-premises to GCP connections.
D) Incorrect. VPC Peering is not applicable for Cloud Storage.
E) Incorrect. VPN is not optimized for high-throughput, low-latency data transfers.

QUESTION 50

Answer – B) Configure Dedicated Interconnect for a direct, high-speed connection to the external service.

A) Incorrect. VPN may not provide the highest throughput necessary for frequent data exchanges.
B) Correct. Dedicated Interconnect offers a high-capacity, direct connection, ideal for high-throughput and low-latency data transfers to non-Google cloud services.
C) Incorrect. Private Google Access is for accessing Google services, not external cloud services.
D) Incorrect. Premium Network Tier enhances general network performance but does not directly address connectivity to external services.
E) Incorrect. While Cloud Interconnect is suitable, it is typically used for on-premises to GCP connections, not for connecting to external cloud services.

PRACTICE TEST 3 - QUESTIONS ONLY

QUESTION 1

You are managing a Google Cloud project with multiple teams. Each team needs its own isolated network within the project. What is the recommended approach to achieve network isolation while maintaining resource separation?

A) Create a separate VPC for each team within the project.
B) Use Shared VPC to share a single VPC across teams.
C) Use a common firewall rule for all teams.
D) Assign each team to a different project.
E) Create separate projects for each team.

QUESTION 2

Your organization is planning to deploy a global Kubernetes cluster on Google Cloud. What should you consider to ensure optimal network performance and low-latency communication between nodes in different regions?

A) Use a single regional cluster for all nodes.
 B) Implement Google Cloud VPN tunnels between nodes.
 C) Deploy Google Cloud CDN for content delivery.
 D) Use Google Cloud Interconnect for dedicated connectivity.
 E) Opt for Google Cloud's managed Kubernetes service (GKE).

QUESTION 3

Your organization is planning to deploy a new application on Google Cloud and wants to ensure secure and controlled communication between microservices. What should you implement to achieve this while maintaining isolation between microservices and controlling traffic flow?

A) Google Cloud Endpoints for API management.
 B) Google Cloud Network Peering between microservices.
 C) Google Cloud VPC Service Controls.
 D) Google Cloud Shared VPC for microservices.
 E) Google Cloud Identity-Aware Proxy (IAP).

QUESTION 4

Your organization is planning to deploy a new application on Google Cloud and wants to ensure secure and controlled communication between microservices. What should you implement to achieve this while maintaining isolation between microservices and controlling traffic flow?

A) Google Cloud Endpoints for API management.
 B) Google Cloud Network Peering between microservices.
 C) Google Cloud VPC Service Controls.

D) Google Cloud Shared VPC for microservices.
E) Google Cloud Identity-Aware Proxy (IAP).

QUESTION 5

Your organization is planning to migrate a large volume of data from an on-premises data warehouse to Google Cloud Storage. You need a high-throughput, reliable solution. What should you consider?

A) Use Google Cloud Storage Transfer Service for data migration.
B) Implement a Cloud VPN with data compression techniques for efficient data transfer.
C) Utilize a Direct Peering connection for dedicated high-speed connectivity.
D) Set up a dedicated fiber optic link for maximum throughput.
E) Explore third-party data migration tools for the migration process.

QUESTION 6

Your organization is expanding its Google Cloud infrastructure to include multiple projects, each with its own set of VPC networks. You need to establish secure communication between projects while maintaining network isolation. What should you prioritize?

A) Assign public IP addresses to instances in each project for direct communication.
B) Implement Cloud VPNs with IPsec encryption between VPC networks in different projects.
C) Set up VPC Network Peering connections between VPC networks in different projects.
D) Utilize Google Cloud Dedicated Interconnect for dedicated, cross-project connectivity.
E) Use Google Cloud Pub/Sub for inter-project messaging.

QUESTION 7

You're tasked with setting up a secure connection between a GCP VPC (10.132.0.0/20) and an external network (192.168.5.0/24) using Cloud VPN. What considerations must you take into account for the BGP session to ensure a secure and reliable connection?

A) Match the ASN across both networks for a secure connection.
B) Utilize pre-shared keys for the VPN and different ASNs for each network.
C) Ensure the same BGP IP is used on both sides for consistency.
D) Use a dynamic routing mode with BGP, with different ASNs and MD5 authentication.
E) Set up static routing with identical BGP IPs on both sides to simplify the setup.

QUESTION 8

Your organization is planning to migrate a large number of virtual machines (VMs) from on-premises data centers to Google Cloud. You want to ensure minimal disruption and downtime during the migration. Which Google Cloud service should you use to facilitate this migration with minimal impact?

A) Google Cloud Transfer Service
B) Google Cloud Dataprep
C) Google Cloud Transfer Appliance
D) Google Cloud Dataflow
E) Google Cloud Migrate for Compute Engine

QUESTION 9

Your organization is planning to deploy a critical application on Google Cloud, and you want to design a highly available architecture. Which design principles should you follow to achieve high availability?

A) Avoid using multiple Availability Zones (AZs) to reduce complexity.
B) Implement a single VPC for all resources to simplify network management.
C) Use multiple regions and Availability Zones (AZs) to distribute resources.
D) Rely on a single instance for critical workloads to minimize points of failure.
E) Separate data storage and compute resources for simplicity.

QUESTION 10

Your organization manages multiple Google Cloud projects, each with its dedicated Virtual Private Cloud (VPC) network. You need to ensure private connectivity between these VPCs, internet access, and connection to an external data center. What architecture should you consider?

A) Establish individual VPN tunnels for each VPC.
B) Create a central hub VPC with VPC Peering connections to project VPCs.
C) Utilize Cloud Interconnect Dedicated for private connections.
D) Implement Cloud VPN for secure project-to-project connectivity.
E) Consolidate all VPCs into a single VPC structure.

QUESTION 11

Your organization is managing a global network infrastructure on Google Cloud with multiple VPCs in different regions. You need to establish private and secure communication between these VPCs while ensuring minimal latency. Additionally, you want to minimize the administrative overhead of managing multiple VPC peering connections. What Google Cloud networking solution should you consider for this complex multi-region VPC connectivity, and what benefits does it offer?

A) Set up Google Cloud VPC Peering connections between all VPCs for direct communication.
B) Implement Google Cloud Interconnect to establish low-latency private connections.
C) Utilize Google Cloud Shared VPC to centralize VPC management and reduce overhead.
D) Configure Google Cloud VPN tunnels for secure communication between VPCs.
E) Deploy Google Cloud Direct Peering to minimize latency between regions.

QUESTION 12

A multinational corporation needs to establish a robust and secure network connection between its primary GCP VPC (10.132.0.0/14) in the us-central1 region and various branch offices worldwide. The solution must prioritize high availability and fault tolerance. Which configuration should you recommend?

A) Set up a global HTTP(S) load balancer for branch office connectivity.
B) Use Cloud VPN with HA configurations for each branch office.
C) Implement multiple Dedicated Interconnects for key branch locations.
D) Create Partner Interconnects with diverse routing for each branch.
E) Deploy a network of Cloud Routers with dynamic BGP routing across all offices.

QUESTION 13

You are designing a network architecture for a data-intensive application in GKE. The application requires high throughput and low latency communication between GKE and BigQuery. Which configuration ensures the most efficient data processing and transfer?

A) Configure Cloud VPN between GKE and BigQuery.
B) Utilize VPC Peering between the GKE cluster's VPC and BigQuery.
C) Implement Dedicated Interconnect for GKE to BigQuery communication.
D) Use a Private Google Access setup for GKE and BigQuery.
E) Deploy the GKE cluster in the same region as the BigQuery dataset.

QUESTION 14

You are designing a network architecture for a global Google Cloud project. The project requires low-latency communication between regions and high availability. What GCP networking approach should you recommend to meet these requirements?

A) Utilize regional load balancers with failover.
B) Deploy the application across multiple regions with a global load balancer.
C) Implement Google Cloud Dedicated Interconnect for direct region-to-region connections.
D) Set up Google Cloud VPN with multiple tunnels for inter-region communication.
E) Use Google Cloud CDN for content delivery across regions.

QUESTION 15

You are setting up a firewall for a GCP project hosting a number of APIs. These APIs should only be accessible from a set of known external partner networks. How should you configure your firewall rules to secure these APIs?

A) Allow ingress on ports used by the APIs only from the partner networks.
B) Deny all ingress and egress, creating exceptions for each partner IP.
C) Set up a rule to allow all ingress traffic on port 443 (HTTPS).
D) Create a rule for stateful inspection of all ingress and egress traffic.
E) Implement a default deny rule and a specific allow rule for partner network IPs.

QUESTION 16

Your organization is adopting a multi-cloud strategy and plans to use Google Cloud in conjunction with other cloud providers. You want to ensure secure and reliable communication between these environments. What GCP networking solution should you recommend for multi-cloud connectivity?

A) Google Cloud Interconnect for dedicated connections.
B) Google Cloud VPN for secure access.
C) Google Cloud Dedicated Interconnect for low-latency connections.
D) Google Cloud Network Peering for inter-cloud communication.
E) Google Cloud CDN for content delivery.

QUESTION 17

Your organization needs to securely connect on-premises data centers to Google Cloud resources. You want to ensure high-speed, dedicated connections with low-latency communication. What GCP networking option should you recommend for this connectivity?

A) Google Cloud VPN for secure access.
B) Google Cloud Interconnect for dedicated connections.
C) Google Cloud Dedicated Interconnect with multiple redundant connections.
D) Google Cloud Network Peering for inter-cloud communication.
E) Google Cloud CDN for content delivery.

QUESTION 18

Your organization is planning to migrate a large database to Google Cloud SQL. Data security and compliance are top priorities. Which database encryption option should you choose to ensure data is encrypted both at rest and in transit?

A) Use SSL/TLS for in-transit encryption and Google Cloud KMS for at-rest encryption.
B) Use Cloud SQL's default encryption settings for both at-rest and in-transit encryption.
C) Implement third-party encryption tools for in-transit and at-rest encryption.
D) Use Cloud SQL's default at-rest encryption and deploy a VPN for in-transit encryption.
E) Configure Google Cloud's network security policies to handle both at-rest and in-transit encryption.

QUESTION 19

You set up a new network infrastructure for your analytics department. You plan to ensure that the system engineers can manage virtual machines within this network securely. How would you adjust your firewall configurations to permit this kind of access?

A) Create two firewall rules: one to deny ingress to all protocols with priority 0, and another to permit ingress on port 22 with priority 1000.
B) Create a single firewall rule to allow port 22 with priority 1000.
C) Create two firewall rules: one to block all traffic with priority 65536, and another to allow port 3389 with priority 1000.
D) Establish a single firewall rule to permit ingress on port 3389 with a priority setting of 1000.
E) Create separate firewall rules for each system engineer with their specific IP addresses.

QUESTION 20

You set up a new network infrastructure for your analytics department. You plan to ensure that the system engineers can manage virtual machines within this network securely. How would you adjust your firewall configurations to permit this kind of access?

A) Create two firewall rules: one to deny ingress to all protocols with priority 0, and another to permit ingress on port 22 with priority 1000.
B) Create a single firewall rule to allow port 22 with priority 1000.
C) Create two firewall rules: one to block all traffic with priority 65536, and another to allow port 3389 with priority 1000.
D) Establish a single firewall rule to permit ingress on port 3389 with a priority setting of 1000.

E) Configure a firewall rule to allow all inbound traffic on all ports.

QUESTION 21

Your Google Cloud project contains a mix of virtual machine (VM) instances, some running on the default network and others on custom VPC networks. You need to set up a network monitoring solution that can capture packet-level data for analysis, including traffic between VM instances. What should you do to achieve this?

A) Enable VPC Flow Logs for each VM instance's subnet.
B) Configure Google Cloud's built-in packet capture feature for each VM instance.
C) Create a shared VPC network and move all VM instances to this network for centralized monitoring.
D) Use Google Cloud's integrated Network Intelligence Center for packet-level data capture.

QUESTION 22

You set up a new network infrastructure for your analytics department. You plan to ensure that the system engineers can manage virtual machines within this network securely. How would you adjust your firewall configurations to permit this kind of access?

A) Create two firewall rules: one to deny ingress to all protocols with priority 0, and another to permit ingress on port 22 with priority 1000.
B) Create a single firewall rule to allow port 22 with priority 1000.
C) Create two firewall rules: one to block all traffic with priority 65536, and another to allow port 3389 with priority 1000.
D) Establish a single firewall rule to permit ingress on port 3389 with a priority setting of 1000.
E) Implement a default-deny firewall rule.

QUESTION 23

For a GCP-hosted service that processes large volumes of data from various sources, you need to ensure both secure data transfer and protection against potential data exfiltration. The data sources include several third-party APIs. What network security configuration would best fit this requirement?

A) Use VPC Service Controls to create a secure perimeter around your data processing resources.
B) Set up Cloud Armor policies to filter incoming data and protect against exfiltration.
C) Configure network tags and corresponding firewall rules for data source endpoints.
D) Implement an internal HTTP(S) load balancer with SSL policies for data transfer.
E) Create a Private Google Access configuration for secure connectivity to third-party APIs.

QUESTION 24

Your organization wants to improve the fault tolerance and availability of its Google Cloud infrastructure. Which two strategies should you recommend to achieve this goal?

A) Deploy all services in a single region for simplicity.
B) Use multiple Google Cloud Load Balancers to distribute traffic.
C) Implement cross-region redundancy for critical services.
D) Set up a single VPC for all projects to centralize management.

E) Rely on Cloud Identity and Access Management (IAM) for access control.

QUESTION 25

Your company is migrating a legacy on-premises application to Google Cloud Platform (GCP). The application relies on a dedicated hardware firewall for security. What two strategies should you recommend to replace the on-premises firewall while maintaining security in GCP?

A) Utilize Google Cloud Security Groups for network security.
B) Set up a Cloud NAT gateway for outbound traffic.
C) Implement a Google Cloud VPN tunnel for secure communication.
D) Deploy a Cloud DNS firewall for DNS-based security.
E) Utilize Google Cloud Armor for DDoS protection.

QUESTION 26

In your GCP environment, you need to set up a network architecture that allows secure, low-latency communication between your GCP-hosted services and a partner's services hosted on another cloud provider. The partner's services require authentication for access. What configuration would best meet these requirements?

A) Configure a Dedicated Interconnect to the partner's cloud and use IAM for authentication.
B) Implement Cloud VPN with a shared secret for secure communication and integrate with Cloud IAM for authentication.
C) Set up VPC Peering with the partner's cloud network and use service accounts for authentication.
D) Use Private Google Access to securely connect to the partner's services and OAuth for authentication.
E) Establish a Cloud Router with custom routes to the partner's cloud and use API keys for authentication.

QUESTION 27

Your global retail chain is expanding its infrastructure to Google Cloud with on-premises data centers in Germany and Japan. You need localized branches across North America and South America as well. What networking approach should you consider for efficient connectivity?

A) Implement dedicated VPN connections to each location.
B) Set up a central VPC in europe-west3 and utilize VPC peering for branch connectivity.
C) Create separate VPCs for each branch location and use VPN tunnels.
D) Use Cloud Interconnect for all locations.
E) None of the above.

QUESTION 28

You are managing a GCP project with multiple Compute Engine instances that need to securely access Google Cloud services without exposure to the public internet. What configuration should you use to achieve this while maintaining private access within the GCP environment?

A) Set up Private Google Access on the subnetworks of the Compute Engine instances.
B) Implement VPC Peering with the networks of the Google Cloud services.

C) Configure Cloud VPN for each Compute Engine instance to access Google Cloud services.
D) Use Cloud Interconnect to establish a private connection to Google Cloud services.
E) Assign external IP addresses to the instances and use Cloud Armor for security.

QUESTION 29

Your organization manages a Google Cloud project that houses multiple App Engine applications. To enforce strict API access control for Memorystore instances and Spanner databases, allowing traffic exclusively from your organization's head office networks, which method should you recommend?

A) Develop an access context policy for each App Engine application, specifying head office network IP ranges, and implement these policies for Memorystore and Spanner.
B) Create a VPC Service Controls perimeter for your project, incorporating an access context policy that encompasses your organization's head office network IP ranges.
C) Generate separate VPC Service Controls perimeters for each App Engine application, each with access context policies specifying your organization's head office network IP ranges.
D) Configure a set of firewall rules to deny API access to Memorystore and Spanner from networks not recognized as part of your head office.
E) None of the above.

QUESTION 30

You are developing a new service and need to connect your Compute Engine instances, which don't have public IP addresses, to Cloud Spanner. What two actions should you execute to accomplish this?

A) Enable the Cloud Memorystore API in your Google Cloud project.
B) Establish a private connection with the Cloud Spanner service producer.
C) Turn on Private Google Access for your subnetwork.
D) Configure a custom static route to direct the traffic to the Cloud Spanner service endpoint.
E) Enable the Service Networking API in your Google Cloud project.

QUESTION 31

You have a distributed campus network with 4 switches connected to Google Cloud through dedicated interconnects. All traffic is routing through a single interconnect instead of being distributed across the 4 links. Investigation reveals that each campus switch has identical BGP ASNs, routes, and priorities configured, and all switches are connected to a single Cloud Router. The interconnect logs show 'no-proposal-chosen' messages during initialization, and BGP session has failed to establish between one of the campus switches and the Cloud Router. What is the primary reason for this issue?

A) An internal firewall is preventing the connection from being established on the second Dedicated Interconnect.
B) One of the Dedicated Interconnects is not configured correctly, causing the BGP session failure.
C) There is no Cloud Load Balancer in place to distribute the network load equally between the interconnects.
D) BGP sessions have failed to establish between all campus switches and the Cloud Router due to identical BGP ASNs and routes.
E) None of the above.

QUESTION 32

For a GCP project involving large-scale data processing, you have a mix of Compute Engine instances and GKE clusters. You need to ensure internal-only communication between these resources, with no exposure to the public internet. What network configuration would you recommend?

A) Enable Private Google Access on all subnetworks.
B) Configure Internal TCP/UDP Load Balancer for inter-resource communication.
C) Use VPC firewall rules to restrict all external communication and allow internal traffic.
D) Implement VPC Network Peering between Compute Engine and GKE resources.
E) Set up a Private Service Connect for internal communication.

QUESTION 33

Your company is planning to deploy a highly available web application in Google Cloud. You want to ensure that the application can withstand region-wide failures and continue operating without interruption. What Google Cloud service should you leverage to achieve this level of high availability?

A) Use Google Cloud Load Balancing to distribute traffic across multiple regions.
B) Deploy multiple instances in a single region and rely on regional redundancy.
C) Implement Google Cloud Autohealing to automatically recover from failures.
D) Use Google Cloud Memorystore for caching to enhance application performance.
E) None of the above.

QUESTION 34

Your organization is running a high-traffic e-commerce website and needs to ensure efficient distribution of traffic across multiple Google Cloud regions while maintaining high availability. What complex load balancing solution should you design to meet this requirement?

A) Regional Load Balancer with Google Cloud CDN
B) Global Load Balancer with HTTP(S) Load Balancer
C) Network Load Balancer with TCP Proxy Load Balancer
D) External TCP/UDP Load Balancer with Internal HTTP(S) Load Balancer
E) SSL Proxy Load Balancer with CDN

QUESTION 35

Your organization is conducting a data center migration to Google Cloud and needs to ensure that specific subnets route their traffic through dedicated firewall instances for security purposes. What complex networking strategy should you employ for this migration?

A) Set up custom routes with more precision than the default network routes, specifying the next hops as the dedicated firewall instances without network tags.
B) Shift the dedicated firewall instances to a separate Virtual Private Cloud (VPC) and establish VPC Peering with the subnets requiring security, optimizing traffic routing.
C) Delete the default network routes and establish distinct custom routes for the subnets, directing traffic through the dedicated firewall instances, with network tags assigned for security.

D) Create more specific custom routes than the default network routes, designating the dedicated firewall instances as next hops, and assign network tags to the subnets for secure routing.
E) Implement Cloud Armor to provide security for the subnets during the migration, ensuring traffic is routed through it for inspection.

QUESTION 36

In a GCP environment, you're tasked with setting up a secure, scalable, and efficient network architecture for a series of microservices that communicate heavily with each other. The microservices will be deployed across multiple GKE clusters within the same region. What configuration provides the best network setup for this scenario?

A) Use VPC Network Peering between GKE clusters and implement network policies based on pod labels.
B) Configure each GKE cluster with a private cluster option and use Internal Load Balancers for service communication.
C) Implement Shared VPC across the GKE clusters and utilize VPC Service Controls for inter-cluster security.
D) Set up a single regional GKE cluster and deploy all microservices within different namespaces.
E) Establish individual VPCs for each GKE cluster and use Cloud VPN for secure cluster-to-cluster communication.

QUESTION 37

In a GCP environment, you need to set up a network solution for an IoT application that involves streaming large volumes of data from devices to a centralized processing system. The system must scale dynamically based on the incoming data volume. What network configuration should you implement?

A) Configure each IoT device to stream data through Cloud VPN to the processing system.
B) Use Cloud Pub/Sub for data ingestion and Dataflow for dynamically scaling the processing.
C) Set up individual VPCs for each IoT device category and use VPC Peering for data streaming.
D) Implement Cloud IoT Core for device management and direct device data to a managed instance group for processing.
E) Establish Cloud Endpoints for each IoT device and use Cloud Run for scalable data processing.

QUESTION 38

You are managing a Google Cloud project and need to ensure high availability and fault tolerance for your virtual machine instances. Which Google Cloud networking solution should you use to automatically replicate your VM instances across multiple zones within a region while maintaining data integrity and redundancy?

A) Google Cloud VPN with VPC peering
B) Regional managed instance groups with Google Cloud Load Balancing
C) Google Cloud Storage with VPC Service Controls
D) Google Cloud SQL with VPC peering
E) Google Cloud Dataprep with Cloud Dataflow

QUESTION 39

Your organization operates a global online gaming platform, and you need to ensure low-latency access to game servers for players around the world. Which Google Cloud networking solution should you implement to achieve this goal while minimizing latency and optimizing player experiences?

A) Google Cloud CDN with Google Cloud Armor
B) Traffic Director with Cloud Spanner
C) Google Cloud Storage with VPC peering
D) Google Cloud Pub/Sub with Google Cloud Load Balancing
E) Google Cloud Dataflow with Google Cloud Storage

QUESTION 40

Your organization is setting up a complex network topology on Google Cloud, connecting multiple VPCs in different regions. Security, efficient data transfer, and minimal latency are top priorities. Which combination of Google Cloud networking products or features should you use to achieve these objectives effectively?

A) Google Cloud VPN and Google Cloud DNS
B) Google Cloud Interconnect and Google Cloud VPC Peering
C) Google Cloud Router and Google Cloud CDN
D) Google Cloud Armor and Google Cloud Load Balancing
E) Google Cloud Spanner and Google Cloud Identity-Aware Proxy (IAP)

QUESTION 41

Your organization is planning to implement a disaster recovery solution for your critical applications on Google Cloud. You need to ensure data replication and failover capabilities between regions. Which combination of Google Cloud services or features should you incorporate into your disaster recovery strategy to achieve these objectives effectively?

A) Google Cloud VPN and Google Cloud Bigtable
B) Google Cloud CDN and Google Cloud Compute Engine Autoscaler
C) Google Cloud Spanner and Google Cloud Interconnect
D) Google Cloud Storage and Google Cloud DNS
E) Google Cloud Load Balancing and Google Cloud VPC Peering

QUESTION 42

You are responsible for securing the network communication between your organization's on-premises data center and Google Cloud. You want to establish a dedicated, high-speed connection that ensures private and reliable communication. Which Google Cloud service or feature should you use to achieve this?

A) Google Cloud VPN and Google Cloud DNS
B) Google Cloud Direct Peering and Google Cloud CDN
C) Google Cloud Dedicated Interconnect and Google Cloud Router
D) Google Cloud VPC Peering and Google Cloud Load Balancing
E) Google Cloud Interconnect and Google Cloud Identity-Aware Proxy (IAP)

QUESTION 43

Your regional headquarters has 4 gateways connected to your Google Cloud environment through a Dedicated Interconnect on each gateway. All services are operational; however, all of the network traffic is being routed through a single gateway instead of being distributed evenly across the 4 connections. Upon investigation, you discover: - Each gateway is configured with a distinct ASN. - Each gateway is set with the same routes and weights. - All gateways are connected to one Cloud Router via a Dedicated Interconnect. - BGP sessions are functioning between each gateway and the Cloud Router. - Only the routes from a single gateway are present in the Cloud Router's route table. What could be the primary reason for this issue?

A) A security rule is obstructing traffic through the additional Dedicated Interconnect.
B) The ASNs utilized on the gateways are unique.
C) There isn't a load balancer in place for distributing network load.
D) The gateways are configured with identical routes.
E) The Cloud Router is not properly configured to handle multiple Dedicated Interconnect connections.

QUESTION 44

Your organization has structured a resource hierarchy with multiple projects and VPCs. You need to establish a way for IAM permissions to be inherited from parent folders to child folders while allowing individual VPCs to set their specific firewall rules. What is the most appropriate way to configure this setup?

A) Enable "Inherit permissions" for each VPC and set firewall rules at the parent folder level.
B) Enable "Inherit permissions" for each VPC and set firewall rules at the organization level.
C) Disable "Inherit permissions" for each VPC and set firewall rules at the parent folder level.
D) Disable "Inherit permissions" for each VPC and set firewall rules at the project level.
E) Enable "Inherit permissions" for each VPC and set firewall rules at the project level.

QUESTION 45

Your organization is planning to migrate a legacy application to Google Cloud. The application relies on a traditional relational database hosted on-premises. The database is large and critical to operations, and you want to minimize downtime during the migration. What database migration strategy should you choose to achieve minimal downtime?

A) Offline migration using data export and import tools.
B) Real-time replication and switchover.
C) Hybrid migration with a combination of data replication and export/import.
D) Cold migration with temporary service interruption.
E) Partial migration with selected tables.

QUESTION 46

Your organization needs to configure a firewall rule in Google Cloud to allow traffic from a specific IP range but deny traffic from a particular set of IP addresses within that range. What is the most appropriate configuration for this rule?

A) Create an allow rule with the specific IP range and a lower priority, followed by a deny rule for the particular IP addresses with a higher priority.

B) Configure a single rule with the specific IP range and specify the particular IP addresses as exceptions within the rule.

C) Create a deny rule for the specific IP range and then an allow rule for the particular IP addresses with higher priority.

D) Use a Cloud Armor security policy to control traffic from the specific IP range and particular IP addresses.

E) Implement a Network Service Tiers policy to manage traffic from both the specific IP range and particular IP addresses.

QUESTION 47

To regulate traffic between two Compute Engines within a VPC, ensuring only traffic from Compute Engine A to B is allowed, what is the correct firewall rule configuration?

A) Ingress; Allow; Target: Compute Engine B's service account; Source: Compute Engine A's service account; Priority: 1000

B) Ingress; Allow; Target: Compute Engine B's network tag; Source: Compute Engine A's network tag; Priority: 100

C) Ingress; Allow; Target: Compute Engine B's network tag; Source: Compute Engine A's network IP range; Priority: 1000

D) Egress; Allow; Target: Compute Engine A's network tag; Destination: Compute Engine B's network tag; Priority: 100

E) Egress; Allow; Target: Compute Engine A's service account; Destination: Compute Engine B's network IP range; Priority: 1000

QUESTION 48

In a GCP environment, you need to set up a network configuration that enables high-speed data transfer between Compute Engine instances and an external, geographically distant data center. The data center hosts critical legacy systems that require low-latency connections. What network configuration optimizes performance for this requirement?

A) Configure Cloud Interconnect for a direct, high-speed connection to the external data center.

B) Implement Cloud VPN with high-throughput tunnels for the data transfer.

C) Use VPC Peering between the Compute Engine network and the external data center's network.

D) Enable Premium Network Tier on Compute Engine instances for enhanced network performance.

E) Set up Dedicated Interconnect with a custom routing configuration for optimized data transfer.

QUESTION 49

In a GCP environment, you need to set up a secure network for a set of applications that process sensitive financial data. The network must restrict all outbound traffic except to a specific set of external financial services. What configuration effectively meets these security requirements?

A) Implement VPC Service Controls to create a secure perimeter for allowed external services.

B) Set up Cloud VPN tunnels to the specific external services with logging enabled.

C) Configure egress firewall rules to restrict traffic to the designated external financial services.

D) Use Private Google Access to restrict outbound traffic to specific external services.

E) Establish Cloud NAT with custom rules to manage outbound traffic to the designated services.

QUESTION 50

In a GCP environment, you need to configure a secure network for applications processing sensitive information. The network must only allow outbound traffic to a specific set of external IP addresses and log all traffic for compliance. What configuration effectively meets these security and compliance requirements?

A) Use VPC Service Controls for secure data transfer and Cloud VPN with logging for restricted connectivity.
B) Configure egress firewall rules to restrict and log traffic to designated external IP addresses.
C) Set up Cloud Interconnect with custom routing and logging to external IP addresses.
D) Implement Private Google Access and Cloud NAT with custom rules and logging.
E) Establish Cloud Endpoints with logging for secure outbound communication to external services.

PRACTICE TEST 3 - ANSWERS ONLY

QUESTION 1

Answer – B) Use Shared VPC to share a single VPC across teams.

Option B - Using Shared VPC is recommended as it allows a single VPC to be shared across teams while maintaining network isolation and resource separation.
Option A - Creating separate VPCs for each team might lead to resource duplication.
Option C - Using a common firewall rule for all teams is not sufficient for network isolation.
Option D - Assigning teams to different projects may not maintain the desired resource separation.
Option E - Creating separate projects for each team may lead to administrative complexity.

QUESTION 2

Answer – D) Use Google Cloud Interconnect for dedicated connectivity.

Option D - Using Google Cloud Interconnect provides dedicated connectivity between nodes in different regions, ensuring optimal network performance and low-latency communication.
Option A - Using a single regional cluster may not provide the desired global reach.
Option B - VPN tunnels between nodes may introduce latency.
Option C - CDN is for content delivery, not node communication.
Option E - GKE is a managed Kubernetes service and does not directly address network performance between nodes in different regions.

QUESTION 3

Answer – D) Google Cloud Shared VPC for microservices.

Option D - Implementing Google Cloud Shared VPC for microservices allows secure and controlled communication while maintaining isolation and control over traffic flow.
Option A - Google Cloud Endpoints is for API management, not microservices communication.
Option B - Network Peering may not provide sufficient isolation.
Option C - VPC Service Controls are for data access controls, not microservices communication.
Option E - Identity-Aware Proxy is for identity and access management, not microservices communication.

QUESTION 4

Answer – D) Google Cloud Shared VPC for microservices.

Option D - Implementing Google Cloud Shared VPC for microservices allows secure and controlled communication while maintaining isolation and control over traffic flow.
Option A - Google Cloud Endpoints is for API management, not microservices communication.
Option B - Network Peering may not provide sufficient isolation.
Option C - VPC Service Controls are for data access controls, not microservices communication.
Option E - Identity-Aware Proxy is for identity and access management, not microservices

communication.

QUESTION 5

Answer - A) Use Google Cloud Storage Transfer Service for data migration.

Option A is the best choice for a high-throughput, reliable data migration to Google Cloud Storage, as it's a specialized service for this purpose.
Option B, while addressing efficiency, may not offer the reliability needed.
Option C is more focused on connectivity and not data migration.
Option D introduces unnecessary complexity and cost.
Option E may not provide the same level of integration as Google's own service.

QUESTION 6

Answer - C) Set up VPC Network Peering connections between VPC networks in different projects.

Option C prioritizes secure communication between projects while maintaining network isolation by using VPC Network Peering connections.
Option A introduces public IP addresses, which may not be desired for security reasons.
Option B with VPNs may add complexity and may not provide the same level of isolation.
Option D, Dedicated Interconnect, may be overkill for inter-project communication.
Option E is related to messaging, not direct VPC communication.

QUESTION 7

Answer – D) Use a dynamic routing mode with BGP, with different ASNs and MD5 authentication.

A) Incorrect. Matching ASN may lead to routing issues.
B) Incorrect. While pre-shared keys are part of VPN security, matching ASNs is not advisable.
C) Incorrect. Using the same BGP IP on both sides can cause IP conflicts.
D) Correct. This setup ensures secure and reliable dynamic routing.
E) Incorrect. Static routing is less flexible and secure than dynamic routing with BGP.

QUESTION 8

Answer - E) Google Cloud Migrate for Compute Engine

Option E is the correct choice for migrating VMs from on-premises data centers to Google Cloud with minimal disruption and downtime. It is specifically designed for this purpose.
 Option A, Google Cloud Transfer Service, is used for data transfers but not VM migration.
 Option B, Google Cloud Dataprep, is for data preparation and transformation, not VM migration.
 Option C, Google Cloud Transfer Appliance, is a physical device for data transfer, not VM migration.
 Option D, Google Cloud Dataflow, is for data processing and transformation, not VM migration.

QUESTION 9

Answer - C) Use multiple regions and Availability Zones (AZs) to distribute resources.

Option C (using multiple regions and AZs) is a key principle for achieving high availability by distributing resources across geographically separated data centers, reducing the impact of single points of failure. Options A, D, and E may not provide the desired level of redundancy and scalability for all components.

QUESTION 10

Answer - B) Create a central hub VPC with VPC Peering connections to project VPCs.

Option A would result in a complex and inefficient setup.
Option C refers to a different Google Cloud service.
Option D provides secure connectivity but doesn't address the central hub requirement.
Option B is the correct choice as it aligns with the requirements, providing a central hub for private connectivity while maintaining separate VPCs for different projects.

QUESTION 11

Answer - C) Utilize Google Cloud Shared VPC to centralize VPC management and reduce overhead.

Option A creates a complex mesh of connections and doesn't minimize administrative overhead.
Option B provides low-latency private connections but doesn't centralize VPC management.
Option D offers secure communication but doesn't address administrative overhead.
Option E focuses on peering with Google services, not VPC-to-VPC connectivity.
Option C is the correct choice as Google Cloud Shared VPC centralizes VPC management, reduces overhead, and simplifies multi-region VPC connectivity, making it suitable for complex multi-region network infrastructures.

QUESTION 12

Answer – D) Create Partner Interconnects with diverse routing for each branch.

A) Incorrect. Load balancers are for traffic distribution, not office connectivity.
B) Incorrect. VPNs might not meet the bandwidth and latency requirements.
C) Incorrect. Dedicated Interconnects are costly for multiple branches.
D) Correct. Ensures high availability and fault tolerance globally.
E) Incorrect. Cloud Routers alone do not establish the physical connectivity needed.

QUESTION 13

Answer – E) Deploy the GKE cluster in the same region as the BigQuery dataset.

A) Incorrect. VPN does not provide the required throughput or latency.
B) Incorrect. BigQuery does not support VPC Peering.
C) Incorrect. Dedicated Interconnect is not used for intra-GCP service communication.
D) Incorrect. Private Google Access is not specific to GKE-BigQuery communication.
E) Correct. Regional deployment minimizes latency and maximizes throughput.

QUESTION 14

Answer - B) Deploy the application across multiple regions with a global load balancer.

B) Deploy the application across multiple regions with a global load balancer - This approach provides low-latency communication and high availability by routing traffic to the healthiest region, aligning with the project's requirements.

 A) Utilize regional load balancers with failover - Regional load balancers may not provide the same level of global high availability and low latency as a global load balancer.

 C) Implement Google Cloud Dedicated Interconnect for direct region-to-region connections - Interconnect may not be the most efficient solution for low-latency communication between regions.

 D) Set up Google Cloud VPN with multiple tunnels - VPNs focus on secure access and may not optimize low-latency communication between regions.

 E) Use Google Cloud CDN for content delivery - CDN is for content caching and may not directly address low-latency communication between VM instances in different regions.

QUESTION 15

Answer – A) Allow ingress on ports used by the APIs only from the partner networks.

A) Correct. Restricts access to the APIs to known partner networks.
B) Incorrect. Too restrictive and may not facilitate API accessibility.
C) Incorrect. Allowing all traffic on HTTPS does not limit access to partner networks.
D) Incorrect. Stateful inspection alone does not restrict access based on source IP.
E) Incorrect. While a default deny rule is good, it needs specific allow rules for API ports and partner networks.

QUESTION 16

Answer - A) Google Cloud Interconnect for dedicated connections.

A) Google Cloud Interconnect for dedicated connections - Interconnect provides dedicated and reliable connections for multi-cloud environments, ensuring secure communication.

 B) Google Cloud VPN for secure access - VPNs provide secure access but may not offer the same level of dedicated connectivity as Interconnect.

 C) Google Cloud Dedicated Interconnect for low-latency connections - While Dedicated Interconnect offers low-latency, it may not be the primary focus for multi-cloud connectivity.

 D) Google Cloud Network Peering for inter-cloud communication - Network Peering is for communication within Google Cloud and may not address multi-cloud connectivity.

 E) Google Cloud CDN for content delivery - CDN is for content caching and may not be directly related to multi-cloud connectivity.

QUESTION 17

Answer - C) Google Cloud Dedicated Interconnect with multiple redundant connections.

C) Google Cloud Dedicated Interconnect with multiple redundant connections - This option ensures high-speed, dedicated connections with low-latency communication between on-premises data centers and Google Cloud resources.

 A) Google Cloud VPN provides secure access but may not offer the same level of dedicated and redundant connections as Dedicated Interconnect.

 B) Google Cloud Interconnect provides dedicated connections but may not emphasize redundancy as much as Dedicated Interconnect with multiple connections.

 D) Google Cloud Network Peering is for communication between VPCs in the cloud, not specifically for

on-premises data centers.
E) Google Cloud CDN is for content delivery, not dedicated connectivity between on-premises and cloud resources.

QUESTION 18

Answer - A) Use SSL/TLS for in-transit encryption and Google Cloud KMS for at-rest encryption.

A) Using SSL/TLS for in-transit encryption and Google Cloud KMS for at-rest encryption is the recommended approach to ensure data security both at rest and in transit.
B) Cloud SQL's default encryption settings may not provide the level of control required for compliance.
C) Implementing third-party tools may add complexity and cost.
D) Using a VPN for in-transit encryption may not be the most efficient method when SSL/TLS is readily available.
E) Network security policies are important but don't handle both at-rest and in-transit encryption directly.

QUESTION 19

Answer - B) Create a single firewall rule to allow port 22 with priority 1000.

B) Creating a single firewall rule to allow port 22 with priority 1000 is a targeted approach to permit secure SSH access for system engineers.
A) Creating two firewall rules, one to deny all protocols and another to allow port 22, may introduce unnecessary complexity.
C) Blocking all traffic with priority 65536 and then allowing port 3389 with priority 1000 is not related to secure VM management.
D) Allowing port 3389 is for RDP, which may not be needed for VM management.
E) Creating separate rules for each engineer's IP address is not scalable and may require frequent updates.

QUESTION 20

Answer - A) Create two firewall rules: one to deny ingress to all protocols with priority 0, and another to permit ingress on port 22 with priority 1000.

A) To permit system engineers to manage virtual machines securely, you can create two firewall rules—one to deny all protocols and another to permit access on a specific port (e.g., port 22) with the appropriate priorities. This allows controlled access while denying all other traffic.
B) Creating a single rule for port 22 does not deny other potentially unneeded traffic.
C) Using port 3389 for RDP may not align with secure practices.
D) Allowing port 3389 for RDP without denying other traffic can be less secure.
E) Allowing all inbound traffic on all ports is not recommended for security reasons.

QUESTION 21

Answer - D) Use Google Cloud's integrated Network Intelligence Center for packet-level data capture.

D) To capture packet-level data for analysis, including traffic between VM instances in various networks, you should use Google Cloud's integrated Network Intelligence Center. It provides comprehensive network monitoring capabilities.

 A) Enabling VPC Flow Logs captures flow-level data, not packet-level data.

 B) Google Cloud's built-in packet capture feature is not a centralized solution for monitoring traffic between VM instances across networks.

 C) Creating a shared VPC network is useful for managing network resources but does not provide packet-level monitoring.

QUESTION 22

Answer - B) Create a single firewall rule to allow port 22 with priority 1000.

B) To securely permit system engineers to manage virtual machines within the network, you can create a single firewall rule that allows ingress on port 22 (SSH) with an appropriate priority. This provides the necessary access for management while maintaining security.

 A) Creating two firewall rules with conflicting priorities is not necessary and can lead to unexpected behavior.

 C) Port 3389 is typically used for Remote Desktop Protocol (RDP), not SSH.

 D) Port 3389 is again referenced here, which is not the typical choice for managing virtual machines.

 E) Implementing a default-deny firewall rule would block all traffic, which is overly restrictive for this scenarlo.

QUESTION 23

Answer – A) Use VPC Service Controls to create a secure perimeter around your data processing resources.

A) Correct. VPC Service Controls provide strong data security and exfiltration protection.
B) Incorrect. Cloud Armor is not designed for internal data flow control.
C) Incorrect. Network tags and firewall rules do not provide comprehensive data exfiltration protection.
D) Incorrect. An internal load balancer focuses on traffic distribution, not on data security or exfiltration.
E) Incorrect. Private Google Access does not offer specific protection against data exfiltration.

QUESTION 24

Answer - B) Use multiple Google Cloud Load Balancers to distribute traffic.
C) Implement cross-region redundancy for critical services.

Option A - Deploying all services in a single region contradicts fault tolerance and high availability.
Option D - Centralizing projects in a single VPC may not enhance fault tolerance or availability.
Option E - While IAM is important, it's not directly related to infrastructure fault tolerance. Choice B (Use multiple Google Cloud Load Balancers to distribute traffic) - Using multiple Google Cloud Load Balancers allows for load distribution and failover across regions or availability zones, enhancing fault tolerance and availability of services. It ensures that traffic is directed to healthy instances even in case of failures. Choice C (Implement cross-region redundancy for critical services) - Implementing cross-region redundancy for critical services ensures that if one region experiences an outage, services remain available in other regions, improving fault tolerance and availability. This can include data replication and failover configurations.

QUESTION 25

Answer - A) Utilize Google Cloud Security Groups for network security.
C) Implement a Google Cloud VPN tunnel for secure communication.

Option B - Cloud NAT gateway is for outbound traffic management, not security like a firewall.
Option D - Cloud DNS firewall is for DNS security, not a direct firewall replacement.
Option E - Google Cloud Armor focuses on security, not traffic management. Choice A - Google Cloud Security Groups provide network-level security controls, allowing you to define firewall rules to control incoming and outgoing traffic, thus replacing the need for a dedicated hardware firewall.
 Choice C - Implementing a Google Cloud VPN tunnel enables secure communication between on-premises and GCP resources, serving as a secure replacement for the dedicated hardware firewall.

QUESTION 26

Answer – B) Implement Cloud VPN with a shared secret for secure communication and integrate with Cloud IAM for authentication.

A) Incorrect. Dedicated Interconnect is not used for connecting to services on other cloud providers.
B) Correct. Cloud VPN ensures secure communication, and Cloud IAM provides robust authentication.
C) Incorrect. VPC Peering is not applicable for connecting to services on another cloud provider.
D) Incorrect. Private Google Access is not intended for secure connections to external clouds.
E) Incorrect. Cloud Router's custom routes do not address the security and authentication requirements.

QUESTION 27

Answer - B) Set up a central VPC in europe-west3 and utilize VPC peering for branch connectivity.

Option A - Implementing dedicated VPN connections for each location may result in complexity and inefficiency.
Option C - Creating separate VPCs for each branch may lead to management overhead.
Option D - Cloud Interconnect is not the best choice for branch connectivity. Choice B - Setting up a central VPC in europe-west3 and utilizing VPC peering for branch connectivity simplifies management and allows for efficient communication between locations.

QUESTION 28

Answer – A) Set up Private Google Access on the subnetworks of the Compute Engine instances.

A) Correct. Private Google Access allows instances without external IPs to access Google services privately.
B) Incorrect. VPC Peering is not applicable for accessing Google Cloud services.
C) Incorrect. Cloud VPN is for connecting external networks, not for private access within GCP.
D) Incorrect. Cloud Interconnect is primarily for connecting on-premises networks to GCP.
E) Incorrect. External IPs expose instances to the public internet, which is not required here.

QUESTION 29

Answer - B) Create a VPC Service Controls perimeter for your project, incorporating an access context policy that encompasses your organization's head office network IP ranges.

Option A - Managing individual access context policies for each application may introduce complexity.
Option C - Creating separate VPC Service Controls perimeters for each application may result in management overhead.
Option D - While firewall rules can provide protection, VPC Service Controls offer a more comprehensive security approach. Choice B - Establishing a VPC Service Controls perimeter for your project with a comprehensive access context policy that covers head office network IP ranges provides centralized and efficient API access control for Memorystore and Spanner across all applications in the project.

QUESTION 30

Answer - B) Establish a private connection with the Cloud Spanner service producer. and C) Turn on Private Google Access for your subnetwork.

Option A - Enabling the Cloud Memorystore API is unrelated to connecting Compute Engine instances to Cloud Spanner.
Option D - Configuring a custom static route is not the standard way to connect Compute Engine instances to Cloud Spanner.
Option E - Enabling the Service Networking API is not required for this specific connection. Explanation for choices B and C - Establishing a private connection with the Cloud Spanner service producer and enabling Private Google Access for your subnetwork are the recommended actions to connect Compute Engine instances without public IP addresses to Cloud Spanner.

QUESTION 31

Answer - B) One of the Dedicated Interconnects is not configured correctly, causing the BGP session failure.

Option A - The issue described doesn't suggest an internal firewall problem.
Option C - The absence of a Cloud Load Balancer is unrelated to BGP session failures.
Option D - BGP session failures with all campus switches are not indicated in the problem description.
Choice B - The issue with BGP sessions failing to establish is most likely due to a misconfiguration in one of the Dedicated Interconnects.

QUESTION 32

Answer – C) Use VPC firewall rules to restrict all external communication and allow internal traffic.

A) Incorrect. Private Google Access is for accessing Google services, not for internal communication between resources.
B) Incorrect. An internal load balancer is not necessary for enabling internal communication.
C) Correct. Firewall rules can effectively enforce internal-only communication.
D) Incorrect. VPC Network Peering is not used for communication within the same project.
E) Incorrect. Private Service Connect is for connecting services, not for general internal communication.

QUESTION 33

Answer - A) Use Google Cloud Load Balancing to distribute traffic across multiple regions.

Option B - Relying on regional redundancy alone may not provide the desired level of high availability.

Option C - While Google Cloud Autohealing is important, it may not address region-wide failures on its own.

Option D - Google Cloud Memorystore is primarily for caching and may not directly contribute to high availability. Choice A - Using Google Cloud Load Balancing to distribute traffic across multiple regions ensures high availability and resilience to region-wide failures.

QUESTION 34

Answer - B) Global Load Balancer with HTTP(S) Load Balancer

A) Regional Load Balancer with Google Cloud CDN - Explanation: This combination operates within a region and may not provide global distribution. Google Cloud CDN focuses on content delivery.

C) Network Load Balancer with TCP Proxy Load Balancer - Explanation: Network Load Balancer and TCP Proxy Load Balancer may distribute traffic, but they may not provide global reach or content delivery.

D) External TCP/UDP Load Balancer with Internal HTTP(S) Load Balancer - Explanation: This combination focuses on TCP/UDP traffic and internal use and may not efficiently distribute traffic across multiple Google Cloud regions.

E) SSL Proxy Load Balancer with CDN - Explanation: SSL Proxy Load Balancer and CDN may not provide the necessary load balancing for high-traffic e-commerce websites across regions.

B) Global Load Balancer with HTTP(S) Load Balancer - Explanation: This combination offers global traffic distribution with the ability to balance traffic effectively across multiple Google Cloud regions, making it suitable for high-traffic e-commerce websites.

QUESTION 35

Answer - D) Create more specific custom routes than the default network routes, designating the dedicated firewall instances as next hops, and assign network tags to the subnets for secure routing.

D) Create more specific custom routes than the default network routes, designating the dedicated firewall instances as next hops, and assign network tags to the subnets for secure routing - Explanation: This approach ensures that specific subnets route their traffic through dedicated firewall instances with the added security of network tags.

A) Set up custom routes with more precision than the default network routes - Explanation: While custom routes are helpful, this option does not consider the use of network tags for security.

B) Shift the dedicated firewall instances to a separate Virtual Private Cloud (VPC) - Explanation: Moving firewall instances to a separate VPC may not be necessary for secure routing.

C) Delete the default network routes and establish distinct custom routes for the subnets - Explanation: Deleting default routes introduces complexity, and this option may not be necessary for secure routing.

E) Implement Cloud Armor - Explanation: Cloud Armor is used for security but may not directly route traffic through dedicated firewall instances, which is the requirement for this migration.

QUESTION 36

Answer – D) Set up a single regional GKE cluster and deploy all microservices within different namespaces.

A) Incorrect. Network Peering is unnecessary for clusters within the same VPC.

B) Incorrect. Private clusters are secure but Internal Load Balancers add unnecessary complexity for intra-cluster communication.

C) Incorrect. Shared VPC is not required for microservices within the same region and VPC Service Controls are for data security, not networking.
D) Correct. A single regional cluster with different namespaces is efficient for communication and resource management.
E) Incorrect. Separate VPCs and VPNs are overly complex and not necessary for microservices within the same region.

QUESTION 37

Answer – B) Use Cloud Pub/Sub for data ingestion and Dataflow for dynamically scaling the processing.

A) Incorrect. VPN is not suitable for high-volume IoT data streams.
B) Correct. Cloud Pub/Sub and Dataflow provide a scalable solution for streaming and processing IoT data.
C) Incorrect. Separate VPCs for each device category is overly complex and unnecessary.
D) Incorrect. While IoT Core manages devices, it doesn't directly address dynamic scaling of data processing.
E) Incorrect. Cloud Endpoints and Cloud Run are not the optimal combination for IoT data streaming and processing.

QUESTION 38

Answer - B) Regional managed instance groups with Google Cloud Load Balancing

A) Google Cloud VPN with VPC peering - VPN and VPC peering provide connectivity but do not replicate VM instances for high availability.
B) Regional managed instance groups with Google Cloud Load Balancing - Correct answer. Regional managed instance groups can replicate instances across zones within a region, achieving high availability.
C) Google Cloud Storage with VPC Service Controls - Storage and Service Controls are used for data storage and access control but do not replicate VM instances.
D) Google Cloud SQL with VPC peering - SQL offers managed databases but may not provide VM instance replication.
E) Google Cloud Dataprep with Cloud Dataflow - These services are used for data preparation and processing but do not replicate VM instances.

QUESTION 39

Answer - B) Traffic Director with Cloud Spanner

A) Google Cloud CDN with Google Cloud Armor - CDN and Armor provide content delivery and security but may not optimize game server latency.
B) Correct answer. Traffic Director with Cloud Spanner provides advanced traffic management and can optimize latency for global game servers.
C) Google Cloud Storage with VPC peering - Storage and VPC peering are for data storage and connectivity, not optimizing game server latency.
D) Google Cloud Pub/Sub with Google Cloud Load Balancing - Pub/Sub and Load Balancing are used for messaging and traffic distribution but may not optimize game server latency.
E) Google Cloud Dataflow with Google Cloud Storage - Dataflow and Storage are used for data processing and storage, not optimizing game server latency.

QUESTION 40

Answer - B) Google Cloud Interconnect and Google Cloud VPC Peering

A) Google Cloud VPN and Google Cloud DNS provide secure connectivity and DNS services but may not offer the same level of dedicated and efficient data transfer between VPCs in different regions.
B) Correct answer. Google Cloud Interconnect provides dedicated and high-speed connections between regions, and Google Cloud VPC Peering connects VPCs, making them suitable for secure and efficient inter-region communication with minimal latency.
C) Google Cloud Router and Google Cloud CDN focus on routing and content delivery but may not provide the dedicated inter-region connections required.
D) Google Cloud Armor and Google Cloud Load Balancing offer security and load distribution but may not address the dedicated inter-region connections for data transfer.
E) Google Cloud Spanner is a database, and Google Cloud Identity-Aware Proxy (IAP) focuses on identity management, but they may not be directly related to inter-region network connectivity.

QUESTION 41

Answer - D) Google Cloud Storage and Google Cloud DNS

A) Google Cloud VPN and Google Cloud Bigtable may not be the primary components for disaster recovery and data replication between regions.
B) Google Cloud CDN and Google Cloud Compute Engine Autoscaler are not primarily designed for disaster recovery and data replication.
C) Google Cloud Spanner and Google Cloud Interconnect focus on database and connectivity but may not be the primary components for disaster recovery.
D) Correct answer. Google Cloud Storage offers data replication between regions, and Google Cloud DNS provides domain name resolution for disaster recovery scenarios.
E) Google Cloud Load Balancing and Google Cloud VPC Peering may not be the primary components for data replication and failover between regions.

QUESTION 42

Answer - C) Google Cloud Dedicated Interconnect and Google Cloud Router

A) Google Cloud VPN and Google Cloud DNS provide secure connectivity and DNS services but may not offer dedicated high-speed connections.
B) Google Cloud Direct Peering and Google Cloud CDN focus on network and content delivery but may not provide dedicated high-speed connections to on-premises data centers.
C) Correct answer. Google Cloud Dedicated Interconnect offers dedicated, high-speed connections, and Google Cloud Router helps manage the routing of traffic between on-premises and Google Cloud resources.
D) Google Cloud VPC Peering and Google Cloud Load Balancing may not provide dedicated connections suitable for on-premises data center communication.
E) Google Cloud Interconnect and Google Cloud Identity-Aware Proxy (IAP) serve different purposes and may not be the primary choices for dedicated, high-speed connections.

QUESTION 43

Answer - B) The ASNs utilized on the gateways are unique.

A) A security rule wouldn't typically affect the routing of traffic between Dedicated Interconnect connections.
B) Correct answer. Each gateway having a distinct ASN can result in BGP routing issues, preventing proper traffic distribution.
C) The absence of a load balancer is not directly related to the routing issue between Dedicated Interconnects.
D) Having identical routes on the gateways is expected for redundancy, and it's not the primary reason for the issue.
E) The Cloud Router should be able to handle multiple Dedicated Interconnect connections, and the issue lies in the ASN configuration.

QUESTION 44

Answer - A) Enable "Inherit permissions" for each VPC and set firewall rules at the parent folder level.

A) Correct answer. Enabling "Inherit permissions" at the VPC level allows IAM permissions to be inherited from parent folders while still allowing specific firewall rules to be set at the parent folder level.
B) Enabling "Inherit permissions" at the organization level would inherit IAM permissions but doesn't allow individual VPCs to set their firewall rules.
C) Disabling "Inherit permissions" would prevent IAM permissions from being inherited, which is not the requirement.
D) Disabling "Inherit permissions" at the project level would not allow for IAM permissions to be inherited from parent folders.
E) Enabling "Inherit permissions" at the project level wouldn't allow for fine-grained control of IAM permissions at the VPC level.

QUESTION 45

Answer - B) Real-time replication and switchover.

A) Offline migration would result in significant downtime.
C) Hybrid migration, while useful, may not achieve minimal downtime for the entire database.
D) Cold migration with service interruption is not aligned with minimizing downtime.
E) Partial migration would not achieve minimal downtime for the entire database.
B) Real-time replication and switchover involve continuously replicating data to Google Cloud and switching over to the cloud database with minimal downtime. This strategy is best suited for critical databases requiring minimal service interruption during migration.

QUESTION 46

Answer - A) Create an allow rule with the specific IP range and a lower priority, followed by a deny rule for the particular IP addresses with a higher priority.

A) This approach allows you to create an allow rule for the specific IP range and a deny rule for the particular IP addresses, ensuring that the deny rule takes precedence.

B) Configuring a single rule with exceptions may not provide the desired level of control.
C) Creating a deny rule for the specific IP range and then an allow rule for the particular IP addresses might not work as intended.
D) Cloud Armor security policies focus on security rather than this specific access control scenario.
E) Network Service Tiers policies are not designed for this level of access control.

QUESTION 47

Answer – B) Ingress; Allow; Target: Compute Engine B's network tag; Source: Compute Engine A's network tag; Priority: 100

A) Incorrect. Service accounts are not used to specify source and target for firewall rules.
B) Correct. This rule allows ingress traffic to Compute Engine B only from Compute Engine A using network tags.
C) Incorrect. Specifying source as IP range is less specific than using network tags.
D) Incorrect. The direction should be ingress, not egress, to control traffic entering Compute Engine B.
E) Incorrect. The direction should be ingress, and service accounts are not used in this context.

QUESTION 48

Answer – A) Configure Cloud Interconnect for a direct, high-speed connection to the external data center.

A) Correct. Cloud Interconnect provides a low-latency, high-throughput connection ideal for linking with external data centers.
B) Incorrect. VPN may not provide the low latency required for legacy systems.
C) Incorrect. VPC Peering is not applicable for connections to external data centers.
D) Incorrect. Premium Network Tier enhances general network performance but does not directly address connectivity to external data centers.
E) Incorrect. While Dedicated Interconnect is suitable, custom routing is not the primary factor in this scenario.

QUESTION 49

Answer – C) Configure egress firewall rules to restrict traffic to the designated external financial services.

A) Incorrect. VPC Service Controls secure data within GCP, not for controlling outbound traffic.
B) Incorrect. VPN tunnels are not necessary for restricting outbound traffic to specific services.
C) Correct. Egress firewall rules with specific allowances are effective for restricting outbound traffic to certain external services.
D) Incorrect. Private Google Access is for accessing Google services, not for restricting traffic to external services.
E) Incorrect. Cloud NAT manages outbound connections but does not provide the same level of control as firewall rules.

QUESTION 50

Answer – B) Configure egress firewall rules to restrict and log traffic to designated external IP addresses.

A) Incorrect. VPC Service Controls and VPN are for data security within GCP, not for controlling and logging outbound traffic to external IPs.
B) Correct. Egress firewall rules with logging effectively control and monitor outbound traffic to specific external IPs for compliance.
C) Incorrect. Cloud Interconnect is typically for on-premises to GCP connections, not for specific external IP connectivity.
D) Incorrect. Private Google Access and Cloud NAT are for managing outbound connections, not for specific IP access control and logging.
E) Incorrect. Cloud Endpoints are for API management, not for logging outbound connections to external IPs.

PRACTICE TEST 4 - QUESTIONS ONLY

QUESTION 1

You want to improve the security of your Google Cloud project by implementing identity and access management (IAM) best practices. Which principle should you follow to ensure the least privilege access for users and resources?

A) Assign the "Owner" role to all users for flexibility.
B) Assign the "Editor" role to all users for collaboration.
C) Assign roles with the fewest permissions needed for specific tasks.
D) Assign roles with full project access to all users.
E) Disable IAM for simplicity.

QUESTION 2

Your organization is setting up a disaster recovery site in Google Cloud for business continuity. What should you implement to ensure data replication and failover in case of a disaster while minimizing downtime?

A) Set up Cloud VPN tunnels between on-premises and Google Cloud.
B) Deploy a multi-region Cloud Storage bucket for data replication.
C) Implement Google Cloud Filestore for data synchronization.
D) Utilize Google Cloud's global load balancer for failover.
E) Create a dedicated VPC for disaster recovery.

QUESTION 3

You are responsible for setting up network connectivity between your on-premises data center and Google Cloud. Your organization requires a dedicated, high-speed connection with low latency. What Google Cloud service should you consider to meet these requirements while ensuring private and secure communication?

A) Google Cloud VPN with a shared VPN gateway.
B) Google Cloud Dedicated Interconnect with a private VLAN.
C) Google Cloud Direct Peering with a public peering connection.
D) Google Cloud VPC Network Peering.
E) Google Cloud Global Load Balancing.

QUESTION 4

Your organization is planning to migrate a large dataset to Google Cloud Storage. The data consists of sensitive customer information, and security is a top priority. What should you do to ensure the highest level of security for this data during and after the migration process?

A) Use Google Cloud Storage Transfer Service to copy the data over an encrypted channel and enable server-side encryption with Customer-Managed Keys (CMEK) in the destination bucket.

B) Use a third-party tool to migrate the data, as it provides better security controls than Google Cloud services.

C) Copy the data manually using a workstation and encrypt the data with a custom encryption tool before uploading it to Google Cloud Storage.

D) Use Google Cloud Storage Transfer Service and enable server-side encryption with Google-managed keys (GMEK) in the destination bucket.

E) Avoid migrating the data to the cloud and continue to store it on-premises to ensure maximum security.

QUESTION 5

Your organization needs to ensure secure, low-latency connectivity to Google Cloud for real-time data processing applications. Which approach should you prioritize?

A) Implement a Google Cloud Dedicated Interconnect for dedicated, low-latency connectivity.
B) Use a Cloud VPN with Quality of Service (QoS) policies to prioritize real-time traffic.
C) Deploy a private fiber optic network connecting your data center to Google Cloud.
D) Set up a dedicated Content Delivery Network (CDN) for data distribution.
E) Explore options for using a hybrid cloud solution.

QUESTION 6

Your organization is planning a hybrid architecture with on-premises data centers and Google Cloud, and you need to ensure high-speed, low-latency connectivity between them. What approach should you consider?

A) Deploy multiple Cloud VPNs with Quality of Service (QoS) policies for optimized connectivity.
B) Utilize Google Cloud Dedicated Interconnect for dedicated, high-speed connectivity.
C) Implement hybrid DNS solutions to route traffic between on-premises and Google Cloud resources.
D) Set up Direct Peering between on-premises data centers and Google Cloud.
E) Establish point-to-point microwave links for direct connectivity.

QUESTION 7

For a global e-commerce company, you're designing a network architecture in GCP to handle sudden traffic spikes during sales events. The company has services deployed in asia-southeast1 and us-central1. Which of the following strategies ensures scalability and high availability?

A) Utilize a single global HTTP(S) load balancer with backend services in both regions.
B) Implement regional Network Load Balancers in each location.
C) Deploy instances in a single region and use Cloud CDN for global reach.
D) Use instance groups in each region with separate regional load balancers.
E) Establish VPC Peering between regions and route traffic based on source IP.

QUESTION 8

Your company's application requires high availability and fault tolerance. You want to deploy instances across multiple Google Cloud regions to achieve this. Which Google Cloud service should you use to efficiently manage and load balance traffic across instances in different regions while minimizing latency?

A) Google Cloud CDN (Content Delivery Network)
B) Google Cloud Armor
C) Google Cloud Load Balancing
D) Google Cloud Interconnect
E) Google Cloud DNS (Domain Name System)

QUESTION 9

Your organization is building a multi-cloud strategy and plans to use both Google Cloud and AWS for various workloads. To ensure secure and efficient network connectivity between the two cloud providers, what architectural approach should you adopt?

A) Set up a Direct Interconnect between Google Cloud and AWS.
B) Use VPN tunnels to establish connectivity between Google Cloud VPCs and AWS VPCs.
C) Deploy a Google Cloud VPN Gateway in AWS and establish VPN tunnels.
D) Utilize a third-party cloud connectivity solution for inter-cloud communication.
E) Establish a dedicated AWS Direct Connect to Google Cloud's backbone network.

QUESTION 10

Your organization manages a multi-project architecture on Google Cloud, each with distinct Virtual Private Cloud (VPC) networks. You need to establish private connectivity between these VPCs, internet access, and a connection to an external data center. Which approach should you consider?

A) Implement VPC Peering connections between all VPCs.
B) Create a central hub VPC and configure VPC Peering connections from all project VPCs to the hub VPC.
C) Use Cloud Interconnect Dedicated for private connectivity.
D) Deploy Cloud VPN for secure project-to-project connections.
E) Consolidate all VPCs into a single VPC network.

QUESTION 11

Your organization is building a microservices-based application architecture on Google Cloud. Each microservice is developed using different programming languages and frameworks, and they need to communicate with each other over a secure and reliable network. What Google Cloud service or feature should you consider for this complex microservices communication, and what advantages does it offer?

A) Google Cloud Cloud Endpoints for API management and communication.
B) Google Cloud VPC Peering for secure inter-VPC communication.
C) Google Cloud Pub/Sub for asynchronous message-based communication.
D) Google Cloud NAT (Network Address Translation) for IP address management.
E) Google Cloud VPN for encrypted communication between microservices.

QUESTION 12

Your company requires a secure, low-latency network solution for transferring large datasets between your on-premises data center and GCP. The data center is already equipped with high-capacity fiber-optic connections. Which GCP networking solution would best meet these requirements?

A) Implement a Cloud VPN with dynamic routing for flexibility.
B) Set up a Dedicated Interconnect for high-throughput connectivity.
C) Utilize Partner Interconnect with a focus on data transfer rates.
D) Deploy Cloud CDN for efficient data distribution.
E) Establish a VPC Peering arrangement with an emphasis on security.

QUESTION 13

In a scenario where you need to establish secure communication between a GKE-based application and an on-premises system, which of the following approaches ensures a secure, high-performance connection?

A) Set up Cloud VPN for encrypted communication.
B) Implement VPC Network Peering between GKE and the on-premises network.
C) Use Dedicated Interconnect for a direct, high-speed connection.
D) Configure Cloud Endpoints in GKE for secure API interactions.
E) Employ Cloud Armor on GKE for enhanced network security.

QUESTION 14

You are configuring network policies for a Google Cloud project that involves multiple VPCs. Each VPC is associated with a different department in your organization, and you want to control the traffic flow between these VPCs while maintaining security. Which GCP networking feature should you implement?

A) Google Cloud Network Peering
B) Google Cloud VPN
C) Google Cloud VPC Service Controls
D) Google Cloud Shared VPC
E) Google Cloud Private Service Connect

QUESTION 15

In a scenario where you have multiple VMs hosting various components of a SaaS application in GCP, you need to ensure that only the web components are accessible from the internet. How would you configure the firewall rules to meet this requirement?

A) Allow ingress on ports 80 and 443 for web components; deny all other ingress.
B) Set up a rule to allow all egress and ingress from any source on all ports.
C) Deny all ingress traffic except on port 443 for all VMs.
D) Create specific rules to allow ingress on web ports only for VMs with web components.
E) Implement a blanket rule to allow ingress on all ports for all VMs.

QUESTION 16

Your organization is planning to migrate its on-premises data center to Google Cloud to reduce operational overhead. You have critical applications that require low-latency communication and minimal disruption during migration. What GCP networking approach should you recommend for this migration?

A) Gradual migration of applications to Google Cloud while maintaining on-premises data center connectivity.
B) A "lift and shift" migration strategy to quickly move all applications to Google Cloud.
C) A phased migration, starting with non-critical applications and gradually moving critical ones.
D) A hybrid approach with permanent coexistence of on-premises and Google Cloud resources.
E) A "big bang" migration where all applications are migrated simultaneously.

QUESTION 17

You are tasked with migrating your organization's applications to Google Cloud while minimizing disruption. What migration strategy should you recommend for achieving this goal?

A) Gradual migration while maintaining on-premises data center connectivity.
B) "Lift and shift" migration of all applications at once.
C) A phased migration, starting with non-critical applications and gradually moving critical ones.
D) A hybrid approach with permanent coexistence of on-premises and cloud resources.
E) "Big bang" migration where all applications are migrated simultaneously.

QUESTION 18

Your organization is deploying a new web application on Google Cloud, and you want to ensure high availability and scalability. Which Google Cloud service or product can help you achieve this for your web application?

A) Google Cloud Functions
B) Google App Engine Standard Environment
C) Google Compute Engine with manual scaling
D) Google Kubernetes Engine (GKE) with a single node pool
E) Google Cloud Run

QUESTION 19

Your organization plans to validate a hybrid cloud setup using Google Cloud. You're tasked with verifying the operability of this arrangement before deploying it into a production environment. This setup involves deploying a service on a Compute Engine instance that must establish a connection with in-house data center servers via private IPs. Your local data centers can access the internet, yet no Cloud Interconnect has been set up so far. You're in charge of selecting the most economical connectivity option that enables your instance and the on-premises servers to communicate, and you need to complete the assessment within 24 hours. Which connectivity option should you opt for?

A) Partner Interconnect without provisioning any VLAN attachments.
B) Cloud VPN.
C) 100-Gbps Partner Interconnect with a redundant VLAN attachment.
D) 10-Gbps Dedicated Interconnect with a single VLAN attachment.
E) Cloud Interconnect with a dedicated VLAN.

QUESTION 20

Your organization plans to validate a hybrid cloud setup using Google Cloud. You're tasked with verifying the operability of this arrangement before deploying it into a production environment. This setup involves deploying a service on a Compute Engine instance that must establish a connection with in-house data center servers via private IPs. Your local data centers can access the internet, yet no Cloud Interconnect has been set up so far. You're in charge of selecting the most economical connectivity option that enables your instance and the on-premises servers to communicate, and you need to complete the assessment within 24 hours. Which connectivity option should you opt for?

A) Partner Interconnect without provisioning any VLAN attachments.
B) Cloud VPN.
C) 100-Gbps Partner Interconnect with a redundant VLAN attachment.
D) 100-Gbps Dedicated Interconnect with a single VLAN attachment.
E) Cloud Router.

QUESTION 21

You have multiple Google Cloud projects, each with its own VPC network. You need to establish private communication between instances in different VPC networks without exposing them to the public internet. What is the recommended solution for achieving this goal?

A) Set up a VPN tunnel between the VPC networks for private communication.
B) Use VPC Peering to connect the VPC networks and enable private communication.
C) Configure Cloud NAT for each VPC network to allow private communication.
D) Create custom firewall rules to allow traffic between the VPC networks.

QUESTION 22

Your organization plans to validate a hybrid cloud setup using Google Cloud. You're tasked with verifying the operability of this arrangement before deploying it into a production environment. This setup involves deploying a service on a Compute Engine instance that must establish a connection with in-house data center servers via private IPs. Your local data centers can access the internet, yet no Cloud Interconnect has been set up so far. You're in charge of selecting the most economical connectivity option that enables your instance and the on-premises servers to communicate, and you need to complete the assessment within 24 hours. Which connectivity option should you opt for?

A) Partner Interconnect without provisioning any VLAN attachments.
B) Cloud VPN.
C) 100-Gbps Partner Interconnect with a redundant VLAN attachment.
D) 10-Gbps Dedicated Interconnect with a single VLAN attachment.
E) Cloud Interconnect with a custom configuration.

QUESTION 23

You have to configure a secure and efficient network for a large-scale analytics platform in GCP. The platform integrates with several external data sources and needs to ensure data integrity and protection against network attacks. What combination of GCP services and configurations would you recommend?

A) Implement Cloud Armor with custom security policies and an external HTTP(S) load balancer.

B) Set up Cloud VPNs for each external data source for secure data transfer.

C) Use VPC Peering with external data sources and configure SSL policies for data integrity.

D) Configure Cloud IDS to monitor and protect network traffic to and from the analytics platform.

E) Establish a Private Google Access setup for secure connectivity to external data sources.

QUESTION 24

Your company is migrating a legacy on-premises application to Google Cloud Platform (GCP). The application relies on a dedicated hardware firewall for security. What two strategies should you recommend to replace the on-premises firewall while maintaining security in GCP?

A) Utilize Google Cloud Security Groups for network security.

B) Set up a Cloud NAT gateway for outbound traffic.

C) Implement a Google Cloud VPN tunnel for secure communication.

D) Deploy a Cloud DNS firewall for DNS-based security.

E) Utilize Google Cloud Armor for DDoS protection.

QUESTION 25

Your organization is running a data analytics workload on Google Cloud's BigQuery. The workload consists of complex queries and data transformations. To optimize query performance and reduce costs, what two actions should you take?

A) Use BigQuery's default caching for query results.

B) Partition large tables based on date or another relevant column.

C) Enable BigQuery's automatic query optimization feature.

D) Create views for frequently used query patterns.

E) Load all data into a single unpartitioned table.

QUESTION 26

You are tasked with designing a network solution in GCP to handle sudden, large-scale data ingest from various external IoT devices. The solution must be secure, able to handle high-volume data, and provide low-latency processing. What combination of GCP components and configurations would you recommend?

A) Use Cloud IoT Core for device management, Cloud Pub/Sub for data ingestion, and edge computing for low-latency processing.

B) Configure multiple Cloud VPNs for data ingestion from IoT devices and use Compute Engine for processing.

C) Implement a series of Cloud Functions triggered by IoT device data, with data stored in Cloud Storage.

D) Establish Cloud Interconnects for each group of IoT devices and process data using BigQuery.

E) Set up a network of Cloud Routers to manage IoT device traffic and use Dataflow for processing.

QUESTION 27

Your organization requires local data processing in europe-west2 and southamerica-east1 regions. What networking strategy should you adopt to facilitate this requirement?

A) Create separate VPCs for each region and establish VPN connections.
B) Deploy a central VPC in europe-west3 and use VPC peering to connect to the other regions.
C) Use Dedicated Interconnects for direct access to both regions.
D) Utilize Cloud Interconnect for low-latency access.
E) None of the above.

QUESTION 28

In a GCP environment, you are tasked with setting up a solution that requires Compute Engine instances to efficiently process a stream of incoming data from a variety of IoT devices. The solution should be scalable and able to handle sudden spikes in data volume. What is the best configuration to handle this scenario?

A) Configure each Compute Engine instance with autoscaling based on CPU usage and integrate with Cloud Pub/Sub for data ingestion.
B) Set up a managed instance group for Compute Engine with an HTTP(S) load balancer for distributing IoT data.
C) Implement Dataflow to process IoT data streams, sending processed data to Compute Engine instances for further analysis.
D) Use Cloud IoT Core for device management and direct data to Compute Engine instances using Cloud Functions.
E) Establish Cloud VPNs for each IoT device group and configure Compute Engine instances to process incoming data streams.

QUESTION 29

Your enterprise oversees a Google Cloud project with multiple App Engine applications. You need to implement robust API access controls for Memorystore instances and Spanner databases, permitting traffic only from your organization's head office networks. What approach should you recommend?

A) Develop an access context policy for each individual App Engine application, specifying head office network IP ranges, and apply these policies to Memorystore and Spanner.
B) Establish a VPC Service Controls perimeter for your project, including an access context policy that encompasses your organization's head office network IP ranges.
C) Create separate VPC Service Controls perimeters for each App Engine application, each with access context policies defining your organization's head office network IP ranges.
D) Define a series of firewall rules to block API access to Memorystore and Spanner from networks not recognized as part of your head office.
E) None of the above.

QUESTION 30

Your team is managing a large-scale IT project for cloud deployment, and you need to address issues related to dedicated interconnects and BGP sessions. What is the primary reason for this issue?

A) An internal firewall is preventing the connection from being established on the second Dedicated Interconnect.
B) One of the Dedicated Interconnects is not configured correctly.
C) There is no Cloud Load Balancer in place to distribute the network load equally.

D) BGP sessions have failed to establish between all campus switches and the Cloud Router.

E) None of the above.

QUESTION 31

You are developing a new service and need to connect your Compute Engine instances, which don't have public IP addresses, to Cloud Spanner. What two actions should you execute to accomplish this?

A) Enable the Cloud Memorystore API in your Google Cloud project.

B) Establish a private connection with the Cloud Spanner service producer.

C) Turn on Private Google Access for your subnetwork.

D) Configure a custom static route to direct the traffic to the Cloud Spanner service endpoint.

E) Enable the Service Networking API in your Google Cloud project.

QUESTION 32

You are setting up a disaster recovery solution for a critical application in GCP. The solution involves replicating data from Cloud SQL in the primary region to a standby Cloud SQL instance in a secondary region. The RPO (Recovery Point Objective) is critical. What additional configuration should you consider to ensure the RPO is met?

A) Configure synchronous replication between the primary and standby Cloud SQL instances.

B) Set up a read replica of the Cloud SQL instance in the secondary region and promote it in case of failure.

C) Use Cloud Dataflow to continuously replicate data from the primary to the standby instance.

D) Implement automated backups and restore to the standby instance in the secondary region.

E) Establish a custom script for incremental backups from the primary to the standby Cloud SQL instance.

QUESTION 33

Your organization has strict data residency requirements, and you need to ensure that all data processed in Google Cloud stays within the European Union (EU). Which Google Cloud service or feature should you use to enforce data residency compliance?

A) Deploy Google Cloud Storage buckets in EU regions and store all data there.

B) Utilize Google Cloud Key Management Service (KMS) to encrypt data and manage keys within EU regions.

C) Set up Google Cloud Identity-Aware Proxy (IAP) to control access to EU-hosted resources.

D) Enable data residency controls in Google Workspace to ensure data stays in the EU.

E) None of the above.

QUESTION 34

Your organization is migrating its existing on-premises data center to Google Cloud and wants to ensure a smooth transition while maintaining high availability. What complex networking strategy should you employ for this migration?

A) Lift and Shift with VPC Peering

B) Rehosting with Cloud Interconnect
C) Replatforming with Dedicated Interconnect
D) Retiring with Cloud VPN
E) Rebuilding with VPN Gateway

QUESTION 35

Your organization is running a distributed application that spans multiple Google Cloud regions and requires precise traffic routing based on geographic locations. What is the most suitable complex load balancing strategy to implement for this application?

A) Set up custom load balancing rules with more precision than the default load balancer settings, specifying geographic regions as criteria for routing.
B) Reconfigure the application to consolidate all components within a single region, simplifying the load balancing requirements.
C) Delete all default load balancing settings and establish distinct custom load balancing rules for each geographic region, using geographic location-based criteria for routing.
D) Create more specific custom load balancing rules than the default settings, designating geographic regions for routing, and assign location tags for precise traffic routing.
E) Implement Google Cloud CDN to optimize content delivery for the distributed application and rely on default load balancing settings for traffic distribution.

QUESTION 36

You are configuring a network in GCP for a set of compute-intensive applications that need to communicate with a managed database service. The applications are sensitive and require a network configuration that minimizes latency and maximizes throughput. What is the most effective network setup for this scenario?

A) Use Cloud VPN to create secure, direct connections to the database service.
B) Set up Dedicated Interconnect to the managed database service for high-performance connectivity.
C) Configure each application with Premium Network Tier and direct peering to the database service.
D) Implement Private Google Access on subnetworks hosting the applications for optimized database connectivity.
E) Establish VPC Service Controls around the applications and database service for enhanced network performance.

QUESTION 37

You are tasked with designing a network architecture for a large-scale, multi-tier web application in GCP. The application requires different network zones for web, application, and database layers, each with specific security and communication needs. What is the most effective network setup for this application?

A) Use a single VPC with separate subnets for each layer and configure firewall rules for inter-layer communication.
B) Set up three different VPCs for each layer and use VPC Peering for communication between them.
C) Implement Shared VPC with dedicated subnets for each application layer.

D) Configure separate subnets within a Shared VPC and use Cloud VPN for inter-layer communication.
E) Establish individual VPCs for each layer and connect them with Cloud Interconnect for secure communication.

QUESTION 38

You are tasked with setting up a network architecture for a global data analytics platform that needs to process large volumes of data efficiently. Your goal is to minimize data transfer costs while ensuring data consistency across regions. Which Google Cloud networking components and services should you combine to achieve these objectives?

A) Cloud Dataflow with Cloud Pub/Sub
B) Google Cloud Bigtable with Google Cloud VPN
C) Google Cloud Pub/Sub with Google Cloud Storage
D) Cloud Interconnect with Cloud Spanner
E) Google Cloud Dataflow with VPC peering

QUESTION 39

Your organization is transitioning to Google Cloud and needs to ensure that data is stored securely and encrypted at rest. You also require fine-grained control over access to data objects and auditing capabilities. Which Google Cloud storage service should you choose to meet these requirements?

A) Google Cloud Storage
B) Google Cloud Bigtable
C) Google Cloud Firestore
D) Google Cloud SQL
E) Google Cloud Spanner

QUESTION 40

Your organization needs to ensure data redundancy and high availability for your cloud-based storage solution on Google Cloud. You are evaluating different storage options. Which combination of Google Cloud storage services or features should you choose to meet these requirements effectively?

A) Google Cloud Storage and Google Cloud Persistent Disk
B) Google Cloud Filestore and Google Cloud Storage Transfer Service
C) Google Cloud Storage Nearline and Google Cloud CDN
D) Google Cloud Spanner and Google Cloud KMS
E) Google Cloud Bigtable and Google Cloud Dataprep

QUESTION 41

To enable a custom SSH key for access on every VM in a healthcare data analysis project in GCP, what is the most efficient method?

A) Add the public SSH key to the project-wide metadata in Google Cloud.
B) Deploy a Compute Engine snapshot containing the public SSH key across all VMs.
C) Manually upload the public SSH key to each VM's metadata.

D) Use the gcloud compute ssh command to distribute the public SSH key to each VM.
E) Create a startup script for VMs that automatically adds the SSH key to each instance.

QUESTION 42

You are tasked with designing a network architecture for a global gaming platform on Google Cloud. The platform needs to ensure low-latency access for players worldwide. Additionally, it should be resilient to regional failures. Which combination of Google Cloud services or features should you use to achieve these objectives effectively?

A) Google Cloud VPN and Google Cloud Bigtable
B) Google Cloud CDN and Google Cloud Compute Engine Autoscaler
C) Google Cloud Spanner and Google Cloud Load Balancing
D) Google Cloud Storage and Google Cloud DNS
E) Google Cloud Global Load Balancing and Google Cloud Memorystore

QUESTION 43

You are transitioning your healthcare organization's VMs to use Google Cloud DNS. You need to transfer your existing BIND zone file to the new service. What is the appropriate command to execute this action?

A) gcloud dns record-sets import ZONE_FILE --zone-file-format --zone MANAGED_ZONE.
B) gcloud dns record-sets import ZONE_FILE --replace-origin-ns --zone MANAGED_ZONE.
C) gcloud dns record-sets import ZONE_FILE --zone MANAGED_ZONE.
D) gcloud dns record-sets import ZONE_FILE --delete-all-existing --zone MANAGED_ZONE.
E) gcloud dns record-sets import ZONE_FILE --update-zone --zone MANAGED_ZONE.

QUESTION 44

Your organization is concerned about data security and wants to encrypt data at rest for virtual machine instances running in Google Compute Engine. Which encryption option should you choose to achieve this while minimizing performance impact?

A) Use application-level encryption within each virtual machine.
B) Enable Google Cloud's default encryption for Compute Engine disks.
C) Implement Cloud HSM for dedicated hardware-based encryption.
D) Use Google Cloud KMS for key management and encrypt VM instances individually.
E) Enable Google Cloud Storage encryption for virtual machine data.

QUESTION 45

For routing traffic through a pair of network virtual appliances in GCP for communication with a corporate network, which configuration ensures redundancy and concurrent utilization of both appliances?

A) Use a Network Load Balancer targeting both appliances, with a route for 172.16.0.0/12 pointing to the load balancer.
B) Configure an Internal TCP/UDP Load Balancer with both appliances as backends and route

172.16.0.0/12 to it.
C) Create two routes for 172.16.0.0/12, each pointing to one of the appliances with different priorities.
D) Set up an Internal HTTP(S) Load Balancer with both appliances as backends, routing 172.16.0.0/12 to this load balancer.
E) Implement an internal network proxy for 172.16.0.0/12, distributing traffic equally to both appliances.

QUESTION 46

Your organization is planning to deploy a globally distributed application on Google Cloud with low-latency access for users around the world. What load balancing solution should you choose to achieve this goal?

A) Network Load Balancing.
B) HTTP(S) Load Balancing with global anycast IP addresses.
C) SSL Proxy Load Balancing.
D) TCP Proxy Load Balancing with regional IP addresses.
E) Internal Load Balancing with regional IP addresses.

QUESTION 47

You are tasked with setting up a GCP network to handle high-volume data transfers between Compute Engine instances and a third-party data analytics service. The instances need to securely send data at high speeds. What network configuration should be implemented to optimize for speed and security?

A) Set up Dedicated Interconnect to the third-party service for direct, high-speed connections.
B) Configure Cloud VPN with high-throughput tunnels for secure data transfer.
C) Enable Premium Network Tier on Compute Engine instances for enhanced performance.
D) Use Private Google Access for secure, high-speed access to external services.
E) Implement VPC Service Controls to secure data transfer and optimize network speed.

QUESTION 48

For a global e-commerce platform on GCP, you need to configure network solutions to handle sudden surges in traffic, optimize content delivery, and protect against web attacks. The network should efficiently distribute traffic to data centers worldwide. Which combination of GCP services and configurations is best suited for this scenario?

A) Use Global HTTP(S) Load Balancer with Cloud Armor and Cloud CDN for traffic distribution and security.
B) Configure regional Network Load Balancers with Cloud IDS for traffic analysis and web attack mitigation.
C) Implement instance groups with Internal Load Balancers for each region and Cloud VPN for global traffic management.
D) Set up TCP/SSL Proxy Load Balancers in each region with VPC Service Controls for security.
E) Deploy Cloud Run instances globally with VPC Network Peering for traffic distribution and security.

QUESTION 49

You are configuring a high-availability setup for a critical application in GCP that requires instant failover in case of a zone failure. The application uses stateful sessions stored on Compute Engine instances. What configuration should you use to achieve high availability and immediate failover?

A) Set up a multi-zone instance group with automatic failover and use persistent disks for session storage.
B) Configure a single-zone instance group with a standby instance in another zone.
C) Use a regional persistent disk with synchronous replication across zones.
D) Implement a custom failover mechanism using Cloud Functions to monitor and initiate failover.
E) Establish Cloud SQL with high availability for stateful session storage.

QUESTION 50

You are setting up a high-availability architecture for a critical application in GCP that requires instant failover in case of a zone failure. The application uses stateful sessions stored on Compute Engine instances. What configuration ensures high availability and immediate failover for the stateful sessions?

A) Configure a multi-zone instance group with automatic failover and use regional persistent disks for session storage.
B) Set up a single-zone instance group with standby instances in another zone.
C) Use Cloud SQL with high availability for managing stateful sessions.
D) Implement a custom failover mechanism using Cloud Functions and regional persistent disks.
E) Establish instance groups with zonal SSD persistent disks and Cloud Load Balancing for traffic distribution.

PRACTICE TEST 4 - ANSWERS ONLY

QUESTION 1

Answer – C) Assign roles with the fewest permissions needed for specific tasks.

Option C - Assigning roles with the fewest permissions needed for specific tasks aligns with the principle of least privilege.
Option A - Assigning the "Owner" role is too permissive and grants excessive access.
Option B - Assigning the "Editor" role is also overly permissive.
Option D - Assigning roles with full project access is not aligned with least privilege.
Option E - Disabling IAM is not a recommended security practice.

QUESTION 2

Answer – B) Deploy a multi-region Cloud Storage bucket for data replication.

Option B - Deploying a multi-region Cloud Storage bucket ensures data replication and failover capabilities, minimizing downtime in case of a disaster.
Option A - Cloud VPN tunnels are for connectivity but do not address data replication.
Option C - Google Cloud Filestore is for file storage, not data replication.
Option D - Global load balancers are for application failover, not data replication.
Option E - Creating a dedicated VPC may not directly address data replication and failover requirements.

QUESTION 3

Answer – B) Google Cloud Dedicated Interconnect with a private VLAN.

Option B - Using Google Cloud Dedicated Interconnect with a private VLAN provides dedicated, high-speed, and low-latency connectivity between on-premises data centers and Google Cloud while ensuring private and secure communication.
Option A - VPNs may not provide the same level of performance and privacy as Dedicated Interconnect.
Option C - Direct Peering is for external connectivity, not private communication with on-premises data centers.
Option D - VPC Network Peering is for VPCs, not on-premises data centers.
Option E - Global Load Balancing is unrelated to dedicated connectivity.

QUESTION 4

Answer – A) Use Google Cloud Storage Transfer Service to copy the data over an encrypted channel and enable server-side encryption with Customer-Managed Keys (CMEK) in the destination bucket.

Option A - Using Google Cloud Storage Transfer Service with encryption and Customer-Managed Keys (CMEK) ensures the highest level of security for sensitive customer data.
Option B - Third-party tools may not necessarily provide better security and can introduce complexity.
Option C - Manual copying and custom encryption may be error-prone and less secure.
Option D - Using Google-managed keys (GMEK) is not as secure as Customer-Managed Keys (CMEK) for

sensitive data.
 Option E - Avoiding migration to the cloud is not a practical solution for most organizations and doesn't leverage cloud security features.

QUESTION 5

Answer - A) Implement a Google Cloud Dedicated Interconnect for dedicated, low-latency connectivity.

Option A provides the best solution for secure, low-latency connectivity to Google Cloud, aligning with the needs of real-time data processing applications.
Option B, while addressing QoS, may not guarantee the low-latency requirements.
Option C introduces complexity and may not be cost-effective.
Option D is more suited for content distribution.
Option E is a broader approach and may not specifically address low-latency connectivity.

QUESTION 6

Answer - B) Utilize Google Cloud Dedicated Interconnect for dedicated, high-speed connectivity.

Option B provides the most appropriate approach for ensuring high-speed, low-latency connectivity between on-premises data centers and Google Cloud, aligning with the organization's needs.
Option A mentions VPNs but focuses on QoS rather than dedicated connectivity.
Option C mentions DNS but doesn't provide the connectivity itself.
Option D may not offer the same level of performance as Dedicated Interconnect.
Option E introduces complexity and may not be as reliable as Dedicated Interconnect.

QUESTION 7

Answer – A) Utilize a single global HTTP(S) load balancer with backend services in both regions.

A) Correct. A global load balancer will distribute traffic efficiently across regions.
B) Incorrect. Regional load balancers do not automatically handle inter-regional traffic.
C) Incorrect. Cloud CDN is not suitable for dynamic e-commerce traffic.
D) Incorrect. This creates isolated regional setups, not a cohesive global solution.
E) Incorrect. VPC Peering is not designed for handling dynamic traffic spikes.

QUESTION 8

Answer - C) Google Cloud Load Balancing

Option C, Google Cloud Load Balancing, is the correct choice for efficiently managing and load balancing traffic across instances in different regions while minimizing latency. It offers global load balancing and is designed for high availability and fault tolerance.
 Option A, Google Cloud CDN, primarily focuses on content delivery and caching to reduce latency but doesn't handle instance load balancing across regions.
 Option B, Google Cloud Armor, is a web application firewall and security service, not a load balancer for regional instances.
 Option D, Google Cloud Interconnect, provides connectivity but doesn't handle traffic load balancing.
 Option E, Google Cloud DNS, is a domain name system service for resolving domain names to IP

addresses, not for traffic load balancing.

QUESTION 9

Answer - D) Utilize a third-party cloud connectivity solution for inter-cloud communication.

Option D (third-party cloud connectivity solution) provides a flexible and efficient way to establish secure network connectivity between Google Cloud and AWS. It allows for optimized routing and network management. Options A and E (Direct Interconnect and AWS Direct Connect) are dedicated but may lack flexibility.
Option B (VPN tunnels) can work but may not offer the same performance and flexibility as a third-party solution.
Option C (Google Cloud VPN Gateway in AWS) is not a standard approach.

QUESTION 10

Answer - B) Create a central hub VPC and configure VPC Peering connections from all project VPCs to the hub VPC.

Option A would result in a complex and inefficient mesh of connections.
Option C refers to a different Google Cloud service.
Option D provides secure connectivity but doesn't address the central hub requirement.
Option B is the correct choice as it aligns with the requirements, providing a central hub for private connectivity while maintaining separate VPCs for different projects.

QUESTION 11

Answer - A) Google Cloud Cloud Endpoints for API management and communication.

Option B is for VPC-to-VPC communication and may not address microservices-specific communication needs.
Option C is suitable for asynchronous messaging but may not cover real-time communication.
Option D focuses on IP address management but doesn't provide communication capabilities.
Option E offers encrypted communication but may not be tailored for microservices communication.
Option A is the correct choice as Google Cloud Cloud Endpoints is designed for API management and communication, allowing secure and reliable communication between microservices developed using different languages and frameworks, making it suitable for complex microservices-based architectures.

QUESTION 12

Answer – B) Set up a Dedicated Interconnect for high-throughput connectivity.

A) Incorrect. VPN may not provide the required throughput or low latency.
B) Correct. Offers high bandwidth and low latency for large data transfers.
C) Incorrect. Partner Interconnect may not fully leverage existing fiber-optic infrastructure.
D) Incorrect. Cloud CDN is primarily for web content distribution.
E) Incorrect. VPC Peering is not suitable for on-premises to cloud connections.

QUESTION 13

Answer – C) Use Dedicated Interconnect for a direct, high-speed connection.

A) Incorrect. VPN may not offer the necessary performance.
B) Incorrect. VPC Peering is not applicable for on-premises connections.
C) Correct. Provides a high-performance, secure connection.
D) Incorrect. Cloud Endpoints are for API management, not direct system communication.
E) Incorrect. Cloud Armor is for security against external threats, not for connectivity.

QUESTION 14

Answer - A) Google Cloud Network Peering

A) Google Cloud Network Peering - Network Peering allows communication between VPCs while maintaining security boundaries, making it suitable for this scenario.
 B) Google Cloud VPN - VPNs are for secure access, not necessarily for inter-VPC communication.
 C) Google Cloud VPC Service Controls - VPC Service Controls focus on isolation and access controls within a VPC, not between VPCs.
 D) Google Cloud Shared VPC - Shared VPC allows shared resources but may not directly address inter-VPC traffic control.
 E) Google Cloud Private Service Connect - Private Service Connect is used for private network connections but may not specifically address inter-VPC communication and traffic control.

QUESTION 15

Answer – D) Create specific rules to allow ingress on web ports only for VMs with web components.

A) Incorrect. This doesn't prevent other VMs from being accessed.
B) Incorrect. Too permissive and exposes non-web components.
C) Incorrect. Restricts access to HTTPS but doesn't differentiate between VMs.
D) Correct. Ensures only web components are accessible from the internet.
E) Incorrect. Allows unnecessary access to non-web VMs.

QUESTION 16

Answer - C) A phased migration, starting with non-critical applications and gradually moving critical ones.

C) A phased migration, starting with non-critical applications and gradually moving critical ones - This approach minimizes disruption and allows for careful testing and optimization of the migration process, ensuring low-latency communication.
 A) Gradual migration while maintaining on-premises data center connectivity - Gradual migration may still involve significant disruption and may not be the best approach for low-latency communication.
 B) "Lift and shift" migration may be faster but can lead to potential issues with low-latency communication and disruption.
 D) A hybrid approach with permanent coexistence may not fully leverage the benefits of Google Cloud and can introduce complexity.
 E) "Big bang" migration simultaneously may result in significant disruption and is generally riskier for critical applications.

QUESTION 17

Answer - C) A phased migration, starting with non-critical applications and gradually moving critical ones.

C) A phased migration, starting with non-critical applications and gradually moving critical ones - This approach minimizes disruption and allows for careful testing and optimization of the migration process, ensuring low-latency communication.
 A) Gradual migration while maintaining on-premises data center connectivity - Gradual migration may still involve significant disruption and may not be the best approach for low-latency communication.
 B) "Lift and shift" migration may be faster but can lead to potential issues with low-latency communication and disruption.
 D) A hybrid approach with permanent coexistence may not fully leverage the benefits of Google Cloud and can introduce complexity.
 E) "Big bang" migration simultaneously may result in significant disruption and is generally riskier for critical applications.

QUESTION 18

Answer - E) Google Cloud Run

E) Google Cloud Run is a managed compute platform that automatically scales containerized applications, making it suitable for achieving high availability and scalability for web applications.
 B) Google App Engine Standard Environment also provides automatic scaling and is suitable for web applications.
 D) Google Kubernetes Engine (GKE) with a single node pool may not provide the same level of automatic scaling and ease of use for web applications.
 C) Google Compute Engine with manual scaling requires manual management and may not offer the same level of scalability as managed platforms.
 A) Google Cloud Functions is more suitable for serverless event-driven tasks rather than web applications.

QUESTION 19

Answer - B) Cloud VPN.

B) Cloud VPN provides an economical and relatively quick connectivity option that allows your Compute Engine instance and in-house servers to communicate securely via private IPs without requiring Cloud Interconnect setup.
 A) Partner Interconnect may involve longer setup times and VLAN attachments.
 C) 100-Gbps Partner Interconnect is overkill for this scenario and may not be available within the given timeframe.
 D) 10-Gbps Dedicated Interconnect is overkill and not the most economical choice.
 E) Cloud Interconnect with a dedicated VLAN introduces complexity and may not meet the 24-hour deadline.

QUESTION 20

Answer - B) Cloud VPN.

B) In this scenario, where you need to establish a connection between a Compute Engine instance and in-house data center servers via private IPs in a cost-effective and timely manner, using Cloud VPN is a suitable option. It provides secure connectivity over the public internet without the need for dedicated hardware like Cloud Interconnect.

A) Partner Interconnect may involve provisioning VLAN attachments and may not be the most economical choice.

C) 100-Gbps Partner Interconnect is overkill for the scenario and not the most economical option.

D) 100-Gbps Dedicated Interconnect is unnecessary and costly for this situation.

E) Cloud Router is used for routing and does not provide the direct connectivity needed.

QUESTION 21

Answer - B) Use VPC Peering to connect the VPC networks and enable private communication.

B) The recommended solution for establishing private communication between instances in different VPC networks without exposing them to the public internet is to use VPC Peering. It allows direct, private communication between VPC networks.

A) Setting up a VPN tunnel may introduce unnecessary complexity and is not as straightforward as VPC Peering.

C) Cloud NAT is used for outbound traffic and does not facilitate direct communication between VPC networks.

D) Creating custom firewall rules may not be as efficient or secure as VPC Peering for private communication between VPC networks.

QUESTION 22

Answer - B) Cloud VPN.

B) Given the requirement for a quick assessment without an existing Cloud Interconnect setup, Cloud VPN is the most practical and economical option to enable communication between the Compute Engine instance and the in-house data center servers via private IPs.

A) Partner Interconnect and its variations (100-Gbps or 10-Gbps) typically require more time for provisioning and setup.

C) High-speed Partner Interconnect options may not be necessary for an initial assessment and can be costlier.

D) Dedicated Interconnect options also involve longer setup times and may not be as economical for this scenario.

E) Configuring Cloud Interconnect with a custom configuration can be complex and time-consuming, making it less suitable for a quick assessment.

QUESTION 23

Answer – D) Configure Cloud IDS to monitor and protect network traffic to and from the analytics platform.

A) Incorrect. Cloud Armor is more suited for web applications, not analytics platforms.
B) Incorrect. Cloud VPNs are for secure connections, not necessarily for large-scale data analytics traffic.
C) Incorrect. VPC Peering is not typically used for connecting to external data sources.
D) Correct. Cloud IDS provides network security monitoring suitable for a large-scale analytics platform.
E) Incorrect. Private Google Access is for accessing Google services, not for broad network security.

QUESTION 24

Answer - A) Utilize Google Cloud Security Groups for network security.
C) Implement a Google Cloud VPN tunnel for secure communication.

Option B - Cloud NAT gateway is for outbound traffic management, not security like a firewall.
Option D - Cloud DNS firewall is for DNS security, not a direct firewall replacement.
Option E - Google Cloud Armor focuses on security, not traffic management. Choice A (Utilize Google Cloud Security Groups for network security) - Google Cloud Security Groups provide network-level security controls, allowing you to define firewall rules to control incoming and outgoing traffic, thus replacing the need for a dedicated hardware firewall.
 Choice C (Implement a Google Cloud VPN tunnel for secure communication) - Implementing a Google Cloud VPN tunnel enables secure communication between on-premises and GCP resources, serving as a secure replacement for the dedicated hardware firewall.

QUESTION 25

Answer - B) Partition large tables based on date or another relevant column.
D) Create views for frequently used query patterns.

Option A - BigQuery's default caching is limited and may not optimize complex queries effectively.
Option C - While BigQuery has automatic query optimization, taking manual actions can further optimize performance.
Option E - Loading all data into a single unpartitioned table can lead to inefficient queries and higher costs. Choice B - Partitioning large tables based on relevant columns allows BigQuery to scan only the required partitions, optimizing query performance and reducing costs by scanning less data.
 Choice D - Creating views for frequently used query patterns simplifies queries and can improve performance by predefining common query logic.

QUESTION 26

Answer – A) Use Cloud IoT Core for device management, Cloud Pub/Sub for data ingestion, and edge computing for low-latency processing.

A) Correct. Provides a comprehensive solution for IoT data management, ingestion, and processing.
B) Incorrect. Cloud VPNs are not optimal for high-volume IoT data ingest.
C) Incorrect. Cloud Functions and Cloud Storage might not handle the volume and latency requirements efficiently.
D) Incorrect. Cloud Interconnects are not typically used for IoT device connectivity.
E) Incorrect. Cloud Routers and Dataflow do not specifically address IoT data ingest and processing needs.

QUESTION 27

Answer - B) Deploy a central VPC in europe-west3 and use VPC peering to connect to the other regions.

Option A - Creating separate VPCs and VPN connections may lead to complexity.
Option C - Dedicated Interconnects are not designed for connecting to specific regions.
Option D - Cloud Interconnect may not be necessary for local data processing. Choice B - Deploying a central VPC in europe-west3 and using VPC peering provides a straightforward and efficient way to

connect to europe-west2 and southamerica-east1 for local data processing while minimizing complexity.

QUESTION 28

Answer – A) Configure each Compute Engine instance with autoscaling based on CPU usage and integrate with Cloud Pub/Sub for data ingestion.

A) Correct. Autoscaling and Cloud Pub/Sub integration provide scalability and efficient data handling.
B) Incorrect. HTTP(S) load balancer is not optimal for IoT data ingestion.
C) Incorrect. Dataflow can process data streams but does not require Compute Engine for further analysis.
D) Incorrect. Direct data handling from Cloud IoT Core to Compute Engine is less scalable.
E) Incorrect. Cloud VPNs are not suitable for high-volume IoT data streams.

QUESTION 29

Answer - B) Establish a VPC Service Controls perimeter for your project, including an access context policy that encompasses your organization's head office network IP ranges.

Option A - Creating individual access context policies for each application may lead to administrative complexity.
Option C - Creating separate VPC Service Controls perimeters for each application may result in management overhead.
Option D - While firewall rules are an option, VPC Service Controls offer a more comprehensive security approach. Choice B - Setting up a VPC Service Controls perimeter for your project with a comprehensive access context policy that covers head office network IP ranges provides centralized and efficient API access control for Memorystore and Spanner across all applications in the project.

QUESTION 30

Answer - B) One of the Dedicated Interconnects is not configured correctly.

Option A - The issue described doesn't suggest an internal firewall problem.
Option C - The absence of a Cloud Load Balancer is unrelated to BGP session failures.
Option D - BGP session failures with all campus switches are not indicated in the problem description.
Choice B - The issue with BGP sessions failing to establish is most likely due to a misconfiguration in one of the Dedicated Interconnects.

QUESTION 31

Answer - B) Establish a private connection with the Cloud Spanner service producer. and C) Turn on Private Google Access for your subnetwork.

Option A - Enabling the Cloud Memorystore API is unrelated to connecting Compute Engine instances to Cloud Spanner.
Option D - Configuring a custom static route is not the standard way to connect Compute Engine instances to Cloud Spanner.
Option E - Enabling the Service Networking API is unrelated to connecting Compute Engine instances to Cloud Spanner. Explanation for choices B and C - To connect Compute Engine instances without public IP

addresses to Cloud Spanner, you should establish a private connection with the Cloud Spanner service producer and turn on Private Google Access for your subnetwork, allowing the instances to reach Cloud Spanner privately.

QUESTION 32

Answer – B) Set up a read replica of the Cloud SQL instance in the secondary region and promote it in case of failure.

A) Incorrect. Cloud SQL does not support synchronous replication across regions.
B) Correct. Read replicas provide an efficient way to replicate data and meet RPO requirements.
C) Incorrect. Cloud Dataflow is not typically used for database replication.
D) Incorrect. Automated backups may not meet the critical RPO requirement.
E) Incorrect. Custom scripts are less reliable and more complex than using built-in Cloud SQL features.

QUESTION 33

Answer - A) Deploy Google Cloud Storage buckets in EU regions and store all data there.

Option B - While encryption is important, it doesn't enforce data residency compliance on its own.
Option C - Google Cloud IAP controls access but doesn't enforce data residency.
Option D - Google Workspace controls are related to user access, not data residency. Choice A - Deploying Google Cloud Storage buckets in EU regions and storing all data there ensures data residency compliance by design.

QUESTION 34

Answer - B) Rehosting with Cloud Interconnect

A) Lift and Shift with VPC Peering - Explanation: Lift and Shift focuses on moving existing workloads, and VPC Peering connects VPCs but may not provide the dedicated connectivity required for data center migration.
C) Replatforming with Dedicated Interconnect - Explanation: Replatforming involves making some changes to workloads, and Dedicated Interconnect provides dedicated, reliable connections for data center migration.
D) Retiring with Cloud VPN - Explanation: Retiring means decommissioning the on-premises data center, and Cloud VPN may not be sufficient for data center migration.
E) Rebuilding with VPN Gateway - Explanation: Rebuilding implies redesigning workloads, and VPN Gateway is used for secure connections but may not be the best choice for data center migration.
B) Rehosting with Cloud Interconnect - Explanation: Rehosting involves moving workloads to Google Cloud with minimal changes, and Cloud Interconnect provides dedicated, reliable connections for a smooth data center migration.

QUESTION 35

Answer - D) Create more specific custom load balancing rules than the default settings, designating geographic regions for routing, and assign location tags for precise traffic routing.

D) Create more specific custom load balancing rules than the default settings, designating geographic regions for routing, and assign location tags for precise traffic routing - Explanation: This approach allows for precise traffic routing based on geographic locations, enhancing the load balancing strategy for the distributed application.

A) Set up custom load balancing rules with more precision than the default load balancer settings - Explanation: While custom load balancing rules are useful, this option does not consider the use of location tags for precise routing.

B) Reconfigure the application to consolidate all components within a single region - Explanation: Consolidating components into a single region may not be practical or efficient for a distributed application spanning multiple regions.

C) Delete all default load balancing settings and establish distinct custom load balancing rules for each geographic region - Explanation: Deleting default settings introduces complexity, and this option may not be necessary for precise geographic routing.

E) Implement Google Cloud CDN - Explanation: CDN focuses on content delivery and may not directly address the requirement of precise geographic traffic routing for the distributed application.

QUESTION 36

Answer – D) Implement Private Google Access on subnetworks hosting the applications for optimized database connectivity.

A) Incorrect. VPNs may introduce additional latency.
B) Incorrect. Dedicated Interconnect is for external connections, not for intra-GCP service communication.
C) Incorrect. Direct peering is not typically used for managed database services.
D) Correct. Private Google Access optimizes connectivity to Google managed services with minimal latency.
E) Incorrect. VPC Service Controls are for securing data, not enhancing network performance.

QUESTION 37

Answer – A) Use a single VPC with separate subnets for each layer and configure firewall rules for inter-layer communication.

A) Correct. This provides efficient network segmentation with controlled access between layers.
B) Incorrect. Multiple VPCs add unnecessary complexity for a single application.
C) Incorrect. Shared VPC is more suitable for multiple projects sharing common resources.
D) Incorrect. VPN within a shared VPC for a single application is not an optimal setup.
E) Incorrect. Cloud Interconnect is typically used for on-premises to cloud connections, not for internal application layering.

QUESTION 38

Answer - D) Cloud Interconnect with Cloud Spanner

A) Cloud Dataflow with Cloud Pub/Sub - Dataflow and Pub/Sub are used for data processing and messaging but do not inherently ensure data consistency across regions.
B) Google Cloud Bigtable with Google Cloud VPN - Bigtable is a NoSQL database, and VPN provides connectivity but may not ensure data consistency.
C) Google Cloud Pub/Sub with Google Cloud Storage - Pub/Sub and Storage are used for messaging and

data storage but may not guarantee data consistency.

D) Cloud Interconnect with Cloud Spanner - Correct answer. Interconnect provides efficient data transfer, and Spanner ensures data consistency across regions for analytics platforms.

E) Google Cloud Dataflow with VPC peering - Dataflow and VPC peering focus on data processing and connectivity but may not address data consistency across regions.

QUESTION 39

Answer - A) Google Cloud Storage

A) Correct answer. Google Cloud Storage allows you to store data securely, encrypt it at rest, and control access with fine-grained permissions and audit logging.

B) Google Cloud Bigtable - While it's a NoSQL database, Bigtable is not primarily designed for general-purpose storage or encryption at rest.

C) Google Cloud Firestore - Firestore is a NoSQL database, and while it offers security features, it is not primarily a storage service.

D) Google Cloud SQL - SQL provides managed databases, not general-purpose storage with fine-grained access control.

E) Google Cloud Spanner - Spanner is a distributed database, not a general-purpose storage service. It offers its own set of features for data storage and management.

QUESTION 40

Answer - B) Google Cloud Filestore and Google Cloud Storage Transfer Service

A) Google Cloud Storage and Google Cloud Persistent Disk offer storage but may not inherently provide data redundancy and high availability without additional configurations.

B) Correct answer. Google Cloud Filestore provides managed file storage with data redundancy and high availability, and Google Cloud Storage Transfer Service assists with data transfer, making them suitable for storage solutions requiring these features.

C) Google Cloud Storage Nearline is designed for archival storage, and Google Cloud CDN focuses on content delivery, but they may not provide the same level of data redundancy and high availability as Filestore.

D) Google Cloud Spanner is a database, and Google Cloud KMS is a key management service, but they may not be the primary solution for achieving data redundancy and high availability in storage.

E) Google Cloud Bigtable is a NoSQL database, and Google Cloud Dataprep is focused on data preparation; they are not primarily storage solutions.

QUESTION 41

Answer – A) Add the public SSH key to the project-wide metadata in Google Cloud.

A) Correct. Project-wide metadata ensures the SSH key is automatically applied to all VMs in the project.

B) Incorrect. A snapshot is used for preserving a disk state, not for distributing SSH keys.

C) Incorrect. Manually uploading to each VM is inefficient for a large number of instances.

D) Incorrect. The gcloud compute ssh command is used for connecting to instances, not for key distribution.

E) Incorrect. While startup scripts can add keys, using project-wide metadata is more efficient.

QUESTION 42

Answer - E) Google Cloud Global Load Balancing and Google Cloud Memorystore

A) Google Cloud VPN and Google Cloud Bigtable may not be the primary components for a low-latency and resilient gaming platform.
B) Google Cloud CDN and Google Cloud Compute Engine Autoscaler focus on content delivery and scaling but may not inherently provide resilience to regional failures.
C) Google Cloud Spanner is a database, and Google Cloud Load Balancing helps distribute traffic but may not be the primary components for resilience to regional failures.
D) Google Cloud Storage and Google Cloud DNS offer storage and DNS services but may not inherently provide low-latency access and resilience to regional failures.
E) Correct answer. Google Cloud Global Load Balancing ensures low-latency access and resilience to regional failures, while Google Cloud Memorystore provides in-memory data storage for high-performance gaming applications.

QUESTION 43

Answer - C) gcloud dns record-sets import ZONE_FILE --zone MANAGED_ZONE.

A) The command format is incorrect, and "zone-file-format" is not a valid option.
B) The option "--replace-origin-ns" is not applicable in this context for transferring zone files.
C) Correct answer. To import a BIND zone file to Google Cloud DNS, you use the command with the appropriate flags and options.
D) The option "--delete-all-existing" is not typically used for importing zone files; it's more for managing existing records.
E) The option "--update-zone" is not used for importing zone files; it's for updating an existing managed zone's DNS settings.

QUESTION 44

Answer - B) Enable Google Cloud's default encryption for Compute Engine disks.

A) Application-level encryption may have performance overhead and can be complex to manage.
B) Correct answer. Enabling Google Cloud's default encryption for Compute Engine disks ensures data at rest is encrypted with minimal performance impact.
C) Cloud HSM is suitable for dedicated hardware-based encryption but may not be necessary for all workloads.
D) Using Google Cloud KMS for individual VM instance encryption can add complexity and performance overhead.
E) Google Cloud Storage encryption is for data at rest in storage buckets, not for virtual machine instances.

QUESTION 45

Answer – B) Configure an Internal TCP/UDP Load Balancer with both appliances as backends and route 172.16.0.0/12 to it.

A) Incorrect. Network Load Balancer is not designed for routing internal traffic in this manner.
B) Correct. An Internal TCP/UDP Load Balancer ensures both redundancy and simultaneous use of the

appliances for traffic management.
C) Incorrect. Separate routes don't guarantee concurrent use of both appliances.
D) Incorrect. Internal HTTP(S) Load Balancer is not suitable for non-HTTP/S traffic routing.
E) Incorrect. An internal network proxy setup does not inherently provide the necessary load balancing and failover capabilities.

QUESTION 46

Answer - B) HTTP(S) Load Balancing with global anycast IP addresses.

A) Network Load Balancing is suitable for network-level traffic but does not provide global anycast IP addresses.
B) HTTP(S) Load Balancing with global anycast IP addresses ensures low-latency access for users around the world.
C) SSL Proxy Load Balancing is focused on SSL termination and may not address latency requirements.
D) TCP Proxy Load Balancing with regional IP addresses is not optimized for global distribution.
E) Internal Load Balancing is designed for internal traffic within a region, not global distribution.

QUESTION 47

Answer – C) Enable Premium Network Tier on Compute Engine instances for enhanced performance.

A) Incorrect. Interconnect is typically for connections to on-premises networks, not third-party services.
B) Incorrect. VPN may not provide the highest available throughput needed for large data transfers.
C) Correct. Premium Network Tier offers optimized network performance for high-speed data transfers.
D) Incorrect. Private Google Access does not apply to third-party services outside of Google Cloud.
E) Incorrect. VPC Service Controls are for securing data within GCP, not optimizing network speed.

QUESTION 48

Answer – A) Use Global HTTP(S) Load Balancer with Cloud Armor and Cloud CDN for traffic distribution and security.

A) Correct. Global Load Balancing, Cloud Armor, and Cloud CDN provide the necessary traffic management, security, and content delivery for a global platform.
B) Incorrect. Network Load Balancers are not suitable for global traffic distribution and DDoS protection.
C) Incorrect. Internal Load Balancers and Cloud VPN are not optimal for a global e-commerce platform.
D) Incorrect. TCP/SSL Proxy Load Balancers are not the best choice for global content distribution.
E) Incorrect. Cloud Run and VPC Peering do not provide the necessary global scaling and DDoS protection.

QUESTION 49

Answer – A) Set up a multi-zone instance group with automatic failover and use persistent disks for session storage.

A) Correct. Multi-zone instance groups with automatic failover and persistent disks provide high availability for stateful sessions.
B) Incorrect. Single-zone instance groups do not offer immediate failover capabilities.

C) Incorrect. Regional persistent disks provide data replication but not automatic failover for instances.
D) Incorrect. Custom failover mechanisms can be complex and may not provide immediate response.
E) Incorrect. Cloud SQL is a database service, not a solution for stateful session storage in Compute Engine instances.

QUESTION 50

Answer – A) Configure a multi-zone instance group with automatic failover and use regional persistent disks for session storage.

A) Correct. Multi-zone instance groups with regional persistent disks provide the necessary high availability and instant failover for stateful sessions.
B) Incorrect. Single-zone instance groups with standby instances do not offer the same level of immediate failover.
C) Incorrect. Cloud SQL is a managed database service, not suitable for storing stateful sessions on Compute Engine instances.
D) Incorrect. Custom failover mechanisms can be complex and may not provide the immediate response required.
E) Incorrect. Zonal SSDs and load balancing do not address the failover requirements for stateful sessions stored on instances.

PRACTICE TEST 5 - QUESTIONS ONLY

QUESTION 1

You need to design a Google Cloud network architecture that can handle bursty traffic patterns efficiently without over-provisioning resources. Which GCP service can automatically scale your network resources based on demand?

A) Google Cloud VPC B) Google Cloud Load Balancing C) Google Cloud Auto Scaling D) Google Cloud VPC Peering E) Google Cloud CDN

QUESTION 2

You are responsible for securing network traffic between your on-premises data center and Google Cloud. What should you set up to ensure encrypted and private communication while allowing access to specific Google Cloud services?

A) Implement Google Cloud VPN with a dedicated tunnel.
B) Use Google Cloud's dedicated Interconnect with a private VLAN.
C) Deploy Google Cloud VPC Network Peering.
D) Configure Google Cloud's Managed SSL Certificates.
E) Set up Google Cloud Firewall Rules for specific services.

QUESTION 3

Your organization operates a Virtual Private Cloud (VPC) with two Partner Interconnect connections serving different regions: europe-westl and europe-northl. Each Partner Interconnect is linked to a Cloud Router in its specific region through a VLAN attachment. You have been tasked with setting up a resilient failover route. Ideally, all ingress traffic from your corporate network should primarily go through the Europe-westl connection. In the event that europe-westl becomes unavailable, traffic should automatically switch over to europe-northl. What should you set the multi-exit discriminator (MED) values to, in order to facilitate this automatic failover configuration?

A) Use regional routing. Set the europe-northl Cloud Router to a base priority of 90, and set the europe-westl Cloud Router to a base priority of 10

B) Use regional routing. Set the europe-northl Cloud Router to a base priority of 800, and set the europe-westl Cloud Router to a base priority of 10

C) Use global routing. Set the europe-northl Cloud Router to a base priority of 90, and set the europe-west 1 Cloud Router to a base priority of 10

D) Use global routing. Set the europe-northl Cloud Router to a base priority of 800, and set the europe-westl Cloud Router to a base pri- ority of 10.

QUESTION 4

Your company operates a Virtual Private Cloud (VPC) with two Partner Interconnect connections serving different regions: europe-west1 and europe-north1. Each Partner Interconnect is linked to a Cloud

Router in its specific region through a VLAN attachment. You have been tasked with setting up a resilient failover route. Ideally, all ingress traffic from your corporate network should primarily go through the Europe-west1 connection. In the event that europe—west1 becomes unavailable, traffic should automatically switch over to europe-north1. What should you set the multi-exit discriminator (MED) values to, in order to facilitate this automatic failover configuration?

A) Use regional routing. Set the europe-north1 Cloud Router to a base priority of 90, and set the europe-west1 Cloud Router to a base priority of 10.

B) Use regional routing. Set the europe-north1 Cloud Router to a base priority of 800, and set the europe—west1 Cloud Router to a base priority of 10.

C) Use global routing. Set the europe-north1 Cloud Router to a base priority of 90, and set the europe-west1 Cloud Router to a base priority of 10.

D) Use global routing. Set the europe-north1 Cloud Router to a base priority of 800, and set the europe-west1 Cloud Router to a base priority of 10.

E) Implement a regional VPC with only one Partner Interconnect connection for simplicity and reliability.

QUESTION 5

Your organization is focused on optimizing costs while maintaining secure connectivity to Google Cloud. You have a requirement for high throughput. What approach should you consider?

A) Utilize a Direct Interconnect connection for dedicated, high-throughput connectivity.
B) Implement a Cloud VPN with data deduplication techniques for efficient data transfer.
C) Explore options for Google Cloud Partner Interconnect to reduce costs.
D) Set up a dedicated microwave link for point-to-point connectivity.
E) Opt for a Content Delivery Network (CDN) for data transfer.

QUESTION 6

Your organization has a global user base, and you need to optimize content delivery for your web application. What networking strategy should you prioritize to achieve this goal?

A) Implement Global Load Balancing with multi-region deployments for traffic distribution.
B) Set up Direct Peering connections with ISPs for improved connectivity.
C) Utilize Google Cloud Dedicated Interconnect for dedicated, high-speed content delivery.
D) Deploy Cloud VPNs with IPsec encryption for secure data transfer.
E) Implement Google Cloud CDN for caching and content optimization.

QUESTION 7

You are implementing a disaster recovery plan for a GCP environment. The primary data center is in us-east1 and the secondary in europe-west2. Considering RTO and RPO objectives, what is the most effective disaster recovery strategy?

A) Hot site in europe-west2 with synchronous data replication.
B) Cold site in europe-west2 with periodic data backups.
C) Warm site in europe-west2 with asynchronous data replication.
D) Pilot light approach, replicating only critical systems.
E) Multi-regional deployment with active-active configuration.

QUESTION 8

You are managing a large-scale Google Kubernetes Engine (GKE) cluster for your microservices-based application. To ensure high availability and performance, you want to distribute the application's pods across multiple zones within a region. Which GKE feature should you use to achieve this?

A) Node Pools
B) Horizontal Pod Autoscaling
C) Regional Clusters
D) Node Locations
E) GKE Autopilot

QUESTION 9

You are managing a BigQuery dataset in Google Cloud project ABC. This dataset contains classified intellectual property. You need to ensure that only computing resources in VPC networks within project ABC have access to this BigQuery dataset. How should you proceed?

A) Set up Private Service Connect to enable private access to BigQuery exclusively from VPCs within project ABC.
B) Configure a VPC Service Controls perimeter around project ABC, and include BigQuery as a restricted service in the service perimeter.
C) Modify the BigQuery dataset's Access Control List (ACL) to grant project-based access for members within project ABC according to their roles.
D) Enable Private Google Access to allow secure access to the BigQuery service using internal IP addresses.
E) Create custom IAM roles for project ABC members and grant them access to the BigQuery dataset.

QUESTION 10

Your organization is managing a complex Google Cloud environment with multiple projects, each containing several Virtual Private Cloud (VPC) networks. You need to ensure secure private connectivity between these VPCs, allow internet access, and establish a connection to an external data center. What strategy should you consider to meet these requirements effectively?

A) Set up individual VPN tunnels for each VPC network.
B) Establish a central hub VPC network and configure VPC Peering connections to all project VPCs.
C) Implement Cloud Interconnect Dedicated for private connectivity.
D) Deploy Cloud VPN for secure project-to-project connections.
E) Merge all project VPCs into a single VPC structure.

QUESTION 11

Your organization is planning to deploy a containerized application on Google Cloud using Kubernetes. You want to ensure high availability, scalability, and efficient resource utilization for your application. What Google Cloud Kubernetes feature or concept should you consider for this complex container orchestration, and what advantages does it offer?

A) Google Cloud Kubernetes Engine (GKE) for containerized application deployment.
B) Google Cloud Kubernetes Horizontal Pod Autoscaling for dynamic scaling based on resource usage.

C) Google Cloud Kubernetes Persistent Volumes for data storage.
D) Google Cloud Kubernetes Custom Resource Definitions (CRDs) for extending Kubernetes capabilities.
E) Google Cloud Kubernetes Ingress for HTTP/HTTPS routing to services.

QUESTION 12

You are setting up a disaster recovery site for a GCP-hosted application in a secondary region. The primary application is hosted in europe-west1 with a VPC range of 10.154.0.0/16, and the disaster recovery site is in asia-east1 with a VPC range of 10.156.0.0/16. What is the most efficient way to ensure seamless failover and data replication?

A) Configure Cloud VPN between the two regions for secure data transfer.
B) Set up VPC Network Peering between the two VPCs.
C) Use Dedicated Interconnects for consistent and high-speed connectivity.
D) Implement a global HTTP(S) load balancer for traffic management.
E) Establish Cloud Storage with multi-regional buckets for data replication.

QUESTION 13

For a GKE-based application that processes sensitive data, you are tasked with configuring network security to restrict access to specific trusted entities. What is the most effective combination of GCP services and configurations to achieve this?

A) Use Cloud Armor for whitelisting IPs and VPC Service Controls for data access.
B) Implement network policies in GKE and configure GCP firewalls for egress control.
C) Configure GKE Ingress with SSL policies and use Identity-Aware Proxy.
D) Set up Binary Authorization in GKE and use VPC Peering for network isolation.
E) Employ Cloud IAM roles for GKE and configure Cloud NAT for outbound traffic.

QUESTION 14

You are tasked with optimizing network performance for a Google Cloud project that involves high-throughput data transfer between virtual machines in the same VPC. The project requires minimal latency and maximum bandwidth. Which GCP networking solution should you recommend?

A) Google Cloud Load Balancer for distributing traffic.
B) Google Cloud CDN for content caching.
C) Google Cloud Interconnect for dedicated high-speed connections.
D) Google Cloud Network Peering for VPC-to-VPC communication.
E) Google Cloud VPN for secure inter-instance communication.

QUESTION 15

You need to set up secure SSH access for a team of developers to VMs in a GCP project. The developers are working remotely and connect from dynamic IP addresses. What is the most secure way to configure firewall rules for SSH access in this scenario?

A) Allow SSH ingress from a range of known IPs and deny all other SSH requests.
B) Set up a VPN for the developers and allow SSH from the VPN's IP range.

C) Allow SSH ingress from any source.
D) Use Identity-Aware Proxy for SSH access control.
E) Implement a rule to allow SSH only during certain hours.

QUESTION 16

Your organization is planning to deploy a high-performance computing workload in Google Cloud that requires maximum network bandwidth and low-latency communication between virtual machines. What GCP networking solution should you recommend for this workload?

A) Google Cloud Load Balancer for distributing traffic.
B) Google Cloud VPN for secure communication.
C) Google Cloud Interconnect for dedicated high-speed connections.
D) Google Cloud Network Peering for inter-VPC communication.
E) Google Cloud CDN for content delivery.

QUESTION 17

Your organization is planning to deploy a high-performance computing workload in Google Cloud that requires maximum network bandwidth and low-latency communication between virtual machines. What GCP networking solution should you recommend for this workload?

A) Google Cloud Load Balancer for distributing traffic.
B) Google Cloud VPN for secure communication.
C) Google Cloud Interconnect for dedicated high-speed connections.
D) Google Cloud Network Peering for inter-VPC communication.
E) Google Cloud CDN for content delivery.

QUESTION 18

Your organization is planning to implement a disaster recovery (DR) strategy for its critical systems on Google Cloud. What should be a key consideration when designing a DR plan for Google Cloud?

A) Ensuring identical hardware and software configurations between primary and DR sites.
B) Deploying DR resources in the same Google Cloud region as the primary resources.
C) Frequent manual backups to on-premises storage for immediate recovery.
D) Using Google Cloud's multi-region redundancy for data and services.
E) Relying solely on Google Cloud's built-in backups for DR.

QUESTION 19

Your mobile application users are concentrated near asia-southeast1 and europe-north1. Their services require frequent interactions with each other. You aim to optimize network performance while keeping costs low. What design should you implement for this architecture?

A) Design a single VPC with 2 regional subnets. Use a global load balancer to manage traffic between the services across the regions.
B) Set up 1 VCP with 2 regional subnets. Position your services within these subnets and enable them to communicate via private RFC1918 IP addresses.

C) Configure 2 VPCs, one in each region, and set up corresponding subnets. Connect the regions using 2 VPN gateways.
D) Establish 2 VPCs, allocating one to each region, with separate subnets. Leverage public IP addresses on the virtual machines to facilitate inter-regional connectivity.
E) Create a single VPC with multiple global subnets and use Cloud NAT to manage traffic between regions.

QUESTION 20

Your mobile application users are concentrated near asia-southeast1 and europe-north1. Their services require frequent interactions with each other. You aim to optimize network performance while keeping costs low. What design should you implement for this architecture?

A) Design a single VPC with 2 regional subnets. Use a global load balancer to manage traffic between the services across the regions.
B) Set up 1 VPC with 2 regional subnets. Position your services within these subnets and enable them to communicate via private RFC1918 IP addresses.
C) Configure 2 VPCs, one in each region, and set up corresponding subnets. Connect the regions using 2 VPN gateways.
D) Establish 2 VPCs, allocating one to each region, with separate subnets. Leverage public IP addresses on the virtual machines to facilitate inter-regional connectivity.
E) Use Cloud NAT to enable private IP communication between the regions.

QUESTION 21

Your organization is planning to migrate its on-premises database to Google Cloud SQL. You want to ensure a secure connection between the application servers in your data center and the Google Cloud SQL instance. What steps should you take to achieve this?

A) Use SSL/TLS for encrypting data in transit and configure the database firewall rules to allow connections from the data center's IP range.
B) Establish a VPN tunnel between the data center and Google Cloud for secure communication.
C) Deploy Google Cloud Armor to protect the Google Cloud SQL instance from unauthorized access.
D) Use Cloud VPN to create a secure connection between the data center and Google Cloud SQL.

QUESTION 22

Your mobile application users are concentrated near asia-southeast1 and europe-north1. Their services require frequent interactions with each other. You aim to optimize network performance while keeping costs low. What design should you implement for this architecture?

A) Design a single VPC with 2 regional subnets. Use a global load balancer to manage traffic between the services across the regions.
B) Set up 1 VPC with 2 regional subnets. Position your services within these subnets and enable them to communicate via private RFC1918 IP addresses.
C) Configure 2 VPCs, one in each region, and set up corresponding subnets. Connect the regions using 2 VPN gateways.
D) Establish 2 VPCs, allocating one to each region, with separate subnets. Leverage public IP addresses on the virtual machines to facilitate inter-regional connectivity.

E) Create a hybrid multi-cloud architecture with different cloud providers for each region.

QUESTION 23

In a highly distributed Google Cloud network, a company utilizes a combination of Google Cloud VPN and Dedicated Interconnect for connectivity to its on-premises data center. They've recently migrated some workloads to a different region within the same Google Cloud project, and connectivity issues have arisen. Traffic between the on-premises data center and the new region is intermittent. What could be a potential cause of this problem?

A) BGP misconfiguration on the Dedicated Interconnect
B) Incorrect firewall rules between the regions
C) VPN tunnel encryption mismatch
D) Suboptimal routes due to Google Cloud's global network backbone
E) Limitations in Google Cloud's VPC peering capabilities

QUESTION 24

Your organization is using Google Cloud's Anthos for managing Kubernetes clusters across hybrid and multi-cloud environments. They want to ensure optimal network connectivity and traffic management. What two Google Cloud services or features should you recommend to achieve this?

A) Implement Google Kubernetes Engine (GKE) for all Kubernetes clusters.
B) Use Google Cloud Load Balancers to distribute traffic to clusters.
C) Set up Google Cloud CDN for caching Kubernetes application data.
D) Utilize Google Cloud VPC Peering for inter-cluster communication.
E) Deploy Google Cloud Armor for container security.

QUESTION 25

Your organization is using Google Cloud's Anthos for managing Kubernetes clusters across hybrid and multi-cloud environments. They want to ensure optimal network connectivity and traffic management. What two Google Cloud services or features should you recommend to achieve this?

A) Implement Google Kubernetes Engine (GKE) for all Kubernetes clusters.
B) Use Google Cloud Load Balancers to distribute traffic to clusters.
C) Set up Google Cloud CDN for caching Kubernetes application data.
D) Utilize Google Cloud VPC Peering for inter-cluster communication.
E) Deploy Google Cloud Armor for container security.

QUESTION 26

For a global content delivery network in GCP, you are implementing a solution to optimize content delivery while protecting against DDoS attacks and reducing latency. The network should efficiently distribute large multimedia files to users worldwide. What combination of GCP services and configurations should you use?

A) Utilize Cloud CDN with Google Cloud Armor and Global HTTP(S) Load Balancing.
B) Set up multiple regional Network Load Balancers and configure Cloud Armor for each.

C) Implement Cloud VPNs to distribute content and use Cloud IDS for security.
D) Configure Cloud Storage as a content repository and use Cloud DNS for distribution.
E) Establish Private Google Access in each region and use Cloud Routers for content routing.

QUESTION 27

Your security and compliance division requires a virtual inline security appliance for deep packet inspection and intrusion prevention. What architectural design should you implement to meet this requirement?

A) Set up a dual-NIC VM in europe-west3 with both NICs connected to the same subnet.
B) Configure a dual-NIC VM in europe-west3 with one NIC connected to a subnet in the Host Project and the other NIC to a subnet in a Service Project.
C) Create two separate VPCs, each with a dual-NIC VM in europe-west3, and establish peering between them.
D) Deploy two separate dual-NIC VMs in europe-west3, one in the Host Project and the other in the Service Project.
E) None of the above.

QUESTION 28

You need to implement a GCP solution that allows a team of data scientists to analyze large datasets stored in Cloud Storage. The team uses Jupyter Notebooks hosted on AI Platform Notebooks. What network configuration ensures secure access to the datasets while maintaining high data processing performance?

A) Configure Private Google Access for the subnetwork where AI Platform Notebooks are deployed.
B) Set up VPC Service Controls around Cloud Storage and AI Platform Notebooks.
C) Use Cloud Interconnect to connect the AI Platform Notebooks with Cloud Storage securely.
D) Implement Cloud VPN to establish a secure connection between AI Platform Notebooks and Cloud Storage.
E) Assign external IP addresses to AI Platform Notebook instances and use Cloud Armor to protect data access.

QUESTION 29

Your organization manages a Google Cloud project with numerous App Engine applications. To restrict API access to your Memorystore instances and Spanner databases to only allow traffic from your organization's head office networks, what approach should you follow?

A) Establish an access context policy that includes your App Engine applications and head office network IP ranges, and then implement the policy for Memorystore and Spanner.
B) Create a VPC Service Controls perimeter for your project with an access context policy that encompasses your organization's head office network IP ranges.
C) Generate a separate VPC Service Controls perimeter for each App Engine application with access context policies specifying your organization's head office network IP ranges.
D) Configure a firewall rule to reject API access to Memorystore and Spanner from all networks not recognized as part of your head office.
E) None of the above.

QUESTION 30

Your distributed campus networks have 4 switches connected to your Google Cloud through dedicated interconnects on each switch. All educational platforms are operational; however, all of the traffic is routing through a single interconnect instead of being distributed across the 4 links as expected. Upon investigation you notice: - Each campus switch is set up with identical BGP ASNs. - Each campus switch has identical routes and priorities configured. - All switches are set up with a dedicated interconnect linked to a single Cloud Router. - The interconnect logs show 'no-proposal—chosen' messages when the interconnects are initializing. - BGP session has failed to establish between one of the campus switches and the Cloud Router. What is the primary reason for this issue?

A) An internal firewall is preventing the connection from being established on the second Dedicated Interconnect.
B) One of the Dedicated Interconnects is not configured correctly.
C) There is no Cloud Load Balancer in place to distribute the network load equally.
D) BGP sessions have failed to establish between all campus switches and the Cloud Router.
E) None of the above.

QUESTION 31

You manage a service that is operating on a managed instance group within Google Cloud. The team has developed an updated instance template that integrates an experimental optimization algorithm. To ensure that any potential issues in the new template have minimal effect on your user base, how should you approach the update process of your instances?

A) Directly apply patches to a fraction of the instances manually, subsequently carrying out a rolling restart on the entire managed instance group.
B) Deploy the updated instance template to carry out a rolling update across the entire scope of instances in the managed instance group. Perform validation of the experimental algorithm once the update has been fully executed.
C) Establish a new managed instance group and utilize it to canary test the updated template. Upon successful verification of the experimental algorithm within the canary group, apply the updated template to the initial managed instance group.
D) Conduct a canary deployment by initiating a rolling update and designating a subset of your instances to adopt the updated template. After confirming the experimental algorithm's stability on the canary instances, proceed to implement the update for the remaining instances.
E) None of the above.

QUESTION 32

Your team is developing a cutting-edge analytics platform that utilizes internal services operating on port 8080. The system also needs to support external communication using both IPv4 and IPv6 over TCP on port 8070, with a focus on maintaining high uptime. How should you configure your setup to ensure maximum reliability?

A) Create a global load balancer that uses backend services, consisting of a single instance group with three instances.
B) Implement an SSL proxy that targets backend services made up of an instance group with three servers.

C) Use a global load balancer with a target pool as the backend, and include three virtual machines.
D) Set up an HTTP(S) load balancer connected to a regional network endpoint group that encompasses a solitary instance.
E) None of the above.

QUESTION 33

You are developing a new service and need to connect your Compute Engine instances, which don't have public IP addresses, to Cloud Spanner. What two actions should you execute to accomplish this?

A) Enable the Cloud Memorystore API in your Google Cloud project.
B) Establish a private connection with the Cloud Spanner service producer.
C) Turn on Private Google Access for your subnetwork.
D) Configure a custom static route to direct the traffic to the Cloud Spanner service endpoint.
E) Enable the Service Networking API in your Google Cloud project.

QUESTION 34

Your organization is running a globally distributed web application that requires secure and efficient access to Google Cloud services, while also maintaining low latency for end users. What complex networking solution should you design to meet these requirements?

A) Google Cloud VPN with Global Load Balancer
B) Direct Peering with VPC Peering
C) Cloud Interconnect with Private Google Access
D) Cloud CDN with SSL Proxy Load Balancer
E) Anycast IP Routing with Cloud Router

QUESTION 35

Your organization is hosting a critical application that requires high availability and fault tolerance across multiple Google Cloud regions. What complex network architecture should you design to achieve these goals effectively?

A) Set up custom routes with more precision than the default network routes, specifying regional failover options for traffic routing.
B) Reconfigure the application to operate within a single region to simplify network management and reduce complexity.
C) Delete all default network routes and establish distinct custom routes for each region with network tags to differentiate traffic for failover.
D) Create more specific custom routes than the default network routes, designating regional failover options for routing, and assign network tags for precise traffic handling.
E) Implement Google Cloud Global Load Balancing with multi-region distribution and ensure application components are distributed across regions for redundancy.

QUESTION 36

In a GCP project, you have an application that requires strict control over network egress to prevent data exfiltration. The application runs on GKE and needs to access specific external APIs securely. How should you configure the network to ensure tight control over network egress while allowing access to required external services?

A) Use VPC Service Controls to create a perimeter that restricts egress, with allowed exceptions for specific external APIs.
B) Implement Cloud NAT with custom routes to control egress and specify allowed destinations.
C) Set up egress-only firewall rules in the GKE cluster to restrict traffic to known external API endpoints.
D) Configure Cloud Armor to block all egress except to the allowed external APIs.
E) Establish Private Google Access for restricted egress and create custom DNS entries for external API access.

QUESTION 37

In a GCP project, you have an application that heavily relies on real-time data analytics. The application ingests streaming data from various sources and needs to process and analyze this data in real time. Considering performance and scalability, what is the best network and service configuration for this application?

A) Use Cloud Pub/Sub for data ingestion, Cloud Dataflow for real-time processing, and BigQuery for immediate analysis.
B) Configure Cloud IoT Core for data ingestion, use Compute Engine for processing, and Cloud Spanner for real-time analysis.
C) Set up Cloud Storage for initial data ingestion, Cloud Functions for data processing, and Bigtable for analysis.
D) Implement direct data streaming to Compute Engine instances and use Cloud SQL for real-time data analysis.
E) Establish Cloud Endpoints for data ingestion, Kubernetes Engine for processing, and Datastore for analysis.

QUESTION 38

You are responsible for implementing a network architecture that provides DDoS protection and intelligent traffic routing for a Google Kubernetes Engine (GKE) application. Your goal is to ensure the application can scale seamlessly based on demand. Which Google Cloud networking service or feature should you integrate with GKE to achieve these objectives?

A) Google Cloud Armor with Google Cloud CDN
B) Traffic Director with Cloud Load Balancing
C) Google Cloud DNS with Cloud IAM
D) Cloud Interconnect with Cloud VPN
E) Google Cloud CDN with VPC peering

QUESTION 39

Your organization operates a critical online marketplace with a global user base. You need to ensure that the application remains highly available and can scale seamlessly based on demand. Which Google Cloud networking service or feature should you integrate with your application to achieve these objectives effectively?

A) Google Cloud Armor with Google Cloud CDN
B) Traffic Director with Cloud Load Balancing
C) Google Cloud DNS with Cloud IAM
D) Cloud Interconnect with Cloud VPN
E) Google Cloud CDN with VPC peering

QUESTION 40

Your organization is migrating its on-premises servers to Google Cloud, and data security is a top concern. You want to ensure data encryption at rest and in transit. Which combination of Google Cloud services or features should you implement to achieve these objectives effectively?

A) Google Cloud VPN and Google Cloud DNS
B) Google Cloud Identity-Aware Proxy (IAP) and Google Cloud CDN
C) Google Cloud Storage and Google Cloud KMS
D) Google Cloud Spanner and Google Cloud Load Balancing
E) Google Cloud Compute Engine Autoscaler and Google Cloud Pub/Sub

QUESTION 41

In a GCP environment, you need to set up a network configuration for a set of applications that require isolation from the internet but must access Google APIs and services securely. What is the most effective network configuration for this requirement?

A) Configure Private Google Access on the subnetworks hosting the applications.
B) Implement VPC Network Peering with Google's network for accessing Google services.
C) Set up Cloud VPN tunnels from the application subnetworks to Google's network.
D) Use Internal TCP/UDP Load Balancers for routing traffic to Google APIs and services.
E) Establish Cloud Endpoints for each application to securely access Google services.

QUESTION 42

Your regional headquarters has 4 gateways connected to your Google Cloud environment through a Dedicated Interconnect on each gateway. All services are operational; however, all of the network traffic is being routed through a single gateway instead of being distributed evenly across the 4 connections. Upon investigation, you discover: - Each gateway is configured with a distinct ASN. - Each gateway is set with the same routes and weights. - All gateways are connected to one Cloud Router via a Dedicated Interconnect. - BGP sessions are functioning between each gateway and the Cloud Router. - Only the routes from a single gateway are present in the Cloud Router's route table. What could be the primary reason for this issue?

A) A security rule is obstructing traffic through the additional Dedicated Interconnect.
B) The ASNs utilized on the gateways are unique.
C) There isn't a load balancer in place for distributing network load.
D) The gateways are configured with identical routes.

E) The Cloud Router is configured with incorrect BGP session parameters.

QUESTION 43

You are configuring a Google Kubernetes Engine (GKE) cluster for an e-commerce platform. The initial deployment is expected to manage 15 nodes, with 30 Pods per node and 250 services. With the onboarding of additional storefronts over the next 18 months, you anticipate an increase to 150 nodes, 250 Pods per node, and 2000 services. You want to adopt VPC-native clusters using alias IP ranges while aiming to use the least amount of addresses possible. What should your network layout look like?

A) Create a subnet of size /24 with 2 secondary ranges of: /16 for Pods and /20 for Services. Establish a VPC-native cluster and designate those ranges.
B) Deploy a VPC-native cluster by executing the gcloud container clusters create [CLUSTER NAME] -- enable-ip-alias command without specifying IP ranges for custom subnet creation.
C) Generate a subnet of size /29 with 2 secondary ranges of: /23 for Pods and /23 for Services. Configure a VPC-native cluster with these ranges. Upon deployment of additional services, expand the subnets as needed.
D) Create a VPC-native cluster using the gcloud container clusters create [CLUSTER NAME] command without enabling alias IPs or specifying IP ranges.
E) Configure a subnet of size /16 with 2 secondary ranges of: /24 for Pods and /16 for Services. Deploy a VPC-native cluster with these settings.

QUESTION 44

Your organization wants to ensure high availability for a mission-critical application in Google Cloud. Which architecture design should you implement to achieve this goal, with minimal downtime in case of failures?

A) Deploy the application in a single zone with automatic instance failover.
B) Deploy the application in a single region with redundant instances and load balancing.
C) Deploy the application in multiple regions with manual failover.
D) Deploy the application in multiple regions with active-active replication.
E) Deploy the application in a single zone with daily backups for disaster recovery.

QUESTION 45

You are designing a network in GCP for an application with a requirement for high network throughput between Compute Engine instances and an external data processing service. The application also requires low latency communication. What network configuration will best meet these requirements?

A) Configure Cloud Interconnect for high-throughput and low-latency connectivity to the external service.
B) Implement a dedicated VPC with optimized routes for traffic to the external data processing service.
C) Use Cloud VPN with dynamic routing for secure and efficient communication.
D) Enable Premium Network Tier on Compute Engine instances for enhanced network performance.
E) Set up Cloud CDN for optimized data delivery to and from the external service.

QUESTION 46

Your organization is planning to set up a disaster recovery strategy for your critical workloads on Google Cloud. What is the recommended approach to achieve a cost-effective and reliable disaster recovery solution?

A) Configure cross-region replication for your data using Cloud Storage.
B) Set up a separate Google Cloud project for disaster recovery purposes.
C) Use Cloud DNS with low TTL settings for DNS records to ensure quick failover.
D) Implement a multi-region architecture for your applications across multiple regions.
E) Rely on Google Cloud's built-in disaster recovery services without additional configuration.

QUESTION 47

In a GCP environment, you need to configure a network solution to support a distributed application that requires state synchronization across multiple Compute Engine instances. The instances are deployed globally and need to maintain constant, low-latency communication. What network configuration best supports these requirements?

A) Implement Global VPC with optimized routing for low-latency communication.
B) Use Cloud VPN to establish dedicated tunnels between instances for state synchronization.
C) Set up Dedicated Interconnect for low-latency, high-throughput connections between instances.
D) Configure Regional Internal Load Balancers in each deployment region for state synchronization.
E) Enable Premium Network Tier on all Compute Engine instances for global low-latency communication.

QUESTION 48

In a GCP environment, your application consists of microservices running on GKE clusters and needs to ensure private and secure communication with a Cloud SQL database. The setup should minimize latency and prevent data exposure to the public internet. What network configuration should you apply?

A) Configure Private Google Access on GKE clusters for secure access to Cloud SQL.
B) Use VPC Peering between the GKE cluster network and Cloud SQL network.
C) Implement Cloud VPN tunnels from GKE clusters to Cloud SQL for secure communication.
D) Set up Cloud Interconnect for a dedicated connection from GKE clusters to Cloud SQL.
E) Enable Cloud SQL Proxy on GKE clusters for secure and private database connectivity.

QUESTION 49

In a GCP deployment, you are setting up a network for a data-intensive service that requires real-time processing and analysis. The service involves streaming data from various sources and needs to process and analyze this data instantly. What network and service configuration optimizes performance for real-time data analytics?

A) Configure Cloud Pub/Sub for data ingestion, Cloud Dataflow for real-time processing, and BigQuery for immediate analysis.
B) Set up Cloud IoT Core for data ingestion, use Compute Engine instances for processing, and Cloud Spanner for real-time analysis.
C) Use Cloud Storage for initial data ingestion, Cloud Functions for data processing, and Cloud Bigtable for analysis.

D) Implement direct data streaming to Compute Engine instances and use Cloud SQL for real-time data analysis.

E) Establish Cloud Endpoints for data ingestion, Kubernetes Engine for processing, and Cloud Firestore for analysis.

QUESTION 50

In a GCP deployment for a data-intensive real-time analytics service, you need to configure a network that supports rapid scaling and efficient data transfer from various sources. The service involves streaming large volumes of data for instant processing and analysis. What network and service configuration optimizes performance for this real-time data analytics service?

A) Configure Cloud Pub/Sub for data ingestion, Cloud Dataflow for real-time processing, and BigQuery for analysis.

B) Set up Cloud IoT Core for data ingestion, Compute Engine for processing, and Cloud Spanner for analysis.

C) Implement Cloud Storage for initial data ingestion, Cloud Functions for processing, and Cloud Bigtable for analysis.

D) Establish direct data streaming to Compute Engine instances and use Cloud SQL for real-time data analysis.

E) Use Cloud Endpoints for data ingestion, Kubernetes Engine for processing, and Cloud Firestore for analysis.

PRACTICE TEST 5 - ANSWERS ONLY

QUESTION 1

Answer – C) Google Cloud Auto Scaling

Option C - Google Cloud Auto Scaling is designed to automatically scale network resources based on demand, making it suitable for bursty traffic patterns.
Option A - Google Cloud VPC is a basic network component.
Option B - Google Cloud Load Balancing distributes traffic but doesn't scale resources.
Option D - Google Cloud VPC Peering connects VPCs.
Option E - Google Cloud CDN is for content delivery, not resource scaling.

QUESTION 2

Answer – B) Use Google Cloud's dedicated Interconnect with a private VLAN.

Option B - Using Google Cloud's dedicated Interconnect with a private VLAN ensures encrypted and private communication while allowing access to specific Google Cloud services.
Option A - VPNs may not provide the dedicated performance required.
Option C - VPC Network Peering is for internal VPC communication, not on-premises connectivity.
Option D - Managed SSL Certificates are for SSL/TLS encryption, not network communication.
Option E - Firewall Rules do not provide dedicated private connectivity.

QUESTION 3

Answer – B) Use regional routing. Set the europe-northl Cloud Router to a base priority of 800, and set the europe-westl Cloud Router to a base priority of 10

Option B - Using regional routing and setting the europe-northl Cloud Router to a higher base priority (800) than the europe-westl Cloud Router (10) ensures that traffic primarily goes through europe-westl but automatically switches to europe-northl in case of unavailability, facilitating automatic failover.
Option A - Setting both Cloud Routers to regional routing with different base priorities may not achieve the desired failover behavior.
Option C - Using global routing with base priorities may not provide the region-specific failover required.
Option D - Setting a higher base priority for europe-northl in global routing may not lead to the desired behavior.

QUESTION 4

Answer – B) Use regional routing. Set the europe-north1 Cloud Router to a base priority of 800, and set the europe—west1 Cloud Router to a base priority of 10.

Option B - Using regional routing with MED values of 800 for europe-north1 and 10 for europe-west1 allows for automatic failover as required.
Option A - Setting europe-west1 to a lower priority may not prioritize it correctly.
Option C - Using global routing may not align with the desired regional failover.

Option D - The MED values should be reversed for the desired failover behavior.
Option E - Implementing a regional VPC does not address the dual connection requirement.

QUESTION 5

Answer - C) Explore options for Google Cloud Partner Interconnect to reduce costs.

Option C offers a cost-effective approach while maintaining secure connectivity to Google Cloud. It aligns with the organization's goal of cost optimization.
Option A provides high throughput but may not be as cost-effective.
Option B addresses efficiency but may not guarantee the required throughput.
Option D introduces complexity and may not be cost-effective.
Option E is more suited for content delivery, not connectivity.

QUESTION 6

Answer - A) Implement Global Load Balancing with multi-region deployments for traffic distribution.
Answer - E) Implement Google Cloud CDN for caching and content optimization.

Option A and E are the networking strategies to prioritize for optimizing content delivery with a global user base.
Option A focuses on traffic distribution across regions, and Option E leverages CDN for caching and content optimization.
Option B with Direct Peering may not directly address content delivery optimization.
Option C, Dedicated Interconnect, is not primarily focused on content delivery.
Option D mentions VPNs but does not specifically address content optimization.

QUESTION 7

Answer – C) Warm site in europe-west2 with asynchronous data replication.

A) Incorrect. Synchronous replication is not always feasible due to latency between regions.
B) Incorrect. A cold site might not meet RTO objectives due to longer recovery times.
C) Correct. This provides a balance between cost and recovery speed.
D) Incorrect. The pilot light approach may not cover all essential services.
E) Incorrect. An active-active configuration is costly and might be overkill for certain RPO/RTO objectives.

QUESTION 8

Answer - C) Regional Clusters

Option C, Regional Clusters, is the appropriate choice for distributing pods across multiple zones within a region in GKE, ensuring high availability and performance.
 Option A, Node Pools, is used for managing groups of nodes within a cluster but doesn't inherently distribute pods across zones.
 Option B, Horizontal Pod Autoscaling, dynamically adjusts the number of pods based on resource usage but doesn't control pod placement across zones.
 Option D, Node Locations, is not a GKE feature.
 Option E, GKE Autopilot, is a mode for managing clusters, but it doesn't focus on regional distribution of

pods.

QUESTION 9

Answer - B) Configure a VPC Service Controls perimeter around project ABC, and include BigQuery as a restricted service in the service perimeter.
Answer - D) Enable Private Google Access to allow secure access to the BigQuery service using internal IP addresses.

Option B (VPC Service Controls perimeter) is the recommended approach to restrict access to the BigQuery dataset from within project ABC's VPC networks.
Option D (Private Google Access) ensures secure access using internal IP addresses.
Option A (Private Service Connect) is not a suitable solution for securing access to BigQuery within project ABC.
Option C (Modifying ACL) is not as comprehensive or centralized as VPC Service Controls.
Option E (custom IAM roles) may not provide the necessary network-level restrictions.

QUESTION 10

Answer - B) Establish a central hub VPC network and configure VPC Peering connections to all project VPCs.

Option A would result in a complex and difficult-to-manage setup.
Option C refers to a different Google Cloud service.
Option D provides secure connectivity but doesn't address the central hub requirement.
Option E would lose the separation between project VPCs.
Option B is the correct choice as it aligns with the requirements, providing a central hub for private connectivity while maintaining separate VPCs for different projects.

QUESTION 11

Answer - B) Google Cloud Kubernetes Horizontal Pod Autoscaling for dynamic scaling based on resource usage.

Option A is for Kubernetes Engine deployment but doesn't focus on autoscaling.
Option C is for data storage but doesn't address scalability requirements.
Option D is for extending Kubernetes capabilities but may not directly relate to autoscaling.
Option E is for Ingress routing but doesn't provide autoscaling capabilities.
Option B is the correct choice as Google Cloud Kubernetes Horizontal Pod Autoscaling allows dynamic scaling of pods based on resource usage, ensuring high availability, scalability, and efficient resource utilization for complex containerized applications deployed on Kubernetes.

QUESTION 12

Answer – B) Set up VPC Network Peering between the two VPCs.

A) Incorrect. VPN may introduce latency.
B) Correct. Provides efficient and direct network connectivity.
C) Incorrect. Overkill for internal GCP region-to-region connectivity.

D) Incorrect. Load balancing does not address data replication needs.

E) Incorrect. Cloud Storage buckets do not address VPC connectivity.

QUESTION 13

Answer – B) Implement network policies in GKE and configure GCP firewalls for egress control.

A) Incorrect. Cloud Armor and VPC Service Controls address different aspects of security.

B) Correct. Network policies and GCP firewalls together provide effective access control.

C) Incorrect. SSL policies and IAP do not restrict network-level access.

D) Incorrect. Binary Authorization and VPC Peering serve different purposes.

E) Incorrect. Cloud IAM and Cloud NAT do not provide the required network-level access control.

QUESTION 14

Answer - C) Google Cloud Interconnect for dedicated high-speed connections.

C) Google Cloud Interconnect - Google Cloud Interconnect provides dedicated, high-throughput, and low-latency connections, making it suitable for projects requiring high-performance data transfer between VM instances in the same VPC.

A) Google Cloud Load Balancer - Load Balancer is used for traffic distribution and may not optimize performance within the same VPC.

B) Google Cloud CDN - CDN focuses on content caching and may not directly address high-throughput data transfer between VM instances.

D) Google Cloud Network Peering - Network Peering is for communication between different VPCs, not necessarily within the same VPC.

E) Google Cloud VPN - VPNs provide secure access but are not designed specifically for high-throughput data transfer within the same VPC.

QUESTION 15

Answer – B) Set up a VPN for the developers and allow SSH from the VPN's IP range.

A) Incorrect. Not feasible due to dynamic IP addresses of developers.

B) Correct. Provides secure access regardless of developers' IP addresses.

C) Incorrect. Too permissive and a security risk.

D) Incorrect. IAP is secure but may not be practical for all remote developers.

E) Incorrect. Time-based rules do not address the dynamic IP issue.

QUESTION 16

Answer - C) Google Cloud Interconnect for dedicated high-speed connections.

C) Google Cloud Interconnect for dedicated high-speed connections - Interconnect provides the dedicated high-speed connections required for high-performance computing workloads with maximum network bandwidth and low-latency communication.

A) Google Cloud Load Balancer for distributing traffic - Load Balancer focuses on traffic distribution, not dedicated high-speed connections.

B) Google Cloud VPN for secure communication - VPNs provide secure access but may not optimize

network performance and bandwidth to the same extent as Interconnect.
 D) Google Cloud Network Peering for inter-VPC communication - Network Peering is for communication between VPCs, not necessarily for high-performance computing workloads.
 E) Google Cloud CDN for content delivery - CDN is for content caching and may not directly address the network requirements of high-performance computing.

QUESTION 17

Answer - C) Google Cloud Interconnect for dedicated high-speed connections.

C) Google Cloud Interconnect for dedicated high-speed connections - Interconnect provides the dedicated high-speed connections required for high-performance computing workloads with maximum network bandwidth and low-latency communication.
 A) Google Cloud Load Balancer for distributing traffic - Load Balancer focuses on traffic distribution, not dedicated high-speed connections.
 B) Google Cloud VPN for secure communication - VPNs provide secure access but may not optimize network performance and bandwidth to the same extent as Interconnect.
 D) Google Cloud Network Peering for inter-VPC communication - Network Peering is for communication between VPCs, not necessarily for high-performance computing workloads.
 E) Google Cloud CDN for content delivery - CDN is for content caching and may not directly address the network requirements of high-performance computing.

QUESTION 18

Answer - D) Using Google Cloud's multi-region redundancy for data and services.

D) Using Google Cloud's multi-region redundancy for data and services is a key consideration for DR as it ensures high availability and data redundancy.
 A) Ensuring identical hardware and software configurations between primary and DR sites may not be cost-effective and could lead to complexity.
 B) Deploying DR resources in the same region as the primary resources may not provide adequate geographic separation in case of region-wide failures.
 C) Frequent manual backups to on-premises storage may not provide the necessary speed and automation for DR.
 E) Relying solely on Google Cloud's built-in backups may not cover all DR requirements, including application-level recovery.

QUESTION 19

Answer - A) Design a single VPC with 2 regional subnets. Use a global load balancer to manage traffic between the services across the regions.

A) Designing a single VPC with 2 regional subnets and utilizing a global load balancer to manage traffic optimizes network performance while minimizing costs by keeping resources within the same project.
 B) Using private RFC1918 IP addresses may restrict communication and is not ideal for frequent interactions.
 C) Configuring 2 VPCs with VPN gateways introduces complexity and may not be the most cost-effective solution.
 D) Leveraging public IP addresses can increase costs and is not necessary for this scenario.

E) Using Cloud NAT for inter-regional traffic introduces additional complexity and may not be as efficient as a global load balancer.

QUESTION 20

Answer - B) Set up 1 VPC with 2 regional subnets. Position your services within these subnets and enable them to communicate via private RFC1918 IP addresses.

B) To optimize network performance while keeping costs low and facilitating interactions between users in different regions, you can set up one VPC with two regional subnets and enable communication between services using private RFC1918 IP addresses. This approach minimizes the complexity of managing multiple VPCs or using public IPs.
 A) Using a global load balancer across regions may introduce unnecessary latency and complexity.
 C) Setting up separate VPCs and connecting them with VPN gateways is more complex than necessary for this scenario.
 D) Leveraging public IPs for inter-regional connectivity may increase costs and complexity.
 E) Cloud NAT is not designed for inter-regional communication and may not optimize performance in this context.

QUESTION 21

Answer - A) Use SSL/TLS for encrypting data in transit and configure the database firewall rules to allow connections from the data center's IP range.

A) To ensure a secure connection between application servers in your data center and a Google Cloud SQL instance, you should use SSL/TLS for encrypting data in transit and configure the database firewall rules to allow connections from the data center's IP range.
 B) Establishing a VPN tunnel is not the recommended solution for securing database connections.
 C) Google Cloud Armor is primarily used for protecting web applications, not database instances.
 D) Cloud VPN is typically used for connecting networks, not for securing database connections specifically.

QUESTION 22

Answer - B) Set up 1 VPC with 2 regional subnets. Position your services within these subnets and enable them to communicate via private RFC1918 IP addresses.

B) To optimize network performance while minimizing costs for users in different regions, you should set up one VPC with two regional subnets. Position your services within these subnets and enable communication via private RFC1918 IP addresses. This approach is cost-effective and efficient for inter-regional communication.
 A) Using a global load balancer with a single VPC may add unnecessary complexity and cost.
 C) Setting up two separate VPCs with VPN gateways can be more complex and may not provide the desired optimization.
 D) Leveraging public IP addresses for inter-regional connectivity may not be cost-effective and can expose security risks.
 E) Creating a hybrid multi-cloud architecture with different providers is a more complex solution than necessary for this scenario.

QUESTION 23

Answer - D) Suboptimal routes due to Google Cloud's global network backbone

Option A - BGP misconfiguration on the Dedicated Interconnect could cause problems but may not lead to intermittent issues.
Option B - Incorrect firewall rules could disrupt traffic, but the issue seems region-specific.
Option C - VPN tunnel encryption mismatch would result in no connectivity, not intermittency.
Option E - Google Cloud's VPC peering capabilities are unlikely to be the primary issue here.

QUESTION 24

Answer - B) Use Google Cloud Load Balancers to distribute traffic to clusters.
D) Utilize Google Cloud VPC Peering for inter-cluster communication.

Option A - GKE is a Kubernetes management solution and not a traffic management tool.
Option C - Google Cloud CDN is for content caching, not cluster-to-cluster traffic management.
Option E - Google Cloud Armor focuses on security, not traffic management. Choice B (Use Google Cloud Load Balancers to distribute traffic to clusters) - Utilizing Google Cloud Load Balancers allows for efficient traffic distribution and load balancing across Kubernetes clusters managed by Anthos, ensuring optimal network connectivity and traffic management.
Choice D (Utilize Google Cloud VPC Peering for inter-cluster communication) - Implementing Google Cloud VPC Peering facilitates inter-cluster communication, enabling efficient data exchange between Kubernetes clusters across hybrid and multi-cloud environments.

QUESTION 25

Answer - B) Use Google Cloud Load Balancers to distribute traffic to clusters.
D) Utilize Google Cloud VPC Peering for inter-cluster communication.

Option A - GKE is a Kubernetes management solution and not a traffic management tool.
Option C - Google Cloud CDN is for content caching, not cluster-to-cluster traffic management.
Option E - Google Cloud Armor focuses on security, not traffic management. Choice B - Utilizing Google Cloud Load Balancers allows for efficient traffic distribution and load balancing across Kubernetes clusters managed by Anthos, ensuring optimal network connectivity and traffic management.
Choice D - Implementing Google Cloud VPC Peering facilitates inter-cluster communication, enhancing network connectivity in a hybrid and multi-cloud environment managed by Anthos.

QUESTION 26

Answer – A) Utilize Cloud CDN with Google Cloud Armor and Global HTTP(S) Load Balancing.

A) Correct. This combination optimizes content delivery and provides security against DDoS.
B) Incorrect. Regional load balancers do not provide the global distribution needed.
C) Incorrect. Cloud VPNs are not designed for content distribution, and Cloud IDS is for network security monitoring.
D) Incorrect. Cloud Storage and Cloud DNS alone are not sufficient for optimized content delivery and protection.
E) Incorrect. Private Google Access and Cloud Routers do not address the global content delivery and security requirements.

QUESTION 27

Answer - B) Configure a dual-NIC VM in europe-west3 with one NIC connected to a subnet in the Host Project and the other NIC to a subnet in a Service Project.

Option A - Both NICs connected to the same subnet may not be ideal for inspection and prevention.
Option C - Creating separate VPCs and peering may add unnecessary complexity.
Option D - Deploying two separate VMs may not be efficient. Choice B - Configuring a dual-NIC VM with one NIC in the Host Project subnet and the other in a Service Project subnet allows for proper placement and inspection capabilities as required for deep packet inspection and intrusion prevention.

QUESTION 28

Answer – A) Configure Private Google Access for the subnetwork where AI Platform Notebooks are deployed.

A) Correct. Private Google Access enables secure and efficient access to Cloud Storage.
B) Incorrect. VPC Service Controls are more for securing data within services, not for network configuration.
C) Incorrect. Cloud Interconnect is for on-premises to GCP connections, not within GCP services.
D) Incorrect. Cloud VPN is for connecting external networks to GCP.
E) Incorrect. External IPs and Cloud Armor are not necessary for this internal GCP configuration.

QUESTION 29

Answer - B) Create a VPC Service Controls perimeter for your project with an access context policy that encompasses your organization's head office network IP ranges.

Option A - Establishing separate access context policies for each application may result in administrative complexity.
Option C - Creating individual VPC Service Controls perimeters for each application may lead to management overhead.
Option D - While configuring firewall rules is a valid approach, VPC Service Controls offer more comprehensive security controls. Choice B - Creating a VPC Service Controls perimeter for your project with a broad access context policy covering head office network IP ranges provides centralized and efficient API access controls for Memorystore and Spanner across all applications in the project.

QUESTION 30

Answer - B) One of the Dedicated Interconnects is not configured correctly.

Option A - The issue described doesn't suggest an internal firewall problem.
Option C - The absence of a Cloud Load Balancer is unrelated to BGP session failures.
Option D - BGP session failures with all campus switches are not indicated in the problem description.
Choice B - The issue with traffic routing through a single interconnect is likely due to a misconfiguration in one of the Dedicated Interconnects.

QUESTION 31

Answer - C) Establish a new managed instance group and utilize it to canary test the updated template.

Upon successful verification of the experimental algorithm within the canary group, apply the updated template to the initial managed instance group.

Option A - Directly applying patches manually is not the most controlled approach for testing a new instance template.
Option B - While deploying the updated template is a step in the right direction, it doesn't address the need for canary testing.
Option D - Conducting a canary deployment without creating a separate group for testing can introduce risk to the entire user base. Choice C - Creating a new managed instance group for canary testing provides a controlled environment to validate the updated template before applying it to the initial group.

QUESTION 32

Answer - D) Set up an HTTP(S) load balancer connected to a regional network endpoint group that encompasses a solitary instance.

Option A - Creating a global load balancer with multiple instances may not be necessary for this scenario.
Option B - Implementing an SSL proxy might not be the most suitable choice for this particular requirement.
Option C - Using a global load balancer with virtual machines may not be the optimal solution for the given objectives. Choice D - Setting up an HTTP(S) load balancer connected to a regional network endpoint group with a single instance ensures maximum reliability for external communication on the specified ports while maintaining high uptime.

QUESTION 33

Answer - B) Establish a private connection with the Cloud Spanner service producer. and C) Turn on Private Google Access for your subnetwork.

Option A - Enabling the Cloud Memorystore API is not related to connecting Compute Engine instances to Cloud Spanner.
Option B and C - These options are correct as they involve establishing a private connection and enabling Private Google Access for the subnetwork, which is necessary to connect Compute Engine instances to Cloud Spanner.
Option D - Configuring a custom static route is not the typical approach for connecting Compute Engine instances to Cloud Spanner.
Option E - Enabling the Service Networking API is not directly related to connecting Compute Engine instances to Cloud Spanner

QUESTION 34

Answer - C) Cloud Interconnect with Private Google Access

A) Google Cloud VPN with Global Load Balancer - Explanation: Google Cloud VPN provides secure connections, but it may not achieve low latency, and Global Load Balancer may not directly optimize network performance.
B) Direct Peering with VPC Peering - Explanation: Direct Peering connects to Google's network, but VPC Peering focuses on connecting VPCs within Google Cloud and may not address global network

optimization.

D) Cloud CDN with SSL Proxy Load Balancer - Explanation: Cloud CDN focuses on content delivery, and SSL Proxy Load Balancer may not optimize network performance for global access.

E) Anycast IP Routing with Cloud Router - Explanation: Anycast IP routing can improve routing efficiency, but Cloud Router is used for dynamic BGP routing within VPCs, and this combination may not directly address the requirements.

C) Cloud Interconnect with Private Google Access - Explanation: This combination provides dedicated, low-latency connections to Google Cloud while allowing secure and efficient access to Google services, making it suitable for the globally distributed web application's needs.

QUESTION 35

Answer - E) Implement Google Cloud Global Load Balancing with multi-region distribution and ensure application components are distributed across regions for redundancy.

E) Implement Google Cloud Global Load Balancing with multi-region distribution and ensure application components are distributed across regions for redundancy - Explanation: This approach leverages Google Cloud's Global Load Balancing for high availability and fault tolerance by distributing application components across multiple regions.

A) Set up custom routes with more precision than the default network routes - Explanation: While custom routes are useful, this option does not directly address the need for regional failover and redundancy.

B) Reconfigure the application to operate within a single region - Explanation: Consolidating components into a single region may reduce complexity but does not provide the desired fault tolerance across regions.

C) Delete all default network routes and establish distinct custom routes for each region - Explanation: Deleting default routes introduces complexity, and this option may not be necessary for regional failover.

D) Create more specific custom routes than the default network routes - Explanation: This option introduces complexity with network tags and may not provide the desired regional failover and redundancy.

QUESTION 36

Answer – C) Set up egress-only firewall rules in the GKE cluster to restrict traffic to known external API endpoints.

A) Incorrect. VPC Service Controls are not designed for granular egress control.

B) Incorrect. Cloud NAT manages outbound connectivity but does not provide the level of control required for this scenario.

C) Correct. Egress-only firewall rules in GKE can effectively restrict outbound traffic to specific endpoints.

D) Incorrect. Cloud Armor is primarily for inbound traffic protection, not egress control.

E) Incorrect. Private Google Access does not provide the necessary control over specific external endpoints.

QUESTION 37

Answer – A) Use Cloud Pub/Sub for data ingestion, Cloud Dataflow for real-time processing, and

BigQuery for immediate analysis.

A) Correct. This setup provides a scalable and efficient pipeline for real-time data analytics.
B) Incorrect. IoT Core is specific to IoT data; Spanner may not be optimal for real-time analytics compared to BigQuery.
C) Incorrect. Cloud Storage is not ideal for real-time data streaming; Bigtable is more for high-throughput, low-latency workloads.
D) Incorrect. Direct streaming to Compute Engine is less scalable; Cloud SQL is not designed for high-volume real-time analytics.
E) Incorrect. Cloud Endpoints and Datastore are not the best fit for high-volume, real-time data analytics workflows.

QUESTION 38

Answer - B) Traffic Director with Cloud Load Balancing

A) Google Cloud Armor with Google Cloud CDN - This combination provides security and content delivery but does not inherently offer intelligent traffic routing or DDoS protection for GKE.
B) Traffic Director with Cloud Load Balancing - Correct answer. Traffic Director and Load Balancing provide advanced traffic management and DDoS protection for GKE, along with seamless scaling based on demand.
C) Google Cloud DNS with Cloud IAM - DNS and IAM are used for DNS resolution and access control, not traffic routing or DDoS protection.
D) Cloud Interconnect with Cloud VPN - Interconnect and VPN provide connectivity but are not used for intelligent traffic routing or DDoS protection for GKE.
E) Google Cloud CDN with VPC peering - CDN and VPC peering focus on content delivery and connectivity but do not inherently offer intelligent traffic routing or DDoS protection.

QUESTION 39

Answer - B) Traffic Director with Cloud Load Balancing

A) Google Cloud Armor with Google Cloud CDN - While this combination offers security and content delivery, Traffic Director with Load Balancing is more suitable for achieving high availability and scalability for an application.
B) Correct answer. Traffic Director with Cloud Load Balancing provides advanced traffic management and scaling capabilities for applications, ensuring high availability.
C) Google Cloud DNS with Cloud IAM - DNS and IAM focus on DNS resolution and access control, not traffic management or scalability.
D) Cloud Interconnect with Cloud VPN - These services provide connectivity but do not inherently offer advanced traffic management or scalability features.
E) Google Cloud CDN with VPC peering - CDN and VPC peering focus on content delivery and connectivity but may not provide the same level of traffic management and scalability as Traffic Director.

QUESTION 40

Answer - C) Google Cloud Storage and Google Cloud KMS

A) Google Cloud VPN and Google Cloud DNS provide secure connectivity and DNS services but may not inherently provide data encryption at rest or in transit for other Google Cloud services.

B) Google Cloud Identity-Aware Proxy (IAP) and Google Cloud CDN focus on identity management and content delivery but may not directly address data encryption requirements.

C) Correct answer. Google Cloud Storage offers data storage with encryption at rest, and Google Cloud KMS (Key Management Service) enables you to manage encryption keys and implement encryption for various Google Cloud services.

D) Google Cloud Spanner is a database, and Google Cloud Load Balancing focuses on traffic distribution; they may not be primarily related to data encryption.

E) Google Cloud Compute Engine Autoscaler and Google Cloud Pub/Sub are not directly related to data encryption at rest and in transit.

QUESTION 41

Answer – A) Configure Private Google Access on the subnetworks hosting the applications.

A) Correct. Private Google Access enables instances in subnetworks to access Google services without exposing them to the internet.

B) Incorrect. VPC Network Peering is not used for accessing Google services.

C) Incorrect. VPN tunnels are not necessary for accessing Google services within GCP.

D) Incorrect. Internal Load Balancers are for internal traffic management, not for accessing Google services.

E) Incorrect. Cloud Endpoints are for creating APIs, not for accessing Google services.

QUESTION 42

Answer - D) The gateways are configured with identical routes.

A) A security rule may affect traffic but may not be the primary reason for the issue.

B) The use of unique ASNs is a good practice and should not cause this routing issue.

C) Load balancers are not typically used for distributing network load across Dedicated Interconnect connections.

D) Correct answer. The gateways having identical routes and weights can cause traffic to be routed through a single gateway instead of being distributed evenly.

E) Incorrect BGP session parameters on the Cloud Router would likely lead to BGP session failures but may not explain this specific routing issue.

QUESTION 43

Answer - C) Generate a subnet of size /29 with 2 secondary ranges of: /23 for Pods and /23 for Services. Configure a VPC-native cluster with these ranges. Upon deployment of additional services, expand the subnets as needed.

A) Creating a /24 subnet for Pods and /20 subnet for Services is too large and inefficient for conserving IP addresses.

B) Deploying a VPC-native cluster without specifying IP ranges won't allow you to use alias IP ranges.

C) Correct answer. Creating a /29 subnet for Pods and /23 subnet for Services conserves IP addresses and allows for expansion.

D) Creating a /16 subnet for Pods and /16 subnet for Services is unnecessarily large and inefficient.

E) It is not the most efficient use of IP addresses.

QUESTION 44

Answer - D) Deploy the application in multiple regions with active-active replication.

A) Single zone deployments may not provide high availability in case of zone failures.
B) While better than single-zone deployments, deploying in a single region with redundant instances and load balancing may not offer the highest level of availability.
C) Deploying in multiple regions with manual failover may introduce downtime during failover events.
D) Correct answer. Deploying in multiple regions with active-active replication provides high availability with minimal downtime in case of failures.
E) Single zone deployments with daily backups are more focused on disaster recovery than high availability.

QUESTION 45

Answer – D) Enable Premium Network Tier on Compute Engine instances for enhanced network performance.

A) Incorrect. Cloud Interconnect is typically for on-premises to cloud connections, not for external service communication.
B) Incorrect. While a dedicated VPC is useful, it doesn't specifically address throughput and latency to an external service.
C) Incorrect. VPNs may introduce latency and are not optimized for high throughput.
D) Correct. The Premium Network Tier provides improved throughput and lower latency for cloud services.
E) Incorrect. Cloud CDN is focused on content delivery, not general data processing service communication.

QUESTION 46

Answer - D) Implement a multi-region architecture for your applications across multiple regions.

A) Cross-region replication in Cloud Storage focuses on data, but a comprehensive disaster recovery strategy involves more than data replication.
B) Setting up a separate project might introduce additional complexity and cost.
C) While low TTL settings in Cloud DNS can help with failover, they are not the sole solution for disaster recovery.
D) Implementing a multi-region architecture for your applications across multiple regions provides redundancy and a cost-effective disaster recovery strategy.
E) Google Cloud offers disaster recovery services, but they may require additional configuration for a comprehensive solution.

QUESTION 47

Answer – E) Enable Premium Network Tier on all Compute Engine instances for global low-latency communication.

A) Incorrect. Global VPC does not inherently reduce latency for global communication.
B) Incorrect. VPN tunnels are not the most efficient for low-latency, high-throughput needs.
C) Incorrect. Interconnect is typically for on-premises to GCP connections.

D) Incorrect. Internal Load Balancers are for distributing internal traffic, not for low-latency state synchronization.

E) Correct. Premium Network Tier provides optimized performance for low-latency, global communication.

QUESTION 48

Answer – E) Enable Cloud SQL Proxy on GKE clusters for secure and private database connectivity.

A) Incorrect. Private Google Access allows access to Google services but does not specifically address secure communication to Cloud SQL.
B) Incorrect. VPC Peering is not used for connecting to managed services like Cloud SQL.
C) Incorrect. Cloud VPN is not necessary for communication within GCP.
D) Incorrect. Cloud Interconnect is for external network connections.
E) Correct. Cloud SQL Proxy ensures secure, private, and low-latency connectivity to the Cloud SQL database.

QUESTION 49

Answer – A) Configure Cloud Pub/Sub for data ingestion, Cloud Dataflow for real-time processing, and BigQuery for immediate analysis.

A) Correct. This configuration provides a scalable and efficient pipeline for real-time data analytics.
B) Incorrect. Cloud IoT Core is specific to IoT data; Spanner may not be optimal for real-time analytics compared to BigQuery.
C) Incorrect. Cloud Storage is not ideal for real-time data streaming; Bigtable is more for high-throughput, low-latency workloads.
D) Incorrect. Direct streaming to Compute Engine is less scalable; Cloud SQL is not designed for high-volume real-time analytics.
E) Incorrect. Cloud Endpoints and Firestore are not the best fit for high-volume, real-time data analytics workflows.

QUESTION 50

Answer – A) Configure Cloud Pub/Sub for data ingestion, Cloud Dataflow for real-time processing, and BigQuery for analysis.

A) Correct. This configuration provides a scalable and efficient solution for real-time data ingestion, processing, and analysis.
B) Incorrect. Cloud IoT Core is specific for IoT data; Spanner may not be the best fit for real-time analytics.
C) Incorrect. Cloud Storage is not ideal for real-time data streaming; Bigtable is for high-throughput, low-latency workloads.
D) Incorrect. Direct streaming to Compute Engine is less scalable; Cloud SQL is not optimized for high-volume real-time analytics.
E) Incorrect. Cloud Endpoints and Firestore are not the best fit for high-volume, real-time data analytics workflows.

QUESTION 1

You are responsible for optimizing network costs in Google Cloud. Your organization frequently transfers large amounts of data between regions. What should you implement to reduce data transfer costs while maintaining low latency?

A) Enable Google Cloud CDN for data transfers
B) Implement Google Cloud Interconnect
C) Use Google Cloud VPN tunnels
D) Set up Google Cloud Storage Transfer Service
E) Deploy Google Cloud Filestore for data transfer

QUESTION 2

You are managing a global e-commerce application in Google Cloud that experiences frequent traffic fluctuations. During peak traffic hours, you notice that some users experience slow response times and latency issues. What GCP service should you implement to optimize the performance and ensure low-latency response for all users?

A) Google Cloud CDN
B) Google Cloud Global Load Balancing
C) Google Cloud Network Peering
D) Google Cloud Traffic Director
E) Google Cloud Regional Load Balancing

QUESTION 3

Your organization operates a Virtual Private Cloud (VPC) with two Partner Interconnect connections serving different regions: europe-westl and europe-northl. Each Partner Interconnect is linked to a Cloud Router in its specific region through a VLAN attachment. You have been tasked with setting up a resilient failover route. Ideally, all ingress traffic from your corporate network should primarily go through the Europe-westl connection. In the event that europe-westl becomes unavailable, traffic should automatically switch over to europe-northl. What should you set the multi-exit discriminator (MED) values to, in order to facilitate this automatic failover configuration?

A) Use regional routing. Set the europe-northl Cloud Router to a base priority of 90, and set the europe-westl Cloud Router to a base priority of 10
B) Use regional routing. Set the europe-northl Cloud Router to a base priority of 800, and set the europe-westl Cloud Router to a base priority of 10
C) Use global routing. Set the europe-northl Cloud Router to a base priority of 90, and set the europe-west 1 Cloud Router to a base priority of 10
D) Use global routing. Set the europe-northl Cloud Router to a base priority of 800, and set the europe-westl Cloud Router to a base pri- ority of 10.

QUESTION 4

Your company is planning to migrate a large dataset to Google Cloud Storage. The data consists of sensitive customer information, and security is a top priority. What should you do to ensure the highest level of security for this data during and after the migration process?

A) Use Google Cloud Storage Transfer Service to copy the data over an encrypted channel and enable server-side encryption with Customer-Managed Keys (CMEK) in the destination bucket.

B) Use a third-party tool to migrate the data, as it provides better security controls than Google Cloud services.

C) Copy the data manually using a workstation and encrypt the data with a custom encryption tool before uploading it to Google Cloud Storage.

D) Use Google Cloud Storage Transfer Service and enable server-side encryption with Google-managed keys (GMEK) in the destination bucket.

E) Avoid migrating the data to the cloud and continue to store it on-premises to ensure maximum security.

QUESTION 5

Your organization operates multiple VPCs across different regions in Google Cloud. You need to ensure low-latency communication between VPCs while maintaining security. What is the most appropriate solution?

A) Utilize Google Cloud Dedicated Interconnect for each VPC.

B) Set up Cloud VPNs with Quality of Service (QoS) policies for VPC-to-VPC communication.

C) Create VPC Peering connections between all VPCs.

D) Implement Google Cloud CDN for VPC-to-VPC data transfer.

E) Establish dedicated fiber optic links between VPCs.

QUESTION 6

Your organization operates a complex multi-tier application in Google Cloud, and you suspect that one of the backend services is experiencing network performance issues. What actions should you take to diagnose the problem?

A) Enable VPC Flow Logs for the entire project and review the log entries for potential network bottlenecks.

B) Use Google Cloud Monitoring to set up custom metrics and alerts for network traffic anomalies.

C) Analyze Google Cloud's Network Intelligence Center data to identify any network performance bottlenecks.

D) Activate Google Cloud's Network Topology insights and examine the network path between components.

E) Deploy Google Cloud's Network Diagnostics tool to capture real-time network performance data.

QUESTION 7

You are configuring a Cloud Interconnect to link a GCP VPC (10.128.0.0/16) with your on-premises network (172.16.0.0/12). You must ensure high availability and redundancy. Which configuration will best achieve this?

A) Use two Dedicated Interconnects, each with a separate physical path.
B) Establish a single Dedicated Interconnect with Cloud VPN as a backup.
C) Implement two Partner Interconnects with diverse routing.
D) Deploy a single Partner Interconnect with direct peering for redundancy.
E) Use a single Dedicated Interconnect with multiple VLAN attachments.

QUESTION 8

You are managing a large-scale Google Kubernetes Engine (GKE) cluster for your microservices-based application. To ensure high availability and performance, you want to distribute the application's pods across multiple zones within a region. Which GKE feature should you use to achieve this?

A) Node Pools
B) Horizontal Pod Autoscaling
C) Regional Clusters
D) Node Locations
E) GKE Autopilot

QUESTION 9

Your organization is migrating a legacy on-premises application to Google Cloud. The application relies on a specific non-standard port for communication, which is different from the default ports used by most Google Cloud services. You want to ensure that this non-standard port can be used without restrictions while maintaining a secure network architecture. What should you do?

A) Use a Cloud NAT gateway to map the non-standard port to a standard port before traffic enters the Google Cloud network.
B) Create a firewall rule that explicitly allows traffic on the non-standard port and apply it to the relevant instances or tags.
C) Modify the application to use a standard port for communication to align with Google Cloud's default configurations.
D) Use Identity-Aware Proxy (IAP) to manage and control access to the application, regardless of the port used.
E) Configure a VPN connection between your on-premises network and Google Cloud to allow unrestricted communication on the non-standard port.

QUESTION 10

Your organization manages a distributed multi-project environment on Google Cloud, with various Virtual Private Cloud (VPC) networks in different regions. You need to ensure secure, private, and low-latency connectivity between these VPCs, along with the capability to route traffic to specific destinations based on custom criteria. What combination of Google Cloud services should you consider for this complex networking requirement?

A) Create dedicated VPC Peering connections between all VPCs.
B) Implement Google Cloud VPN for secure communication between VPCs.
C) Set up Google Cloud External HTTP(S) Load Balancers for routing traffic.
D) Deploy Google Cloud Network Service Tiers for low-latency communication.
E) Configure Google Cloud Traffic Director for advanced traffic routing based on custom criteria.

QUESTION 11

Your organization has multiple development teams working on separate projects, and you want to enforce network segmentation and isolate their environments securely. Each team should have its own isolated network for testing and development. What Google Cloud networking solution should you consider for this complex multi-team isolation, and what advantages does it offer?

A) Google Cloud Shared VPC for centralized network administration and segmentation.
B) Google Cloud VPC Network Peering for inter-VPC communication and isolation.
C) Google Cloud Identity and Access Management (IAM) for role-based access control.
D) Google Cloud Security Command Center for security assessment and monitoring.
E) Google Cloud Private Service Connect for secure communication with external services.

QUESTION 12

You are tasked with configuring a secure, resilient connection between your GCP VPC and a third-party service provider. The provider requires a dedicated physical link for data transfer. Your GCP environment already uses several Cloud VPN instances. What steps should you take to meet these requirements?

A) Establish a Dedicated Interconnect and configure Cloud Router for dynamic routing.
B) Use existing Cloud VPN instances for the connection.
C) Set up a Partner Interconnect and configure custom routes for the third-party provider.
D) Create additional Cloud VPN instances with static routing.
E) Implement a hybrid approach using both Dedicated Interconnect and Cloud VPN.

QUESTION 13

You are responsible for optimizing the network cost of a GCP project that spans multiple regions. The project consists of various virtual machine instances, and you need to minimize data transfer costs between these instances. Which GCP networking solution should you recommend?

A) Google Cloud Private Service Connect
B) Google Cloud Network Peering
C) Google Cloud Dedicated Interconnect
D) Google Cloud CDN for content caching
E) Google Cloud Router with BGP dynamic routing

QUESTION 14

You are setting up a secure network environment for system engineers to manage VMs in GCP. What firewall configurations would you apply to allow secure remote management while maintaining network security?

A) Allow all ingress on port 22, deny all other ports.
B) Deny all ingress traffic by default and allow port 22 for SSH access.
C) Allow all ingress and egress traffic on ports 22 and 3389 for SSH and RDP.
D) Implement stateful inspection for ingress on port 22 and egress on port 3389.
E) Create a rule to deny all ingress traffic and another to allow ingress on port 3389 for RDP.

QUESTION 15

You set up a new network infrastructure for your analytics department. You plan to ensure that the system engineers can manage virtual machines within this network securely. How would you adjust your firewall configurations to permit this kind of access?

A) Create two firewall rules: one to deny ingress to all protocols with priority 0, and another to permit ingress on port 22 with priority 1000.
 B) Create a single firewall rule to allow port 22 with priority 1000.
 C) Create two firewall rules: one to block all traffic with priority 65536, and another to allow port 3389 with priority 1000.
 D) Establish a single firewall rule to permit ingress on port 3389 with a priority setting of 1000.
 E) Configure a firewall rule to allow ingress on all ports and protocols.

QUESTION 16

Your organization needs to ensure high availability and fault tolerance for a critical application deployed in Google Cloud. What GCP networking feature should you recommend to achieve this goal?

A) Google Cloud CDN for content caching.
 B) Google Cloud VPN for secure access.
 C) Google Cloud Load Balancing for distributing traffic.
 D) Google Cloud Interconnect for dedicated connections.
 E) Google Cloud DNS for domain management.

QUESTION 17

In setting up a disaster recovery plan, you configured Cloud NAT for your virtual machines in Google Cloud. You notice that a particular VM isn't using Cloud NAT when connecting to external services. What is the primary reason for this behavior?

A) There are custom-defined routes directing traffic to private IP ranges.
 B) The VM has been assigned a publicly routable IP address.
 C) The VM is deployed with several network interfaces.
 D) The VM is reachable through an external IP address provided by a Google Cloud load balancer.
 E) The VM is running a custom firewall rule preventing Cloud NAT usage.

QUESTION 18

You need to ensure that VMs in your company's Shared VPC in GCP can resolve internal domain names using your on-premises DNS through a Dedicated Interconnect. What configuration would achieve this in the most efficient manner?

A) Set up a Cloud DNS private zone in the core project and enable DNS forwarding to on-premises DNS servers.
B) Configure each VM's network settings to directly point to the on-premises DNS servers.
C) Create a Cloud DNS forwarding zone in each service project, pointing to the on-premises DNS servers.
D) Implement a DNS policy in the core project to resolve names using on-premises DNS servers as primary resolvers.
E) Establish a Cloud Router custom route to redirect all DNS queries to the on-premises network.

QUESTION 19

You're tasked with configuring high availability for your Google Cloud project. Which combination of services and settings will provide the highest level of redundancy and availability for your virtual machines?

A) Create regional managed instance groups with autoscaling enabled and utilize regional persistent disks.
B) Implement Zonal managed instance groups with autoscaling and utilize instance templates.
C) Configure instance groups with preemptible instances and use zonal persistent disks.
D) Use unmanaged instance groups with manually assigned static IP addresses and local SSDs.
E) Utilize sole-tenant nodes for your virtual machines.

QUESTION 20

In setting up a disaster recovery plan, you configured Cloud NAT for your virtual machines in Google Cloud. You notice that a particular VM isn't using Cloud NAT when connecting to external services. What is the primary reason for this behavior?

A) There are custom-defined routes directing traffic to private IP ranges.
B) The VM has been assigned a publicly routable IP address.
C) The VM is deployed with several network interfaces.
D) The VM is reachable through an external IP address provided by a Google Cloud load balancer.
E) Cloud NAT is not enabled for the project.

QUESTION 21

As the Organization Admin for a multinational corporation, an engineer in your team is tasked with deploying several main storage buckets across different departments and enabling uniform access to service accounts. You need to configure the Identity and Access Management (IAM) settings for the engineer so they can accomplish this with minimal effort. What action should you take?

A) Provide the engineer with the Storage Admin IAM role and Project IAM Admin role at the organization level.
B) Assign the engineer the Storage Admin IAM role at the department level.
C) Grant the engineer both the Storage Admin IAM role and Project IAM Admin role at the department level.
D) Assign the engineer the Storage Admin IAM role at the organization level.
E) Create a custom IAM role for the engineer with the necessary permissions.

QUESTION 22

As the Organization Admin for a multinational corporation, an engineer in your team is tasked with deploying several main storage buckets across different departments and enabling uniform access to service accounts. You need to configure the Identity and Access Management (IAM) settings for the engineer so they can accomplish this with minimal effort. What action should you take?

A) Provide the engineer with the Storage Admin IAM role and Project IAM Admin role at the organization level.
B) Assign the engineer the Storage Admin IAM role at the department level.

C) Grant the engineer both the Storage Admin IAM role and Project IAM Admin role at the department level.
D) Assign the engineer the Storage Admin IAM role at the organization level.
E) Create a custom IAM role specifically for this task.

QUESTION 23

A company has multiple Google Cloud projects with VPCs, and they want to establish secure communication between VMs in different projects. They've set up VPC peering but are facing challenges with connectivity. The VMs can ping each other, but other protocols fail to work. What might be the issue?

A) Insufficient IAM permissions
B) Google Cloud's default network service account limitations
C) Network firewall rules blocking non-ping traffic
D) MTU mismatches between projects
E) Incompatible OS versions on the VMs

QUESTION 24

Your company Is planning to set up a disaster recovery (DR) solution in Google Cloud. The DR plan requires data replication to a secondary region for failover. What two Google Cloud services should you recommend to achieve this data replication and failover capability?

A) Use Google Cloud Spanner for real-time data replication.
B) Set up Google Cloud Storage for object-level replication.
C) Implement Google Cloud Pub/Sub for event-driven data synchronization.
D) Utilize Google Cloud Bigtable for analytical data replication.
E) Configure Google Cloud Storage Nearline for data archiving.

QUESTION 25

You manage a service that is operating on a managed instance group within Google Cloud. The team has developed an updated instance template that integrates an experimental optimization algorithm. To ensure that any potential issues in the new template have minimal effect on your user base, how should you approach the update process of your instances?

A) Directly apply patches to a fraction of the instances manually, subsequently carrying out a rolling restart on the entire managed instance group.
B) Deploy the updated instance template to carry out a rolling update across the entire scope of instances in the managed instance group. Perform validation of the experimental algorithm once the update has been fully executed.
C) Establish a new managed instance group and utilize it to canary test the updated template. Upon successful verification of the experimental algorithm within the canary group, apply the updated template to the initial managed instance group.
D) Conduct a canary deployment by initiating a rolling update and designating a subset of your instances to adopt the updated template. After confirming the experimental algorithm's stability on the canary instances, proceed to implement the update for the remaining instances.

QUESTION 26

You are deploying a hybrid cloud solution where your GCP environment needs secure connectivity with an on-premises data center. The on-premises data center hosts critical legacy systems. What configuration ensures secure, reliable, and low-latency communication between GCP and the on-premises data center?

A) Use Cloud VPN with dynamic routing for secure communication.
B) Implement Dedicated Interconnect for a direct, high-speed connection.
C) Configure VPC Peering between the GCP VPC and the on-premises network.
D) Utilize Cloud CDN to optimize communication between the environments.
E) Establish Partner Interconnect with diverse routing for redundancy.

QUESTION 27

To ensure unified network management, your organization plans to centralize network management tasks. What networking approach should you adopt for this requirement?

A) Create separate VPCs for each branch office and assign network management tasks to each VPC.
B) Set up a dedicated VPC in europe-west3 for network management and use VPC peering to connect to other VPCs.
C) Implement separate network management tools for each location with no centralization.
D) Utilize Cloud Interconnect for centralized network management.
E) None of the above.

QUESTION 28

In a GCP environment, you are tasked with ensuring high availability and fault tolerance for an application that heavily relies on Cloud Spanner. The application must remain operational even if an entire region becomes unavailable. What configuration should you use?

A) Implement a multi-regional instance of Cloud Spanner.
B) Set up multiple single-region Cloud Spanner instances and replicate data using Cloud Dataflow.
C) Use a regional Cloud Spanner instance with Cloud SQL as a failover.
D) Configure Cloud Spanner with synchronous replication across two regions.
E) Deploy Cloud Spanner instances in each region and use Pub/Sub for data synchronization.

QUESTION 29

Your organization manages a Google Cloud project that houses multiple App Engine applications. To enforce strict API access control for Memorystore instances and Spanner databases, allowing traffic exclusively from your organization's head office networks, which method should you recommend?

A) Develop an access context policy for each individual App Engine application, specifying head office network IP ranges, and apply these policies to Memorystore and Spanner.
B) Establish a VPC Service Controls perimeter for your project, including an access context policy that encompasses your organization's head office network IP ranges.
C) Create separate VPC Service Controls perimeters for each App Engine application, each with access context policies defining your organization's head office network IP ranges.
D) Configure a set of firewall rules to deny API access to Memorystore and Spanner from networks not

recognized as part of your head office.
E) None of the above.

QUESTION 30

In a multi-cloud setup with GCP and an on-premises data center connected via HA VPN, you need to configure DNS for Cloud SQL instances to resolve both internal and Google Cloud hostnames. What is the most appropriate configuration?

A) Set up a private forwarding zone in Cloud DNS pointing to the internal DNS server and update firewall to allow ingress from the Cloud SQL network.
B) Create a Cloud DNS private zone and update Cloud SQL instances' /etc/resolv.conf to use the internal DNS server.
C) Implement DNS Server Policies in Cloud DNS directing to the internal DNS server, and update the firewall to allow traffic from Cloud SQL's network.
D) Establish a private forwarding zone in Cloud DNS for internal DNS resolution and advertise a custom route on Cloud Router for the Cloud SQL network.
E) Configure a custom DNS server on each Cloud SQL instance to directly communicate with the internal DNS server.

QUESTION 31

You are configuring network settings for a data-intensive application deployed in multiple GCP regions. The application needs to minimize latency in inter-region communication. Which network configuration would best support this requirement?

A) Use Cloud VPN with dynamic routing between regions.
B) Configure Dedicated Interconnect for each region for high-throughput connectivity.
C) Implement a Global HTTP(S) Load Balancer for inter-region traffic distribution.
D) Utilize Premium Network Tier for optimized inter-region network performance.
E) Establish VPC Peering between regions with custom routes for low-latency connectivity.

QUESTION 32

You have set up an HTTPS load balancer in the healthcare industry, but health checks to port 443 on your Google Cloud Compute Engine instances are failing, leading to no traffic being directed to your servers. How can you rectify this issue?

A) gcloud compute health-checks update https create-my-check --unhealthy-threshold 1 5.
B) gcloud compute firewall-rules create health-check-rule --network my-health-network --allow tcp2443 --source-ranges 130.211.0.0/22,35.191.0.0/16 --direction INGRESS.
C) gcloud compute instances add-access-config my-instance.
D) gcloud compute firewall-rules create health-check-rule --network my-health-network --allow tcp2443 --destination-ranges 130.211.0.0/22,35.191.0.0/16 --direction EGRESS.
E) None of the above.

QUESTION 33

You manage a service that is operating on a managed instance group within Google Cloud. The team has developed an updated instance template that integrates an experimental optimization algorithm. To ensure that any potential issues in the new template have minimal effect on your user base, how should you approach the update process of your instances?

A) Directly apply patches to a fraction of the instances manually, subsequently carrying out a rolling restart on the entire managed instance group.

B) Deploy the updated instance template to carry out a rolling update across the entire scope of instances in the managed instance group. Perform validation of the experimental algorithm once the update has been fully executed.

C) Establish a new managed instance group and utilize it to canary test the updated template. Upon successful verification of the experimental algorithm within the canary group, apply the updated template to the initial managed instance group.

D) Conduct a canary deployment by initiating a rolling update and designating a subset of your instances to adopt the updated template. After confirming the experimental algorithm's stability on the canary instances, proceed to implement the update for the remaining instances.

E) None of the above.

QUESTION 34

Your organization is running a global media streaming platform that requires low-latency access and high availability for viewers across the world. You want to ensure that your content is delivered securely with encryption. Which complex Google Cloud networking solution should you implement to meet these requirements effectively?

A) HTTP(S) Load Balancer with CDN
B) SSL Proxy Load Balancer with Anycast IP Routing
C) TCP Proxy Load Balancer with Network Load Balancer
D) Global Load Balancer with Private Google Access
E) Cloud VPN with Dedicated Interconnect

QUESTION 35

Your organization needs to establish secure communication between on-premises data centers and Google Cloud resources. You also want to optimize network performance for data transfer. What complex networking solution should you design to achieve these goals effectively?

A) Set up custom routes with more precision than the default network routes, specifying secure VPN connections for communication and network tags for optimized performance.

B) Reconfigure the on-premises data centers to move all resources to Google Cloud, simplifying the network architecture and enhancing security.

C) Delete all default network routes and establish distinct custom routes for VPN connections, using network tags to differentiate traffic and optimize performance.

D) Create more specific custom routes than the default network routes, designating secure VPN connections for communication, and assign network tags for precise routing and optimized performance.

E) Implement Google Cloud Dedicated Interconnect with Cloud Router for secure and optimized communication between on-premises data centers and Google Cloud.

QUESTION 36

You are setting up a network in GCP for a distributed application that requires strong isolation between production and development environments, but still needs some level of controlled interaction for data updates and testing. What network configuration should you implement?

A) Use VPC Network Peering between production and development VPCs with restricted firewall rules.
B) Set up two separate VPCs and connect them with Cloud VPN for controlled interaction.
C) Implement Shared VPC with separate subnets for production and development, and firewall rules for controlled access.
D) Configure separate VPCs for each environment and use VPC Service Controls for data exchange.
E) Establish a Private Service Connect between the two environments for secure and controlled data interaction.

QUESTION 37

You are designing a highly available network architecture for a global e-commerce platform. To ensure low-latency access for customers worldwide, you need to choose a global load balancing solution. Which Google Cloud networking service should you select to provide advanced traffic distribution and global failover capabilities?

A) Global external load balancer
B) Cloud CDN with Google Cloud Armor
C) Traffic Director with Cloud Spanner
D) Google Cloud VPN with VPC peering
E) Regional managed instance groups with Cloud Interconnect

QUESTION 38

Your organization operates a critical online video streaming service, and you want to enhance security by restricting access to your backend servers to only allow connections from a specific DDoS protection service. Which Google Cloud networking solution should you implement to achieve this goal?

A) Create a VPC Service Controls Perimeter that blocks all traffic except for the DDoS protection service.
B) Create a Cloud Armor Security Policy that blocks all traffic except for the DDoS protection service.
C) Create a VPC Firewall rule that blocks all traffic except for the DDoS protection service.
D) Implement iptables firewall rules on your servers that block all traffic except for the DDoS protection service.
E) Deploy Google Cloud Armor with Google Cloud CDN to filter traffic from the DDoS protection service.

QUESTION 39

You are responsible for implementing a network architecture that provides DDoS protection and intelligent traffic routing for a Google Kubernetes Engine (GKE) application. Your goal is to ensure the application can scale seamlessly based on demand. Which Google Cloud networking service or feature should you integrate with GKE to achieve these objectives?

A) Google Cloud Armor with Google Cloud CDN
B) Traffic Director with Cloud Load Balancing
C) Google Cloud DNS with Cloud IAM

D) Cloud Interconnect with Cloud VPN
E) Google Cloud CDN with VPC peering

QUESTION 40

Your organization operates a multi-tier application on Google Cloud that requires horizontal scaling and load balancing to handle variable workloads. You want to ensure efficient resource utilization and minimal downtime. Which combination of Google Cloud service or feature should you leverage to achieve these objectives effectively?

A) Google Compute Engine Autoscaler and Google Cloud Bigtable
B) Google Kubernetes Engine (GKE) and Google Cloud Pub/Sub
C) Google Cloud Load Balancing and Google Cloud CDN
D) Google Cloud Dataprep and Google Cloud Filestore
E) Google Cloud Spanner and Google Cloud Identity-Aware Proxy (IAP)

QUESTION 41

For a set of GCP Compute Engine instances that handle sensitive data processing, you need to ensure that all outgoing internet connections are logged for security and compliance. What configuration should you use to achieve this logging?

A) Enable VPC Flow Logs for the subnetworks where the instances reside.
B) Configure individual logging for each Compute Engine instance using Cloud Monitoring.
C) Set up a NAT gateway with integrated logging for all outbound connections.
D) Implement Cloud IDS to log and analyze all outgoing traffic from the instances.
E) Use Cloud Armor with custom logging policies for outbound traffic monitoring.

QUESTION 42

Your organization operates a high-traffic online video streaming service. Your servers are configured with private IP addresses, and users connect through a regional load balancer. To enhance security, you've enlisted a DDoS protection service and need to limit your backend servers to accept connections solely from this DDoS mitigation provider. How should you proceed?

A) Create a VPC Service Controls Perimeter that blocks all traffic except for the DDoS protection service.
B) Create a Cloud Armor Security Policy that blocks all traffic except for the DDoS protection service.
C) Create a VPC Firewall rule that blocks all traffic except for the DDoS protection service.
D) Implement iptables firewall rules on your servers that block all traffic except for the DDoS protection service.

QUESTION 43

Your regional headquarters has 4 gateways connected to your Google Cloud environment through a Dedicated Interconnect on each gateway. All services are operational; however, all of the network traffic is being routed through a single gateway instead of being distributed evenly across the 4 connections. Upon investigation, you discover: - Each gateway is configured with a distinct ASN. - Each gateway is set with the same routes and weights. - All gateways are connected to one Cloud Router via a Dedicated Interconnect. - BGP sessions are functioning between each gateway and the Cloud Router. - Only the routes from a single gateway are present in the Cloud Router's route table. What could be the primary reason for this issue?

A) A security rule is obstructing traffic through the additional Dedicated Interconnect.
B) The ASNs utilized on the gateways are unique.
C) There isn't a load balancer in place for distributing network load.
D) The gateways are configured with identical routes.
E) The Cloud Router is not properly configured to distribute traffic among multiple gateways.

QUESTION 44

You are tasked with designing a highly available and fault-tolerant architecture for a critical application in Google Cloud. The application requires low-latency access to a regional Cloud SQL database and must survive the failure of a zone without downtime. What architecture should you recommend?

A) Deploy the application and the database in the same zone with zone redundancy enabled.
B) Use an instance group with instances in multiple zones, each connecting to the regional Cloud SQL database.
C) Deploy the application and the database in separate zones within the same region.
D) Utilize a global load balancer to distribute traffic to instances in different zones, each connecting to the regional Cloud SQL database.
E) Deploy the application in a multi-region configuration and use a global load balancer to route traffic to the nearest region.

QUESTION 45

In a GCP environment, your company's application needs to ensure zero downtime and immediate failover in case of a zone failure. The application uses a stateful database hosted on Compute Engine instances. What configuration should you use to achieve this high availability and failover capability?

A) Set up instance groups with automatic failover across multiple zones and a regional persistent disk for the database.
B) Configure a single-zone instance group with a standard persistent disk and regular snapshots for backup.
C) Use a multi-regional database service like Cloud Spanner instead of Compute Engine instances.
D) Implement a custom failover mechanism using Cloud Functions to monitor and initiate failover for Compute Engine instances.
E) Establish a zonal instance group with SSD persistent disks and Cloud Load Balancing for traffic distribution.

QUESTION 46

Your organization is using Google Kubernetes Engine (GKE) to manage containerized applications. You want to ensure the security of your GKE cluster by limiting which IP ranges can access the cluster's master endpoint. What is the recommended approach to achieve this?

A) Use a Network Policy in GKE to restrict access to the master endpoint based on IP ranges.
B) Configure a firewall rule in Google Cloud to allow traffic only from specific IP ranges to the master endpoint's public IP address.

C) Use GKE's built-in master authorized networks feature to specify allowed IP ranges for master endpoint access.
D) Implement a Cloud Armor security policy to control access to the master endpoint's IP address.
E) Set up a Google Cloud Identity-Aware Proxy (IAP) to manage access to the GKE master endpoint.

QUESTION 47

For a GCP project with strict regulatory compliance requirements, you are configuring network access for a set of applications that process sensitive data. The applications must only communicate with a designated set of external IP addresses. What configuration ensures compliance with these communication restrictions?

A) Use VPC Service Controls to create a secure perimeter around the applications and allowed external IPs.
B) Implement egress firewall rules in the VPC to restrict traffic to the designated external IP addresses.
C) Set up Cloud VPN tunnels to the designated external IP addresses for secure, restricted communication.
D) Configure Private Google Access to restrict outbound traffic from the applications to specific external IP addresses.
E) Establish Cloud NAT with custom rules to allow traffic only to the designated external IP addresses.

QUESTION 48

You are tasked with setting up a disaster recovery solution in GCP for a critical application. The application relies on a regional Cloud Spanner database for data storage. To ensure minimal downtime and data loss, what configuration would you recommend for the disaster recovery solution?

A) Set up a multi-regional Cloud Spanner instance for high availability.
B) Configure regular exports of the Cloud Spanner database to Cloud Storage in another region.
C) Implement a read replica of the Cloud Spanner database in a different region.
D) Use Cloud Dataflow for continuous replication of data to a secondary Cloud Spanner instance in another region.
E) Establish a custom script for incremental backups from Cloud Spanner to another database service in a different region.

QUESTION 49

In a GCP environment, you need to optimize the network for a set of applications that involve heavy data transfers to and from BigQuery. The setup requires maximizing throughput and minimizing latency for these data transfers. What network configuration would you recommend?

A) Use Cloud VPN with high-throughput tunnels for data transfer.
B) Configure each application instance with Premium Network Tier.
C) Implement Cloud Interconnect for direct, high-throughput connections to BigQuery.
D) Enable Private Google Access on the subnetworks hosting the applications.
E) Set up VPC Peering between the application's network and BigQuery's network.

QUESTION 50

You are configuring a network in GCP for applications that require high throughput and low-latency communication with Cloud SQL. What configuration ensures optimal performance for these database connections?

A) Use Cloud VPN with high-throughput tunnels to Cloud SQL.
B) Configure Private Google Access on the subnetworks hosting the applications.
C) Implement Dedicated Interconnect to Cloud SQL for direct connectivity.
D) Enable Premium Network Tier on the Compute Engine instances hosting the applications.
E) Set up VPC Peering between the applications' network and Cloud SQL.

PRACTICE TEST 6 - ANSWERS ONLY

QUESTION 1

Answer – B) Implement Google Cloud Interconnect

Option B - Implementing Google Cloud Interconnect allows for dedicated, cost-effective, and low-latency data transfers between regions.
Option A - Google Cloud CDN is for content delivery, not data transfers between regions.
Option C - Google Cloud VPN may not offer the cost-efficiency required for large data transfers.
Option D - Google Cloud Storage Transfer Service is for managing data transfers, but it doesn't directly reduce transfer costs.
Option E - Google Cloud Filestore is for file storage, not data transfers.

QUESTION 2

Answer – B) Google Cloud Global Load Balancing

Option B - Implementing Google Cloud Global Load Balancing ensures optimal performance and low-latency response times by distributing traffic across multiple regions.
Option A - Google Cloud CDN improves content delivery but may not address application latency.
Option C - Network Peering is for connecting networks, not optimizing application performance.
Option D - Traffic Director is for traffic management, not global load balancing.
Option E - Regional Load Balancing is not global and may not provide the desired low-latency response.

QUESTION 3

Answer – B) Use regional routing. Set the europe-northl Cloud Router to a base priority of 800, and set the europe-westl Cloud Router to a base priority of 10

Option B - Using regional routing and setting the europe-northl Cloud Router to a higher base priority (800) than the europe-westl Cloud Router (10) ensures that traffic primarily goes through europe-westl but automatically switches to europe-northl in case of unavailability, facilitating automatic failover.
Option A - Setting both Cloud Routers to regional routing with different base priorities may not achieve the desired failover behavior.
Option C - Using global routing with base priorities may not provide the region-specific failover required.
Option D - Setting a higher base priority for europe-northl in global routing may not lead to the desired behavior.

QUESTION 4

Answer – A) Use Google Cloud Storage Transfer Service to copy the data over an encrypted channel and enable server-side encryption with Customer-Managed Keys (CMEK) in the destination bucket.

Option A - Using Google Cloud Storage Transfer Service with encryption and Customer-Managed Keys (CMEK) ensures the highest level of security for sensitive customer data.

Option B - Third-party tools may not necessarily provide better security and can introduce complexity.
Option C - Manual copying and custom encryption may be error-prone and less secure.
Option D - Using Google-managed keys (GMEK) is not as secure as Customer-Managed Keys (CMEK) for sensitive data.
Option E - Avoiding migration to the cloud is not a practical solution for most organizations and doesn't leverage cloud security features.

QUESTION 5

Answer - C) Create VPC Peering connections between all VPCs.

Option C is the most suitable solution for low-latency communication between multiple VPCs while maintaining security.
Option A, Dedicated Interconnect, can be expensive and may not be necessary for all VPCs.
Option B with Cloud VPNs and QoS policies may not guarantee the required low-latency.
Option D is related to content delivery, not VPC-to-VPC communication.
Option E is costly and may introduce unnecessary complexity.

QUESTION 6

Answer - B) Use Google Cloud Monitoring to set up custom metrics and alerts for network traffic anomalies.
Answer - C) Analyze Google Cloud's Network Intelligence Center data to identify any network performance bottlenecks.

Options B and C are the appropriate actions for diagnosing network performance issues in a complex multi-tier application in Google Cloud.
Option B focuses on setting up custom metrics and alerts in Google Cloud Monitoring, while Option C leverages Google Cloud's Network Intelligence Center data.
Option A mentions VPC Flow Logs, which may not provide the detailed insights needed for network performance issues.
Option D discusses Network Topology insights, which may not directly address performance bottlenecks.
Option E mentions Network Diagnostics, but its applicability may vary based on the specific issue.

QUESTION 7

Answer – A) Use two Dedicated Interconnects, each with a separate physical path.

A) Correct. Provides redundancy and high availability.
B) Incorrect. Cloud VPN may not offer the same throughput.
C) Incorrect. Partner Interconnects may not provide sufficient control over routing.
D) Incorrect. Single Interconnect lacks redundancy.
E) Incorrect. Multiple VLANs do not address physical path redundancy.

QUESTION 8

Answer - C) Regional Clusters

Option C, Regional Clusters, is the appropriate choice for distributing pods across multiple zones within a region in GKE, ensuring high availability and performance.

Option A, Node Pools, is used for managing groups of nodes within a cluster but doesn't inherently distribute pods across zones.

Option B, Horizontal Pod Autoscaling, dynamically adjusts the number of pods based on resource usage but doesn't control pod placement across zones.

Option D, Node Locations, is not a GKE feature.

Option E, GKE Autopilot, is a mode for managing clusters, but it doesn't focus on regional distribution of pods.

QUESTION 9

Answer - B) Create a firewall rule that explicitly allows traffic on the non-standard port and apply it to the relevant instances or tags.

Answer - D) Use Identity-Aware Proxy (IAP) to manage and control access to the application, regardless of the port used.

Option B is the recommended approach to allow traffic on the non-standard port by creating a firewall rule specifically for that port.

Option D can be used in conjunction with Option B to manage access to the application securely. Options A, C, and E are not the most suitable choices for accommodating non-standard port traffic while maintaining security.

QUESTION 10

Answer - E) Configure Google Cloud Traffic Director for advanced traffic routing based on custom criteria.

Option A would create a complex mesh of connections that may not provide the required custom routing.

Option B provides secure communication but doesn't address custom routing criteria.

Option C is suitable for external traffic but doesn't cover VPC-to-VPC routing.

Option D is related to networking tiers but doesn't address custom routing.

Option E is the correct choice as Google Cloud Traffic Director allows advanced traffic routing based on custom criteria, addressing the complex requirements effectively.

QUESTION 11

Answer - A) Google Cloud Shared VPC for centralized network administration and segmentation.

Option B mentions VPC Network Peering but doesn't specifically address multi-team isolation.

Option C focuses on IAM but may not directly relate to network segmentation.

Option D is for security assessment but may not provide network isolation capabilities.

Option E is for secure communication but may not cover multi-team isolation within a network.

Option A is the correct choice as Google Cloud Shared VPC allows centralized network administration and segmentation, ensuring each development team has its own isolated network for testing and development, meeting the complex multi-team isolation requirements.

QUESTION 12

Answer – A) Establish a Dedicated Interconnect and configure Cloud Router for dynamic routing.

A) Correct. Dedicated Interconnect provides a dedicated physical link and Cloud Router enables dynamic routing.
B) Incorrect. Cloud VPN does not provide a dedicated physical link.
C) Incorrect. Partner Interconnect might not meet the dedicated link requirement.
D) Incorrect. Cloud VPN with static routing does not provide a dedicated physical link.
E) Incorrect. A hybrid approach is unnecessary for a dedicated link requirement.

QUESTION 13

Answer - B) Google Cloud Network Peering

B) Google Cloud Network Peering - Google Cloud Network Peering allows you to establish private connections between VPCs within the same organization, minimizing data transfer costs.
 A) Google Cloud Private Service Connect - Private Service Connect is used for private network connections but may not specifically minimize data transfer costs.
 C) Google Cloud Dedicated Interconnect - Dedicated Interconnect provides high-speed connections but may not directly minimize data transfer costs.
 D) Google Cloud CDN for content caching - CDN is for content caching, not for minimizing data transfer costs between instances.
 E) Google Cloud Router with BGP dynamic routing - Router with BGP is used for routing within GCP, not specifically for minimizing data transfer costs.

QUESTION 14

Answer – B) Deny all ingress traffic by default and allow port 22 for SSH access.

A) Incorrect. Allowing all ingress on port 22 is insecure.
B) Correct. Denying all by default and allowing SSH is secure practice.
C) Incorrect. Allowing all traffic on both ports is excessive.
D) Incorrect. Stateful inspection is good but doesn't specify port restrictions.
E) Incorrect. Port 3389 is for RDP, which might not be needed for system engineers.

QUESTION 15

Answer - D) Establish a single firewall rule to permit ingress on port 3389 with a priority setting of 1000.

D) Establish a single firewall rule to permit ingress on port 3389 with a priority setting of 1000 - This rule specifically allows access on port 3389, which is typically used for remote desktop services, providing the required secure access for system engineers.
 A) Create two firewall rules: one to deny ingress to all protocols with priority 0, and another to permit ingress on port 22 with priority 1000 - The first rule denies all traffic, which may be overly restrictive, and the second allows port 22, which is commonly used for SSH, not necessarily for system management.
 B) Create a single firewall rule to allow port 22 with priority 1000 - Allowing port 22 may not provide the necessary access for system engineers.
 C) Create two firewall rules: one to block all traffic with priority 65536, and another to allow port 3389 with priority 1000 - The first rule blocking all traffic is overly restrictive, and the second allows port 3389,

which is appropriate but can be simplified into a single rule.
 E) Configure a firewall rule to allow ingress on all ports and protocols - Allowing all traffic is not recommended for security reasons.

QUESTION 16

Answer - C) Google Cloud Load Balancing for distributing traffic.

C) Google Cloud Load Balancing for distributing traffic - Load Balancing helps achieve high availability and fault tolerance by distributing traffic across multiple instances or regions.
 A) Google Cloud CDN for content caching - CDN is for content caching and may not directly address high availability and fault tolerance at the application level.
 B) Google Cloud VPN for secure access - VPNs provide secure access but are not primarily focused on high availability and fault tolerance for applications.
 D) Google Cloud Interconnect for dedicated connections - Interconnect is for connectivity, not high availability at the application level.
 E) Google Cloud DNS for domain management - DNS manages domain resolution but does not inherently provide high availability or fault tolerance for applications.

QUESTION 17

Answer - B) The VM has been assigned a publicly routable IP address.

B) The VM has been assigned a publicly routable IP address - When a VM has a publicly routable IP address, it bypasses Cloud NAT, which is designed for private IP address translation.
 A) There are custom-defined routes directing traffic to private IP ranges - Custom routes may influence traffic routing but do not directly affect Cloud NAT behavior.
 C) The VM is deployed with several network interfaces - The number of network interfaces does not determine Cloud NAT usage.
 D) The VM is reachable through an external IP address provided by a Google Cloud load balancer - Load balancers don't necessarily impact Cloud NAT behavior.
 E) The VM running a custom firewall rule preventing Cloud NAT usage - Firewall rules may affect traffic, but this is not the primary reason for the behavior described.

QUESTION 18

Answer – A) Set up a Cloud DNS private zone in the core project and enable DNS forwarding to on-premises DNS servers.

A) Correct. Efficiently integrates Cloud DNS with on-premises DNS.
B) Incorrect. Direct VM configuration is less scalable and bypasses Cloud DNS.
C) Incorrect. Centralizing in the core project is more efficient than per service project.
D) Incorrect. Policy should not override but rather complement on-premises DNS.
E) Incorrect. Using Cloud Router for DNS redirection is not a standard or efficient method.

QUESTION 19

Answer - A) Create regional managed instance groups with autoscaling enabled and utilize regional persistent disks.

A) Creating regional managed instance groups with autoscaling and using regional persistent disks provides the highest level of redundancy and availability for virtual machines, spanning multiple zones within a region.
B) Zonal managed instance groups are limited to a single zone, reducing redundancy.
C) Preemptible instances are not suitable for high availability as they can be terminated at any time.
D) Unmanaged instance groups and local SSDs lack the redundancy required for high availability.
E) Sole-tenant nodes do not inherently provide higher availability.

QUESTION 20

Answer - A) There are custom-defined routes directing traffic to private IP ranges.

A) When custom-defined routes direct traffic to private IP ranges, it can bypass Cloud NAT, leading to the behavior described.
B) Having a publicly routable IP address doesn't affect Cloud NAT behavior.
C) The number of network interfaces on a VM is not the primary factor for Cloud NAT usage.
D) VMs reachable through external IP addresses from a load balancer may still use Cloud NAT.
E) Assuming Cloud NAT is enabled at the project level, it's the custom routes that take precedence.

QUESTION 21

Answer - C) Grant the engineer both the Storage Admin IAM role and Project IAM Admin role at the department level.

C) To enable the engineer to deploy storage buckets across different departments and enable uniform access to service accounts with minimal effort, you should grant the engineer both the Storage Admin IAM role and Project IAM Admin role at the department level. This provides the necessary permissions without granting overly broad access at the organization level.
A) Providing the engineer with these roles at the organization level may grant excessive privileges.
B) Assigning the Storage Admin IAM role at the department level alone may not provide the engineer with all the necessary permissions.
D) Assigning the Storage Admin IAM role at the organization level may grant excessive privileges.
E) Creating a custom IAM role may be more complex and may not be necessary in this scenario.

QUESTION 22

Answer - C) Grant the engineer both the Storage Admin IAM role and Project IAM Admin role at the department level.

C) To enable the engineer to deploy storage buckets across different departments and enable access to service accounts with minimal effort, granting them both the Storage Admin IAM role and Project IAM Admin role at the department level would provide the necessary permissions and flexibility.
A) Providing both roles at the organization level may grant unnecessary permissions across the entire organization.
B) Assigning the Storage Admin IAM role at the department level alone may not cover all the required permissions for managing service accounts.
D) Assigning the Storage Admin IAM role at the organization level without the Project IAM Admin role may limit the engineer's ability to manage projects effectively.
E) Creating a custom IAM role might be an option but could be more complex and time-consuming

compared to granting the existing roles.

QUESTION 23

Answer - D) MTU mismatches between projects

Option A - IAM permissions wouldn't affect protocol-specific issues.
Option B - Default network service accounts are generally not related to this kind of connectivity problem.
Option C - Network firewall rules blocking non-ping traffic could cause this issue, but the question implies ping is working.
Option E - OS versions typically don't impact protocol-specific connectivity in Google Cloud.

QUESTION 24

Answer - B) Set up Google Cloud Storage for object-level replication.
C) Implement Google Cloud Pub/Sub for event-driven data synchronization.

Option A - Google Cloud Spanner is a relational database service and not designed for real-time data replication across regions.
Option D - Google Cloud Bigtable is for analytical data and not suitable for replication for failover.
Option E - Google Cloud Storage Nearline is for data archiving, not real-time replication. Choice B (Set up Google Cloud Storage for object-level replication) - Setting up Google Cloud Storage for object-level replication allows for data replication between regions, ensuring data availability and failover capability in a disaster recovery scenario.
Choice C (Implement Google Cloud Pub/Sub for event-driven data synchronization) - Implementing Google Cloud Pub/Sub enables event-driven data synchronization between regions, ensuring real-time data updates and failover capability in a disaster recovery scenario.

QUESTION 25

Answer - C) Establish a new managed instance group and utilize it to canary test the updated template. Upon successful verification of the experimental algorithm within the canary group, apply the updated template to the initial managed instance group.

Option A - Directly applying patches manually does not test the new template or experimental algorithm.
Option B - Deploying the updated template to all instances may risk user impact before validation.
Option D - Conducting a canary deployment without a separate group may impact the entire user base if issues arise. Choice C - Establishing a new managed instance group for canary testing allows for verification of the experimental algorithm's stability before applying it to the initial group, minimizing potential user impact.

QUESTION 26

Answer – B) Implement Dedicated Interconnect for a direct, high-speed connection.

A) Incorrect. VPN may not offer the low latency required for legacy systems.
B) Correct. Provides a private, high-performance connection.
C) Incorrect. VPC Peering is not applicable for on-premises connections.

D) Incorrect. Cloud CDN is for content delivery, not for legacy application traffic.
E) Incorrect. Partner Interconnect might not offer the consistent performance needed for legacy systems.

QUESTION 27

Answer - B) Set up a dedicated VPC in europe-west3 for network management and use VPC peering to connect to other VPCs.

Option A - Creating separate VPCs may lead to fragmentation of network management.
Option C - Implementing separate tools does not achieve centralized management.
Option D - Cloud Interconnect is not designed for network management tasks. Choice B - Establishing a dedicated VPC for network management in europe-west3 and using VPC peering provides a centralized and efficient approach to unified network management.

QUESTION 28

Answer – A) Implement a multi-regional instance of Cloud Spanner.

A) Correct. Multi-regional Cloud Spanner provides high availability and fault tolerance across regions.
B) Incorrect. This approach is complex and does not leverage Cloud Spanner's built-in capabilities.
C) Incorrect. Cloud SQL as a failover for Cloud Spanner is not a viable solution.
D) Incorrect. Cloud Spanner's multi-regional configuration inherently includes synchronous replication.
E) Incorrect. Manual synchronization with Pub/Sub is less efficient and reliable than Cloud Spanner's native capabilities.

QUESTION 29

Answer - B) Establish a VPC Service Controls perimeter for your project, including an access context policy that encompasses your organization's head office network IP ranges.

Option A - Managing individual access context policies for each application may introduce complexity.
Option C - Creating separate VPC Service Controls perimeters for each application may result in management overhead.
Option D - While firewall rules can provide protection, VPC Service Controls offer a more comprehensive security approach. Choice B - Establishing a VPC Service Controls perimeter for your project with a comprehensive access context policy that covers head office network IP ranges provides centralized and efficient API access control for Memorystore and Spanner across all applications in the project.

QUESTION 30

Answer – A) Set up a private forwarding zone in Cloud DNS pointing to the internal DNS server and update firewall to allow ingress from the Cloud SQL network.

A) Correct. This setup enables Cloud SQL instances to resolve internal domain names and Google Cloud service names, adhering to best practices.
B) Incorrect. Directly editing /etc/resolv.conf on Cloud SQL instances is not a standard practice.
C) Incorrect. DNS Server Policies in Cloud DNS don't directly address the needs of Cloud SQL instances.
D) Incorrect. Advertised custom routes on Cloud Router are not necessary for DNS resolution.

E) Incorrect. Configuring custom DNS servers on each Cloud SQL instance is not recommended and inefficient.

QUESTION 31

Answer – D) Utilize Premium Network Tier for optimized inter-region network performance.

A) Incorrect. VPN may introduce additional latency.
B) Incorrect. Dedicated Interconnect is typically for on-premises to GCP connections.
C) Incorrect. Load Balancer is not used for general inter-region network communication.
D) Correct. Premium Network Tier provides optimized routing for reduced latency.
E) Incorrect. VPC Peering is not typically used for inter-region communication within GCP.

QUESTION 32

Answer - B) gcloud compute firewall-rules create health-check-rule --network my-health-network --allow tcp2443 --source-ranges 130.211.0.0/22,35.191.0.0/16 --direction INGRESS.

Option A - Updating a health check might not address the underlying issue related to firewall rules.
Option C - Adding an access config to an instance is unlikely to resolve the health check failures.
Option D - Creating firewall rules for EGRESS traffic may not be necessary to fix health check failures.
Choice B - Creating a firewall rule allowing traffic on port 2443 from specific source IP ranges (as specified in the health checks) can rectify the issue by permitting health checks to reach the instances.

QUESTION 33

Answer - C) Establish a new managed instance group and utilize it to canary test the updated template. Upon successful verification of the experimental algorithm within the canary group, apply the updated template to the initial managed instance group.

Option A - Directly applying patches manually is not an effective approach for ensuring minimal impact during updates.
Option B - While deploying the updated template is a step, it does not specifically address minimizing the impact of potential issues.
Option C - This is the correct approach for minimizing the impact of potential issues by canary testing the updated template before applying it to the initial managed instance group.
Option D - Conducting a canary deployment is a good practice, but it is not the same as establishing a new managed instance group for testing.
Option E - None of the options adequately address the best approach for minimizing the impact of potential issues

QUESTION 34

Answer - B) SSL Proxy Load Balancer with Anycast IP Routing

A) HTTP(S) Load Balancer with CDN - Explanation: HTTP(S) Load Balancer is designed for web applications and content delivery, but it may not focus on low-latency access or encryption for various protocols.
C) TCP Proxy Load Balancer with Network Load Balancer - Explanation: TCP Proxy Load Balancer may handle network traffic, but it may not provide the same level of encryption and content delivery as

needed.

D) Global Load Balancer with Private Google Access - Explanation: Global Load Balancer provides distribution but may not offer the same encryption or content delivery capabilities.

E) Cloud VPN with Dedicated Interconnect - Explanation: Cloud VPN and Dedicated Interconnect focus on secure connections but may not optimize content delivery and low-latency access for a media streaming platform.

B) SSL Proxy Load Balancer with Anycast IP Routing - Explanation: SSL Proxy Load Balancer specializes in SSL certificate management and encryption while Anycast IP Routing improves routing efficiency, making it the best choice for secure, low-latency access with encryption for the media streaming platform.

QUESTION 35

Answer - E) Implement Google Cloud Dedicated Interconnect with Cloud Router for secure and optimized communication between on-premises data centers and Google Cloud.

E) Implement Google Cloud Dedicated Interconnect with Cloud Router for secure and optimized communication between on-premises data centers and Google Cloud - Explanation: Google Cloud Dedicated Interconnect provides dedicated, secure, and high-performance connections between on-premises data centers and Google Cloud, and Cloud Router manages dynamic BGP routing for optimal performance.

A) Set up custom routes with more precision than the default network routes - Explanation: While custom routes are useful, this option does not provide the dedicated and optimized connection needed for secure communication and network performance.

B) Reconfigure the on-premises data centers to move all resources to Google Cloud - Explanation: This option may not be practical and does not address the need for secure communication between on-premises and Google Cloud resources.

C) Delete all default network routes and establish distinct custom routes for VPN connections - Explanation: Deleting default routes introduces complexity, and this option may not be necessary for secure and optimized communication.

D) Create more specific custom routes than the default network routes - Explanation: This option introduces complexity with network tags and may not provide the dedicated and optimized connection required for secure communication and network performance.

QUESTION 36

Answer – C) Implement Shared VPC with separate subnets for production and development, and firewall rules for controlled access.

A) Incorrect. Network Peering might not provide the strong isolation required.

B) Incorrect. Cloud VPN is not the most efficient method for inter-VPC communication within GCP.

C) Correct. Shared VPC with dedicated subnets and firewall rules offers both isolation and controlled interaction.

D) Incorrect. VPC Service Controls are more focused on securing data within GCP services, not network interaction.

E) Incorrect. Private Service Connect is more suitable for connecting services, not for environment isolation.

QUESTION 37

Answer - C) Traffic Director with Cloud Spanner

A) Global external load balancer - While it distributes traffic globally, it doesn't provide the advanced traffic management features offered by Traffic Director.
B) Cloud CDN with Google Cloud Armor - This combination is focused on content delivery and security, not global failover.
C) Traffic Director with Cloud Spanner - Correct answer. Traffic Director and Cloud Spanner provide advanced traffic distribution and global failover capabilities.
D) Google Cloud VPN with VPC peering - VPN and VPC peering focus on connectivity, not traffic distribution.
E) Regional managed instance groups with Cloud Interconnect - These components do not offer the same level of global traffic management as Traffic Director and Cloud Spanner.

QUESTION 38

Answer - C) Create a VPC Firewall rule that blocks all traffic except for the DDoS protection service.

A) Create a VPC Service Controls Perimeter - Service Controls focus on access control for Google APIs, not specific IP-based traffic blocking.
B) Create a Cloud Armor Security Policy - While Cloud Armor can block traffic, it's not the best choice for restricting access to specific IPs.
C) Create a VPC Firewall rule - Correct answer. A VPC Firewall rule can be configured to allow traffic only from specific IP addresses, such as the DDoS protection service.
D) Implement iptables firewall rules on your servers - While this can work, managing server-level firewall rules can be complex and less scalable.
E) Deploy Google Cloud Armor with Google Cloud CDN - This combination focuses on security and content delivery, not IP-based access control.

QUESTION 39

Answer - B) Traffic Director with Cloud Load Balancing

A) Google Cloud Armor with Google Cloud CDN - This combination provides security and content delivery but does not inherently offer intelligent traffic routing or DDoS protection for GKE.
B) Correct answer. Traffic Director with Cloud Load Balancing provides advanced traffic management and DDoS protection for GKE, along with seamless scaling based on demand.
C) Google Cloud DNS with Cloud IAM - DNS and IAM are used for DNS resolution and access control, not traffic routing or DDoS protection.
D) Cloud Interconnect with Cloud VPN - Interconnect and VPN provide connectivity but are not used for intelligent traffic routing or DDoS protection for GKE.
E) Google Cloud CDN with VPC peering - CDN and VPC peering focus on content delivery and connectivity but do not inherently offer intelligent traffic routing or DDoS protection.

QUESTION 40

Answer - C) Google Cloud Load Balancing and Google Cloud CDN

A) Google Compute Engine Autoscaler and Google Cloud Bigtable may not inherently address load balancing and resource utilization for multi-tier applications.

B) Google Kubernetes Engine (GKE) and Google Cloud Pub/Sub focus on container orchestration and messaging but may not provide the same level of load balancing and resource management as Load Balancing and CDN.

C) Correct answer. Google Cloud Load Balancing provides efficient load distribution, and Google Cloud CDN helps with content delivery, ensuring resource utilization and minimal downtime for multi-tier applications.

D) Google Cloud Dataprep and Google Cloud Filestore are not primarily related to load balancing and resource utilization for multi-tier applications.

E) Google Cloud Spanner is a database, and Google Cloud Identity-Aware Proxy (IAP) focuses on identity management; they are not primarily load balancing solutions.

QUESTION 41

Answer – A) Enable VPC Flow Logs for the subnetworks where the instances reside.

A) Correct. VPC Flow Logs capture network traffic logs, ideal for security and compliance.

B) Incorrect. Cloud Monitoring on each instance does not specifically capture all outgoing internet connections.

C) Incorrect. NAT gateways log traffic, but VPC Flow Logs provide more comprehensive coverage for compliance.

D) Incorrect. Cloud IDS is primarily for intrusion detection, not for logging all outbound connections.

E) Incorrect. Cloud Armor is focused on inbound traffic protection and logging, not outbound.

QUESTION 42

Answer - C) Create a VPC Firewall rule that blocks all traffic except for the DDoS protection service.

A) VPC Service Controls Perimeter is more focused on data protection and may not be the right choice for limiting backend server access.

B) Cloud Armor Security Policy can help with web application security but may not be ideal for limiting server access.

C) Correct answer. Creating a VPC Firewall rule is a suitable approach to limit backend server access.

D) Implementing iptables firewall rules on individual servers is not as centralized and manageable as using VPC Firewall rules.

QUESTION 43

Answer - D) The gateways are configured with identical routes.

A) A security rule would not typically obstruct traffic between gateways and Cloud Router.

B) The ASNs being distinct is the expected configuration for multiple gateways.

C) While a load balancer could be used for distributing traffic, it's not the primary reason for the issue.

D) Correct answer. The gateways having identical routes would cause traffic to be routed through only one of them, leading to an imbalance.

E) The Cloud Router configuration is more likely responsible for load balancing traffic between gateways.

QUESTION 44

Answer - D) Utilize a global load balancer to distribute traffic to instances in different zones, each connecting to the regional Cloud SQL database.

A) Deploying the application and the database in the same zone with zone redundancy does not provide fault tolerance across zones.
B) While using instances in multiple zones is a step in the right direction, it does not address the database's high availability requirements.
C) Deploying the application and the database in separate zones is a good start but does not provide automatic failover.
E) Deploying the application in a multi-region configuration adds unnecessary complexity and may increase latency.
D) Using a global load balancer with instances in different zones ensures high availability and fault tolerance, with low-latency access to the regional database.

QUESTION 45

Answer – A) Set up instance groups with automatic failover across multiple zones and a regional persistent disk for the database.

A) Correct. Multi-zone instance groups with a regional persistent disk ensure high availability and immediate failover.
B) Incorrect. Single-zone instance groups don't provide immediate failover across zones.
C) Incorrect. While Cloud Spanner offers high availability, it requires changing the database system.
D) Incorrect. Custom failover mechanisms are complex and might not provide immediate response.
E) Incorrect. Zonal instance groups do not provide failover across zones, and load balancing doesn't address database failover.

QUESTION 46

Answer - C) Use GKE's built-in master authorized networks feature to specify allowed IP ranges for master endpoint access.

A) Network Policies in GKE primarily focus on pod-to-pod traffic, not master endpoint access control.
B) Configuring a firewall rule for the master endpoint's public IP address may not provide the intended access control.
C) GKE's master authorized networks feature allows you to specify IP ranges that are allowed to access the master endpoint.
D) Cloud Armor security policies are more suitable for protecting web applications from DDoS attacks.
E) Google Cloud IAP is used for securing applications and services, not the GKE master endpoint.

QUESTION 47

Answer – B) Implement egress firewall rules in the VPC to restrict traffic to the designated external IP addresses.

A) Incorrect. VPC Service Controls are for securing data within GCP, not for controlling network traffic to external IPs.
B) Correct. Egress firewall rules effectively restrict outbound traffic to specific external IP addresses.

C) Incorrect. VPN tunnels are not necessary for restricting traffic to specific external IPs.
D) Incorrect. Private Google Access is for accessing Google services, not for restricting traffic to external IPs.
E) Incorrect. Cloud NAT is used for outbound traffic management, not for specific IP restrictions.

QUESTION 48

Answer – A) Set up a multi-regional Cloud Spanner instance for high availability.

A) Correct. Multi-regional instances of Cloud Spanner provide built-in high availability and are ideal for disaster recovery.
B) Incorrect. Regular exports to Cloud Storage may not meet stringent downtime and data loss requirements.
C) Incorrect. Read replicas are for scaling reads, not for disaster recovery purposes.
D) Incorrect. Continuous replication using Cloud Dataflow adds complexity and is not the optimal solution for Spanner.
E) Incorrect. Custom backup scripts are less reliable and efficient compared to using Spanner's built-in capabilities.

QUESTION 49

Answer – B) Configure each application instance with Premium Network Tier.

A) Incorrect. VPN may not offer the highest throughput necessary for heavy data transfers.
B) Correct. Premium Network Tier is optimized for high-throughput and low-latency network performance, ideal for BigQuery data transfers.
C) Incorrect. Cloud Interconnect is typically for on-premises to GCP connections.
D) Incorrect. Private Google Access is for accessing Google services but does not inherently improve throughput or reduce latency.
E) Incorrect. VPC Peering is not used for accessing BigQuery.

QUESTION 50

Answer – B) Configure Private Google Access on the subnetworks hosting the applications.

A) Incorrect. VPN may not provide the lowest latency for database connections.
B) Correct. Private Google Access allows secure and efficient connectivity to Cloud SQL from within GCP without traversing the public internet, optimizing for performance.
C) Incorrect. Dedicated Interconnect is typically for on-premises to GCP connections.
D) Incorrect. Premium Network Tier enhances general network performance but is not specific to Cloud SQL connectivity.
E) Incorrect. VPC Peering is not applicable for Cloud SQL.

PRACTICE TEST 7 - QUESTIONS ONLY

QUESTION 1

You are managing a Google Cloud project with multiple VPCs in different regions. There is a need for VPCs to communicate securely across regions. What should you implement to achieve this while ensuring security and isolation between VPCs?

A) Use VPC Network Peering between all VPCs
B) Deploy a Shared VPC across regions
C) Implement VPC VPN tunnels between VPCs
D) Create a common firewall rule for all VPCs
E) Connect all VPCs to the same VPC Network

QUESTION 2

Your organization is planning to set up a hybrid cloud architecture, with some applications running in Google Cloud and others on-premises. Security and data privacy are top priorities. What GCP service should you use to establish a secure and private connection between your on-premises data center and Google Cloud while ensuring minimal latency?

A) Google Cloud VPN
B) Google Cloud Dedicated Interconnect
C) Google Cloud Interconnect
D) Google Cloud VPC Peering
E) Google Cloud CDN

QUESTION 3

You are responsible for setting up network connectivity between your on-premises data center and Google Cloud. Your organization requires a dedicated, high-speed connection with low latency. What Google Cloud service should you consider to meet these requirements while ensuring private and secure communication?

A) Google Cloud VPN with a shared VPN gateway.
B) Google Cloud Dedicated Interconnect with a private VLAN.
C) Google Cloud Direct Peering with a public peering connection.
D) Google Cloud VPC Network Peering.
E) Google Cloud Global Load Balancing.

QUESTION 4

Your organization is planning to deploy a new application on Google Cloud and wants to ensure secure and controlled communication between microservices. What should you implement to achieve this while maintaining isolation between microservices and controlling traffic flow?

A) Google Cloud Endpoints for API management.

B) Google Cloud Network Peering between microservices.
C) Google Cloud VPC Service Controls.
D) Google Cloud Shared VPC for microservices.
E) Google Cloud Identity-Aware Proxy (IAP).

QUESTION 5

Your organization has a hybrid architecture with on-premises data centers and Google Cloud. You need to establish secure, high-speed connectivity between them. What approach should you prioritize?

A) Set up Direct Peering between on-premises data centers and Google Cloud.
B) Deploy Cloud VPNs with IPsec encryption for data transfer.
C) Utilize Google Cloud Dedicated Interconnect for dedicated, high-speed connectivity.
D) Implement a hybrid DNS solution to route traffic between on-premises and Google Cloud resources.
E) Establish point-to-point microwave links for direct connectivity.

QUESTION 6

Your organization is experiencing intermittent network connectivity problems between on-premises data centers and Google Cloud. You need to troubleshoot and identify the root cause. What approach should you prioritize?

A) Set up Google Cloud Network Diagnostics for real-time network performance monitoring.
B) Implement Google Cloud's Network Intelligence Center to analyze connectivity issues.
C) Enable VPC Flow Logs for the affected VPC and review logs for network anomalies.
D) Deploy Google Cloud's Network Topology insights to visualize network paths.
E) Use Google Cloud Monitoring to create custom dashboards for network performance analysis.

QUESTION 7

In setting up a secure and efficient connection between two GCP projects, you need to configure VPC Peering. Project A's network is 192.168.0.0/16, and Project B's is 10.156.0.0/16. What is the most effective way to configure the peering?

A) Establish bi-directional peering between both VPCs.
B) Set up uni-directional peering from Project A to B.
C) Implement Shared VPC for both projects.
D) Use Cloud VPN instead of VPC Peering for enhanced security.
E) Configure peering with dynamic routing using BGP.

QUESTION 8

Your company's application requires high availability and fault tolerance. You want to deploy instances across multiple Google Cloud regions to achieve this. Which Google Cloud service should you use to efficiently manage and load balance traffic across instances in different regions while minimizing latency?

A) Google Cloud CDN (Content Delivery Network)
B) Google Cloud Armor

C) Google Cloud Load Balancing
D) Google Cloud Interconnect
E) Google Cloud DNS (Domain Name System)

QUESTION 9

Your organization is setting up a disaster recovery (DR) solution in Google Cloud. You need to ensure that your virtual machine (VM) instances are running in a different region from your primary setup for high availability in case of a regional failure. Which configuration should you choose for your DR setup?

A) Use Google Cloud Storage to regularly back up your VM instances and restore them in another region if needed.
B) Set up a Cloud VPN between regions to replicate VM instances in real-time.
C) Deploy your VM instances in a separate region from the primary setup and use Cloud Load Balancing to distribute traffic between regions.
D) Create a snapshot of your VM instances and use Compute Engine's automatic snapshot scheduling to maintain a copy in a different region.
E) Use Google Kubernetes Engine (GKE) to containerize your applications, making them region-independent for disaster recovery purposes.

QUESTION 10

Your organization operates a large-scale, globally distributed web application on Google Cloud. To ensure high availability and low-latency access for users worldwide, you need to distribute application traffic across multiple regions and data centers. What Google Cloud load balancing solution should you consider for this complex scenario, and what key feature sets it apart?

A) Google Cloud Internal TCP/UDP Load Balancer with global backend services.
B) Google Cloud External HTTP(S) Load Balancer with global forwarding rules.
C) Google Cloud Network Load Balancer with cross-region distribution.
D) Google Cloud Regional HTTP(S) Load Balancer with multi-region failover.
E) Google Cloud Traffic Director with custom traffic routing policies.

QUESTION 11

Your organization is planning to set up a disaster recovery solution for your Google Cloud resources. You want to ensure minimal data loss and rapid failover in the event of a disaster. What Google Cloud service or feature should you consider for this complex disaster recovery architecture, and what benefits does it offer?

A) Google Cloud Datastore for NoSQL data storage and recovery capabilities.
B) Google Cloud Memorystore for Redis for in-memory data replication.
C) Google Cloud Storage for data backup and recovery.
D) Google Cloud Backup for automated backup and recovery of VM instances.
E) Google Cloud Site Recovery for disaster recovery orchestration and rapid failover.

QUESTION 12

In a GCP setup with multiple VPCs across different projects, you need to ensure private connectivity and centralized network management. The VPCs have overlapping IP ranges. What is the best approach to accomplish this?

A) Use VPC Network Peering with exported and imported custom routes.
B) Implement Shared VPC across all projects.
C) Configure Cloud VPN with dynamic routing between VPCs.
D) Set up a Dedicated Interconnect for each VPC.
E) Employ a hub-and-spoke model using Cloud Routers.

QUESTION 13

You are designing a GCP network for a highly secure application that requires strict control over incoming and outgoing traffic. Which GCP service should you choose to manage and control the firewall rules effectively?

A) Google Cloud Armor
B) Google Cloud Firewall
C) Google Cloud NAT
D) Google Cloud Load Balancer
E) Google Cloud VPN

QUESTION 14

In a GCP environment, you need to configure firewall rules for a set of VMs used by the development team. The goal is to enable secure access to these VMs while restricting unnecessary traffic. What firewall settings should you apply?

A) Allow ingress on ports 22 (SSH) and 443 (HTTPS), and deny all other ingress.
B) Create a rule to deny all ingress and egress traffic, except for port 80 (HTTP).
C) Allow ingress on port 22 (SSH) for specific IP ranges only.
D) Set up a firewall rule to allow all egress traffic and deny all ingress traffic.
E) Implement firewall rules to allow ingress on port 3389 (RDP) and deny all egress.

QUESTION 15

You are responsible for securing a Google Cloud project that processes sensitive customer data. The project involves multiple virtual machines in a VPC. To enhance security, you want to control the traffic flow between instances within the same VPC while preventing unauthorized communication. What GCP networking feature should you recommend?

A) Google Cloud Firewall Rules
B) Google Cloud VPN with dedicated tunnels
C) Google Cloud VPC Service Controls
D) Google Cloud Network Peering
E) Google Cloud Shared VPC

QUESTION 16

Your organization is planning to expand its Google Cloud infrastructure globally to accommodate increased demand. You want to ensure low-latency access for users across the world. What GCP networking strategy should you recommend for this expansion?

A) Establish a single global VPC to centralize resources.
B) Deploy multiple regional VPCs in key geographical locations.
C) Utilize Google Cloud Load Balancers for global traffic distribution.
D) Implement Google Cloud VPN for secure connections.
E) Use Google Cloud CDN for content delivery.

QUESTION 17

As the Organization Admin for a multinational corporation, an engineer in your team is tasked with deploying several main storage buckets across different departments and enabling uniform access to service accounts. You need to configure the Identity and Access Management (IAM) settings for the engineer so they can accomplish this with minimal effort. What action should you take?

A) Provide the engineer with the Storage Admin IAM role and Project IAM Admin role at the organization level.
B) Assign the engineer the Storage Admin IAM role at the department level.
C) Grant the engineer both the Storage Admin IAM role and Project IAM Admin role at the department level.
D) Assign the engineer the Storage Admin IAM role at the organization level.
E) Create a custom IAM role for the engineer with specific permissions.

QUESTION 18

In a GCP environment with a Shared VPC setup, you are tasked with configuring network access so that specific service projects can communicate with a set of restricted APIs deployed in another project. What approach should you take to configure this securely and efficiently?

A) Use VPC Service Controls to create a perimeter around the target APIs and allow access from the specified service projects.
B) Set up VPC Peering between each service project's VPC and the API project's VPC.
C) Implement firewall rules in the Shared VPC to allow traffic to the API project's network.
D) Configure Private Google Access in the service projects for access to the APIs.
E) Create custom routes in the Shared VPC to direct traffic to the API project's network.

QUESTION 19

You're designing a network architecture in Google Cloud for your e-commerce application. The application has a global user base, and you want to ensure low-latency access for all users. Which Google Cloud networking service or feature should you leverage to achieve this goal?

A) Cloud Load Balancing with global backend services.
B) Regional VPC peering.
C) VPN tunnels with multi-region redundancy.
D) Cloud CDN with regional caches.

E) Cloud NAT for outbound traffic optimization.

QUESTION 20

As the Organization Admin for a multinational corporation, an engineer in your team is tasked with deploying several main storage buckets across different departments and enabling uniform access to service accounts. You need to configure the Identity and Access Management (IAM) settings for the engineer so they can accomplish this with minimal effort. What action should you take?

A) Provide the engineer with the Storage Admin IAM role and Project IAM Admin role at the organization level.
B) Assign the engineer the Storage Admin IAM role at the department level.
C) Grant the engineer both the Storage Admin IAM role and Project IAM Admin role at the department level.
D) Assign the engineer the Storage Admin IAM role at the organization level.
E) Create a custom IAM role with the required permissions and assign it to the engineer.

QUESTION 21

You set up a new network infrastructure for your analytics department. You plan to ensure that the system engineers can manage virtual machines within this network securely. How would you adjust your firewall configurations to permit this kind of access?

A) Create two firewall rules: one to deny ingress to all protocols with priority 0, and another to permit ingress on port 22 with priority 1000.
B) Create a single firewall rule to allow port 22 with priority 1000.
C) Create two firewall rules: one to block all traffic with priority 65536, and another to allow port 3389 with priority 1000.
D) Establish a single firewall rule to permit ingress on port 3389 with a priority setting of 1000.
E) Use a Network Service Tier to manage access.

QUESTION 22

You set up a new network infrastructure for your analytics department. You plan to ensure that the system engineers can manage virtual machines within this network securely. How would you adjust your firewall configurations to permit this kind of access?

A) Create two firewall rules: one to deny ingress to all protocols with priority 0, and another to permit ingress on port 22 with priority 1000.
B) Create a single firewall rule to allow port 22 with priority 1000.
C) Create two firewall rules: one to block all traffic with priority 65536, and another to allow port 3389 with priority 1000.
D) Establish a single firewall rule to permit ingress on port 3389 with a priority setting of 1000.
E) Use Google Cloud Identity-Aware Proxy (IAP) instead of firewall rules for secure access.

QUESTION 23

A company is experiencing inconsistent performance of its Google Cloud Load Balancer. While some requests are served quickly, others experience significant delays. The company uses auto-scaling with instance groups behind the load balancer. What could be a potential cause of this performance variation?

A) Misconfigured health checks for instances
B) Load balancer backend service scaling settings
C) Inadequate network bandwidth for instances
D) Google Cloud's global load balancer design
E) IP address conflicts within the instance groups

QUESTION 24

Your organization is deploying a multi-tier application in Google Cloud. The application consists of web servers, application servers, and a database tier. You want to ensure that each tier is isolated from the others for security and scalability. Which Google Cloud service or feature should you utilize to achieve this isolation effectively?

A) Create separate Google Cloud Projects for each application tier.
B) Implement VPC Service Controls for strict access control.
C) Use Google Cloud IAM Roles to manage access to each tier.
D) Configure a single VPC network with firewall rules for isolation.
E) Utilize Google Cloud Endpoints for API management.

QUESTION 25

Your organization is designing a highly available and globally distributed application on Google Cloud. What two Google Cloud services should you consider for distributing traffic to different regions while ensuring low-latency access for users worldwide?

A) Use Google Cloud VPN for secure global connectivity.
B) Deploy Google Cloud Load Balancers for regional traffic routing.
C) Utilize Google Cloud CDN for content caching.
D) Set up Google Cloud NAT for outbound traffic management.
E) Implement Google Cloud Interconnect for dedicated network connections.

QUESTION 26

For a GCP-hosted application requiring high availability and disaster recovery, you plan to replicate data between regions. The application is critical and uses Cloud SQL and Compute Engine instances. How should you set up your environment to ensure data replication and application availability across regions?

A) Use Regional Persistent Disks for Compute Engine instances and configure Cloud SQL for cross-region replication.
B) Implement a multi-regional GKE cluster and use Cloud Spanner for database needs.
C) Set up Compute Engine instances with Local SSDs and replicate data using Cloud Data Transfer.
D) Configure regional Network Load Balancers and use Cloud Bigtable for data storage.
E) Deploy instances in one region and use Cloud Storage Multi-Regional buckets for data.

QUESTION 27

Your organization has on-premises data centers in Europe and Asia with Dedicated Interconnects to Google Cloud regions. To ensure redundancy and failover capabilities, what networking strategy should you implement for your Dedicated Interconnects?

A) Establish a single Dedicated Interconnect in the primary region with no redundancy.
B) Set up two Dedicated Interconnects in separate regions and configure them for failover.
C) Utilize VPN connections for redundancy instead of Dedicated Interconnects.
D) Deploy Cloud Interconnect for redundancy and scalability.
E) None of the above.

QUESTION 28

You are configuring a secure network architecture for a set of sensitive applications in GCP. These applications should only be accessible from your corporate office network. Which approach ensures that only traffic from your corporate network can access these applications?

A) Use VPC firewall rules to allow traffic only from your corporate network's IP ranges.
B) Set up Cloud VPN with your corporate network and route all application traffic through it.
C) Implement Cloud Armor with rules to permit traffic exclusively from your corporate network.
D) Configure Private Google Access for the applications' subnetworks and restrict access to corporate IPs.
E) Use VPC Service Controls to create a service perimeter around the applications.

QUESTION 29

Your enterprise oversees a Google Cloud project with multiple App Engine applications. You need to implement robust API access controls for Memorystore instances and Spanner databases, permitting traffic only from your organization's head office networks. What approach should you recommend?

A) Develop an access context policy for each individual App Engine application, specifying head office network IP ranges, and apply these policies to Memorystore and Spanner.
B) Establish a VPC Service Controls perimeter for your project, including an access context policy that encompasses your organization's head office network IP ranges.
C) Create separate VPC Service Controls perimeters for each App Engine application, each with access context policies defining your organization's head office network IP ranges.
D) Define a series of firewall rules to block API access to Memorystore and Spanner from networks not recognized as part of your head office.
E) None of the above.

QUESTION 30

You're setting up a network architecture in GCP for an application that requires secure, private connectivity to external SaaS providers. The connectivity should bypass the public internet for security reasons. Which configuration ensures secure and private connectivity to these external services?

A) Use Cloud Interconnect to establish direct physical connections to the SaaS providers.
B) Implement Cloud VPN to create encrypted tunnels to the SaaS providers.
C) Configure Private Google Access for secure access to external SaaS services.
D) Set up VPC Network Peering with each SaaS provider for private connectivity.

E) Utilize Cloud Endpoints to securely connect to the external SaaS services.

QUESTION 31

In a GCP environment, you are setting up a network for an application that requires strict segregation of administrative and user traffic. Administrative traffic should be highly restricted and monitored. What combination of network configurations and monitoring tools should you use?

A) Set up separate subnets for administrative and user traffic with VPC firewall rules for segregation and Stackdriver for monitoring.
B) Use Network Tags to differentiate traffic and apply corresponding firewall rules, with Cloud Monitoring for traffic analysis.
C) Implement Private Google Access for administrative traffic and Internet NEG for user traffic, with Cloud Logging for monitoring.
D) Configure separate VPCs for each traffic type and use VPC Peering with Cloud Trace for monitoring.
E) Establish Cloud VPN tunnels for administrative traffic and Cloud Load Balancing for user traffic, with Cloud Monitoring.

QUESTION 32

Your team is developing a new service and needs to connect Compute Engine instances, which don't have public IP addresses, to Cloud Spanner. What two actions should you execute to accomplish this?

A) Enable the Cloud Memorystore API in your Google Cloud project.
B) Establish a private connection with the Cloud Spanner service producer.
C) Turn on Private Google Access for your subnetwork.
D) Configure a custom static route to direct the traffic to the Cloud Spanner service endpoint.
E) Enable the Service Networking API in your Google Cloud project.

QUESTION 33

Your enterprise manages a single Google Cloud project with a multitude of App Engine applications. You are tasked with safeguarding API access to your Memorystore instances and Spanner databases to ensure that only API traffic from your organization's head office networks is permitted. How should you proceed?

A) Establish an access context policy that includes your App Engine applications and head office network IP ranges, and then implement the policy for Memorystore and Spanner.
B) Create a VPC Service Controls perimeter for your project with an access context policy that includes your organization's head office network IP ranges.
C) Generate a VPC Service Controls perimeter for each App Engine application with an access context policy that includes your organization's head office network IP ranges.
D) Configure a firewall rule to reject API access to Memorystore and Spanner from all networks not recognized as part of your head office.
E) None of the above.

QUESTION 34

Your organization is managing a critical financial application that requires strong encryption for data in transit and strict access control. However, SSL certificate management is not within your control. Which combination of Google Cloud networking services and features should you implement to meet these complex security requirements effectively?

A) VPN Gateway with Firewall Rules
B) VPC Service Controls with Cloud Armor
C) Private Google Access with VPC Peering
D) Transit Gateway with Identity-Aware Proxy
E) Dedicated Interconnect with Network Peering

QUESTION 35

Your organization is managing a complex multi-cloud environment with workloads distributed across Google Cloud, AWS, and Azure. You need a solution for efficient traffic routing and secure communication between the clouds. What complex networking strategy should you employ to achieve this goal effectively?

A) Set up custom routes with more precision than the default network routes, specifying cross-cloud connections for traffic routing, and use network tags for secure communication.
B) Migrate all workloads to a single cloud provider to simplify network management and enhance security.
C) Delete all default network routes and establish distinct custom routes for cross-cloud connections, using network tags for traffic differentiation and secure communication.
D) Create more specific custom routes than the default network routes, designating cross-cloud connections for routing, and assign network tags for secure communication and precise traffic handling.
E) Implement a multi-cloud network orchestrator service to manage traffic routing and secure communication efficiently across Google Cloud, AWS, and Azure.

QUESTION 36

For a GCP project involving a mix of Compute Engine instances and serverless functions, you need to configure network settings to optimize for cost, performance, and security. The serverless functions need to access a Cloud SQL database securely. What is the best network setup for this scenario?

A) Enable Private Google Access on the subnetworks hosting the Compute Engine instances and use VPC Connector for serverless functions.
B) Configure VPC Peering between the Compute Engine instances and serverless function networks.
C) Set up Cloud VPN for secure communication from serverless functions to the Cloud SQL database.
D) Use Internal TCP/UDP Load Balancer for communication between Compute Engine and serverless functions.
E) Implement Shared VPC across Compute Engine and serverless functions for unified network management.

QUESTION 37

You need to ensure secure, private communication between your on-premises data center and Google Cloud. Additionally, you require dynamic routing for optimal traffic distribution. Which Google Cloud networking solution should you implement to meet both requirements?

A) Google Cloud VPN
B) VPC peering with Cloud Router
C) Cloud Interconnect with Google Cloud Router
D) Google Cloud DNS with Cloud CDN
E) Regional managed instance groups with Google Cloud Load Balancing

QUESTION 38

You need to establish a highly available and secure connection between your on-premises data center and Google Cloud. Additionally, you want to ensure low-latency access to Google Cloud services. Which Google Cloud networking solution should you implement to achieve these objectives, considering both high availability and low latency?

A) Google Cloud VPN with VPC peering
B) Cloud Interconnect with Google Cloud Router
C) VPC peering with Cloud VPN
D) Google Cloud Armor with Cloud CDN
E) Google Cloud DNS with Cloud Identity-Aware Proxy (IAP)

QUESTION 39

Your organization is planning to deploy a large-scale microservices architecture on Google Cloud. Each microservice needs its own dedicated storage with strict access control. Which Google Cloud storage service should you choose to meet these requirements effectively while ensuring data isolation and fine-grained access control?

A) Google Cloud Storage
B) Google Cloud Bigtable
C) Google Cloud Firestore
D) Google Cloud SQL
E) Google Cloud Spanner

QUESTION 40

Your organization is planning to implement a disaster recovery solution for your critical applications on Google Cloud. You need to ensure data replication and failover capabilities between regions. Which combination of Google Cloud services or features should you incorporate into your disaster recovery strategy to achieve these objectives effectively?

A) Google Cloud VPN and Google Cloud Bigtable
B) Google Cloud CDN and Google Cloud Compute Engine Autoscaler
C) Google Cloud Spanner and Google Cloud Interconnect
D) Google Cloud Storage and Google Cloud DNS
E) Google Cloud Load Balancing and Google Cloud VPC Peering

QUESTION 41

In a multi-regional GCP deployment, you have a requirement to route user traffic to the nearest regional endpoint to minimize latency. The application is structured to handle stateless requests at each endpoint. What is the most suitable load balancing configuration for this scenario?

A) Use a Global HTTP(S) Load Balancer with multi-regional backend services.
B) Configure regional Network Load Balancers in each user region.
C) Implement regional Internal Load Balancers for each application endpoint.
D) Set up a TCP/SSL Proxy Load Balancer with instance groups in each region.
E) Establish regional HTTP(S) Load Balancers connected through VPC Peering.

QUESTION 42

You are transitioning your healthcare organization's VMs to use Google Cloud DNS. You need to transfer your existing BIND zone file to the new service. What is the appropriate command to execute this action?

A) gcloud dns record-sets import ZONE_FILE --zone-file-format --zone MANAGED_ZONE
B) gcloud dns record-sets import ZONE_FILE --replace-origin-ns --zone MANAGED_ZONE
C) gcloud dns record-sets import ZONE_FILE --zone MANAGED_ZONE
D) gcloud dns record-sets import ZONE_FILE --delete-all-existing --zone MANAGED_ZONE.

QUESTION 43

You want to enable your tailored SSH key for access on every virtual machine within your healthcare data analysis project as simply as possible. How do you achieve this?

A) Create a specialized Google Compute Engine snapshot that includes your public SSH key.
B) Upload your public SSH key to the project-wide metadata.
C) Upload your public SSH key individually to each virtual machine's metadata.
D) Utilize the gcloud compute ssh command to propagate your public SSH key across each virtual machine.
E) Create a custom image with your public SSH key and use it for all virtual machines in the project.

QUESTION 44

Your organization operates a high-traffic online video streaming service. Your servers are configured with private IP addresses, and users connect through a regional load balancer. To enhance security, you've enlisted a DDoS protection service and need to limit your backend servers to accept connections solely from this DDoS mitigation provider. How should you proceed?

A) Create a VPC Service Controls Perimeter that blocks all traffic except for the DDoS protection service.
B) Create a Cloud Armor Security Policy that blocks all traffic except for the DDoS protection service.
C) Create a VPC Firewall rule that blocks all traffic except for the DDoS protection service.
D) Implement iptables firewall rules on your servers that block all traffic except for the DDoS protection service.
E) Configure the backend servers to accept traffic only from the DDoS mitigation provider's IP addresses using a custom script.

QUESTION 45

For a large-scale data analysis project in GCP, you need to configure network access to allow secure, private connectivity between Compute Engine instances and BigQuery. The setup should minimize public internet exposure and maintain high data transfer performance. Which network configuration meets these criteria?

A) Use VPC Service Controls for secure data access and Cloud VPN for private connectivity to BigQuery.
B) Configure Private Google Access on subnetworks hosting Compute Engine instances for direct access to BigQuery.
C) Implement Cloud Interconnect for a dedicated, private connection to BigQuery.
D) Set up Internal TCP/UDP Load Balancers to route traffic from Compute Engine to BigQuery.
E) Establish a dedicated VPC for Compute Engine instances with custom routes for optimized access to BigQuery.

QUESTION 46

Your organization needs to maintain a high level of security for data stored in Google Cloud Storage. You want to implement encryption at rest and in transit for the data. What are the appropriate steps to achieve this?

A) Enable Google-managed keys for data encryption at rest and use HTTPS for data in transit.
B) Use a customer-managed encryption key (CMEK) for data encryption at rest and configure SSL/TLS for data in transit.
C) Rely on Google Cloud's default encryption settings for both data at rest and in transit.
D) Enable Cloud Identity-Aware Proxy (IAP) for data encryption at rest and use IPsec for data in transit.
E) Implement VPC Service Controls to secure data at rest and use Cloud CDN for data in transit.

QUESTION 47

In a GCP deployment for a real-time gaming platform, you need to configure a network that supports rapid scaling and global distribution of game servers. The servers require instantaneous communication with a central database and global players with minimal latency. What is the most suitable network and server configuration for this gaming platform?

A) Configure Global HTTP(S) Load Balancer for traffic distribution and use Cloud Spanner for the central database.
B) Use regional Network Load Balancers for each game server cluster and a multi-regional Cloud SQL database.
C) Implement instance groups in each region with an Internal TCP/UDP Load Balancer and use Cloud Bigtable for the database.
D) Set up a global network of Compute Engine instances with Premium Network Tier and Cloud Firestore for the database.
E) Establish Cloud Run instances for game servers in each region and Cloud Spanner for low-latency database access.

QUESTION 48

You are configuring a network in GCP for a distributed database system that requires synchronized state across multiple Compute Engine instances. The instances are deployed globally and need to maintain continuous, low-latency communication. What network configuration best supports these requirements?

A) Implement Global VPC with optimized routing for low-latency communication.
B) Use Cloud VPN to establish dedicated tunnels between instances for state synchronization.
C) Set up Dedicated Interconnect for low-latency, high-throughput connections between instances.
D) Configure Regional Internal Load Balancers in each deployment region for state synchronization.
E) Enable Premium Network Tier on all Compute Engine instances for global low-latency communication.

QUESTION 49

For a global e-commerce platform on GCP, which configuration is best suited to handle varying traffic loads, optimize content delivery, and secure against web attacks while efficiently distributing traffic to data centers worldwide?

A) Global HTTP(S) Load Balancer with Cloud Armor and Cloud CDN.
B) Regional Network Load Balancers with Cloud IDS for traffic analysis and DDoS mitigation.
C) TCP/SSL Proxy Load Balancers in each region with VPC Service Controls.
D) Internal Load Balancers for each region and Cloud VPN for global traffic management.
E) Cloud Run instances globally with Cloud Endpoints for security and traffic distribution.

QUESTION 50

For a global e-commerce platform on GCP, which network setup is most appropriate to manage traffic surges, optimize content delivery, and secure against web attacks, while efficiently distributing traffic to data centers globally?

A) Global HTTP(S) Load Balancer with Cloud Armor and Cloud CDN.
B) Regional Network Load Balancers with Cloud IDS for traffic analysis and DDoS protection.
C) TCP/SSL Proxy Load Balancers in each region with VPC Service Controls for security.
D) Internal Load Balancers in each region and Cloud VPN for global traffic management.
E) Cloud Run instances globally with Cloud Endpoints for security and traffic distribution.

PRACTICE TEST 7 - ANSWERS ONLY

QUESTION 1

Answer – B) Deploy a Shared VPC across regions

Option B - Deploying a Shared VPC across regions allows secure communication between VPCs while maintaining isolation.
 Option A - VPC Network Peering may not provide sufficient isolation between regions.
 Option C - VPC VPN tunnels are for connecting to on-premises networks, not between VPCs in different regions.
 Option D - A common firewall rule may not ensure secure communication between VPCs.
 Option E - Connecting all VPCs to the same VPC Network may lead to complexity and reduced isolation.

QUESTION 2

Answer – B) Google Cloud Dedicated Interconnect

Option B - Using Google Cloud Dedicated Interconnect provides a secure and private connection between on-premises data centers and Google Cloud with minimal latency.
 Option A - Google Cloud VPN may introduce latency and is not as dedicated as Interconnect.
 Option C - Google Cloud Interconnect is related to connectivity but may not provide the same level of privacy as Dedicated Interconnect.
 Option D - VPC Peering is for connecting VPCs, not on-premises data centers.
 Option E - CDN is for content delivery and not suitable for direct data center connectivity.

QUESTION 3

Answer – B) Google Cloud Dedicated Interconnect with a private VLAN.

Option B - Using Google Cloud Dedicated Interconnect with a private VLAN provides dedicated, high-speed, and low-latency connectivity between on-premises data centers and Google Cloud while ensuring private and secure communication.
 Option A - VPNs may not provide the same level of performance and privacy as Dedicated Interconnect.
 Option C - Direct Peering is for external connectivity, not private communication with on-premises data centers.
 Option D - VPC Network Peering is for VPCs, not on-premises data centers.
 Option E - Global Load Balancing is unrelated to dedicated connectivity.

QUESTION 4

Answer – D) Google Cloud Shared VPC for microservices.

Option D - Implementing Google Cloud Shared VPC for microservices allows secure and controlled communication while maintaining isolation and control over traffic flow.
 Option A - Google Cloud Endpoints is for API management, not microservices communication.
 Option B - Network Peering may not provide sufficient isolation.

Option C - VPC Service Controls are more about data access controls.
Option E - Identity-Aware Proxy (IAP) is primarily for securing access to applications, not microservices communication.

QUESTION 5

Answer - C) Utilize Google Cloud Dedicated Interconnect for dedicated, high-speed connectivity.

Option C provides the most appropriate solution for secure, high-speed connectivity between on-premises data centers and Google Cloud, aligning with the organization's needs.
Option A with Direct Peering may not offer the same level of performance.
Option B, while secure, may not guarantee the required high-speed connectivity.
Option D addresses DNS but doesn't provide the connectivity itself.
Option E introduces complexity and may not be as reliable as Dedicated Interconnect.

QUESTION 6

Answer - B) Implement Google Cloud's Network Intelligence Center to analyze connectivity issues.
Answer - E) Use Google Cloud Monitoring to create custom dashboards for network performance analysis.

Options B and E are the appropriate approaches for troubleshooting intermittent network connectivity problems between on-premises data centers and Google Cloud.
Option B leverages Google Cloud's Network Intelligence Center to analyze connectivity issues, while Option E focuses on creating custom dashboards for network performance analysis.
Option A mentions Network Diagnostics, which may not address the specific intermittent issues.
Option C suggests VPC Flow Logs, which may provide log data but may not pinpoint the root cause of intermittent problems.
Option D discusses Network Topology insights, which may not directly address connectivity problems.

QUESTION 7

Answer – A) Establish bi-directional peering between both VPCs.

A) Correct. Ensures seamless connectivity between both networks.
B) Incorrect. Uni-directional peering won't allow two-way communication.
C) Incorrect. Shared VPC is not suitable for separate projects.
D) Incorrect. Cloud VPN is not as efficient as VPC Peering for this purpose.
E) Incorrect. VPC Peering does not utilize BGP.

QUESTION 8

Answer - C) Google Cloud Load Balancing

Option C, Google Cloud Load Balancing, is the correct choice for efficiently managing and load balancing traffic across instances in different regions while minimizing latency. It offers global load balancing and is designed for high availability and fault tolerance.
Option A, Google Cloud CDN, primarily focuses on content delivery and caching to reduce latency but doesn't handle instance load balancing across regions.

Option B, Google Cloud Armor, is a web application firewall and security service, not a load balancer for regional instances.
Option D, Google Cloud Interconnect, provides connectivity but doesn't handle traffic load balancing.
Option E, Google Cloud DNS, is a domain name system service for resolving domain names to IP addresses, not for traffic load balancing.

QUESTION 9

Answer - C) Deploy your VM instances in a separate region from the primary setup and use Cloud Load Balancing to distribute traffic between regions.
Answer - D) Create a snapshot of your VM instances and use Compute Engine's automatic snapshot scheduling to maintain a copy in a different region.

Option C is the recommended approach for setting up a disaster recovery solution in a different region with high availability through Cloud Load Balancing.
Option D provides additional backup capabilities. Options A, B, and E are not aligned with the best practices for disaster recovery in different regions.

QUESTION 10

Answer - B) Google Cloud External HTTP(S) Load Balancer with global forwarding rules.

Option A is for internal traffic and doesn't address global user access.
Option C is for network-level load balancing and lacks Layer 7 capabilities.
Option D provides regional load balancing but not global distribution.
Option E is for service mesh traffic management, not external traffic distribution.
Option B is the correct choice as it offers global distribution of external HTTP(S) traffic with low-latency access and high availability, setting it apart from other options.

QUESTION 11

Answer - E) Google Cloud Site Recovery for disaster recovery orchestration and rapid failover.

Option A focuses on data storage but may not provide disaster recovery orchestration.
Option B is for in-memory data replication and may not cover disaster recovery architecture.
Option C is for data backup but may not offer rapid failover capabilities.
Option D involves automated backup but may not address rapid failover in the event of a disaster.
Option E is the correct choice as Google Cloud Site Recovery provides disaster recovery orchestration and enables rapid failover, ensuring minimal data loss and quick recovery in complex disaster scenarios.

QUESTION 12

Answer – E) Employ a hub-and-spoke model using Cloud Routers.

A) Incorrect. VPC Peering does not support overlapping IP ranges.
B) Incorrect. Shared VPC does not allow overlapping IP ranges.
C) Incorrect. Cloud VPN doesn't solve the overlapping IP issue.
D) Incorrect. Dedicated Interconnect does not address overlapping IPs.
E) Correct. A hub-and-spoke model can manage overlapping IPs and centralize network management.

QUESTION 13

Answer - B) Google Cloud Firewall

B) Google Cloud Firewall - Google Cloud Firewall allows you to define and manage firewall rules for controlling incoming and outgoing traffic effectively.
 A) Google Cloud Armor - Google Cloud Armor is used for security policies, not firewall rule management.
 C) Google Cloud NAT - Google Cloud NAT is for network address translation and does not focus on firewall rule management.
 D) Google Cloud Load Balancer - Load Balancer distributes traffic and does not directly manage firewall rules.
 E) Google Cloud VPN - Google Cloud VPN provides secure access but is not primarily designed for firewall rule management.

QUESTION 14

Answer – C) Allow ingress on port 22 (SSH) for specific IP ranges only.

A) Incorrect. Allowing HTTPS may not be necessary for VM management.
B) Incorrect. Denying all egress restricts legitimate outbound traffic.
C) Correct. Restricting SSH access to specific IPs enhances security.
D) Incorrect. Denying all ingress could block legitimate access.
E) Incorrect. Allowing only RDP and denying all egress is restrictive and not typically required for development VMs.

QUESTION 15

Answer - A) Google Cloud Firewall Rules

A) Google Cloud Firewall Rules - Firewall rules allow you to control traffic within the same VPC and enhance security by preventing unauthorized communication between instances.
 B) Google Cloud VPN with dedicated tunnels - VPNs focus on secure access, not necessarily on traffic control within the same VPC.
 C) Google Cloud VPC Service Controls - VPC Service Controls are used for isolation and access controls but may not directly address traffic control within a VPC.
 D) Google Cloud Network Peering - Network Peering is for communication between different VPCs, not necessarily for controlling traffic within the same VPC.
 E) Google Cloud Shared VPC - Shared VPC allows shared resources but does not specifically address traffic control within a VPC.

QUESTION 16

Answer - B) Deploy multiple regional VPCs in key geographical locations.

B) Deploy multiple regional VPCs in key geographical locations - Deploying regional VPCs allows you to distribute resources closer to users, ensuring low-latency access as you expand globally.
 A) Establishing a single global VPC may introduce latency for users in distant regions.
 C) Utilizing Google Cloud Load Balancers distributes traffic but does not necessarily address resource placement.
 D) Implementing Google Cloud VPN for secure connections is not directly related to optimizing low-

latency access.

E) Using Google Cloud CDN for content delivery focuses on caching content, not resource placement for low-latency access.

QUESTION 17

Answer - A) Provide the engineer with the Storage Admin IAM role and Project IAM Admin role at the organization level.

A) Provide the engineer with the Storage Admin IAM role and Project IAM Admin role at the organization level - This allows for easy management of storage buckets and service accounts across different departments within the organization.

B) Assigning the engineer the Storage Admin IAM role at the department level may not provide sufficient permissions for managing resources across departments.

C) Granting both roles at the department level can lead to unnecessary complexity and may not align with minimal effort.

D) Assigning the Storage Admin role at the organization level without Project IAM Admin may limit the engineer's capabilities.

E) Creating a custom IAM role can be more complex and may not align with minimal effort.

QUESTION 18

Answer – A) Use VPC Service Controls to create a perimeter around the target APIs and allow access from the specified service projects.

A) Correct. Provides secure and controlled access to specific resources.
B) Incorrect. VPC Peering is not necessary within a Shared VPC setup.
C) Incorrect. Firewall rules alone don't provide the necessary access control for specific APIs.
D) Incorrect. Private Google Access is for Google services, not for specific inter-project communication.
E) Incorrect. Custom routes are not used for access control to specific APIs.

QUESTION 19

Answer - A) Cloud Load Balancing with global backend services.

A) Cloud Load Balancing with global backend services allows you to distribute traffic globally, ensuring low-latency access for users around the world.

B) Regional VPC peering does not inherently optimize for low-latency global access.

C) VPN tunnels focus on secure connectivity, not low-latency access.

D) Cloud CDN improves content delivery but may not provide the same benefits as load balancing for application access.

E) Cloud NAT is primarily used for outbound traffic and does not address low-latency access concerns.

QUESTION 20

Answer - C) Grant the engineer both the Storage Admin IAM role and Project IAM Admin role at the department level.

C) To minimize effort and enable the engineer to deploy storage buckets and manage service accounts across different departments, granting both the Storage Admin IAM role and Project IAM Admin role at the department level provides the necessary permissions.

A) Providing these roles at the organization level may grant excessive permissions.

B) Assigning only the Storage Admin IAM role at the department level may not cover all required actions.

D) Assigning the Storage Admin IAM role at the organization level is overly permissive and lacks granularity.

E) Creating a custom IAM role may require more effort than necessary.

QUESTION 21

Answer - B) Create a single firewall rule to allow port 22 with priority 1000.

B) To allow system engineers to manage virtual machines securely, you should create a single firewall rule that permits ingress on port 22 with priority 1000. This rule allows SSH access, which is commonly used for secure remote management.

A) Creating two firewall rules with complex priority settings and different ports may lead to unintended behavior and potential security issues.

C) Blocking all traffic with priority 65536 is overly restrictive, and allowing port 3389 may not be necessary for system engineers.

D) Allowing port 3389 (RDP) may not be the most secure choice for virtual machine management.

E) Network Service Tiers are related to load balancing and may not be directly applicable to firewall configurations for virtual machine management.

QUESTION 22

Answer - B) Create a single firewall rule to allow port 22 with priority 1000.

B) To securely allow system engineers to manage virtual machines, you can create a single firewall rule to allow SSH traffic on port 22 with a priority of 1000. This provides secure access for managing VMs.

A) Creating two firewall rules, one to deny all protocols and another to permit port 22, is unnecessarily complex.

C) Creating firewall rules with priorities like 65536 and allowing port 3389 may not be the best practice for secure access.

D) Allowing port 3389 (typically used for RDP) may not be suitable for managing VMs unless that is the specific protocol required.

E) While Google Cloud Identity-Aware Proxy (IAP) is a valid option for secure access, the question asks about adjusting firewall configurations.

QUESTION 23

Answer - B) Load balancer backend service scaling settings

Option A - Misconfigured health checks would impact instance health but may not cause inconsistent performance.

Option C - Network bandwidth issues could lead to performance problems but wouldn't explain variation in performance.

Option D - Google Cloud's global load balancer design is unlikely to be the primary cause of inconsistent performance.

Option E - IP address conflicts may lead to connectivity issues but not inconsistent performance.

QUESTION 24

Answer - B) Implement VPC Service Controls for strict access control.

Option A - Creating separate projects can help with isolation but may not provide fine-grained control and access restrictions between tiers.
Option C - IAM Roles are for identity and access management but may not provide sufficient network-level isolation.
Option D - While configuring firewall rules can isolate traffic to some extent, VPC Service Controls offer more comprehensive access control.
Option E - Google Cloud Endpoints is focused on API management and does not directly address tier isolation. Choice B (Implement VPC Service Controls for strict access control) - VPC Service Controls allow you to define and enforce security perimeters around your Google Cloud resources, including specific tiers of your multi-tier application. This ensures strict access control and isolation between the tiers for security and compliance.

QUESTION 25

Answer - B) Deploy Google Cloud Load Balancers for regional traffic routing.
C) Utilize Google Cloud CDN for content caching.

Option A - Google Cloud VPN is for secure connectivity but not for traffic distribution.
Option D - Google Cloud NAT manages outbound traffic but doesn't distribute incoming traffic globally.
Option E - Google Cloud Interconnect provides dedicated connections but doesn't distribute traffic globally. Choice B - Google Cloud Load Balancers can distribute incoming traffic to different regions, ensuring low-latency access for users worldwide, and regional traffic routing is a key feature for this purpose.
 Choice C - Google Cloud CDN caches content at edge locations, reducing latency for users by serving content from nearby locations, enhancing the global user experience.

QUESTION 26

Answer – A) Use Regional Persistent Disks for Compute Engine instances and configure Cloud SQL for cross-region replication.

A) Correct. Ensures high availability and disaster recovery for both Compute Engine and Cloud SQL.
B) Incorrect. Cloud Spanner is an alternative but doesn't address Compute Engine requirements.
C) Incorrect. Local SSDs are ephemeral and not suitable for disaster recovery.
D) Incorrect. Network Load Balancers are regional, not cross-regional; Cloud Bigtable doesn't inherently provide cross-region replication.
E) Incorrect. Multi-Regional buckets offer storage redundancy but don't address Compute Engine instance availability.

QUESTION 27

Answer - B) Set up two Dedicated Interconnects in separate regions and configure them for failover.

Option A - A single Dedicated Interconnect with no redundancy may lead to downtime in case of a failure.

Option C - VPN connections may not provide the same level of performance and reliability as Dedicated Interconnects.

Option D - Cloud Interconnect is not designed for the same purpose as Dedicated Interconnects. Choice B - Setting up two Dedicated Interconnects in separate regions and configuring them for failover ensures redundancy and failover capabilities for improved reliability.

QUESTION 28

Answer – A) Use VPC firewall rules to allow traffic only from your corporate network's IP ranges.

A) Correct. Firewall rules effectively restrict access to specified IP ranges.
B) Incorrect. VPN is for connectivity, not selective traffic restriction.
C) Incorrect. Cloud Armor is more suited for external web-facing applications.
D) Incorrect. Private Google Access does not restrict based on external IP ranges.
E) Incorrect. VPC Service Controls are for securing data within GCP services, not network traffic.

QUESTION 29

Answer - B) Establish a VPC Service Controls perimeter for your project, including an access context policy that encompasses your organization's head office network IP ranges.

Option A - Creating individual access context policies for each application may lead to administrative complexity.

Option C - Creating separate VPC Service Controls perimeters for each application may result in management overhead.

Option D - While firewall rules are an option, VPC Service Controls offer a more comprehensive security approach. Choice B - Setting up a VPC Service Controls perimeter for your project with a comprehensive access context policy covering head office network IP ranges provides centralized and efficient API access control for Memorystore and Spanner across all applications in the project.

QUESTION 30

Answer – A) Use Cloud Interconnect to establish direct physical connections to the SaaS providers.

A) Correct. Cloud Interconnect provides secure, private connectivity that bypasses the public internet.
B) Incorrect. VPN uses the public internet, which doesn't meet the requirement for bypassing it.
C) Incorrect. Private Google Access is for Google services, not for external SaaS connectivity.
D) Incorrect. VPC Network Peering is typically for intra-cloud connectivity, not for connecting to external SaaS providers.
E) Incorrect. Cloud Endpoints are for developing APIs, not for establishing network connections to SaaS providers.

QUESTION 31

Answer – A) Set up separate subnets for administrative and user traffic with VPC firewall rules for segregation and Stackdriver for monitoring.

A) Correct. Subnet segregation with firewall rules and Stackdriver provides the required control and monitoring.
B) Incorrect. Network Tags alone do not provide strict segregation.
C) Incorrect. Private Google Access and Internet NEGs are not suitable for segregating admin and user traffic.
D) Incorrect. Separate VPCs are overly complex for this requirement, and VPC Peering does not address segregation.
E) Incorrect. VPN and Load Balancing are not the primary tools for traffic segregation within GCP.

QUESTION 32

Answer - B) Establish a private connection with the Cloud Spanner service producer. and C) Turn on Private Google Access for your subnetwork.

Option A - Enabling the Cloud Memorystore API is unrelated to connecting Compute Engine instances to Cloud Spanner.
Option D - Configuring a custom static route is not the recommended approach for connecting instances to Cloud Spanner.
Option E - Enabling the Service Networking API is not necessary for this specific task. Explanation for choices B and C - To connect Compute Engine instances to Cloud Spanner without public IP addresses, you should establish a private connection with the Cloud Spanner service producer and turn on Private Google Access for your subnetwork to allow the necessary communication.

QUESTION 33

Answer - B) Create a VPC Service Controls perimeter for your project with an access context policy that includes your organization's head office network IP ranges.

Option A - While access context policies are important, they do not directly address creating a VPC Service Controls perimeter.
Option B - This is the correct approach for creating a VPC Service Controls perimeter with the appropriate access context policy.
Option C - Creating separate perimeters for each App Engine application may not be the most efficient way to achieve the goal.
Option D - Configuring a firewall rule is a good security measure but may not provide the level of control described in the scenario.
Option E - None of the options directly address the best approach for safeguarding API access from head office networks

QUESTION 34

Answer - D) Transit Gateway with Identity-Aware Proxy

A) VPN Gateway with Firewall Rules - Explanation: VPN Gateway provides secure connections, but it may not handle encryption or access control at the desired level. Firewall Rules can restrict traffic but may not provide strong encryption.
B) VPC Service Controls with Cloud Armor - Explanation: VPC Service Controls focus on access control, but Cloud Armor may not provide the necessary encryption for data in transit.
C) Private Google Access with VPC Peering - Explanation: Private Google Access enables private access to

Google services, but VPC Peering may not provide the required encryption and access control.
E) Dedicated Interconnect with Network Peering - Explanation: Dedicated Interconnect provides dedicated connectivity, but Network Peering may not focus on encryption and access control for the financial application.
D) Transit Gateway with Identity-Aware Proxy - Explanation: Transit Gateway connects VPCs while Identity-Aware Proxy provides access control. This combination ensures strong encryption and access control for the critical financial application.

QUESTION 35

Answer - E) Implement a multi-cloud network orchestrator service to manage traffic routing and secure communication efficiently across Google Cloud, AWS, and Azure.

E) Implement a multi-cloud network orchestrator service to manage traffic routing and secure communication efficiently across Google Cloud, AWS, and Azure - Explanation: A multi-cloud network orchestrator service is designed to efficiently manage traffic routing and secure communication across different cloud providers, making it a suitable choice for a complex multi-cloud environment.
A) Set up custom routes with more precision than the default network routes - Explanation: While custom routes are useful, this option does not directly address the need for efficient cross-cloud traffic routing and secure communication.
B) Migrate all workloads to a single cloud provider - Explanation: Migrating all workloads to a single cloud provider may not be feasible or desirable in a multi-cloud environment.
C) Delete all default network routes and establish distinct custom routes for cross-cloud connections - Explanation: Deleting default routes introduces complexity, and this option may not be necessary for efficient cross-cloud traffic routing and secure communication.
D) Create more specific custom routes than the default network routes - Explanation: This option introduces complexity with network tags and may not provide the comprehensive solution needed for a complex multi-cloud environment.

QUESTION 36

Answer – A) Enable Private Google Access on the subnetworks hosting the Compute Engine instances and use VPC Connector for serverless functions.

A) Correct. Private Google Access and VPC Connector provide secure, cost-effective, and performance-optimized networking.
B) Incorrect. VPC Peering is not applicable for serverless functions.
C) Incorrect. Cloud VPN is not necessary for internal GCP communication.
D) Incorrect. An internal load balancer is not needed for this setup and does not address serverless functions.
E) Incorrect. Shared VPC is more for resource sharing across projects, not for Compute Engine and serverless function integration.

QUESTION 37

Answer - C) Cloud Interconnect with Google Cloud Router

A) Google Cloud VPN - VPNs provide encrypted connections but may not offer dynamic routing.
B) VPC peering with Cloud Router - While it supports dynamic routing, it does not provide the same level

of dedicated connectivity as Cloud Interconnect.

C) Cloud Interconnect with Google Cloud Router - Correct answer. Cloud Interconnect provides private connectivity with dynamic routing capabilities through Google Cloud Router.

D) Google Cloud DNS with Cloud CDN - These services focus on DNS resolution and content delivery, not private connectivity and dynamic routing.

E) Regional managed instance groups with Google Cloud Load Balancing - These components are used for traffic distribution and do not provide dedicated private connections.

QUESTION 38

Answer - B) Cloud Interconnect with Google Cloud Router

A) Google Cloud VPN with VPC peering - VPN and VPC peering provide connectivity but may not guarantee low-latency access.

B) Cloud Interconnect with Google Cloud Router - Correct answer. Cloud Interconnect offers high availability and low-latency connectivity, and Router handles dynamic routing.

C) VPC peering with Cloud VPN - This combination focuses on connectivity but may not provide the same level of low latency as Interconnect.

D) Google Cloud Armor with Cloud CDN - These services are for security and content delivery, not dedicated connectivity.

E) Google Cloud DNS with Cloud Identity-Aware Proxy (IAP) - DNS and IAP provide DNS resolution and identity-based access, not low-latency connectivity.

QUESTION 39

Answer - A) Google Cloud Storage

A) Correct answer. Google Cloud Storage allows you to create dedicated storage buckets for each microservice, ensuring data isolation and offering fine-grained access control through IAM policies.

B) Google Cloud Bigtable is a NoSQL database and may not provide the same level of isolation and fine-grained access control as dedicated storage buckets.

C) Google Cloud Firestore is a NoSQL database focused on document storage and may not offer dedicated storage for microservices.

D) Google Cloud SQL provides managed databases, which are not designed for dedicated storage with fine-grained access control.

E) Google Cloud Spanner is a distributed database and may not be the most efficient choice for microservice storage with strict access control.

QUESTION 40

Answer - D) Google Cloud Storage and Google Cloud DNS

A) Google Cloud VPN and Google Cloud Bigtable may not be the primary components for disaster recovery and data replication between regions.

B) Google Cloud CDN and Google Cloud Compute Engine Autoscaler are not primarily designed for disaster recovery and data replication.

C) Google Cloud Spanner and Google Cloud Interconnect focus on database and connectivity but may not be the primary components for disaster recovery.

D) Correct answer. Google Cloud Storage offers data replication between regions, and Google Cloud DNS

provides domain name resolution for disaster recovery scenarios.
E) Google Cloud Load Balancing and Google Cloud VPC Peering may not be the primary components for data replication and failover between regions.

QUESTION 41

Answer – A) Use a Global HTTP(S) Load Balancer with multi-regional backend services.

A) Correct. Global HTTP(S) Load Balancer efficiently routes traffic to the nearest regional endpoint.
B) Incorrect. Network Load Balancers are not suitable for global traffic distribution.
C) Incorrect. Internal Load Balancers are for internal network load balancing, not global routing.
D) Incorrect. TCP/SSL Proxy Load Balancer does not provide the same geographic routing capabilities as an HTTP(S) Load Balancer.
E) Incorrect. Regional HTTP(S) Load Balancers with VPC Peering complicate the setup without offering better geographic routing.

QUESTION 42

Answer - C) gcloud dns record-sets import ZONE_FILE --zone MANAGED_ZONE

A) Option A has extra parameters that are not required for this action.
B) Option B includes --replace-origin-ns, which is not necessary for importing a BIND zone file.
C) Correct answer.
Option C is the appropriate command to import a BIND zone file to Google Cloud DNS.
D) Option D includes --delete-all-existing, which is not needed for the import process.

QUESTION 43

Answer - B) Upload your public SSH key to the project-wide metadata.

A) Creating a specialized snapshot is not the most straightforward way to enable SSH access with a public key.
B) Correct answer. Uploading the public SSH key to project-wide metadata simplifies access management.
C) Uploading the key individually to each virtual machine's metadata can be cumbersome for large projects.
D) Using the gcloud compute ssh command for each virtual machine is manual and not the simplest approach.
E) Creating a custom image with the SSH key is an option but not the most straightforward one.

QUESTION 44

Answer - B) Create a Cloud Armor Security Policy that blocks all traffic except for the DDoS protection service.

A) VPC Service Controls Perimeter is designed for data protection, not controlling traffic to backend servers.
C) While VPC Firewall rules can be used, Cloud Armor provides more granular control and is better suited for this scenario.

D) Implementing iptables on servers adds complexity and is less manageable at scale.
E) Configuring servers individually with custom scripts is not a scalable solution and may lead to maintenance challenges.
B) Creating a Cloud Armor Security Policy allows you to easily restrict traffic to the backend servers to only allow connections from the DDoS protection service.

QUESTION 45

Answer – B) Configure Private Google Access on subnetworks hosting Compute Engine instances for direct access to BigQuery.

A) Incorrect. VPC Service Controls secure data but don't address network connectivity; VPN is not required for internal GCP communication.
B) Correct. Private Google Access provides secure, private connectivity to BigQuery without public internet exposure.
C) Incorrect. Cloud Interconnect is for external connections, not necessary for intra-GCP services.
D) Incorrect. Internal Load Balancers are for internal traffic management, not for service-specific connectivity like BigQuery.
E) Incorrect. A dedicated VPC with custom routes adds complexity without specific benefits for BigQuery connectivity.

QUESTION 46

Answer - B) Use a customer-managed encryption key (CMEK) for data encryption at rest and configure SSL/TLS for data in transit.

A) Google-managed keys are suitable for some scenarios, but customer-managed encryption keys (CMEK) provide more control over encryption at rest.
B) Using CMEK for data encryption at rest and SSL/TLS for data in transit is a secure and customizable approach.
C) Relying on default settings may not provide the desired level of security.
D) Cloud Identity-Aware Proxy (IAP) is primarily for access control, not data encryption. IPsec is for network-level encryption, not data in transit.
E) VPC Service Controls focus on access control, and Cloud CDN is a content delivery network service, not specifically for data encryption.

QUESTION 47

Answer – D) Set up a global network of Compute Engine instances with Premium Network Tier and Cloud Firestore for the database.

A) Incorrect. HTTP(S) Load Balancer is not optimal for real-time gaming traffic.
B) Incorrect. Network Load Balancers do not provide the global scaling needed, and Cloud SQL may have latency issues.
C) Incorrect. Internal Load Balancers are for internal traffic, not for global player communication.
D) Correct. Compute Engine with Premium Network Tier and Cloud Firestore offers low-latency and scalability for global gaming platforms.
E) Incorrect. Cloud Run is not ideal for real-time gaming servers, and Spanner, while fast, may not be the best fit for game data.

QUESTION 48

Answer – E) Enable Premium Network Tier on all Compute Engine instances for global low-latency communication.

A) Incorrect. Global VPC does not inherently reduce latency for global communication.
B) Incorrect. VPN tunnels are not the most efficient for low-latency, high-throughput needs.
C) Incorrect. Interconnect is typically for on-premises to GCP connections.
D) Incorrect. Internal Load Balancers are for distributing internal traffic, not for low-latency state synchronization.
E) Correct. Premium Network Tier provides optimized performance for low-latency, global communication.

QUESTION 49

Answer – A) Global HTTP(S) Load Balancer with Cloud Armor and Cloud CDN.

A) Correct. This setup provides dynamic scaling, DDoS protection, efficient content delivery, and global traffic distribution.
B) Incorrect. Network Load Balancers are not ideal for dynamic content delivery and global traffic management.
C) Incorrect. TCP/SSL Proxy Load Balancers are not the best for global content distribution and DDoS protection.
D) Incorrect. Internal Load Balancers and VPNs are not suitable for a high-traffic, global e-commerce platform.
E) Incorrect. Cloud Run and Endpoints do not provide the necessary scaling and DDoS protection for a global e-commerce platform.

QUESTION 50

Answer – A) Global HTTP(S) Load Balancer with Cloud Armor and Cloud CDN.

A) Correct. Global HTTP(S) Load Balancing with Cloud Armor and Cloud CDN provides the necessary dynamic scaling, security, and efficient content delivery for a global e-commerce platform.
B) Incorrect. Network Load Balancers are not ideal for dynamic content delivery and global traffic management.
C) Incorrect. TCP/SSL Proxy Load Balancers are not the best for global traffic distribution and security needs.
D) Incorrect. Internal Load Balancers and Cloud VPN are not suitable for high-traffic, global online platforms.
E) Incorrect. Cloud Run and Endpoints do not provide the necessary scaling and advanced security for a global e-commerce platform.

PRACTICE TEST 8 - QUESTIONS ONLY

QUESTION 1

You are tasked with optimizing network performance between a Google Cloud VPC and an on-premises data center. You notice that the latency is high, and data transfer rates are suboptimal. Which GCP service should you consider to improve connectivity and reduce latency?

A) Use Google Cloud Dedicated Interconnect with a dedicated VLAN.
B) Deploy Google Cloud VPN with a shared VPN gateway.
C) Implement Google Cloud Direct Peering with a public peering connection.
D) Set up Google Cloud Interconnect with a 1 Gbps bandwidth.
E) Enable Google Cloud CDN with global caching.

QUESTION 2

Your organization operates a critical business application on Google Cloud, and you want to ensure high availability and disaster recovery. What should you set up to replicate data and configurations between two Google Cloud regions, ensuring minimal downtime in case of an outage?

A) Use Google Cloud DNS for traffic management.
B) Implement Google Cloud VPN tunnels for data replication.
C) Deploy Google Cloud CDN for content delivery.
D) Configure Google Cloud Storage Transfer Service for data transfer.
E) Utilize multi-region Google Cloud Storage buckets.

QUESTION 3

Your organization is planning to deploy a new application on Google Cloud and wants to ensure secure and controlled communication between microservices. What should you implement to achieve this while maintaining isolation between microservices and controlling traffic flow?

A) Google Cloud Endpoints for API management.
B) Google Cloud Network Peering between microservices.
C) Google Cloud VPC Service Controls.
D) Google Cloud Shared VPC for microservices.
E) Google Cloud Identity-Aware Proxy (IAP).

QUESTION 4

You are responsible for configuring the networking setup for a multi-tier application in Google Cloud. The application consists of web servers hosted on Compute Engine instances in separate VPCs, configured in a hub-and-spoke network topology. You need to set up Cloud DNS to allow the web servers to resolve private DNS zones internally and from a remote corporate office. What should you do?

A) Establish private zones within the satellite VPCs, then configure DNS peering to the central VPC.
B) Apply a DNS policy in the central VPC that sets up the corporate office DNS as a fallback DNS server.

C) Implement a DNS policy in the central VPC for inbound query forwarding from the other VPCs.
D) Create a private DNS zone within the central VPC, and utilize DNS forwarding to the corporate location's DNS server.
E) Use public DNS servers for all DNS resolutions to ensure accessibility from the remote office.

QUESTION 5

Your organization needs to enable communication between two separate GCP projects, each with its own VPC network. The communication should be secure and efficient. What should you consider?

A) Assign public IP addresses to instances in both projects for direct communication.
B) Set up a Cloud VPN with IPsec encryption between the VPC networks in each project.
C) Create a VPC Peering connection between the two VPC networks.
D) Implement a dedicated Google Cloud Interconnect for each project.
E) Use Google Cloud Pub/Sub for inter-project communication.

QUESTION 6

Your organization is concerned about a potential DDoS (Distributed Denial of Service) attack on your Google Cloud resources. What measures should you take to investigate and mitigate this threat?

A) Enable VPC Flow Logs for the entire project and review the logs for unusual traffic patterns.
B) Set up Google Cloud's DDoS Protection service to monitor and mitigate potential attacks.
C) Analyze Google Cloud Monitoring metrics related to network traffic and resource utilization.
D) Deploy Google Cloud's Traffic Director to reroute traffic and minimize the impact of potential DDoS attacks.
E) Implement Google Cloud's Network Security Scanner to identify vulnerabilities.

QUESTION 7

You're tasked with optimizing network traffic for a set of GCP Compute Engine instances that frequently access data in a multi-regional Cloud Storage bucket. What is the most efficient configuration to reduce latency and costs?

A) Use Premium Network Tier for all instances.
B) Implement Cloud CDN for the storage bucket.
C) Configure each instance with a Local SSD for caching.
D) Enable multi-regional data locations for the Cloud Storage bucket.
E) Utilize Network Service Tiers to select an optimal network path.

QUESTION 8

Your organization is planning to migrate a large number of virtual machines (VMs) from on-premises data centers to Google Cloud. You want to ensure minimal disruption and downtime during the migration. Which Google Cloud service should you use to facilitate this migration with minimal impact?

A) Google Cloud Transfer Service
B) Google Cloud Dataprep
C) Google Cloud Transfer Appliance

D) Google Cloud Dataflow
E) Google Cloud Migrate for Compute Engine

QUESTION 9

You are responsible for a multi-tier web application running in Google Cloud that consists of virtual machines (VMs) distributed across different zones within a region. Your application requires low-latency communication between these VMs. What networking solution should you implement to achieve low-latency communication while ensuring high availability?

A) Deploy the VMs in a single zone within the region and use zonal networking for low-latency communication.
B) Implement a regional peering arrangement between the VMs' subnetworks to reduce latency across zones within the region.
C) Use Google Cloud's Content Delivery Network (CDN) to cache and deliver content close to users, reducing the load on VMs.
D) Set up a dedicated interconnect between the zones to minimize latency for communication between VMs.
E) Configure global load balancing to distribute traffic to the nearest available zone, ensuring low-latency access to the VMs.

QUESTION 10

Your organization is planning to set up a hybrid cloud environment with Google Cloud and on-premises data centers. The requirement is to establish secure and private connectivity between the on-premises data centers and Google Cloud, allowing for high bandwidth and low-latency data transfer. Which combination of Google Cloud networking solutions should you recommend for this complex hybrid cloud setup?

A) Use Google Cloud VPN for secure communication between on-premises and Google Cloud.
B) Deploy Google Cloud Dedicated Interconnect for high-bandwidth, low-latency connectivity.
C) Establish Google Cloud Partner Interconnect for secure data transfer.
D) Implement Google Cloud Cloud VPN for a combination of secure and high-bandwidth communication.
E) Set up Google Cloud Direct Peering for low-latency data transfer.

QUESTION 11

Your organization is running a critical, high-traffic web application on Google Cloud, and you need to ensure maximum uptime and reliability. Downtime can result in significant revenue loss. What Google Cloud service or feature should you consider for this complex high-availability architecture, and what advantages does it offer?

A) Google Cloud Endpoints for API management and load balancing.
B) Google Cloud Kubernetes Engine (GKE) for containerized application deployment.
C) Google Cloud Load Balancing for distributing traffic across multiple regions.
D) Google Cloud AutoML for automated machine learning and predictive maintenance.
E) Google Cloud Memorystore for Redis for in-memory data caching.

QUESTION 12

Your organization plans to migrate a critical application to GCP, requiring minimal latency and maximum throughput between compute instances and a managed database service. The application has components spread across multiple VPCs in the same region. Which network setup would be most effective for this scenario?

A) Configure VPC Peering between all VPCs hosting the application components.
B) Use Dedicated Interconnects for each VPC.
C) Implement a single Shared VPC for all application components.
D) Set up Cloud VPN with dynamic routing for inter-VPC communication.
E) Create a custom network with subnets for each application component.

QUESTION 13

You are managing a Google Cloud project that requires real-time data analysis and processing. The project involves multiple VM instances communicating with each other over the network. To ensure low-latency communication, which GCP networking solution should you choose?

A) Google Cloud VPN with multiple tunnels
B) Google Cloud Private Service Connect for private network connections
C) Google Cloud Network Peering for direct VPC-to-VPC connections
D) Google Cloud Dedicated Interconnect for dedicated high-speed connections
E) Google Cloud NAT for network address translation

QUESTION 14

For a newly deployed network in GCP, you are tasked with configuring firewalls to secure communication to and from web servers. These servers should only respond to web traffic. How would you set up the firewall rules?

A) Allow ingress on ports 80 (HTTP) and 443 (HTTPS), deny all other ports.
B) Create a rule to deny all egress traffic and allow ingress on port 443 only.
C) Set up rules to allow ingress and egress on ports 80 and 443.
D) Allow ingress on port 8080 for internal web traffic and deny all other traffic.
E) Implement rules to allow egress on port 443 and deny all ingress traffic.

QUESTION 15

You are configuring a Google Cloud project that requires high availability and low-latency communication between regions. The project involves multiple virtual machines in different regions. What GCP networking approach should you recommend to meet these requirements?

A) Utilize regional load balancers with failover.
B) Deploy the application across multiple regions with a global load balancer.
C) Implement Google Cloud Dedicated Interconnect for direct region-to-region connections.
D) Set up Google Cloud VPN with multiple tunnels for inter-region communication.
E) Use Google Cloud CDN for content delivery across regions.

QUESTION 16

Your organization is adopting a multi-cloud strategy and plans to use Google Cloud in conjunction with other cloud providers. You want to ensure secure and reliable communication between these environments. What GCP networking solution should you recommend for multi-cloud connectivity?

A) Google Cloud Interconnect for dedicated connections.
B) Google Cloud VPN for secure access.
C) Google Cloud Dedicated Interconnect for low-latency connections.
D) Google Cloud Network Peering for inter-cloud communication.
E) Google Cloud CDN for content delivery.

QUESTION 17

You set up a new network infrastructure for your analytics department. You plan to ensure that the system engineers can manage virtual machines within this network securely. How would you adjust your firewall configurations to permit this kind of access?

A) Create two firewall rules: one to deny ingress to all protocols with priority 0, and another to permit ingress on port 22 with priority 1000.
B) Create a single firewall rule to allow port 22 with priority 1000.
C) Create two firewall rules: one to block all traffic with priority 65536, and another to allow port 3389 with priority 1000.
D) Establish a single firewall rule to permit ingress on port 3389 with a priority setting of 1000.
E) Implement a deny-all firewall rule and then create specific allow rules for necessary ports and services.

QUESTION 18

You are configuring network settings for a set of VMs in a GCP Shared VPC that need to securely connect to an external partner's network. The connection requires encryption and must not be exposed to the public internet. Which configuration would you choose to establish this connection?

A) Set up a Cloud VPN tunnel from the Shared VPC to the partner's network.
B) Implement Dedicated Interconnect to create a direct physical link to the partner's network.
C) Use VPC Peering between the Shared VPC and the partner's network.
D) Configure a Private Google Access setup for secure communication.
E) Establish a Cloud NAT instance in the Shared VPC for outbound connections to the partner.

QUESTION 19

You're tasked with optimizing your Google Cloud costs by minimizing egress data transfer charges. Which strategy would be most effective in achieving this goal?

A) Utilize CDN services to cache and serve content closer to end-users.
B) Move frequently accessed data to regional storage buckets.
C) Implement data compression and efficient encoding techniques for outbound data.
D) Reduce the overall amount of data transferred by optimizing application code and queries.
E) Increase the network bandwidth to reduce the time spent on data transfers.

QUESTION 20

You set up a new network infrastructure for your analytics department. You plan to ensure that the system engineers can manage virtual machines within this network securely. How would you adjust your firewall configurations to permit this kind of access?

A) Create two firewall rules: one to deny ingress to all protocols with priority 0, and another to permit ingress on port 22 with priority 1000.
 B) Create a single firewall rule to allow port 22 with priority 1000.
 C) Create two firewall rules: one to block all traffic with priority 65536, and another to allow port 3389 with priority 1000.
 D) Establish a single firewall rule to permit ingress on port 3389 with a priority setting of 1000.
 E) Create a firewall rule to allow all incoming and outgoing traffic from the system engineers' IP addresses.

QUESTION 21

Your organization plans to validate a hybrid cloud setup using Google Cloud. You're tasked with verifying the operability of this arrangement before deploying it into a production environment. This setup involves deploying a service on a Compute Engine instance that must establish a connection with in-house data center servers via private IPs. Your local data centers can access the internet, yet no Cloud Interconnect has been set up so far. You're in charge of selecting the most economical connectivity option that enables your instance and the on-premises servers to communicate, and you need to complete the assessment within 24 hours. Which connectivity option should you opt for?

A) Partner Interconnect without provisioning any VLAN attachments.
 B) Cloud VPN.
 C) 100-Gbps Partner Interconnect with a redundant VLAN attachment.
 D) 10-Gbps Dedicated Interconnect with a single VLAN attachment.

QUESTION 22

Your organization plans to validate a hybrid cloud setup using Google Cloud. You're tasked with verifying the operability of this arrangement before deploying it into a production environment. This setup involves deploying a service on a Compute Engine instance that must establish a connection with in-house data center servers via private IPs. Your local data centers can access the internet, yet no Cloud Interconnect has been set up so far. You're in charge of selecting the most economical connectivity option that enables your instance and the on-premises servers to communicate, and you need to complete the assessment within 24 hours. Which connectivity option should you opt for?

A) Partner Interconnect without provisioning any VLAN attachments.
 B) Cloud VPN.
 C) 100-Gbps Partner Interconnect with a redundant VLAN attachment.
 D) 10-Gbps Dedicated Interconnect with a single VLAN attachment.
 E) Create a Cloud Router instance to establish BGP peering.

QUESTION 23

A company is using Google Cloud CDN to accelerate the delivery of their web content. However, they've noticed that some of their static assets still have slow loading times. What might be a reason for this suboptimal CDN performance?

A) Incorrect DNS configuration
B) Cache expiration settings
C) Low TTL values on DNS records
D) Incomplete HTTP header optimizations
E) CDN misconfiguration in Google Cloud's global network

QUESTION 24

Your organization is running a data analytics workload on Google Cloud's BigQuery. The workload consists of complex queries and data transformations. To optimize query performance and reduce costs, what two actions should you take?

A) Use BigQuery's default caching for query results.
B) Partition large tables based on date or another relevant column.
C) Enable BigQuery's automatic query optimization feature.
D) Create views for frequently used query patterns.
E) Load all data into a single unpartitioned table.

QUESTION 25

Your team is responsible for managing a multi-tier web application hosted on Google Cloud. The application relies on a relational database running on Cloud SQL. To optimize database performance, what two actions should you take into consideration?

A) Configure automated backups for the database.
B) Implement Google Cloud Memorystore for in-memory caching.
C) Enable automated scaling for the database instance.
D) Utilize read replicas for read-heavy workloads.
E) Migrate the database to Google Cloud Bigtable for improved scalability.

QUESTION 26

You need to design a network in GCP for an application with strict compliance and security requirements. The application must only allow network connections from specific, pre-approved external IP addresses. What is the best approach to enforce this network access policy?

A) Create VPC firewall rules to allow traffic only from the pre-approved IP addresses.
B) Implement Cloud Armor to create security policies based on the source IPs.
C) Use Cloud VPN with pre-shared keys, allowing connections only from specific external IPs.
D) Configure Private Google Access to restrict external access, allowing only specific IPs.
E) Set up VPC Service Controls to allow traffic from designated external IP ranges.

QUESTION 27

Your organization requires low-latency connectivity between on-premises data centers in Europe and Google Cloud regions europe-west3 and europe-west2. What networking approach should you consider to achieve this?

A) Configure a single Dedicated Interconnect to europe-west3 for connectivity to both regions.
B) Set up separate Dedicated Interconnects for each region to optimize latency.
C) Deploy a VPN connection for cost-effective connectivity.
D) Use Cloud Interconnect for low-latency access.
E) None of the above.

QUESTION 28

For a global application deployed in GCP, you need to ensure data consistency and low-latency read/write access for users worldwide. The application uses Cloud Firestore for data storage. What configuration would you recommend to meet these requirements?

A) Configure Cloud Firestore in Datastore mode with multi-regional settings.
B) Use Cloud Firestore in Native mode and implement Cloud CDN for content delivery.
C) Set up Cloud Firestore in Native mode with a multi-regional instance.
D) Implement regional Cloud Firestore instances and use Cloud Load Balancing for data distribution.
E) Deploy Cloud Firestore in Native mode, replicating data across regions using Cloud Dataflow.

QUESTION 29

Your distributed campus networks have 4 switches connected to your Google Cloud through dedicated interconnects on each switch. All educational platforms are operational; however, all of the traffic is routing through a single interconnect instead of being distributed across the 4 links as expected. Upon investigation you notice: - Each campus switch is set up with identical BGP ASNs. - Each campus switch has identical routes and priorities configured. - All switches are set up with a dedicated interconnect linked to a single Cloud Router. - The interconnect logs show 'no-proposal—chosen' messages when the interconnects are initializing. - BGP session has failed to establish between one of the campus switches and the Cloud Router. What is the primary reason for this issue?

A) An internal firewall is preventing the connection from being established on the second Dedicated Interconnect.
B) One of the Dedicated Interconnects is not configured correctly.
C) There is no Cloud Load Balancer in place to distribute the network load equally.
D) BGP sessions have failed to establish between all campus switches and the Cloud Router.
E) None of the above.

QUESTION 30

For a large e-commerce platform on GCP, you need to configure a network solution that optimizes content delivery to users worldwide while protecting against DDoS attacks. The solution should also cache static content to reduce load times. What combination of GCP services would be most effective?

A) Implement Global HTTP(S) Load Balancing with Cloud Armor and Cloud CDN.
B) Use regional Network Load Balancers and configure Cloud Armor for each region.
C) Set up Cloud VPN for each user region and use Cloud Storage for content caching.
D) Configure Cloud Endpoints for global API management and Cloud CDN for content caching.
E) Utilize Cloud Functions for dynamic content delivery and Cloud CDN for static content.

QUESTION 31

You are designing a network architecture in GCP for an application that needs to ensure the security of data in transit between microservices. The application consists of services deployed across multiple GCP projects. What configuration ensures secure communication between these services?

A) Implement VPC Service Controls and use Private Google Access within each project.
B) Set up VPC Network Peering between projects with TLS encryption for data in transit.
C) Use Cloud VPN to encrypt data between services across different projects.
D) Configure a Shared VPC with SSL/TLS encryption for inter-service communication.
E) Utilize Cloud Endpoints with HTTPS for secure communication between microservices.

QUESTION 32

You manage a series of IoT devices within a secure network in an existing Google Cloud Virtual Private Cloud (VPC). You're tasked with integrating additional data processing components using Cloud Run and Cloud Functions to process information from the IoT devices. The network traffic load between your serverless data processors and the IoT devices is minimal. Each serverless component must ensure seamless communication with any of the IoT devices. Your goal is to deploy a solution that minimizes costs. What should you do?

A) Generate an individual serverless VPC access connector for each Cloud Run and Cloud Function. Tailor the connectors to provide connectivity pathways between the serverless components and the IoT devices.
B) Deploy your serverless data processing components directly into the secure network of the existing VPC. Adjust firewall rules to facilitate communication paths between the serverless components and the IoT devices.
C) Set up your serverless components within a new serverless-dedicated VPC. Establish VPC peering between this new VPC and your current VPC, and update firewall rules to permit communication between the serverless components and the IoT devices.
D) Create a single serverless VPC access connector. Configure the serverless components to leverage the connector to interface with the IoT devices.
E) None of the above.

QUESTION 33

You are developing a cutting-edge analytics platform that utilizes internal services operating on port 8080. The system also needs to support external communication using both IPv4 and IPv6 over TCP on port 8070, with a focus on maintaining high uptime. How should you configure your setup to ensure maximum reliability?

A) Create a global load balancer that uses backend services, consisting of a single instance group with three instances.
B) Implement an SSL proxy that targets backend services made up of an instance group with three servers.
C) Use a global load balancer with a target pool as the backend, and include three virtual machines.
D) Set up an HTTP(S) load balancer connected to a regional network endpoint group that encompasses a solitary instance.
E) None of the above.

QUESTION 34

Your organization is migrating a legacy application to Google Cloud, and it requires low-latency access to on-premises resources over multiple VPN connections. You also want to ensure efficient data transfer between Google Cloud and the on-premises environment. What complex networking solution should you design for this migration?

A) VPN Gateway with Dedicated Interconnect
B) Cloud VPN with VPC Peering
C) Cloud Interconnect with Private Google Access
D) Cloud Router with Direct Peering
E) Dedicated Interconnect with Cloud NAT

QUESTION 35

Your organization is running a critical application that requires real-time data processing with low-latency communication between microservices deployed in different regions. What complex networking solution should you design to achieve this goal effectively?

A) Set up custom routes with more precision than the default network routes, specifying low-latency paths for traffic routing, and use network tags for microservice differentiation.
B) Reconfigure the application to consolidate all microservices within a single region to simplify network management and reduce latency.
C) Delete all default network routes and establish distinct custom routes for low-latency paths, using network tags for microservice differentiation and precise routing.
D) Create more specific custom routes than the default network routes, designating low-latency paths for routing, and assign network tags for microservice differentiation and precise traffic handling.
E) Implement Google Cloud's Global Edge Network for real-time data processing and low-latency communication between microservices deployed in different regions.

QUESTION 36

You are deploying a multi-regional web application in GCP that requires geographic load balancing and protection against regional outages. The application must serve users from the closest region to reduce latency. What combination of GCP services should be used to meet these requirements?

A) Use Global HTTP(S) Load Balancer with Cloud Armor and configure multi-regional backend services.
B) Set up regional Network Load Balancers in each user region and use Cloud VPN for inter-region failover.
C) Implement Global Load Balancing with Cloud CDN for content distribution and Cloud DNS for regional failover.
D) Configure a series of regional Internal Load Balancers and Cloud Endpoints for regional traffic management.
E) Establish Cloud Run instances in each region and use VPC Peering for regional failover and load distribution.

QUESTION 37

You are responsible for designing a network architecture that ensures high availability and data redundancy for a financial application. Your solution must include automatic failover and replication of data across multiple zones within a region. Which Google Cloud networking components should you choose to achieve these objectives?

A) VPC peering with regional managed instance groups
B) Google Cloud Load Balancing with Cloud Spanner
C) Google Cloud VPN with Google Cloud Storage
D) Internal load balancer with Compute Engine snapshots
E) Cloud Interconnect with Cloud SQL regional instance

QUESTION 38

You are tasked with setting up a network architecture that ensures the highest level of data security and compliance for a financial application running on Google Cloud. Your goal is to encrypt data at rest and in transit while maintaining control over encryption keys. Which Google Cloud networking components and services should you integrate to meet these requirements?

A) Google Cloud VPN with Cloud Identity-Aware Proxy (IAP)
B) VPC Service Controls with VPC Flow Logs
C) Google Cloud Armor with Cloud Security Scanner
D) Google Cloud Key Management Service (KMS) with Google Cloud Storage
E) Cloud IAM with Google Cloud SQL

QUESTION 39

You are responsible for setting up a highly available and globally distributed application on Google Cloud. The application needs to handle traffic from multiple regions and ensure low-latency access for users. Which Google Cloud networking feature should you implement to achieve these objectives effectively?

A) Google Cloud Armor with Cloud CDN
B) Traffic Director with Cloud Load Balancing
C) Google Cloud DNS with Cloud IAM
D) Cloud Interconnect with Cloud VPN
E) Google Cloud CDN with VPC peering

QUESTION 40

You are tasked with designing a highly available architecture for your organization's mission-critical application on Google Cloud. The application must withstand regional failures and maintain low latency. Which combination of Google Cloud services or features should you incorporate into your design to achieve these objectives effectively?

A) Google Cloud VPN and Google Cloud Storage
B) Google Cloud Load Balancing and Google Cloud Pub/Sub
C) Google Cloud Spanner and Google Cloud CDN
D) Google Cloud Interconnect and Google Cloud Armor
E) Google Cloud VPC Peering and Google Cloud Bigtable

QUESTION 41

You are configuring network security for a set of GKE clusters in GCP, where each cluster hosts different aspects of a large-scale web application. You need to enforce network segmentation between clusters while allowing controlled communication for specific services. What is the most efficient way to configure this inter-cluster communication?

A) Set up VPC Network Peering between cluster networks and define firewall rules for allowed services.
B) Use Network Security Policies in GKE based on labels to control traffic between clusters.
C) Implement Shared VPC for all clusters with selective firewall rules governing inter-cluster traffic.
D) Configure separate VPCs for each cluster and use Cloud VPN for secure communication between them.
E) Establish a private network with Cloud Interconnect and set custom routes for inter-cluster service communication.

QUESTION 42

You need to provide each member of your healthcare analytics team the minimal level of access needed to create, alter, and remove BigQuery datasets and table schemas. What is the appropriate action to take?

A) Grant each user only the following permissions: bigquery.datasets.create, bigquery.tables.get.
B) Assign each user the bigquery.dataOwner role.
C) Assign each user the roles/owner role.
D) Grant each user only the following permissions: bigquery.datasets.create, bigquery.tables.get, bigquery.tables.update.

QUESTION 43

You have implemented a pilot project on Compute Engine with instances manually configured in one zone of the finance sector. As the project transitions to a fully operational production stage, you aim to enhance the reliability of your application and provide scaling capabilities based on demand. What is the best approach to set up your instances for this purpose?

A) Configure an unmanaged instance group in a solitary zone and proceed to deploy an HTTP load balancer targeting this instance group.
B) Establish individual managed instance groups for each sector, opt for a Single zone setting, and evenly distribute your instances across various zones within the same sector.
C) Set up a regional managed instance group, designate the preferred region, and pick the option for distributing instances across multiple zones.
D) Put together separate unmanaged instance groups for every zone needed and allocate the instances among the zones on your own discretion.
E) Implement a single managed instance group in a single zone with automatic scaling enabled.

QUESTION 44

When reviewing the server health dashboard, you notice that your online retail application is no longer connecting to your inventory management system hosted on-premises. The inventory system's server IP is 192.168.30.50. During a recent maintenance window, the only recorded change was the introduction of 3 new VPC subnets in Google Cloud. The new subnets are 192.168.20.0/24, 192.168.30.0/24, and 192.168.40.0/24. Your corporate router is configured to broadcast routes to the new subnets. What is the most likely cause of the connectivity issue?

A) The new subnets are misconfigured, causing a network conflict.
B) The corporate router is not properly configured to broadcast routes to Google Cloud.
C) The VPC peering between the new subnets and the on-premises network is not established.
D) The inventory management system's firewall rules in Google Cloud are misconfigured.
E) The online retail application's virtual machines are not properly configured to use the new subnets.

QUESTION 45

You are deploying a high-traffic web application in GCP that requires global scaling and DDoS protection. The application is distributed across multiple regions and needs to handle large surges in traffic. What combination of GCP services and configurations should be implemented for this scenario?

A) Use Global HTTP(S) Load Balancer with Cloud Armor and Cloud CDN for traffic distribution and DDoS protection.
B) Configure regional Network Load Balancers in each region with Cloud IDS for traffic analysis and DDoS mitigation.
C) Implement a series of regional Internal Load Balancers and Cloud VPN for global traffic management.
D) Set up TCP/SSL Proxy Load Balancers in each region and use VPC Service Controls for security.
E) Establish Global Load Balancing with instance groups in each region and Cloud Endpoints for API management.

QUESTION 46

Your organization has multiple Google Cloud projects, each with its own billing setup. You want to consolidate billing for all projects under a single billing account for better cost management. What is the recommended approach to achieve this consolidation?

A) Create a new Google Cloud project and move all existing projects under it to consolidate billing.
B) Contact Google Cloud Support to manually consolidate billing for your projects.
C) Use the Google Cloud Console to link all your projects to a single billing account.
D) Cancel the existing billing accounts for each project and create a new billing account for consolidation.
E) Export billing data from each project and manually calculate the total costs for consolidation.

QUESTION 47

To troubleshoot connectivity issues over a Cloud VPN connection using Border Gateway Protocol (BGP), what Cloud Logging filter should you use to review the relevant logs?

A) resource.type="vpn_tunnel"
B) resource.type="gce_router"
C) resource.type="vpn_gateway"
D) resource.type="gce_subnetwork"
E) resource.type="gce_network"

QUESTION 48

For a GCP project with strict regulatory compliance requirements, you need to configure network access to allow secure communication with a set of external IP addresses. The setup must log all traffic for audit purposes and restrict access to only allowed IPs. What configuration ensures compliance with these communication restrictions?

A) Use VPC Service Controls to create a perimeter around the allowed external IPs.
B) Implement egress firewall rules in the VPC to restrict and log traffic to the designated external IP addresses.
C) Set up Cloud VPN tunnels to the allowed external IP addresses with logging enabled.
D) Configure Private Google Access to restrict outbound traffic from GCP to specific external IP addresses.
E) Establish Cloud NAT with custom rules and logging to manage traffic to the designated external IP addresses.

QUESTION 49

In a GCP environment, you need to configure a network solution for an application that processes sensitive data. The network must log all outbound connections to external IP addresses and restrict traffic to a specific set of external services. What configuration meets these security requirements?

A) Use VPC Service Controls for secure data transfer and Cloud VPN for restricted connectivity.
B) Configure egress firewall rules to restrict and log traffic to designated external services.
C) Set up Cloud Interconnect with custom routing to external services and enable logging.
D) Implement Private Google Access and Cloud NAT with custom rules for traffic management.
E) Establish Cloud Endpoints with logging for secure communication to external services.

QUESTION 50

In a GCP environment, you are tasked with configuring a secure network for applications that process highly sensitive data. The network must restrict all outbound traffic except to a verified set of external IP addresses, and all traffic must be logged for audit purposes. What configuration would best meet these security and compliance requirements?

A) Use VPC Service Controls for secure data transfer and Cloud VPN with logging for restricted connectivity.
B) Configure egress firewall rules to restrict and log traffic to the designated external IP addresses.
C) Set up Cloud Interconnect with custom routing and logging for outbound traffic to external IPs.
D) Implement Private Google Access and Cloud NAT with custom rules and logging for outbound traffic management.
E) Establish Cloud Endpoints with logging for secure communication to external services.

PRACTICE TEST 8 - ANSWERS ONLY

QUESTION 1

Answer – A) Use Google Cloud Dedicated Interconnect

Option A - Using Google Cloud Dedicated Interconnect with a dedicated VLAN provides a high-performance and low-latency connection between Google Cloud and the on-premises data center, addressing the latency and performance issues. Other options do not provide the same level of dedicated and high-performance connectivity.

QUESTION 2

Answer – E) Utilize multi-region Google Cloud Storage buckets.

Option E - Utilizing multi-region Google Cloud Storage buckets allows for data replication and ensures minimal downtime in case of an outage.
 Option A - Google Cloud DNS is for traffic management, not data replication.
 Option B - VPN tunnels may not be the most efficient way to replicate data between regions.
 Option C - CDN is for content delivery, not data replication.
 Option D - Google Cloud Storage Transfer Service is for managing data transfers, not data replication.

QUESTION 3

Answer – D) Google Cloud Shared VPC for microservices.

Option D - Implementing Google Cloud Shared VPC for microservices allows secure and controlled communication while maintaining isolation and control over traffic flow.
 Option A - Google Cloud Endpoints is for API management, not microservices communication.
 Option B - Network Peering may not provide sufficient isolation.
 Option C - VPC Service Controls are for data access controls, not microservices communication.
 Option E - Identity-Aware Proxy is for identity and access management, not microservices communication.

QUESTION 4

Answer – A) Establish private zones within the satellite VPCs, then configure DNS peering to the central VPC.

Option A - Setting up private zones in satellite VPCs and configuring DNS peering to the central VPC allows for private DNS resolution.
 Option B - Using a DNS policy for fallback DNS may not provide private DNS resolution.
 Option C - Inbound query forwarding is typically for public DNS resolution.
 Option D - DNS forwarding to a corporate location may not ensure private DNS resolution.
 Option E - Using public DNS servers may expose sensitive DNS queries and doesn't ensure private DNS resolution.

QUESTION 5

Answer - C) Create a VPC Peering connection between the two VPC networks.

Option C is the most suitable solution for enabling secure and efficient communication between separate GCP projects with VPC networks.
Option A introduces public IP addresses, which may not be necessary and could pose security risks.
Option B with VPNs may add complexity and may not guarantee the required efficiency.
Option D with dedicated Interconnects might be overkill for inter-project communication.
Option E is related to messaging, not direct VPC communication.

QUESTION 6

Answer - B) Set up Google Cloud's DDoS Protection service to monitor and mitigate potential attacks.
Answer - C) Analyze Google Cloud Monitoring metrics related to network traffic and resource utilization.

Options B and C are the appropriate measures to investigate and mitigate potential DDoS attacks on Google Cloud resources.
Option B involves setting up Google Cloud's DDoS Protection service, while Option C involves analyzing Google Cloud Monitoring metrics.
Option A mentions VPC Flow Logs, which may not directly address DDoS threats.
Option D discusses Traffic Director, which is more about traffic management than DDoS mitigation.
Option E mentions Network Security Scanner, which is focused on vulnerability scanning, not DDoS prevention.

QUESTION 7

Answer – E) Utilize Network Service Tiers to select an optimal network path.

A) Incorrect. Premium Tier may not always be cost-efficient.
B) Incorrect. Cloud CDN is for static web content, not instance-to-bucket traffic.
C) Incorrect. Local SSDs do not affect network traffic.
D) Incorrect. Multi-regional data locations increase costs.
E) Correct. Allows for optimized network performance and cost.

QUESTION 8

Answer - E) Google Cloud Migrate for Compute Engine

Option E is the correct choice for migrating VMs from on-premises data centers to Google Cloud with minimal disruption and downtime. It is specifically designed for this purpose.
Option A, Google Cloud Transfer Service, is used for data transfers but not VM migration.
Option B, Google Cloud Dataprep, is for data preparation and transformation, not VM migration.
Option C, Google Cloud Transfer Appliance, is a physical device for data transfer, not VM migration.
Option D, Google Cloud Dataflow, is for data processing and transformation, not VM migration.

QUESTION 9

Answer - B) Implement a regional peering arrangement between the VMs' subnetworks to reduce latency across zones within the region.

Answer - D) Set up a dedicated interconnect between the zones to minimize latency for communication between VMs.

Option B is the recommended approach for achieving low-latency communication between VMs distributed across different zones within a region.
Option D provides additional low-latency capabilities by setting up a dedicated interconnect. Options A, C, and E do not address the requirement for low-latency communication across zones effectively.

QUESTION 10

Answer - B) Deploy Google Cloud Dedicated Interconnect for high-bandwidth, low-latency connectivity.

Option A provides secure communication but may not offer the required high bandwidth.
Option C is more for connecting to service providers, not data centers.
Option D, while secure, doesn't focus on high-bandwidth requirements.
Option E is for peering with Google services, not for direct data center connections.
Option B is the correct choice as Google Cloud Dedicated Interconnect is designed for high-bandwidth, low-latency connectivity between on-premises data centers and Google Cloud, meeting the complex requirements effectively.

QUESTION 11

Answer - C) Google Cloud Load Balancing for distributing traffic across multiple regions.

Option A focuses on API management but may not address high-availability architecture.
Option B is for containerized applications but may not specifically relate to high-availability.
Option D involves machine learning and predictive maintenance but doesn't target high-availability requirements.
Option E is for data caching but may not cover high-availability for web applications.
Option C is the correct choice as Google Cloud Load Balancing provides high-availability by distributing traffic across multiple regions, ensuring maximum uptime and reliability for critical, high-traffic web applications.

QUESTION 12

Answer – C) Implement a single Shared VPC for all application components.

A) Incorrect. VPC Peering could introduce latency and complexity.
B) Incorrect. Dedicated Interconnects are for external connections, not intra-regional.
C) Correct. Shared VPC offers centralized management and high network performance.
D) Incorrect. VPNs may not provide the necessary latency or throughput.
E) Incorrect. A custom network does not inherently solve inter-component latency and throughput issues.

QUESTION 13

Answer - B) Google Cloud Private Service Connect for private network connections

B) Google Cloud Private Service Connect - Google Cloud Private Service Connect allows you to establish private, low-latency network connections between VM instances, making it suitable for real-time data communication.

A) Google Cloud VPN - Google Cloud VPN provides secure access but is not primarily focused on low-latency communication.

C) Google Cloud Network Peering - Google Cloud Network Peering is for communication between different VPCs, not within the same VPC.

D) Google Cloud Dedicated Interconnect - Google Cloud Dedicated Interconnect provides high-speed connections but may not specifically address low-latency communication.

E) Google Cloud NAT - Google Cloud NAT is for network address translation and does not enhance low-latency communication.

QUESTION 14

Answer – A) Allow ingress on ports 80 (HTTP) and 443 (HTTPS), deny all other ports.

A) Correct. This ensures servers respond only to web traffic.
B) Incorrect. Denying all egress can hinder necessary outbound communications.
C) Incorrect. Allowing all egress on these ports is unnecessary.
D) Incorrect. Port 8080 is not standard for external web traffic.
E) Incorrect. Denying all ingress would prevent web servers from receiving traffic.

QUESTION 15

Answer - B) Deploy the application across multiple regions with a global load balancer.

B) Deploy the application across multiple regions with a global load balancer - This approach provides high availability and low-latency communication between regions, aligning with the project's requirements.

A) Utilize regional load balancers with failover - Regional load balancers may not provide the same level of global high availability and low latency as a global load balancer.

C) Implement Google Cloud Dedicated Interconnect for direct region-to-region connections - Interconnect may not be the most efficient solution for low-latency communication between regions.

D) Set up Google Cloud VPN with multiple tunnels - VPNs focus on secure access and may not optimize low-latency communication between regions.

E) Use Google Cloud CDN for content delivery - CDN is for content caching and may not directly address low-latency communication between VM instances in different regions.

QUESTION 16

Answer - A) Google Cloud Interconnect for dedicated connections.

A) Google Cloud Interconnect for dedicated connections - Interconnect provides dedicated and reliable connections for multi-cloud environments, ensuring secure communication.

B) Google Cloud VPN for secure access - VPNs provide secure access but may not offer the same level of dedicated connectivity as Interconnect.

C) Google Cloud Dedicated Interconnect for low-latency connections - While Dedicated Interconnect offers low-latency, it may not be the primary focus for multi-cloud connectivity.

D) Google Cloud Network Peering for inter-cloud communication - Network Peering is for communication within Google Cloud and may not address multi-cloud connectivity.

E) Google Cloud CDN for content delivery - CDN is for content caching and may not be directly related to multi-cloud connectivity.

QUESTION 17

Answer - E) Implement a deny-all firewall rule and then create specific allow rules for necessary ports and services.

E) Implement a deny-all firewall rule and then create specific allow rules for necessary ports and services - This approach ensures that access is restricted by default, and only required ports and services are allowed, enhancing security.
 A) Creating two rules with a deny rule for all protocols and a separate rule for port 22 with high priority may not be the best practice for secure access.
 B) Creating a single rule for port 22 allows SSH access but does not address other necessary access requirements.
 C) Creating rules with high priority to block all traffic and then allow specific ports can be complex and not efficient.
 D) Allowing port 3389 (commonly used for RDP) without proper restrictions can be a security risk.

QUESTION 18

Answer – A) Set up a Cloud VPN tunnel from the Shared VPC to the partner's network.

A) Correct. Provides secure, encrypted communication to the external network.
B) Incorrect. Dedicated Interconnect is for high-capacity connections, not necessarily secure or encrypted.
C) Incorrect. VPC Peering is not feasible for connections to external, non-GCP networks.
D) Incorrect. Private Google Access is for accessing Google services, not external networks.
E) Incorrect. Cloud NAT is for outbound internet access, not secure partner connections.

QUESTION 19

Answer - A) Utilize CDN services to cache and serve content closer to end-users.

A) Utilizing CDN services to cache and serve content closer to end-users reduces the egress data transfer charges by serving content from edge locations, minimizing long-distance data transfer.
 B) Moving data to regional storage buckets does not address egress charges; it mainly affects storage costs.
 C) Data compression and encoding techniques may help but may not provide as significant savings as using a CDN.
 D) Optimizing application code and queries can help but may not directly reduce egress charges.
 E) Increasing network bandwidth may not have a significant impact on egress charges and can increase costs in other areas.

QUESTION 20

Answer - A) Create two firewall rules: one to deny ingress to all protocols with priority 0, and another to permit ingress on port 22 with priority 1000.

A) To securely allow system engineers to manage virtual machines, you can create two firewall rules: one to deny all protocols with a low priority and another to permit SSH (port 22) with a higher priority, ensuring secure access.

B) Allowing port 22 directly without additional rules may not provide the required security.

C) Blocking all traffic and then allowing port 3389 may lead to unnecessary restrictions.

D) Permitting port 3389 directly without additional rules may not provide the desired security.

E) Allowing all traffic from specific IP addresses may be too permissive and less secure.

QUESTION 21

Answer - B) Cloud VPN.

B) In this scenario, where you need to quickly establish connectivity between a Compute Engine instance and in-house data center servers via private IPs, Cloud VPN is the most economical and suitable option. It allows secure communication over the public internet without the need for dedicated interconnects, which can take more time and resources to set up.

A) Partner Interconnect and dedicated interconnect options typically require more planning and provisioning time.

C) 100-Gbps Partner Interconnect is overkill for this scenario, and it would require VLAN attachments.

D) 10-Gbps Dedicated Interconnect is also more than what's needed and may take longer to set up than Cloud VPN.

QUESTION 22

Answer - B) Cloud VPN.

B) Given the requirement for an economical connectivity option that enables communication between a Compute Engine instance and in-house data center servers via private IPs and the need to complete the assessment within 24 hours, Cloud VPN is a suitable choice. It allows secure and cost-effective connectivity over the internet without the need for physical hardware setup, making it a practical choice for testing.

A) Partner Interconnect and the options with VLAN attachments may not be as quickly provisioned and may involve more complex configurations.

C) 100-Gbps Partner Interconnect may be overkill for a validation setup, and the time frame may not allow for its implementation.

D) 10-Gbps Dedicated Interconnect may also be more than what's needed for a validation setup and could take longer to set up.

E) Creating a Cloud Router instance for BGP peering is not necessary for a simple validation setup and may introduce complexity.

QUESTION 23

Answer - D) Incomplete HTTP header optimizations

Option A - DNS configuration issues could affect initial routing but not ongoing static asset loading times.

Option B - Cache expiration settings might affect content freshness but not necessarily loading times.

Option C - Low TTL values would lead to frequent DNS resolution but shouldn't impact static asset loading times.

Option E - CDN misconfiguration in Google Cloud's global network would likely affect all assets uniformly.

QUESTION 24

Answer - B) Partition large tables based on date or another relevant column.
D) Create views for frequently used query patterns.

Option A - BigQuery's default caching is limited and may not optimize complex queries effectively.
Option C - While BigQuery has automatic query optimization, taking manual actions can further optimize performance.
Option E - Loading all data into a single unpartitioned table can lead to inefficient queries and higher costs. Choice B (Partition large tables based on date or another relevant column) - Partitioning large tables based on relevant columns allows BigQuery to scan only the required partitions, optimizing query performance and reducing costs by scanning less data.
 Choice D (Create views for frequently used query patterns) - Creating views for frequently used query patterns simplifies queries and can improve performance by predefining common query logic.

QUESTION 25

Answer - D) Utilize read replicas for read-heavy workloads.
B) Implement Google Cloud Memorystore for in-memory caching.

Option A - Automated backups are important but do not directly optimize database performance.
Option C - Automated scaling is valuable for managing load but may not directly optimize database performance.
Option E - Migrating to Google Cloud Bigtable is a different database service and not related to optimizing performance on Cloud SQL. Choice D - Using read replicas offloads read-heavy workloads from the primary database, enhancing performance by distributing the read traffic.
 Choice B - Implementing Google Cloud Memorystore for caching can reduce the load on the database by serving frequently accessed data from in-memory cache, improving overall performance.

QUESTION 26

Answer – A) Create VPC firewall rules to allow traffic only from the pre-approved IP addresses.

A) Correct. Firewall rules effectively enforce access based on source IP addresses.
B) Incorrect. Cloud Armor is more suited for web application security, not for enforcing network-level IP allowlists.
C) Incorrect. VPNs are not typically configured to restrict traffic based on source IPs.
D) Incorrect. Private Google Access does not control access based on external IP addresses.
E) Incorrect. VPC Service Controls are designed for securing data within GCP services, not for IP-based traffic filtering.

QUESTION 27

Answer - B) Set up separate Dedicated Interconnects for each region to optimize latency.

Option A - A single Dedicated Interconnect may not provide optimal latency to both regions.
Option C - VPN connections may not deliver the low-latency performance required.
Option D - Cloud Interconnect is not designed for the same purpose as Dedicated Interconnects. Choice B - Configuring separate Dedicated Interconnects for each region optimizes latency and ensures low-latency connectivity between on-premises data centers and Google Cloud regions.

QUESTION 28

Answer – C) Set up Cloud Firestore in Native mode with a multi-regional instance.

A) Incorrect. Firestore in Datastore mode does not address global low-latency requirements.
B) Incorrect. Cloud CDN is not applicable for database read/write operations.
C) Correct. Multi-regional Firestore in Native mode provides low-latency access globally.
D) Incorrect. Firestore manages its own distribution; Load Balancing is not applicable.
E) Incorrect. Replicating data with Dataflow adds unnecessary complexity; Firestore handles replication natively.

QUESTION 29

Answer - B) One of the Dedicated Interconnects is not configured correctly.

Option A - The issue appears to be related to configuration, not an internal firewall.
Option C - The presence of a Cloud Load Balancer is not directly related to BGP session failures.
Option D - While there are BGP session issues, they are not failing on all campus switches. Choice B - The 'no-proposal—chosen' messages during interconnect initialization indicate a configuration problem on one of the Dedicated Interconnects, which is likely causing the BGP session failure.

QUESTION 30

Answer – A) Implement Global HTTP(S) Load Balancing with Cloud Armor and Cloud CDN.

A) Correct. Global Load Balancing with Cloud Armor and Cloud CDN optimizes content delivery and provides security.
B) Incorrect. Regional load balancers are not optimal for global content distribution.
C) Incorrect. VPN is not suitable for user content delivery, and Cloud Storage alone does not optimize caching.
D) Incorrect. Cloud Endpoints are for API management, not for content delivery optimization.
E) Incorrect. Cloud Functions are not primarily for content delivery, and CDN alone doesn't address DDoS protection.

QUESTION 31

Answer – D) Configure a Shared VPC with SSL/TLS encryption for inter-service communication.

A) Incorrect. VPC Service Controls are for data access control, not transit.
B) Incorrect. Network Peering does not inherently encrypt data in transit.
C) Incorrect. VPN is not necessary for communication within GCP.
D) Correct. Shared VPC with SSL/TLS ensures secure, centralized network management.
E) Incorrect. Cloud Endpoints are for API management, not for internal service communication.

QUESTION 32

Answer - B) Deploy your serverless data processing components directly into the secure network of the existing VPC. Adjust firewall rules to facilitate communication paths between the serverless components and the IoT devices.

Option A - Creating individual VPC access connectors for each component may not be the most cost-effective solution.

Option C - Setting up a new serverless-dedicated VPC with VPC peering may add unnecessary complexity and cost.

Option D - Creating a single VPC access connector for all components might not provide the desired minimal cost solution. Choice B - Deploying serverless components directly into the existing secure network VPC and adjusting firewall rules allows for seamless communication with minimal cost.

QUESTION 33

Answer - D) Set up an HTTP(S) load balancer connected to a regional network endpoint group that encompasses a solitary instance.

Option A - Creating a global load balancer may not be necessary for the described scenario.

Option B - Implementing an SSL proxy is not directly related to the requirements for supporting external communication over TCP on port 8070.

Option C - Using a global load balancer with virtual machines is a valid approach but may introduce complexity.

Option D - Setting up an HTTP(S) load balancer connected to a regional network endpoint group with a solitary instance is a simple and cost-effective way to achieve the goal.

Option E - None of the options directly address the best approach for ensuring maximum reliability while meeting the described requirements

QUESTION 34

Answer - A) VPN Gateway with Dedicated Interconnect

B) Cloud VPN with VPC Peering - Explanation: Cloud VPN provides secure connections, but it may not provide the same level of low-latency access as Dedicated Interconnect. VPC Peering is used for connecting VPCs within Google Cloud.

C) Cloud Interconnect with Private Google Access - Explanation: Cloud Interconnect connects to Google Cloud, but it may not offer efficient data transfer between Google Cloud and on-premises resources. Private Google Access focuses on Google services access.

D) Cloud Router with Direct Peering - Explanation: Cloud Router is used for dynamic BGP routing within VPCs, and Direct Peering connects to Google's network. This combination may not provide the low-latency access required for on-premises resources.

E) Dedicated Interconnect with Cloud NAT - Explanation: Dedicated Interconnect provides dedicated connections, and Cloud NAT is used for network address translation, but this combination may not offer low-latency access.

A) VPN Gateway with Dedicated Interconnect - Explanation: VPN Gateway provides secure connections with low-latency access, and Dedicated Interconnect offers dedicated connections, making it the right choice for this migration scenario.

QUESTION 35

Answer - E) Implement Google Cloud's Global Edge Network for real-time data processing and low-latency communication between microservices deployed in different regions.

E) Implement Google Cloud's Global Edge Network for real-time data processing and low-latency communication between microservices deployed in different regions - Explanation: Google Cloud's Global Edge Network is designed to optimize real-time data processing and low-latency communication across different regions, making it suitable for this critical application.

A) Set up custom routes with more precision than the default network routes - Explanation: While custom routes are useful, this option does not directly address the need for a global edge network and may not provide the required low-latency communication.

B) Reconfigure the application to consolidate all microservices within a single region - Explanation: Consolidating microservices into a single region may not be practical and does not achieve the goal of low-latency communication between different regions.

C) Delete all default network routes and establish distinct custom routes for low-latency paths - Explanation: Deleting default routes introduces complexity, and this option may not be necessary for achieving low-latency communication.

D) Create more specific custom routes than the default network routes - Explanation: This option introduces complexity with network tags and may not provide the comprehensive solution needed for real-time data processing and low-latency communication between microservices in different regions.

QUESTION 36

Answer – A) Use Global HTTP(S) Load Balancer with Cloud Armor and configure multi-regional backend services.

A) Correct. This setup provides geographic load balancing, regional failover, and security.
B) Incorrect. Network Load Balancers are not suitable for global traffic distribution.
C) Incorrect. Cloud CDN is for content delivery, not application load balancing.
D) Incorrect. Internal Load Balancers are for intra-region, not multi-region setups.
E) Incorrect. Cloud Run with VPC Peering does not provide the necessary geographic load balancing and failover.

QUESTION 37

Answer - A) VPC peering with regional managed instance groups

A) VPC peering with regional managed instance groups - Correct answer. VPC peering connects networks, and regional managed instance groups provide automatic failover and data redundancy across zones within a region.
B) Google Cloud Load Balancing with Cloud Spanner - Load balancing and Cloud Spanner focus on different aspects and do not replicate instances across zones.
C) Google Cloud VPN with Google Cloud Storage - VPN and Google Cloud Storage do not provide automatic failover and data replication across zones.
D) Internal load balancer with Compute Engine snapshots - These components are used for different purposes and do not achieve the specified objectives.
E) Cloud Interconnect with Cloud SQL regional instance - While Cloud Interconnect provides connectivity, it does not inherently offer automatic failover and data replication across zones.

QUESTION 38

Answer - D) Google Cloud Key Management Service (KMS) with Google Cloud Storage

A) Google Cloud VPN with Cloud Identity-Aware Proxy (IAP) - VPN and IAP focus on access control but

may not provide control over encryption keys.
B) VPC Service Controls with VPC Flow Logs - While these enhance access control and visibility, they don't manage encryption keys.
C) Google Cloud Armor with Cloud Security Scanner - These services focus on security but do not manage encryption keys.
D) Google Cloud Key Management Service (KMS) with Google Cloud Storage - Correct answer. KMS manages encryption keys, and Storage offers data storage with encryption options.
E) Cloud IAM with Google Cloud SQL - IAM is about access control, not managing encryption keys. SQL provides managed databases but may not control encryption keys to the same degree as KMS.

QUESTION 39

Answer - B) Traffic Director with Cloud Load Balancing

A) Google Cloud Armor with Cloud CDN - While this combination provides security and content delivery, Traffic Director with Load Balancing is more suitable for achieving high availability and low-latency access for globally distributed applications.
B) Correct answer. Traffic Director with Cloud Load Balancing offers advanced traffic management and global load balancing capabilities to ensure low-latency access and high availability.
C) Google Cloud DNS with Cloud IAM - DNS and IAM focus on DNS resolution and access control, not traffic management or low-latency access.
D) Cloud Interconnect with Cloud VPN - Interconnect and VPN provide connectivity but do not inherently offer advanced traffic management or low-latency access for globally distributed applications.
E) Google Cloud CDN with VPC peering - CDN and VPC peering focus on content delivery and connectivity but may not provide the same level of traffic management and low-latency access as Traffic Director.

QUESTION 40

Answer - C) Google Cloud Spanner and Google Cloud CDN

A) Google Cloud VPN and Google Cloud Storage provide secure connectivity and storage but may not inherently address high availability and low latency in the event of regional failures.
B) Google Cloud Load Balancing and Google Cloud Pub/Sub offer load distribution and messaging capabilities but may not directly address high availability and low latency requirements.
C) Correct answer. Google Cloud Spanner is a globally distributed, horizontally scalable database, and Google Cloud CDN focuses on content delivery, making them suitable for achieving high availability and low latency even in the face of regional failures.
D) Google Cloud Interconnect and Google Cloud Armor provide dedicated connections and security but may not inherently address regional failure tolerance and latency.
E) Google Cloud VPC Peering connects VPCs, and Google Cloud Bigtable is a NoSQL database, but they may not directly address the specified high availability and low latency requirements.

QUESTION 41

Answer – C) Implement Shared VPC for all clusters with selective firewall rules governing inter-cluster traffic.

A) Incorrect. Network Peering might not provide the necessary control over inter-cluster communication.
B) Incorrect. Network Security Policies control traffic within a cluster but are not designed for inter-

cluster communication.

C) Correct. Shared VPC with selective firewall rules provides both network segmentation and controlled inter-cluster communication.

D) Incorrect. Separate VPCs and Cloud VPN add unnecessary complexity for inter-cluster communication.

E) Incorrect. Cloud Interconnect is typically used for external network connections, not for intra-GCP cluster communication.

QUESTION 42

Answer - D) Grant each user only the following permissions: bigquery.datasets.create, bigquery.tables.get, bigquery.tables.update.

A) Granting only bigquery.datasets.create and bigquery.tables.get would not allow users to alter or remove datasets and table schemas.

B) Assigning the bigquery.dataOwner role grants more permissions than necessary and may allow users to perform actions beyond creating, altering, and removing datasets and table schemas.

C) Assigning the roles/owner role is a broad permission that includes more than what is needed for this specific task.

D) Correct answer. Granting bigquery.datasets.create, bigquery.tables.get, and bigquery.tables.update permissions provides users with the minimal level of access required for these actions.

QUESTION 43

Answer - C) Set up a regional managed instance group, designate the preferred region, and pick the option for distributing instances across multiple zones.

A) Configuring an unmanaged instance group is not the best way to enhance reliability and scalability.

B) Creating individual managed instance groups for each sector in a single zone does not provide high availability and scalability across zones.

C) Correct answer. Setting up a regional managed instance group with distribution across multiple zones provides high availability and scalability.

D) Managing separate unmanaged instance groups for different zones can be complex and does not provide automatic scaling.

E) Implementing a single managed instance group in a single zone may not provide the desired reliability and scalability across zones.

QUESTION 44

Answer - B) The corporate router is not properly configured to broadcast routes to Google Cloud.

A) Misconfigured subnets would likely result in different errors or routing issues, but not necessarily a complete loss of connectivity.

C) VPC peering issues would also result in different symptoms and error messages.

D) Misconfigured firewall rules would not necessarily affect the corporate router's ability to broadcast routes.

E) Misconfigured virtual machines would also not impact the corporate router's routing capabilities.

B) The most likely cause of the issue is that the corporate router is not broadcasting routes to the new Google Cloud subnets, leading to a loss of connectivity.

QUESTION 45

Answer – A) Use Global HTTP(S) Load Balancer with Cloud Armor and Cloud CDN for traffic distribution and DDoS protection.

A) Correct. This setup provides global load balancing, DDoS protection, and efficient content delivery.
B) Incorrect. Network Load Balancers are not suitable for global traffic distribution and DDoS protection.
C) Incorrect. Internal Load Balancers and VPNs are not optimal for high-traffic, global web applications.
D) Incorrect. TCP/SSL Proxy Load Balancers and VPC Service Controls do not provide the necessary global scaling and protection.
E) Incorrect. Global Load Balancing with instance groups is suitable, but Cloud Endpoints are for API management, not for DDoS protection or traffic distribution.

QUESTION 46

Answer - C) Use the Google Cloud Console to link all your projects to a single billing account.

A) Moving projects under a new project does not automatically consolidate billing.
B) Google Cloud Support can assist with billing issues but may not manually consolidate billing.
C) Using the Google Cloud Console to link projects to a single billing account is the recommended approach for consolidation.
D) Canceling existing billing accounts may lead to loss of historical billing data and is not necessary for consolidation.
E) Manually exporting and calculating billing data is a time-consuming and error-prone process compared to using the built-in billing account linking feature.

QUESTION 47

Answer – A) resource.type="vpn_tunnel"

A) Correct. The "vpn_tunnel" resource type in Cloud Logging is used to review logs specific to VPN tunnels, which is relevant for troubleshooting VPN connectivity issues.
B) Incorrect. While "gce_router" is related to routing, it does not specifically log VPN tunnel activity.
C) Incorrect. "vpn_gateway" does not provide detailed logs about the VPN tunnel's operational status.
D) Incorrect. "gce_subnetwork" logs are for subnetwork activities, not for VPN tunnel status.
E) Incorrect. "gce_network" logs are related to the overall network, not specifically for VPN tunnels.

QUESTION 48

Answer – B) Implement egress firewall rules in the VPC to restrict and log traffic to the designated external IP addresses.

A) Incorrect. VPC Service Controls secure data within GCP, not for controlling network traffic to external IPs.
B) Correct. Egress firewall rules with logging effectively restrict and monitor outbound traffic to specific external IP addresses.
C) Incorrect. VPN tunnels are not necessary for restricting traffic to specific external IPs.
D) Incorrect. Private Google Access is for accessing Google services, not for restricting traffic to external IPs.
E) Incorrect. Cloud NAT is for managing outbound connections, not for specific IP access control and

logging.

QUESTION 49

Answer – B) Configure egress firewall rules to restrict and log traffic to designated external services.

A) Incorrect. VPC Service Controls and VPN are not primarily used for controlling and logging outbound traffic.
B) Correct. Egress firewall rules with logging effectively restrict and monitor outbound traffic to specific external services.
C) Incorrect. Cloud Interconnect is typically for on-premises to GCP connections, not for specific external service connectivity.
D) Incorrect. Private Google Access and Cloud NAT do not provide the same level of control and logging as firewall rules.
E) Incorrect. Cloud Endpoints are for API management, not for logging all outbound connections.

QUESTION 50

Answer – B) Configure egress firewall rules to restrict and log traffic to the designated external IP addresses.

A) Incorrect. VPC Service Controls and VPN are more about securing data within GCP, not for controlling and logging outbound traffic.
B) Correct. Egress firewall rules with logging effectively control and monitor outbound traffic to specified external IPs for compliance.
C) Incorrect. Cloud Interconnect is typically for on-premises to GCP connections, not for specific external IP connectivity.
D) Incorrect. Private Google Access and Cloud NAT do not provide the same level of outbound traffic control and logging as firewall rules.
E) Incorrect. Cloud Endpoints are for API management, not for logging all outbound connections.

PRACTICE TEST 9 - QUESTIONS ONLY

QUESTION 1

Your organization is using Google Cloud's global load balancing for its web applications. You want to ensure high availability and minimal downtime in case of an outage in one region. What should you configure to achieve this?

A) Set up a global VPN network
B) Enable HTTP(S) load balancing
C) Implement multi-region VPCs
D) Use Google Cloud CDN
E) Deploy regional load balancers

QUESTION 2

Your organization is planning to deploy a new application on Google Cloud and wants to ensure secure and controlled communication between microservices. What should you implement to achieve this while maintaining isolation between microservices and controlling traffic flow?

A) Google Cloud Endpoints for API management.
B) Google Cloud Network Peering between microservices.
C) Google Cloud VPC Service Controls.
D) Google Cloud Shared VPC for microservices.
E) Google Cloud Identity-Aware Proxy (IAP).

QUESTION 3

Your company has recently initiated a new streaming service. Upon deploying the service for high availability utilizing managed instance groups, autoscaling, and a network load balancer at the front, you observe intermittent but intense traffic spikes causing autoscaling to hit its peak capacity, leading to streaming disrup— tions for users. After reviewing the situation, you suspect a DDoS attack. You want to swiftly re-establish service for users and ensure continuous streaming while keeping costs down. What two actions should you perform? (Select two.)

A) Expand the maximum capacity of the autoscaling mechanism of the backend to manage the unexpected traffic surge.
B) Temporarily take down the streaming platform from Google Cloud for several hours to deter the ongoing attack.
C) Implement Cloud Armor to block the IP addresses linked to the attacking source.
D) Switch to a global HTTP(s) load balancer and redirect your streaming service backend onto this load balancer.
E) Directly access the backend Compute Engine instances via SSH to check the authentication and system logs for deeper insights into the attack.

QUESTION 4

Your company has recently initiated a new streaming service. Upon deploying the service for high availability utilizing managed instance groups, autoscaling, and a network load balancer at the front, you observe intermittent but intense traffic spikes causing autoscaling to hit its peak capacity, leading to streaming disruptions for users. After reviewing the situation, you suspect a DDoS attack. You want to swiftly re-establish service for users and ensure continuous streaming while keeping costs down. What two actions should you perform? (Select two.)

A) Expand the maximum capacity of the autoscaling mechanism of the backend to manage the unexpected traffic surge.

B) Temporarily take down the streaming platform from Google Cloud for several hours to deter the ongoing attack.

C) Implement Cloud Armor to block the IP addresses linked to the attacking source.

D) Switch to a global HTTP(s) load balancer and redirect your streaming service backend onto this load balancer.

E) Directly access the backend Compute Engine instances via SSH to check the authentication and system logs for deeper insights into the attack.

QUESTION 5

Your organization is migrating a large-scale application to Google Cloud, and you need to ensure high availability and redundancy. What networking approach should you prioritize?

A) Implement Global Load Balancing for application traffic distribution.
B) Set up a Direct Peering connection with Google Cloud for low-latency access.
C) Utilize Google Cloud Dedicated Interconnect for dedicated, high-availability connectivity.
D) Deploy Cloud VPNs with active-active tunnels for failover.
E) Implement Google Cloud CDN for content delivery and redundancy.

QUESTION 6

Your organization operates a critical application in Google Cloud and has experienced unexpected network outages. To diagnose the issue, what actions should you take?

A) Enable VPC Flow Logs for the entire project and review the logs for potential network disruptions.
B) Implement Google Cloud's Network Intelligence Center to analyze network health and diagnose outages.
C) Analyze Google Cloud Monitoring metrics related to network latency and packet loss.
D) Deploy Google Cloud's Traffic Director to reroute traffic during network outages.
E) Set up Google Cloud's Network Diagnostics tool to capture real-time network performance data.

QUESTION 7

For a distributed application in GCP, you need to establish secure communication between services in different VPCs within the same organization. The VPCs are non-overlapping with CIDRs 10.1.0.0/16 and 10.2.0.0/16. Which approach ensures secure and efficient inter-service communication?

A) Set up VPC Network Peering between the two VPCs.
B) Use Cloud VPN to connect the VPCs.

C) Implement Shared VPC across the services.
D) Configure a Dedicated Interconnect for the VPCs.
E) Establish a Private Google Access for each VPC.

QUESTION 8

Your organization needs to ensure that data stored in Google Cloud Storage buckets within a specific project is encrypted at rest using customer-managed encryption keys (CMEK). What should you do to achieve this?

A) Enable Cloud Storage default encryption for the project and select Google-managed keys for encryption.
B) Create a Cloud Storage custom encryption policy that enforces the use of CMEK for all buckets in the project.
C) Set up a Google Cloud Key Management Service (KMS) key ring and grant permissions to the project for using customer-managed keys.
D) Configure a Cloud Identity and Access Management (IAM) policy that restricts access to buckets in the project, ensuring data encryption.
E) Utilize the Cloud Storage Uniform Bucket-level Access feature to enforce CMEK for all objects in the project's buckets.

QUESTION 9

You are tasked with designing a network architecture that ensures secure and efficient communication between on-premises data centers and Google Cloud. Your organization requires a high-speed, dedicated connection with low latency. What Google Cloud product or feature should you use for this purpose?

A) Google Cloud VPN for secure, site-to-site connectivity with on-premises data centers.
B) Google Cloud Interconnect for high-speed, dedicated connections with on-premises data centers.
C) Google Cloud CDN for content caching and delivery.
D) Google Cloud Direct Peering for low-latency, direct connectivity to Google's network.
E) Google Kubernetes Engine (GKE) for containerized application deployment.

QUESTION 10

Your organization is planning to implement a serverless application architecture on Google Cloud. The goal is to leverage Google Cloud's managed services and automatically scale resources based on demand. What Google Cloud service or feature should you consider for this complex serverless architecture, and what key benefits does it offer?

A) Google Cloud Kubernetes Engine (GKE) for container orchestration.
B) Google Cloud App Engine for building and deploying serverless applications.
C) Google Cloud Compute Engine for custom virtual machine setups.
D) Google Cloud Functions for event-driven serverless computing.
E) Google Cloud AI Platform for machine learning integration.

QUESTION 11

Your organization operates a multi-region application on Google Cloud that requires real-time data processing and analytics. You need to ensure low-latency access to data across regions and leverage serverless architecture. What Google Cloud service or feature should you consider for this complex multi-region, real-time data processing, and analytics architecture, and what benefits does it offer?

A) Google Cloud Dataprep for data preparation and transformation.
B) Google Cloud Pub/Sub for real-time message ingestion and processing.
C) Google Cloud Dataflow for real-time data processing pipelines.
D) Google Cloud Bigtable for high-performance NoSQL data storage.
E) Google Cloud Firestore for serverless, scalable, multi-region NoSQL database.

QUESTION 12

For a multi-regional application in GCP, you need to optimize network traffic and ensure low-latency access to Cloud Storage. The application is heavily used in North America and Europe. How should you configure the network for optimal performance?

A) Use a global HTTP(S) load balancer with backend buckets in both regions.
B) Implement multi-regional Cloud Storage buckets and direct traffic via Cloud CDN.
C) Set up regional Network Load Balancers in each major user region.
D) Configure Cloud VPN to route traffic to the nearest storage location.
E) Use Premium Network Service Tiers for all instances and storage buckets.

QUESTION 13

You are responsible for designing a highly available network architecture for a global Google Cloud project. The architecture should withstand regional failures while ensuring optimal performance. Which GCP networking approach should you recommend?

A) Implement a single-region architecture with automatic failover.
B) Deploy the application across multiple regions with a global load balancer.
C) Utilize regional load balancers within each zone for redundancy.
D) Set up an external VPN connection to a backup data center.
E) Use Cloud Router with BGP for dynamic routing.

QUESTION 14

In setting up a GCP environment for a database server, you need to ensure that the server is accessible only by application servers within your network. What firewall configuration would best suit this requirement?

A) Allow ingress on port 5432 (PostgreSQL) from application server IPs.
B) Deny all egress traffic from the database server and allow ingress on port 3306 (MySQL).
C) Create a rule to allow ingress and egress on all ports for internal network IPs.
D) Set up a firewall to deny all traffic, both ingress and egress, except for internal network communication.
E) Implement rules to allow egress on standard database ports and deny all ingress.

QUESTION 15

You are designing a network architecture for a Google Cloud project that involves multiple VPCs, each associated with a different department in your organization. You want to control the traffic flow between these VPCs to maintain security and isolation. Which GCP networking feature should you implement?

A) Google Cloud Network Peering
B) Google Cloud VPN
C) Google Cloud VPC Service Controls
D) Google Cloud Shared VPC
E) Google Cloud Private Service Connect

QUESTION 16

Your organization is planning to migrate its on-premises data center to Google Cloud to reduce operational overhead. You have critical applications that require low-latency communication and minimal disruption during migration. What GCP networking approach should you recommend for this migration?

A) Gradual migration of applications to Google Cloud while maintaining on-premises data center connectivity.
B) A "lift and shift" migration strategy to quickly move all applications to Google Cloud.
C) A phased migration, starting with non-critical applications and gradually moving critical ones.
D) A hybrid approach with permanent coexistence of on-premises and Google Cloud resources.
E) A "big bang" migration where all applications are migrated simultaneously.

QUESTION 17

Your organization plans to validate a hybrid cloud setup using Google Cloud. You're tasked with verifying the operability of this arrangement before deploying it into a production environment. This setup involves deploying a service on a Compute Engine instance that must establish a connection with in-house data center servers via private IPs. Your local data centers can access the internet, yet no Cloud Interconnect has been set up so far. You're in charge of selecting the most economical connectivity option that enables your instance and the on-premises servers to communicate, and you need to complete the assessment within 24 hours. Which connectivity option should you opt for?

A) Partner Interconnect without provisioning any VLAN attachments.
B) Cloud VPN
C) 100-Gbps Partner Interconnect with a redundant VLAN attachment
D) 10-Gbps Dedicated Interconnect with a single VLAN attachment.
E) Dedicated Interconnect with a private VLAN attachment.

QUESTION 18

In a GCP environment, you need to ensure that a specific set of GKE clusters in a service project can only communicate with certain on-premises resources over a Dedicated Interconnect. What is the most effective way to configure network access controls for this requirement?

A) Implement network tags on the GKE clusters and create corresponding firewall rules.

B) Use VPC Service Controls to restrict the GKE clusters' communication to specified on-premises resources.
C) Configure Cloud VPN for the GKE clusters to route traffic to the on-premises resources.
D) Set up a Private Google Access for the service project's subnets.
E) Create custom routes and firewall rules in the Shared VPC to direct and control traffic to the on-premises resources.

QUESTION 19

Your organization is planning to migrate its on-premises data center to Google Cloud. Security and data privacy are top priorities. Which Google Cloud networking service should you consider to securely connect your on-premises network to the Google Cloud VPC?

A) Google Cloud Interconnect.
B) Google Cloud VPN.
C) Google Cloud Direct Peering.
D) Google Cloud VPN with Shared VPC.
E) Google Cloud Partner Interconnect.

QUESTION 20

Your organization plans to validate a hybrid cloud setup using Google Cloud. You're tasked with verifying the operability of this arrangement before deploying it into a production environment. This setup involves deploying a service on a Compute Engine instance that must establish a connection with in-house data center servers via private IPs. Your local data centers can access the internet, yet no Cloud Interconnect has been set up so far. You're in charge of selecting the most economical connectivity option that enables your instance and the on-premises servers to communicate, and you need to complete the assessment within 24 hours. Which connectivity option should you opt for?

A) Partner Interconnect without provisioning any VLAN attachments.
B) Cloud VPN.
C) 100-Gbps Partner Interconnect with a redundant VLAN attachment.
D) 100-Gbps Dedicated Interconnect with a single VLAN attachment.
E) Cloud Router.

QUESTION 21

Your mobile application users are concentrated near asia-southeast1 and europe-north1. Their services require frequent interactions with each other. You aim to optimize network performance while keeping costs low. What design should you implement for this architecture?

A) Design a single VPC with 2 regional subnets. Use a global load balancer to manage traffic between the services across the regions.
B) Set up 1 VPC with 2 regional subnets. Position your services within these subnets and enable them to communicate via private RFC1918 IP addresses.
C) Configure 2 VPCs, one in each region, and set up corresponding subnets. Connect the regions using 2 VPN gateways.
D) Establish 2 VPCs, allocating one to each region, with separate subnets. Leverage public IP addresses on the virtual machines to facilitate inter-regional connectivity.

QUESTION 22

Your mobile application users are concentrated near asia-southeast1 and europe-north1. Their services require frequent interactions with each other. You aim to optimize network performance while keeping costs low. What design should you implement for this architecture?

A) Design a single VPC with 2 regional subnets. Use a global load balancer to manage traffic between the services across the regions.

B) Set up 1 VPC with 2 regional subnets. Position your services within these subnets and enable them to communicate via private RFC1918 IP addresses.

C) Configure 2 VPCs, one in each region, and set up corresponding subnets. Connect the regions using 2 VPN gateways.

D) Establish 2 VPCs, allocating one to each region, with separate subnets. Leverage public IP addresses on the virtual machines to facilitate inter-regional connectivity.

E) Create a hybrid deployment with Cloud VPNs connecting the two regions.

QUESTION 23

A company is using Google Cloud Identity-Aware Proxy (IAP) to secure access to its internal applications. However, some users report that they are unable to access the applications even though they have the required permissions. What could be a potential reason for this access issue?

A) Misconfigured IAP policies
B) IP address whitelisting issues
C) Insufficient VPN access
D) Identity provider synchronization problems
E) Lack of MFA (Multi-Factor Authentication)

QUESTION 24

Your organization is using Google Cloud's Identity and Access Management (IAM) to manage permissions for Google Cloud resources. You want to grant a group of users the ability to create and manage virtual machine instances in a specific project, but you want to restrict them from making changes to network configurations. Which IAM role should you assign to this group to meet these requirements?

A) Compute Instance Admin (v1)
B) Network Admin
C) Compute Instance Admin (Beta)
D) Compute OS Login
E) Compute Security Admin

QUESTION 25

Your organization is managing a Kubernetes cluster on Google Cloud using Google Kubernetes Engine (GKE). You want to ensure that the cluster remains highly available in the event of a zone failure. What two strategies should you consider for achieving high availability in GKE clusters?

A) Utilize multiple node pools distributed across different zones.
B) Configure GKE's default auto-scaling to adapt to zone failures.
C) Enable GKE's automatic node repair feature.

D) Set up a separate GKE cluster in a different region for redundancy.
E) Implement GKE's automatic version upgrades for enhanced stability.

QUESTION 26

In a GCP project, you have a requirement to segregate internal management traffic from application traffic within the same VPC. The goal is to enhance security and network organization. How should you configure your network to meet this requirement effectively?

A) Utilize network tags and firewall rules to segregate and control traffic between management and application instances.
B) Implement separate subnets within the VPC for management and application traffic.
C) Create two different VPCs, one for management and one for application traffic, and connect them using VPC Peering.
D) Use Cloud VPN to create separate tunnels for management and application traffic.
E) Configure Private Google Access to differentiate management traffic from application traffic.

QUESTION 27

Your organization has multiple branch offices in North America and South America. You want to provide secure and efficient connectivity for these branches to Google Cloud. What networking approach should you adopt for branch connectivity?

A) Implement a separate VPN connection for each branch office.
B) Set up dedicated Cloud Interconnects for each branch office.
C) Create a single VPC for all branch offices and use VPC peering.
D) Establish a central VPC in a designated region and utilize VPC peering for branch connectivity.
E) None of the above.

QUESTION 28

In a complex GCP environment with multiple projects and networks, you need to configure network routes to optimize traffic flow between Compute Engine instances, Cloud Functions, and Cloud Storage. What approach ensures efficient routing while maintaining network security?

A) Use custom static routes in VPC networks for targeted traffic flow.
B) Implement VPC Network Peering between projects and configure appropriate firewall rules.
C) Set up Cloud VPN tunnels between projects for dedicated routing paths.
D) Configure Cloud Router with dynamic routing for automatic route adjustments.
E) Use Private Google Access in subnetworks for optimized access to Google Cloud services.

QUESTION 29

You are developing a new service and need to connect your Compute Engine instances, which don't have public IP addresses, to Cloud Spanner. What two actions should you execute to accomplish this?

A) Enable the Cloud Memorystore API in your Google Cloud project.
B) Establish a private connection with the Cloud Spanner service producer.
C) Turn on Private Google Access for your subnetwork.

D) Configure a custom static route to direct the traffic to the Cloud Spanner service endpoint.
E) Enable the Service Networking API in your Google Cloud project.

QUESTION 30

In a GCP environment with multiple Kubernetes Engine clusters, you need to set up network policies to control traffic flow between pods in different clusters. The goal is to enhance security by allowing only specific inter-cluster communications. How should you configure these network policies?

A) Use VPC firewall rules to control traffic between the clusters.
B) Implement network policies in GKE based on pod labels for each cluster.
C) Set up Cloud VPN tunnels between clusters for secure pod communication.
D) Configure VPC Peering between cluster networks and apply appropriate firewall rules.
E) Establish Cloud Interconnect for inter-cluster communications and control traffic with Cloud Armor.

QUESTION 31

In a GCP environment, your application requires real-time data processing and analysis. The application ingests streaming data from external IoT devices and processes it using a combination of Cloud Functions and BigQuery. Considering performance and scalability, what is the best network configuration for this use case?

A) Configure Cloud Pub/Sub for data ingestion, Cloud Dataflow for stream processing, and BigQuery for analysis.
B) Use Cloud IoT Core for device management, direct data to Cloud Functions for processing, and BigQuery for storage and analysis.
C) Set up Cloud Storage for data ingestion, Cloud Functions for processing, and Cloud Spanner for real-time analysis.
D) Implement direct HTTPS endpoints in Cloud Functions for data ingestion and use BigQuery for analysis.
E) Establish Cloud VPN tunnels for secure data ingestion from IoT devices and utilize BigQuery for analysis.

QUESTION 32

You are the IT architect for a global retail chain that is expanding its infrastructure to Google Cloud. These are the infrastructure requirements:
- On-premises data centers situated in Germany and Japan with Dedicated Interconnects linked to Google Cloud regions europe-west3 (central hub) and asia-northeast1 (secondary site)
- Various localized branches across North America and South America
- Local data processing needs in europe-west2 and southamerica-east1
- Unified Network Management Team
Your security and compliance division insists on a virtual inline security appliance for deep packet inspection and intrusion prevention. You aim to implement this appliance in europe-west3. What steps should you take?

A) Formulate a single VPC in a Shared VPC Host Project.
B) Configure a dual-NIC VM in zone europe-west3-b within the Host Project.
C) Link NIC0 to the europe-west3 subnet of the Host Project.

D) Link NIC1 to the same europe-west3 subnet of the Host Project.
E) Initiate the VM deployment.
F) Define the necessary routing and firewalls to facilitate traffic flow through the VM.

QUESTION 33

You have set up an HTTPS load balancer in the healthcare industry, but health checks to port 443 on your Google Cloud Compute Engine instances are failing, leading to no traffic being directed to your servers. How can you rectify this issue?

A) gcloud compute health-checks update https create-my-check --unhealthy-threshold 1 5.
B) gcloud compute firewall-rules create health-check-rule --network my-health-network --allow tcp2443 --source-ranges 130.211.0.0/22,35.19.1.0.0/16 --direction INGRESS.
C) gcloud compute instances add-access-config my-instance.
D) gcloud compute firewall-rules create health-check-rule --network my-health-network --allow tcp2443 --destination-ranges 130.211.0.0/22,35.19.1.0.0/16 --direction EGRESS.
E) None of the above.

QUESTION 34

Your organization is running a global online gaming platform that experiences variable traffic patterns throughout the day. You need a load balancing solution that can efficiently distribute traffic across multiple Google Cloud regions while ensuring high availability and security. What complex load balancing strategy should you design for this platform?

A) Regional Load Balancer with Cloud CDN
B) HTTP(S) Load Balancer with SSL Proxy Load Balancer
C) Network Load Balancer with Anycast IP Routing
D) Global Load Balancer with Google Cloud Armor
E) TCP Proxy Load Balancer with Health Checks

QUESTION 35

Your organization is planning to deploy a containerized application with microservices that require secure communication within the same Google Cloud project. What complex networking strategy should you implement to ensure secure communication between microservices while minimizing external exposure?

A) Set up custom routes with more precision than the default network routes, specifying microservice-to-microservice connections, and use network tags for security.
B) Isolate each microservice in its separate Virtual Private Cloud (VPC) to ensure secure communication and minimal external exposure.
C) Delete all default network routes and establish distinct custom routes for microservice-to-microservice connections, using network tags for security and precise routing.
D) Create more specific custom routes than the default network routes, designating microservice-to-microservice connections, and assign network tags for secure communication and precise traffic handling.

E) Implement Google Cloud's Anthos Service Mesh for secure and policy-driven communication between microservices within the same Google Cloud project.

QUESTION 36

In a GCP environment with high data transfer requirements between Compute Engine instances and BigQuery, you need to ensure maximum network throughput and minimize latency. The Compute Engine instances perform heavy data analytics tasks. What network configuration optimizes performance for this workload?

A) Configure Dedicated Interconnect for high-throughput connectivity to BigQuery.
B) Use Cloud VPN with dynamic routing for optimized network performance.
C) Enable Premium Network Tier on Compute Engine instances for enhanced throughput.
D) Set up VPC Peering between Compute Engine and BigQuery for direct network paths.
E) Implement Network Service Tiers, selecting the tier based on each instance's network load.

QUESTION 37

Your organization requires a networking solution that can enforce strict access controls, provide visibility into network traffic, and prevent unauthorized data exfiltration. Which Google Cloud networking components and services should you combine to meet these security and compliance requirements?

A) Google Cloud VPN with Cloud Identity-Aware Proxy (IAP)
B) VPC Service Controls with VPC Flow Logs
C) Google Cloud Armor with Cloud Security Scanner
D) Regional managed instance groups with VPC Service Controls
E) Cloud DNS with Cloud Identity and Access Management (IAM)

QUESTION 38

Your organization is deploying a global microservices architecture and needs to ensure traffic is intelligently routed based on performance metrics and health checks. You also want to minimize latency. Which Google Cloud networking feature can help you achieve this by providing advanced traffic management and health checks?

A) Google Cloud CDN with Google Cloud Armor
B) Traffic Director with Cloud Load Balancing
C) Google Cloud DNS with Cloud IAM
D) Cloud Interconnect with Cloud VPN
E) Google Cloud CDN with VPC peering

QUESTION 39

Your organization is planning to migrate its legacy on-premises database to Google Cloud to take advantage of scalability and managed services. Data security and encryption are top priorities, and you want to ensure that sensitive data is protected at all times. Which Google Cloud service should you choose to meet these requirements while maintaining fine-grained control over access to the data?

A) Google Cloud Storage

B) Google Cloud Bigtable
C) Google Cloud Firestore
D) Google Cloud SQL
E) Google Cloud Spanner

QUESTION 40

Your organization is setting up a complex network topology on Google Cloud, connecting multiple VPCs in different regions. Security, efficient data transfer, and minimal latency are top priorities. Which combination of Google Cloud networking products or features should you use to achieve these objectives effectively?

A) Google Cloud VPN and Google Cloud DNS
B) Google Cloud Interconnect and Google Cloud VPC Peering
C) Google Cloud Router and Google Cloud CDN
D) Google Cloud Armor and Google Cloud Load Balancing
E) Google Cloud Spanner and Google Cloud Identity-Aware Proxy (IAP)

QUESTION 41

You are architecting a highly available and scalable web application on Google Cloud. The application requires real-time data processing and analysis. Which combination of Google Cloud services and features should you use to meet these requirements effectively?

A) Google Cloud Storage and Google Cloud Pub/Sub
B) Google Cloud Dataflow and Google Cloud Bigtable
C) Google Cloud Dataprep and Google Cloud Spanner
D) Google Cloud Firestore and Google Cloud Functions
E) Google Cloud Memorystore and Google Cloud SQL

QUESTION 42

You are configuring a hybrid cloud connectivity solution using Dedicated Interconnect for seamless networking across two seismically active regions. You need to ensure fault-tolerance between the following region/metro pairs: - (region A/metro A) - (region B/metro B) According to Google's best practices, how should you structure your setup?

A) Create a Cloud Router in region A with two VLAN attachments connected to metroA-zoneA-x. Create a Cloud Router in region B with two VLAN attachments connected to metroA-zoneB-x.
B) Create a Cloud Router in region A with one VLAN attachment connected to metroA-zoneA-x. Create a Cloud Router in region B with two VLAN attachments connected to metroB-zoneB-x.
C) Create a Cloud Router in region A with one VLAN attachment connected to metroA-zoneA-x and one VLAN attachment connected to metroA-zoneB-x. Create a Cloud Router in region B with one VLAN attachment connected to metroB-zoneA-x and one VLAN attachment to metroB-zoneB-x.
D) Create a Cloud Router in region A with one VLAN attachment connected to metroA-zoneB-x. Create a Cloud Router in region B with one VLAN attachment connected to metroB-zoneB-x.

QUESTION 43

Your organization has a cybersecurity division that administers network safeguards and digital certificates. An infrastructure division is in charge of handling network configurations. The infrastructure division requires the capability to view firewall configurations, but they should not have permissions to create, amend, or remove them. How would you configure the access rights for the infrastructure division in Google Cloud?

A) Assign members of the infrastructure team the roles/compute.networkViewer role.
B) Assign members of the infrastructure team a custom role with permissions including computesubnetworks.* and compute.firewalls.get.
C) Assign members of the infrastructure team the roles/compute.networkUser role.
D) Assign members of the infrastructure team the roles/compute.networkViewer role and grant them the compute.subnetworks.useExternal permission.
E) Create a custom role for the infrastructure team with read-only permissions for compute.firewalls.* and assign it to them.

QUESTION 44

Your organization is planning to migrate a legacy on-premises database to Google Cloud. The database is critical for your business operations, and you need to ensure minimal downtime during the migration. Which Google Cloud service or feature should you use to replicate and migrate the database while minimizing downtime?

A) Use Cloud VPN to establish a secure connection and manually copy the database to Google Cloud Storage before importing it into Google Cloud SQL.
B) Use Google Cloud Dataflow to continuously stream data from the on-premises database to Google Cloud SQL.
C) Use Google Cloud Transfer Service to transfer the database to Google Cloud Storage and then restore it in Google Cloud SQL.
D) Use Google Cloud Database Migration Service to perform a live migration of the database with minimal downtime.
E) Use Google Cloud Pub/Sub to publish changes from the on-premises database to Google Cloud SQL and apply them in real-time.

QUESTION 45

Your organization is planning to migrate a legacy application to Google Cloud. The application relies on a monolithic architecture with a large relational database. What is the recommended approach to modernize this application for scalability and performance?

A) Lift and shift the entire application to Compute Engine instances.
B) Rewrite the entire application using microservices and Cloud Spanner for the database.
C) Refactor the application into containers and deploy it on Google Kubernetes Engine (GKE).
D) Implement a serverless architecture using Cloud Functions for the application logic and Cloud SQL for the database.
E) Maintain the monolithic architecture but optimize it for Google Cloud services.

QUESTION 46

You are tasked with optimizing a Google Kubernetes Engine (GKE) cluster's network performance for your e-commerce application. You need to select the most appropriate network mode for your GKE cluster. Which network mode should you choose?

A) Legacy network mode.
B) Routes-based network mode.
C) Alias IP ranges network mode.
D) VPC-native network mode.
E) GKE-native network mode.

QUESTION 47

You are implementing a network in GCP for a set of applications that require high network throughput and low-latency communication between themselves and Cloud Spanner. What configuration should you apply to optimize for these performance requirements?

A) Enable Premium Network Tier on the Compute Engine instances hosting the applications.
B) Set up Dedicated Interconnect to Cloud Spanner for low-latency connections.
C) Use Cloud VPN with dynamic routing for optimized performance between the applications and Cloud Spanner.
D) Configure a Global VPC with optimized routes for low-latency communication to Cloud Spanner.
E) Implement VPC Peering between the application's network and Cloud Spanner's network.

QUESTION 48

In a GCP environment hosting a high-traffic web application, you need to set up a network solution that dynamically scales to handle varying traffic loads and protects against DDoS attacks. The network should also optimize the delivery of dynamic and static content to users globally. Which combination of GCP services and configurations should be implemented?

A) Use Global HTTP(S) Load Balancer with Cloud Armor and Cloud CDN.
B) Configure regional Network Load Balancers with Cloud IDS for traffic analysis and DDoS mitigation.
C) Implement a series of regional Internal Load Balancers and Cloud VPN for global traffic management.
D) Set up TCP/SSL Proxy Load Balancers in each region and use VPC Service Controls for security.
E) Deploy Cloud Run instances globally with VPC Network Peering for traffic distribution and security.

QUESTION 49

You are setting up a high-availability solution for a stateful application in GCP that requires instant failover in case of a zone failure. The application stores stateful sessions on Compute Engine instances. What is the best configuration to ensure high availability and immediate failover for the stateful sessions?

A) Use a multi-zone instance group with automatic failover and regional persistent disks.
B) Configure a single-zone instance group with automated backups and standby instances in another zone.
C) Implement Cloud SQL with high availability for managing stateful sessions.
D) Set up a custom failover mechanism using Cloud Functions and regional persistent disks.
E) Establish instance groups with regional SSD persistent disks and use Cloud Load Balancing.

QUESTION 50

You are setting up a disaster recovery solution in GCP for a critical application that relies on a regional Cloud Spanner database for data storage. To ensure minimal downtime and data loss, what configuration would you recommend for the disaster recovery plan?

A) Use a multi-regional Cloud Spanner instance for high availability.
B) Configure regular exports of the Cloud Spanner database to Cloud Storage in another region.
C) Implement a read replica of the Cloud Spanner database in a different region.
D) Use Cloud Dataflow for continuous replication of data to a secondary Cloud Spanner instance in another region.
E) Set up a custom script for incremental backups from Cloud Spanner to a different database service in another region.

PRACTICE TEST 9 - ANSWERS ONLY

QUESTION 1

Answer – B) Enable HTTP(S) load balancing

Option B - Enabling HTTP(S) load balancing with Google's global load balancers ensures high availability and minimal downtime during regional outages.
Option A - Setting up a global VPN network is unrelated to load balancing.
Option C - Multi-region VPCs do not directly improve load balancing availability.
Option D - Google Cloud CDN improves content delivery but is not load balancing.
Option E - Regional load balancers are not global and may not provide the desired high availability.

QUESTION 2

Answer – D) Google Cloud Shared VPC for microservices.

Option D - Implementing Google Cloud Shared VPC for microservices allows secure and controlled communication while maintaining isolation and control over traffic flow.
Option A - Google Cloud Endpoints is for API management, not microservices communication.
Option B - Network Peering may not provide sufficient isolation.
Option C - VPC Service Controls are for data access controls, not microservices communication.
Option E - Identity-Aware Proxy is for identity and access management, not microservices communication.

QUESTION 3

Answer – A) Expand the maximum capacity of the autoscaling mechanism of the backend to manage the unexpected traffic surge.
E) Directly access the backend Compute Engine instances via SSH to check the authentication and system logs for deeper insights into the attack.

Option A - Increasing the backend's capacity through autoscaling can help manage the traffic surge.
Option E - Directly accessing the backend instances via SSH can provide insights into the attack and aid in mitigation.
Option B - Taking down the streaming platform may disrupt legitimate users and is not a recommended response to a DDoS attack.
Option C - Implementing Cloud Armor to block IP addresses may help but is not sufficient on its own.
Option D - Switching to a global load balancer may not directly address the DDoS attack.

QUESTION 4

Answer – A) Expand the maximum capacity of the autoscaling mechanism of the backend to manage the unexpected traffic surge.
C) Implement Cloud Armor to block the IP addresses linked to the attacking source.

Option A - Expanding the autoscaling capacity allows for handling traffic surges efficiently.
Option C - Implementing Cloud Armor to block attacking IP addresses provides immediate protection

against DDoS attacks.
 Option B - Taking down the service disrupts user experience and is not a proactive DDoS mitigation strategy.
 Option D - Switching to a global load balancer may not directly address the DDoS attack.
 Option E - Accessing instances via SSH is not a recommended DDoS mitigation strategy and may not provide immediate relief.

QUESTION 5

Answer - A) Implement Global Load Balancing for application traffic distribution.

Option A provides the best approach for ensuring high availability and redundancy by distributing application traffic globally.
Option B, while low-latency, does not address high availability.
Option C, Dedicated Interconnect, is not primarily focused on application-level redundancy.
Option D introduces complexity and may not guarantee high availability.
Option E is more focused on content delivery, not application-level redundancy.

QUESTION 6

Answer - B) Implement Google Cloud's Network Intelligence Center to analyze network health and diagnose outages.
Answer - C) Analyze Google Cloud Monitoring metrics related to network latency and packet loss.

Options B and C are the appropriate actions to diagnose unexpected network outages in a critical application in Google Cloud.
Option B involves implementing Google Cloud's Network Intelligence Center to analyze network health, while Option C involves analyzing Google Cloud Monitoring metrics for latency and packet loss.
Option A mentions VPC Flow Logs, which may not provide the specific insights needed for network outages.
Option D discusses Traffic Director, which is more about traffic management and may not address network outages.
Option E mentions Network Diagnostics, but its applicability may vary depending on the issue.

QUESTION 7

Answer – A) Set up VPC Network Peering between the two VPCs.

A) Correct. Ensures direct and secure communication between VPCs.
B) Incorrect. VPN is less efficient for this use case.
C) Incorrect. Shared VPC is for different projects, not services within the same org.
D) Incorrect. Overkill for intra-organization communication.
E) Incorrect. Private Google Access does not facilitate VPC-to-VPC communication.

QUESTION 8

Answer - B) Create a Cloud Storage custom encryption policy that enforces the use of CMEK for all buckets in the project.

Option B is the correct approach as it allows you to create a custom encryption policy that enforces the use of customer-managed encryption keys (CMEK) for all buckets in the project, ensuring data encryption at rest with CMEK.

Option A enables default encryption but with Google-managed keys, not CMEK.

Option C is related to Google Cloud Key Management Service (KMS) but doesn't enforce encryption directly on Cloud Storage buckets.

Option D addresses IAM policies for access control but doesn't enforce encryption.

Option E is not a valid feature for enforcing CMEK on Cloud Storage buckets.

QUESTION 9

Answer - B) Google Cloud Interconnect for high-speed, dedicated connections with on-premises data centers.

Answer - D) Google Cloud Direct Peering for low-latency, direct connectivity to Google's network.

Option B is the recommended choice for establishing high-speed, dedicated connections with low latency between on-premises data centers and Google Cloud.

Option D provides additional low-latency capabilities. Options A, C, and E are not the most suitable for achieving dedicated, low-latency connectivity.

QUESTION 10

Answer - B) Google Cloud App Engine for building and deploying serverless applications.

Option A is for container orchestration and doesn't provide serverless benefits.

Option C requires manual management and doesn't offer serverless scalability.

Option D is for event-driven serverless computing but doesn't cover serverless application deployment.

Option E is for machine learning and not suitable for serverless applications.

Option B is the correct choice as Google Cloud App Engine is designed for serverless application development and deployment, automatically scaling resources based on demand, and simplifying serverless architecture complexities.

QUESTION 11

Answer - C) Google Cloud Dataflow for real-time data processing pipelines.

Option A is for data preparation but may not cover real-time processing.

Option B focuses on message ingestion but may not address data processing architecture.

Option D offers NoSQL data storage but doesn't provide real-time processing capabilities.

Option E is for NoSQL database but may not cover real-time data processing architecture.

Option C is the correct choice as Google Cloud Dataflow allows the creation of real-time data processing pipelines, ensuring low-latency access to data across regions and leveraging serverless architecture for complex multi-region analytics.

QUESTION 12

Answer – B) Implement multi-regional Cloud Storage buckets and direct traffic via Cloud CDN.

A) Incorrect. Load balancers are not used for Cloud Storage access.

B) Correct. Multi-regional buckets and Cloud CDN optimize access and latency.

C) Incorrect. Network Load Balancers don't apply to Cloud Storage.

D) Incorrect. VPN does not optimize for storage latency.

E) Incorrect. Premium Network Service Tiers do not directly impact Cloud Storage access.

QUESTION 13

Answer - B) Deploy the application across multiple regions with a global load balancer.

B) Deploy the application across multiple regions with a global load balancer - This approach provides high availability and optimal performance by routing traffic to the healthiest region, even in the case of regional failures.

A) Implement a single-region architecture with automatic failover - This approach lacks geographic redundancy.

C) Utilize regional load balancers within each zone for redundancy - While providing redundancy, this approach may not achieve global high availability.

D) Set up an external VPN connection to a backup data center - VPNs are for secure access, not global high availability.

E) Use Cloud Router with BGP for dynamic routing - Dynamic routing does not directly address the requirement for global high availability.

QUESTION 14

Answer – A) Allow ingress on port 5432 (PostgreSQL) from application server IPs.

A) Correct. Allows secure communication from specific servers.

B) Incorrect. Denying all egress could block necessary outbound communications.

C) Incorrect. Allowing all traffic for internal IPs can be a security risk.

D) Incorrect. Too restrictive and may block necessary traffic.

E) Incorrect. Denying all ingress prevents the database from receiving necessary queries.

QUESTION 15

Answer - A) Google Cloud Network Peering

A) Google Cloud Network Peering - Network Peering allows communication between VPCs while maintaining security boundaries, making it suitable for this scenario.

B) Google Cloud VPN - VPNs are for secure access, not necessarily for inter-VPC communication.

C) Google Cloud VPC Service Controls - VPC Service Controls focus on isolation and access controls within a VPC, not between VPCs.

D) Google Cloud Shared VPC - Shared VPC allows shared resources but may not directly address traffic control between different VPCs.

E) Google Cloud Private Service Connect - Private Service Connect is used for private network connections but may not specifically address inter-VPC communication and traffic control.

QUESTION 16

Answer - C) A phased migration, starting with non-critical applications and gradually moving critical ones.

C) A phased migration, starting with non-critical applications and gradually moving critical ones - This approach minimizes disruption and allows for careful testing and optimization of the migration process, ensuring low-latency communication.

A) Gradual migration while maintaining on-premises data center connectivity - Gradual migration may still involve significant disruption and may not be the best approach for low-latency communication.

B) "Lift and shift" migration may be faster but can lead to potential issues with low-latency communication and disruption.

D) A hybrid approach with permanent coexistence may not fully leverage the benefits of Google Cloud and can introduce complexity.

E) "Big bang" migration simultaneously may result in significant disruption and is generally riskier for critical applications.

QUESTION 17

Answer - B) Cloud VPN

B) Cloud VPN - Cloud VPN offers a cost-effective and relatively quick way to establish a secure connection between your Compute Engine instance and in-house data center servers via private IPs, making it suitable for a rapid assessment.

A) Partner Interconnect may require VLAN attachments and can be less economical than Cloud VPN.

C) 100-Gbps Partner Interconnect is likely overkill for this assessment and would take longer to set up.

D) 10-Gbps Dedicated Interconnect is also excessive for the assessment's requirements.

E) Dedicated Interconnect with a private VLAN attachment adds complexity and may not be the most economical choice for a quick assessment.

QUESTION 18

Answer – E) Create custom routes and firewall rules in the Shared VPC to direct and control traffic to the on-premises resources.

A) Incorrect. Network tags and firewall rules alone do not address routing over Dedicated Interconnect.
B) Incorrect. VPC Service Controls are more for securing data within GCP services.
C) Incorrect. Cloud VPN is not required when using Dedicated Interconnect.
D) Incorrect. Private Google Access is for accessing Google services, not specific on-premises resources.
E) Correct. Custom routing and firewalling can effectively manage traffic between GKE and on-premises resources.

QUESTION 19

Answer - A) Google Cloud Interconnect.

A) Google Cloud Interconnect offers dedicated, high-speed, and secure connections between on-premises networks and Google Cloud VPCs, making it suitable for security and data privacy considerations.

B) Google Cloud VPN provides secure connectivity but may not offer the same level of performance as Interconnect.

C) Google Cloud Direct Peering is focused on public internet peering, not private connectivity to on-premises networks.

D) Google Cloud VPN with Shared VPC doesn't inherently provide more security than regular VPN.

E) Google Cloud Partner Interconnect may involve third-party vendors and is not dedicated to your organization's network.

QUESTION 20

Answer - B) Cloud VPN.

B) In this scenario, where you need to establish a connection between a Compute Engine instance and in-house data center servers via private IPs in a cost-effective and timely manner, using Cloud VPN is a suitable option. It provides secure connectivity over the public internet without the need for setting up a physical Cloud Interconnect.
 A) Partner Interconnect typically involves provisioning VLAN attachments and may not align with the quick assessment requirement.
 C) 100-Gbps Partner Interconnect is a high-capacity option and may be excessive for a validation task.
 D) 100-Gbps Dedicated Interconnect is a high-capacity option and may be overkill for a validation task.
 E) Cloud Router is used for dynamic routing within Google Cloud networks and doesn't address the connectivity to on-premises servers.

QUESTION 21

Answer - B) Set up 1 VPC with 2 regional subnets. Position your services within these subnets and enable them to communicate via private RFC1918 IP addresses.

B) To optimize network performance while minimizing costs for users concentrated in two regions, you should set up 1 VPC with 2 regional subnets and enable communication via private RFC1918 IP addresses. This approach allows for efficient, low-latency communication between services.
 A) While using a global load balancer is a valid option, it may introduce additional complexity and cost that is not necessary for this scenario.
 C) Configuring 2 VPCs with VPN gateways would likely introduce unnecessary complexity and may not be the most cost-effective solution.
 D) Leveraging public IP addresses for inter-regional communication could lead to increased costs and may not be necessary for optimizing network performance.

QUESTION 22

Answer - B) Set up 1 VPC with 2 regional subnets. Position your services within these subnets and enable them to communicate via private RFC1918 IP addresses.

B) To optimize network performance while keeping costs low, you should set up one VPC with two regional subnets, positioning your services within these subnets, and enabling communication via private RFC1918 IP addresses. This approach minimizes data transfer costs between regions and provides efficient communication.
 A) While using a global load balancer is useful for distributing traffic, it may not be necessary for optimizing communication between two regions in this scenario.
 C) Configuring two separate VPCs with VPN gateways introduces unnecessary complexity for optimizing communication between two regions.
 D) Leveraging public IP addresses for inter-regional communication may increase costs and expose services to the public internet unnecessarily.
 E) Creating a hybrid deployment with Cloud VPNs adds complexity and may not be the most cost-

effective solution for optimizing communication between two regions.

QUESTION 23

Answer - A) Misconfigured IAP policies

Option B - IP address whitelisting issues would affect connectivity, but the question mentions users having the required permissions.
 Option C - VPN access is unrelated to Google Cloud IAP access.
 Option D - Identity provider synchronization issues may affect authentication but not necessarily access permissions.
 Option E - Lack of MFA, while a security concern, wouldn't prevent users with proper permissions from accessing applications.

QUESTION 24

Answer - A) Compute Instance Admin (v1)

Option B - Network Admin would provide permissions to make changes to network configurations, which is not desired.
Option C - Compute Instance Admin (Beta) is a similar role to option A, but it's in beta and may have limited features.
Option D - Compute OS Login grants access to OS login configurations but not VM instance management.
Option E - Compute Security Admin grants permissions related to security, not VM instance management. Choice A (Compute Instance Admin (v1)) - The Compute Instance Admin (v1) role provides the necessary permissions to create and manage virtual machine instances within a specific project while restricting changes to network configurations, aligning with the requirements.

QUESTION 25

Answer - A) Utilize multiple node pools distributed across different zones.
C) Enable GKE's automatic node repair feature.

Option B - While auto-scaling is important, it doesn't directly address zone failures.
Option D - Setting up a separate cluster in a different region is a form of redundancy but may not be cost-effective or necessary for all scenarios.
Option E - Automatic version upgrades are important for stability but don't directly address zone failures.
Choice A - Using multiple node pools distributed across different zones ensures that the cluster can continue operating even if a zone experiences a failure, enhancing high availability.
 Choice C - Enabling GKE's automatic node repair feature helps maintain the health of nodes, reducing the impact of node failures on cluster availability.

QUESTION 26

Answer – B) Implement separate subnets within the VPC for management and application traffic.

A) Incorrect. Network tags and firewall rules help with control but do not segregate traffic.
B) Correct. Separate subnets provide clear segregation and organization of traffic types.
C) Incorrect. Separate VPCs are more complex and not necessary for segregation within the same

project.
D) Incorrect. VPN tunnels are not used for segregating internal VPC traffic.
E) Incorrect. Private Google Access does not segregate internal VPC traffic types.

QUESTION 27

Answer - D) Establish a central VPC in a designated region and utilize VTC peering for branch connectivity.

Option A - Managing separate VPN connections for each branch may lead to complexity.
Option B - Cloud Interconnects may not be necessary for branch office connectivity.
Option C - Creating a single VPC for all branch offices may not provide the desired level of segmentation and control. Choice D - Establishing a central VPC in a designated region and using VPC peering for branch connectivity allows for efficient and secure connectivity while centralizing management.

QUESTION 28

Answer – D) Configure Cloud Router with dynamic routing for automatic route adjustments.

A) Incorrect. Custom static routes require manual management and may not be optimal for dynamic environments.
B) Incorrect. VPC Network Peering is useful for connectivity but does not by itself optimize traffic flow.
C) Incorrect. Cloud VPN is not intended for internal GCP traffic routing.
D) Correct. Cloud Router with dynamic routing optimizes traffic flow and adjusts to network changes.
E) Incorrect. Private Google Access improves access to Google services but doesn't optimize inter-project traffic.

QUESTION 29

Answer - B) Establish a private connection with the Cloud Spanner service producer. and C) Turn on Private Google Access for your subnetwork.

Option A - Enabling the Cloud Memorystore API is unrelated to connecting Compute Engine instances to Cloud Spanner.
Option D - Configuring a custom static route is not the standard way to connect Compute Engine instances to Cloud Spanner.
Option E - Enabling the Service Networking API is not required for this specific connection. Explanation for choices B and C - Establishing a private connection with the Cloud Spanner service producer and enabling Private Google Access for your subnetwork are the recommended actions to connect Compute Engine instances without public IP addresses to Cloud Spanner.

QUESTION 30

Answer – B) Implement network policies in GKE based on pod labels for each cluster.

B) Correct. Network policies in GKE using pod labels effectively control inter-cluster communications.
A) Incorrect. VPC firewall rules are not granular enough for specific pod-to-pod communication.
C) Incorrect. VPN tunnels are not necessary or optimal for pod communication within GCP.
D) Incorrect. VPC Peering is not required for pod communication within the same GCP environment.

E) Incorrect. Cloud Interconnect and Cloud Armor are not relevant for pod-to-pod communication within GKE.

QUESTION 31

Answer – A) Configure Cloud Pub/Sub for data ingestion, Cloud Dataflow for stream processing, and BigQuery for analysis.

A) Correct. This setup is optimal for real-time data processing and scalable analytics.
B) Incorrect. Cloud IoT Core is not necessary for all IoT scenarios, and direct processing in Cloud Functions may not be as scalable.
C) Incorrect. Cloud Storage is not ideal for real-time data ingestion, and Cloud Spanner is not primarily for analytics.
D) Incorrect. Direct HTTPS endpoints may not handle high-volume IoT data efficiently.
E) Incorrect. VPNs are not suitable for high-volume, real-time IoT data streams.

QUESTION 32

Answer - A) Formulate a single VPC in a Shared VPC Host Project.
B) Configure a dual-NIC VM in zone europe-west3-b within the Host Project.
C) Link NIC0 to the europe-west3 subnet of the Host Project.
D) Link NIC1 to the same europe-west3 subnet of the Host Project. F) Define the necessary routing and firewalls to facilitate traffic flow through the VM.

Option E - Initiating VM deployment is missing from the steps required to implement the security appliance. Explanation for choices A, B, C, D, and F - To implement the virtual inline security appliance, you should formulate a single VPC in a Shared VPC Host Project, configure a dual-NIC VM, link NICs to the subnet, and define the necessary routing and firewalls to facilitate traffic flow through the VM.

QUESTION 33

Answer - B) gcloud compute firewall-rules create health-check-rule --network my-health-network --allow tcp2443 --source-ranges 130.211.0.0/22,35.19.1.0.0/16 --direction INGRESS.

Option A - Updating the health checks may not directly address the issue with failing health checks.
Option A - Updating the health checks may not directly address the issue with failing health checks.

Option B - This is the correct option as it creates a firewall rule to allow incoming traffic on port 2443 from specified source ranges, which can resolve the issue with failing health checks.

Option C - Adding an access config to an instance is unlikely to resolve the issue with failing health checks.

Option D - Creating a firewall rule for EGRESS traffic may not address the issue with failing health checks for incoming traffic.

Option E - None of the options provided directly address the issue with failing health checks.

QUESTION 34

Answer - D) Global Load Balancer with Google Cloud Armor

A) Regional Load Balancer with Cloud CDN - Explanation: Regional Load Balancer operates within a region and may not provide global distribution. Cloud CDN focuses on content delivery.
B) HTTP(S) Load Balancer with SSL Proxy Load Balancer - Explanation: This combination may provide load balancing and security features, but it may not focus on global distribution or variable traffic patterns.
C) Network Load Balancer with Anycast IP Routing - Explanation: Network Load Balancer can handle network traffic, but Anycast IP Routing alone may not provide the required load balancing and security features for the gaming platform.
E) TCP Proxy Load Balancer with Health Checks - Explanation: TCP Proxy Load Balancer may handle traffic, but it may not offer the same level of load balancing and security as needed for the gaming platform.
D) Global Load Balancer with Google Cloud Armor - Explanation: Global Load Balancer provides global distribution with high availability, and Google Cloud Armor offers security features. This combination ensures efficient traffic distribution with security for the online gaming platform.

QUESTION 35

Answer - E) Implement Google Cloud's Anthos Service Mesh for secure and policy-driven communication between microservices within the same Google Cloud project.

E) Implement Google Cloud's Anthos Service Mesh for secure and policy-driven communication between microservices within the same Google Cloud project - Explanation: Google Cloud's Anthos Service Mesh provides a secure and policy-driven approach to microservice communication within the same project, ensuring both security and precise control.
A) Set up custom routes with more precision than the default network routes - Explanation: While custom routes are useful, this option does not directly address the need for a service mesh for microservice communication.
B) Isolate each microservice in its separate Virtual Private Cloud (VPC) - Explanation: Isolating microservices in separate VPCs may introduce unnecessary complexity and may not be the most efficient approach.
C) Delete all default network routes and establish distinct custom routes for microservice-to-microservice connections - Explanation: Deleting default routes introduces complexity, and this option may not be necessary for secure microservice communication.
D) Create more specific custom routes than the default network routes - Explanation: This option introduces complexity with network tags and may not provide the comprehensive solution needed for secure microservice communication within the same project.

QUESTION 36

Answer – C) Enable Premium Network Tier on Compute Engine instances for enhanced throughput.

A) Incorrect. Dedicated Interconnect is for on-premises connections, not for Compute Engine to BigQuery.
B) Incorrect. VPN is not designed for high throughput required for data analytics.
C) Correct. Premium Network Tier optimizes network performance for data-intensive tasks.
D) Incorrect. VPC Peering is not used for Compute Engine to BigQuery connectivity.

E) Incorrect. Network Service Tiers offer different performance levels, but Premium Tier is optimal for this scenario.

QUESTION 37

Answer - B) VPC Service Controls with VPC Flow Logs

A) Google Cloud VPN with Cloud Identity-Aware Proxy (IAP) - While IAP enhances identity-based access, it doesn't inherently provide visibility and flow log monitoring.
B) VPC Service Controls with VPC Flow Logs - Correct answer. VPC Service Controls enforce strict access controls, and VPC Flow Logs provide visibility into network traffic.
C) Google Cloud Armor with Cloud Security Scanner - These services focus on security but not visibility and access controls.
D) Regional managed instance groups with VPC Service Controls - Managed instance groups do not inherently enforce access controls.
E) Cloud DNS with Cloud Identity and Access Management (IAM) - DNS and IAM provide identity-based access control but do not provide network visibility and flow logs.

QUESTION 38

Answer - B) Traffic Director with Cloud Load Balancing

A) Google Cloud CDN with Google Cloud Armor - While CDN offers content delivery, it doesn't provide advanced traffic management or health checks.
B) Traffic Director with Cloud Load Balancing - Correct answer. Traffic Director and Load Balancing provide advanced traffic management and health checks for microservices, minimizing latency.
C) Google Cloud DNS with Cloud IAM - DNS and IAM are about DNS resolution and access control, not traffic management.
D) Cloud Interconnect with Cloud VPN - These services provide connectivity but do not offer advanced traffic management.
E) Google Cloud CDN with VPC peering - CDN and VPC peering are for content delivery and connectivity but not advanced traffic management.

QUESTION 39

Answer - D) Google Cloud SQL

A) Google Cloud Storage - While it provides secure data storage, Cloud SQL offers more control over database access and encryption, making it a better choice for database migration.
B) Google Cloud Bigtable - Bigtable is a NoSQL database and may not offer the same fine-grained access control as Cloud SQL for sensitive data.
C) Google Cloud Firestore - Firestore is a NoSQL database primarily focused on document storage and may not align with the requirements for a legacy database migration.
D) Correct answer. Google Cloud SQL provides managed databases with fine-grained access control and encryption options, making it suitable for migrating a legacy database with sensitive data.
E) Google Cloud Spanner is a distributed database and may not be the most efficient choice for database migration with fine-grained access control.

QUESTION 40

Answer - B) Google Cloud Interconnect and Google Cloud VPC Peering

A) Google Cloud VPN and Google Cloud DNS provide secure connectivity and DNS services but may not inherently provide data redundancy and high availability without additional configurations.
B) Correct answer. Google Cloud Interconnect provides dedicated and high-speed connections between regions, and Google Cloud VPC Peering connects VPCs, making them suitable for secure and efficient inter-region communication with minimal latency.
C) Google Cloud Router and Google Cloud CDN focus on routing and content delivery but may not provide the dedicated inter-region connections required.
D) Google Cloud Armor and Google Cloud Load Balancing offer security and load distribution but may not address the dedicated inter-region connections for data transfer.
E) Google Cloud Spanner is a database, and Google Cloud Identity-Aware Proxy (IAP) focuses on identity management; they are not primarily related to inter-region network connectivity.

QUESTION 41

Answer - B) Google Cloud Dataflow and Google Cloud Bigtable

A) Google Cloud Storage and Google Cloud Pub/Sub are suitable for storing and publishing data but may not provide real-time data processing and analysis capabilities.
B) Correct answer. Google Cloud Dataflow enables real-time data processing, and Google Cloud Bigtable is a highly scalable NoSQL database for storing and analyzing large volumes of data in real-time.
C) Google Cloud Dataprep and Google Cloud Spanner focus on data preparation and database operations but may not provide real-time data processing.
D) Google Cloud Firestore and Google Cloud Functions offer serverless application development but may not be the best choice for real-time data processing and analysis.
E) Google Cloud Memorystore is a managed Redis service, and Google Cloud SQL is a managed database service, which may not be the primary services for real-time data processing and analysis.

QUESTION 42

Answer - C) Create a Cloud Router in region A with one VLAN attachment connected to metroA-zoneA-x and one VLAN attachment connected to metroA-zoneB-x. Create a Cloud Router in region B with one VLAN attachment connected to metroB-zoneA-x and one VLAN attachment to metroB-zoneB-x.

A) Option A does not align the Cloud Router configurations correctly with the desired region/metro pairs.
B) Option B does not provide an optimal configuration for fault tolerance between region/metro pairs.
C) Correct answer.
Option C creates Cloud Routers with VLAN attachments that span the desired region/metro pairs, ensuring fault tolerance.
D) Option D does not distribute the VLAN attachments appropriately for fault tolerance across the specified region/metro pairs.

QUESTION 43

Answer - B) Assign members of the infrastructure team a custom role with permissions including computesubnetworks.* and compute.firewalls.get.

A) The compute.networkViewer role allows viewing but also includes other permissions that the infrastructure team should not have.
B) Correct answer. Creating a custom role with specific read-only permissions is the most appropriate way to grant access to view firewall configurations without allowing other actions.
C) The compute.networkUser role does not provide the necessary permissions to view firewall configurations.
D) Adding compute.subnetworks.useExternal permission to compute.networkViewer grants additional permissions that are not required for viewing firewall configurations.
E) Creating a custom role with read-only permissions for compute.firewalls.* is a good approach, but using an existing role with the required permissions is more efficient.

QUESTION 44

Answer - D) Use Google Cloud Database Migration Service to perform a live migration of the database with minimal downtime.

A) Manually copying the database and importing it would result in significant downtime.
B) Google Cloud Dataflow may not provide the real-time migration capabilities required.
C) Google Cloud Transfer Service is not designed for live database migrations.
E) While Google Cloud Pub/Sub can be used for real-time data synchronization, it may not cover all database migration scenarios.
D) Google Cloud Database Migration Service is specifically designed for migrating databases with minimal downtime and is the recommended solution for critical database migrations.

QUESTION 45

Answer - C) Refactor the application into containers and deploy it on Google Kubernetes Engine (GKE).

A) Lift and shift may not provide the desired scalability and performance benefits.
B) While microservices are modern, transitioning to Cloud Spanner might not be necessary for all applications.
C) Refactoring into containers and using GKE allows for modernization, scalability, and performance improvements.
D) Serverless architecture may not be suitable for all parts of a legacy application.
E) Maintaining the monolithic architecture may not fully leverage Google Cloud's capabilities.

QUESTION 46

Answer - D) VPC-native network mode.

A) Legacy network mode is outdated and not recommended for modern GKE clusters.
B) Routes-based network mode is not a valid network mode for GKE clusters.
C) Alias IP ranges network mode is an option but may not offer the same performance benefits as VPC-native network mode.
D) VPC-native network mode is the recommended mode for improved network performance, as it provides native integration with VPC networking.
E) GKE-native network mode is not a recognized network mode for GKE clusters.

QUESTION 47

Answer – A) Enable Premium Network Tier on the Compute Engine instances hosting the applications.

A) Correct. Premium Network Tier provides optimized network performance for high throughput and low latency.
B) Incorrect. Dedicated Interconnect is typically for on-premises to GCP connections, not within GCP services.
C) Incorrect. VPNs may introduce additional latency, not suitable for high-performance requirements.
D) Incorrect. Global VPC does not inherently optimize latency to Cloud Spanner.
E) Incorrect. VPC Peering is not used for accessing managed services like Cloud Spanner.

QUESTION 48

Answer – A) Use Global HTTP(S) Load Balancer with Cloud Armor and Cloud CDN.

A) Correct. Global HTTP(S) Load Balancing with Cloud Armor and Cloud CDN provides dynamic scaling, DDoS protection, and efficient content delivery.
B) Incorrect. Network Load Balancers are not ideal for dynamic content delivery and global traffic management.
C) Incorrect. Internal Load Balancers and Cloud VPN are not suitable for a high-traffic, global web application.
D) Incorrect. TCP/SSL Proxy Load Balancers are not the best choice for global content distribution.
E) Incorrect. Cloud Run and VPC Network Peering do not provide the necessary scaling and DDoS protection for a global web application.

QUESTION 49

Answer – A) Use a multi-zone instance group with automatic failover and regional persistent disks.

A) Correct. Multi-zone instance groups with regional persistent disks provide the necessary high availability and instant failover for stateful sessions.
B) Incorrect. Single-zone instance groups with standby instances do not offer the same level of immediate failover.
C) Incorrect. Cloud SQL is a managed database service, not suitable for storing instance-based stateful sessions.
D) Incorrect. Custom failover mechanisms can be complex and may not provide the immediate response required.
E) Incorrect. Load balancing does not address the failover requirements for stateful sessions stored on instances.

QUESTION 50

Answer – A) Use a multi-regional Cloud Spanner instance for high availability.

A) Correct. Multi-regional Cloud Spanner instances offer built-in high availability and are ideal for disaster recovery.
B) Incorrect. Regular exports to Cloud Storage may not meet the stringent downtime and data loss requirements.
C) Incorrect. Read replicas are for scaling read operations, not for disaster recovery.
D) Incorrect. Continuous replication using Cloud Dataflow adds complexity and is not the optimal solution for Spanner.
E) Incorrect. Custom backup scripts are less reliable and efficient compared to Spanner's built-in capabilities.

PRACTICE TEST 10 - QUESTIONS ONLY

QUESTION 1

You are designing a Google Cloud network architecture for a multinational company with offices in various countries. Each office needs its own isolated network, but there should be a secure and controlled way to communicate between them. What should you implement to achieve this?

A) Use Shared VPC across all offices
B) Create separate projects for each office
C) Establish VPC Network Peering between offices
D) Deploy Google Cloud VPN for each office
E) Use Google Cloud Interconnect for all offices

QUESTION 2

You are responsible for setting up network connectivity between your on-premises data center and Google Cloud. Your organization requires a dedicated, high-speed connection with low latency. What Google Cloud service should you consider to meet these requirements while ensuring private and secure communication?

A) Google Cloud VPN with a shared VPN gateway.
B) Google Cloud Dedicated Interconnect with a private VLAN.
C) Google Cloud Direct Peering with a public peering connection.
D) Google Cloud VPC Network Peering.
E) Google Cloud Global Load Balancing.

QUESTION 3

You are the network administrator responsible for hybrid connec- tivity at your organization. Your finance team intends to leverage Bnguery for data analytics in the europe—northl region within your Shared VPC. You have established a Partner Interconnect con- nection and a Cloud Router in europe-northl, and the connectivity between your Shared VPC and corporate network is operational. Recently, you set up the private services access connection needed for Bnguery using the allocated IP address range with default con- figurations. Nevertheless, your finance analysts are unable to query Bnguery datasets from the corporate network. You need to resolve this issue. What should you do?

A) Change the VPC routing mode to regional.
B) Modify the VPC Network Peering connection used for Bnguery, and enable the import and export of routes.
C) Deploy an additional Cloud Router in europe-north2. Create a new Border Gateway Protocol (BGP) session for your corporate network. Modify the VPC Network Peering connection used for Big- Query, and enable the import and export of routes.
D) Change the VPC routing mode to regional. Modify the VPC Net- work Peering connection used for Bnguery, and enable the import and export of routes.

QUESTION 4

Your company operates a Virtual Private Cloud (VPC) with two Partner Interconnect connections serving different regions: europe-west1 and europe-north1. Each Partner Interconnect is linked to a Cloud Router in its specific region through a VLAN attachment. You have been tasked with setting up a resilient failover route. Ideally, all ingress traffic from your corporate network should primarily go through the Europe-west1 connection. In the event that europe—west1 becomes unavailable, traffic should automatically switch over to europe-north1. What should you set the multi-exit discriminator (MED) values to, in order to facilitate this automatic failover configuration?

A) Use regional routing. Set the europe-north1 Cloud Router to a base priority of 90, and set the europe-west1 Cloud Router to a base priority of 10.

B) Use regional routing. Set the europe-north1 Cloud Router to a base priority of 800, and set the europe—west1 Cloud Router to a base priority of 10.

C) Use global routing. Set the europe-north1 Cloud Router to a base priority of 90, and set the europe-west1 Cloud Router to a base priority of 10.

D) Use global routing. Set the europe-north1 Cloud Router to a base priority of 800, and set the europe-west1 Cloud Router to a base priority of 10.

E) Implement a regional VPC with only one Partner Interconnect connection for simplicity and reliability.

QUESTION 5

Your organization needs to enable secure, cross-regional communication between VPCs in different Google Cloud regions. What would be the most appropriate solution?

A) Set up multiple Cloud VPNs with IPsec encryption between VPCs in each region.
B) Implement VPC Network Peering connections between the VPCs.
C) Utilize Google Cloud Dedicated Interconnect for dedicated, cross-regional connectivity.
D) Deploy Google Cloud DNS for routing traffic between VPCs.
E) Establish a private fiber optic network connecting VPCs in different regions.

QUESTION 6

Your organization needs to ensure compliance with regulatory requirements regarding network activity monitoring. What approach should you prioritize to meet these requirements?

A) Enable VPC Flow Logs for all VPCs and store them in a secure, compliant data store for auditing purposes.
B) Implement Google Cloud's Network Intelligence Center to monitor and report on network activities for compliance.
C) Analyze Google Cloud Monitoring metrics related to network usage and traffic patterns to ensure compliance.
D) Deploy Google Cloud's Traffic Director with access controls to restrict network access as per compliance requirements.
E) Use Google Cloud Security Command Center to scan for potential compliance violations in network configurations.

QUESTION 7

You are implementing a hybrid cloud setup involving a GCP VPC (172.20.0.0/16) and an on-premises network (10.0.0.0/8). To ensure secure data transfer and network efficiency, which of the following Cloud VPN configurations should you employ?

A) Dynamic routing with BGP and matching ASN on both sides.
B) Static routing with manual route updates as needed.
C) HA VPN with Cloud Router on GCP and dynamic BGP routing.
D) Single-tunnel VPN with pre-shared key and static routes.
E) HA VPN with redundant tunnels and Cloud Router using OSPF.

QUESTION 8

Your team is responsible for managing a Google Kubernetes Engine (GKE) cluster hosting a microservices-based application. You want to ensure that the cluster can automatically adjust its size based on resource utilization to optimize costs and performance. Which GKE feature should you leverage for this purpose?

A) Node Pools
B) Cluster Autoscaler
C) Horizontal Pod Autoscaling
D) GKE Autopilot
E) Google Kubernetes Engine Usage Metering

QUESTION 9

Your organization needs to provide a secure and scalable way for external partners to access specific resources in your Google Cloud environment. These resources are distributed across multiple Virtual Private Clouds (VPCs) within your organization's projects. What should you implement to meet these requirements?

A) Configure a Cloud VPN to allow partner organizations to connect securely to your VPCs.
B) Use Google Cloud CDN to cache and deliver content to partner organizations more efficiently.
C) Set up VPC Network Peering to establish private connections between your VPCs and partner VPCs.
D) Implement Identity-Aware Proxy (IAP) to control and manage partner access to specific resources.
E) Deploy VPC Shared VPC for partners to access resources securely across multiple VPCs.

QUESTION 10

Your organization operates a global e-commerce platform on Google Cloud. To ensure high availability and low-latency access for customers worldwide, you need to replicate data across multiple regions and synchronize it in real-time. What Google Cloud database solution should you consider for this complex global data replication, and what advantages does it offer?

A) Google Cloud Cloud SQL for managed relational databases.
B) Google Cloud Spanner for a globally distributed, strongly consistent database.
C) Google Cloud Bigtable for scalable NoSQL storage.
D) Google Cloud Datastore for a managed NoSQL database.
E) Google Cloud Memorystore for in-memory data caching.

QUESTION 11

Your organization is planning to migrate a legacy on-premises application to Google Cloud. This application heavily relies on static IP addresses for communication, and any changes in IP addresses could cause disruptions. What Google Cloud networking feature or concept should you consider for this complex migration, and what advantages does it offer?

A) Google Cloud Global Load Balancing for global traffic distribution and IP address preservation.
B) Google Cloud DNS for managing domain names and IP address resolution.
C) Google Cloud External IP Addresses with static assignment for persistent IP addresses.
D) Google Cloud VPN with static routes for secure communication with on-premises resources.
E) Google Cloud CDN for content delivery with low-latency routing.

QUESTION 12

You are integrating a GCP VPC (10.150.0.0/16) with an on-premises network (192.168.0.0/16) using Cloud VPN. The on-premises network hosts critical legacy systems that need to communicate with GCP-based services. Which configuration ensures a secure, reliable, and high-performance connection?

A) Set up a single Cloud VPN tunnel with dynamic routing.
B) Use HA VPN with Cloud Router for each on-premises connection.
C) Implement multiple Cloud VPN tunnels with static routing.
D) Deploy Dedicated Interconnect for direct physical connectivity.
E) Configure Partner Interconnect with a focus on high availability.

QUESTION 13

You have configured a Google Cloud project with multiple VPC networks, each containing instances for different departments within your organization. You want to enable communication between instances in different VPCs while maintaining security. Which GCP networking solution should you implement to achieve this?

A) Google Cloud VPN
B) Google Cloud Interconnect
C) Google Cloud Network Peering
D) Google Cloud Shared VPC
E) Google Cloud VPC Peering

QUESTION 14

You are configuring a set of VMs on GCP for a team of remote developers. The team needs secure access to these VMs for software development and testing. What is the most appropriate firewall configuration for this scenario?

A) Allow ingress on port 22 (SSH) from the developers' IP addresses.
B) Create a rule to allow all traffic on all ports from any source.
C) Set up ingress on ports 22 (SSH) and 3389 (RDP) from any source.
D) Implement firewall rules to allow ingress on port 22 and egress on port 443.
E) Allow egress on all ports and restrict ingress to port 22 from known IPs.

QUESTION 15

You are responsible for optimizing network performance for a Google Cloud project that involves high-throughput data transfer between virtual machines in different VPCs. The project requires minimal latency and maximum bandwidth. What GCP networking solution should you recommend?

A) Google Cloud Load Balancer for distributing traffic.
B) Google Cloud CDN for content caching.
C) Google Cloud Interconnect for dedicated high-speed connections.
D) Google Cloud Network Peering for inter-VPC communication.
E) Google Cloud VPN for secure communication.

QUESTION 16

Your organization is planning to deploy a high-performance computing workload in Google Cloud that requires maximum network bandwidth and low-latency communication between virtual machines. What GCP networking solution should you recommend for this workload?

A) Google Cloud Load Balancer for distributing traffic.
B) Google Cloud VPN for secure communication.
C) Google Cloud Interconnect for dedicated high-speed connections.
D) Google Cloud Network Peering for inter-VPC communication.
E) Google Cloud CDN for content delivery.

QUESTION 17

Your mobile application users are concentrated near asia-southeast1 and europe-north1. Their services require frequent interactions with each other. You aim to optimize network performance while keeping costs low. What design should you implement for this architecture?

A) Design a single VPC with 2 regional subnets. Use a global load balancer to manage traffic between the services across the regions.
B) Set up 1 VPC with 2 regional subnets. Position your services within these subnets and enable them to communicate via private RFC1918 IP addresses.
C) Configure 2 VPCs, one in each region, and set up corresponding subnets. Connect the regions using 2 VPN gateways.
D) Establish 2 VPCs, allocating one to each region, with separate subnets. Leverage public IP addresses on the virtual machines to facilitate inter-regional connectivity.
E) Create 2 VPCs, each with a single regional subnet, and establish VPC peering between them for inter-VPC communication.

QUESTION 18

Your organization is using a Shared VPC in GCP to host a variety of applications. For compliance reasons, you need to ensure that all outbound traffic from the service projects' VMs to the internet goes through a centralized inspection and control point. What configuration should you implement?

A) Set up Cloud NAT instances in each service project for outbound traffic control.
B) Use a centralized Cloud NAT in the Shared VPC's host project to route all outbound internet traffic.
C) Implement individual egress-only firewall rules in each service project.

D) Configure a dedicated egress proxy or firewall appliance in the Shared VPC.
E) Create VPC Peering connections between service projects and the host project for outbound traffic management.

QUESTION 19

You're managing a Google Cloud project for a research institution that involves large-scale data processing. The researchers need high-performance network connectivity to transfer data between Google Cloud and their local research center. What Google Cloud networking option should you consider for this scenario?

A) Google Cloud VPN.
B) Google Cloud Dedicated Interconnect.
C) Google Cloud Partner Interconnect.
D) Google Cloud Interconnect with Carrier Peering.
E) Google Cloud Direct Peering.

QUESTION 20

Your mobile application users are concentrated near asia-southeast1 and europe-north1. Their services require frequent interactions with each other. You aim to optimize network performance while keeping costs low. What design should you implement for this architecture?

A) Design a single VPC with 2 regional subnets. Use a global load balancer to manage traffic between the services across the regions.
B) Set up 1 VCP with 2 regional subnets. Position your services within these subnets and enable them to communicate via private RFC1918 IP addresses.
C) Configure 2 VPCs, one in each region, and set up corresponding subnets. Connect the regions using 2 VPN gateways.
D) Establish 2 VPCs, allocating one to each region, with separate subnets. Leverage public IP addresses on the virtual machines to facilitate inter-regional connectivity.
E) Deploy a hybrid architecture with a mix of on-premises servers and Google Cloud resources to optimize performance.

QUESTION 21

Your organization's media processing system is transitioning its compute-heavy video rendering servers from an on-site data center to Google Cloud. The video rendering servers vary significantly in terms of their libraries and setups. This transition to Google Cloud will be a straightforward rehosting, and a unified network load balancer will cater to all incoming rendering requests. You are inclined to utilize Google Cloud-native solutions when applicable. What is the appropriate method to accomplish this deployment on Google Cloud?

A) Leverage the Equal Cost Multipath (ECMP) routing feature of Google Cloud to evenly distribute the traffic to your rendering servers by setting up several static routes with identical priority directed to the rendering server instances.
B) Implement a third-party front-end solution tailored to handle the diversity in configuration of your rendering servers, setting this up in front of the servers.
C) Set up a managed instance group using one of the virtual machine images from your in-house

rendering servers, and associate this managed instance group with a target pool that is connected to your network load balancer.

D) Establish a target pool, incorporate all the rendering instances within this pool, and configure this pool to work in conjunction with your network load balancer.

QUESTION 22

Your organization's media processing system is transitioning its compute-heavy video rendering servers from an on-site data center to Google Cloud. The video rendering servers vary significantly in terms of their libraries and setups. This transition to Google Cloud will be a straightforward rehosting, and a unified network load balancer will cater to all incoming rendering requests. You are inclined to utilize Google Cloud-native solutions when applicable. What is the appropriate method to accomplish this deployment on Google Cloud?

A) Leverage the Equal Cost Multipath (ECMP) routing feature of Google Cloud to evenly distribute the traffic to your rendering servers by setting up several static routes with identical priority directed to the rendering server instances.

B) Implement a third-party front-end solution tailored to handle the diversity in configuration of your rendering servers, setting this up in front of the servers.

C) Set up a managed instance group using one of the virtual machine images from your in-house rendering servers, and associate this managed instance group with a target pool that is connected to your network load balancer.

D) Establish a target pool, incorporate all the rendering instances within this pool, and configure this pool to work in conjunction with your network load balancer.

E) Deploy a dedicated Kubernetes cluster to manage the rendering servers and use Google Kubernetes Engine (GKE) to orchestrate their deployment and scaling.

QUESTION 23

A company has set up Google Cloud Private Google Access to allow its VM instances in a subnet to access Google services without external IP addresses. However, some VMs in that subnet still cannot access Google services. What could be a likely reason for this access problem?

A) Inconsistent service account permissions
B) VPC firewall rules blocking egress traffic
C) Google Cloud project quotas exceeded
D) Misconfigured DNS settings
E) Lack of required OS packages on the VMs

QUESTION 24

Your company is deploying a highly available web application on Google Cloud. The application is composed of web servers distributed across multiple zones for redundancy. You want to ensure that the web servers can automatically scale based on traffic demand and that the load is evenly distributed across zones. Which Google Cloud services or features should you use to achieve this?

A) Configure a regional instance group with autoscaling enabled.
B) Use Google Cloud CDN for content delivery.
C) Implement Google Cloud HTTP(S) Load Balancing with regional backend services.

D) Set up an external HTTP(S) load balancer with a single instance group.
E) Utilize Google Cloud Armor for security.

QUESTION 25

Your organization is planning to set up a global, distributed file storage solution on Google Cloud to serve files to users around the world. What two Google Cloud services or features should you recommend to achieve low-latency access for users and high availability of file storage?

A) Implement Google Cloud Storage for storing files.
B) Utilize Google Cloud Filestore for NFS-based file storage.
C) Deploy Google Cloud CDN for content caching.
D) Set up Google Cloud Memorystore for in-memory file serving.
E) Configure Google Cloud Storage Coldline for file archiving.

QUESTION 26

You are setting up a real-time data analytics solution in GCP. The solution requires streaming data from various sources, processing it in real-time, and making it available for immediate analysis. What combination of GCP services would best meet these requirements?

A) Use Cloud Pub/Sub for data streaming, Dataflow for real-time processing, and BigQuery for analysis.
B) Implement Cloud IoT Core for data ingestion, Compute Engine for processing, and Cloud SQL for storage and analysis.
C) Configure Cloud Storage for data ingestion, use Cloud Functions for processing, and Bigtable for analysis.
D) Set up a series of Cloud Data Fusion instances for ingestion, Cloud Dataproc for processing, and Cloud Spanner for analysis.
E) Employ Cloud Endpoints for data ingestion, Kubernetes Engine for processing, and Firestore for real-time data storage and analysis.

QUESTION 27

Your organization is planning to deploy a high-availability application in Google Cloud across multiple regions. What networking strategy should you consider to ensure redundancy and failover capabilities for this application?

A) Use a single region with multiple availability zones for redundancy.
B) Deploy separate instances of the application in each region and configure DNS for failover.
C) Implement global load balancing with Google Cloud Load Balancers.
D) Utilize VPN connections for redundancy instead of regional deployments.
E) None of the above.

QUESTION 28

You are building a data processing pipeline in GCP that involves ingesting large datasets from external sources, processing the data in Dataproc, and storing results in BigQuery. Security and data privacy are paramount. How should you configure the network to securely handle and process this data?

A) Utilize VPC Service Controls to protect data across Dataproc and BigQuery.
B) Set up a dedicated VPC for Dataproc with restricted firewall rules and private access to BigQuery.
C) Implement Cloud Interconnect for secure data ingestion and use Private Google Access for BigQuery.
D) Configure Cloud VPN for secure data transfer and deploy Dataproc clusters with private IPs only.
E) Use Cloud Armor to protect data in transit and configure Dataproc for internal IP communication with BigQuery.

QUESTION 29

You manage a service that is operating on a managed instance group within Google Cloud. The team has developed an updated instance template that integrates an experimental optimization algorithm. To ensure that any potential issues in the new template have minimal effect on your user base, how should you approach the update process of your instances?

A) Directly apply patches to a fraction of the instances manually, subsequently carrying out a rolling restart on the entire managed instance group.
B) Deploy the updated instance template to carry out a rolling update across the entire scope of instances in the managed instance group. Perform validation of the experimental algorithm once the update has been fully executed.
C) Establish a new managed instance group and utilize it to canary test the updated template. Upon successful verification of the experimental algorithm within the canary group, apply the updated template to the initial managed instance group.
D) Conduct a canary deployment by initiating a rolling update and designating a subset of your instances to adopt the updated template. After confirming the experimental algorithm's stability on the canary instances, proceed to implement the update for the remaining instances.
E) None of the above.

QUESTION 30

You are designing a disaster recovery strategy for a mission-critical application in GCP. The application uses Cloud Spanner for data storage and needs to maintain a recovery point objective (RPO) of 15 minutes. What configuration would you recommend to achieve this RPO with Cloud Spanner?

A) Configure multi-regional replication in Cloud Spanner.
B) Set up automated exports of Cloud Spanner data to Cloud Storage every 15 minutes.
C) Implement a custom script to perform incremental backups of Cloud Spanner every 15 minutes.
D) Use Cloud Spanner's read replicas in a different region for disaster recovery.
E) Establish a secondary Cloud Spanner instance in another region and synchronize data every 15 minutes.

QUESTION 31

You are implementing a global application in GCP with a requirement for low-latency access to a Cloud SQL database from Compute Engine instances located in multiple regions. What configuration ensures optimal database performance for all regions?

A) Configure a multi-regional Cloud SQL instance.
B) Deploy read replicas of the Cloud SQL database in each region.
C) Use Cloud Spanner instead of Cloud SQL for global distribution.

D) Set up Cloud VPN tunnels from each region to the Cloud SQL instance region.
E) Implement Global Load Balancing with a backend service for Cloud SQL.

QUESTION 32

Your organization is migrating to Google Cloud, and you need to establish a highly available and low-latency connection between your on-premises data center in New York and Google Cloud's us-east1 region. What networking solution should you implement to meet these requirements?

A) Create a VPN tunnel between your on-premises data center and Google Cloud us-east1 region.
B) Deploy Cloud Interconnect Dedicated to establish a dedicated, high-speed connection.
C) Utilize Google Cloud Direct Peering for a low-latency, high-bandwidth connection.
D) Set up an Interconnect connection using a Partner Interconnect provider.
E) None of the above.

QUESTION 33

Your organization is designing a global network architecture for its applications, with a focus on low-latency access and high availability. Which combination of Google Cloud networking services and features should you consider to achieve this complex goal effectively?

A) Global Load Balancer with Cloud CDN
B) Anycast IP Routing with Global VPN
C) Transit Gateway with Private Google Access
D) Regional Load Balancer with Cloud Interconnect
E) Network Peering with Dedicated Interconnect

QUESTION 34

Your organization is planning to establish a hybrid cloud setup, with some workloads hosted in Google Cloud and others on-premises. You need a secure and reliable connection between the two environments, and you want to optimize the use of Google Cloud resources. What complex networking solution should you design to achieve this goal?

A) Cloud VPN with VPC Peering
B) Cloud Interconnect with Cloud Router
C) Dedicated Interconnect with VPN Gateway
D) Transit Gateway with Network Peering
E) VPC Peering with Private Google Access

QUESTION 35

Your organization is running a global e-commerce platform with customers in various regions. You need to ensure low-latency access for customers while maintaining data residency compliance. What complex networking strategy should you employ to achieve these goals effectively?

A) Set up custom routes with more precision than the default network routes, specifying low-latency paths and regional data residency zones for traffic routing, and use network tags for compliance.
B) Replicate the entire e-commerce platform in each region to guarantee low-latency access and data residency compliance, reducing network complexity.
C) Delete all default network routes and establish distinct custom routes for low-latency paths and data residency zones, using network tags for traffic differentiation and compliance.
D) Create more specific custom routes than the default network routes, designating low-latency paths and data residency zones for routing, and assign network tags for secure communication, compliance, and precise traffic handling.
E) Implement Google Cloud's Global Load Balancing with regional distribution and leverage Google's network infrastructure for low-latency access while configuring data residency zones for compliance.

QUESTION 36

You are designing a network in GCP for an application that processes sensitive data and requires secure communication between Compute Engine instances and Cloud Storage. The data must not traverse the public internet and needs encryption in transit. What configuration ensures the security and privacy of data transfer?

A) Use VPC Service Controls to isolate Compute Engine and Cloud Storage, and enable Private Google Access for secure communication.
B) Configure each Compute Engine instance with a private IP and use Cloud VPN to encrypt data to Cloud Storage.
C) Implement Cloud Interconnect for a dedicated connection to Cloud Storage and enable TLS for data encryption.
D) Set up Private Service Connect between Compute Engine and Cloud Storage for private data transfer.
E) Enable default encryption on Cloud Storage and restrict Compute Engine instances to internal IPs only.

QUESTION 37

You need to design a network architecture that allows for seamless scaling of your Google Kubernetes Engine (GKE) clusters based on application demand while providing DDoS protection. Which Google Cloud networking service or feature should you integrate with GKE to achieve these objectives?

A) Google Cloud CDN with Google Cloud Armor
B) Traffic Director with Cloud Load Balancing
C) Google Cloud DNS with Cloud IAM
D) Cloud Interconnect with Cloud VPN
E) Google Cloud CDN with VPC peering

QUESTION 38

You are managing a Google Cloud project and need to set up a secure, private network connection between two Google Cloud Virtual Private Clouds (VPCs) located in different regions. Your goal is to ensure data isolation and low-latency communication between the VPCs. Which Google Cloud networking solution should you implement to achieve these objectives?

A) Google Cloud VPN with VPC peering
B) Cloud Interconnect with Google Cloud Router

C) VPC peering with Cloud VPN
D) Google Cloud Load Balancing with VPC Service Controls
E) Google Cloud CDN with VPC peering

QUESTION 39

Your organization operates a mission-critical e-commerce platform, and you need to ensure that the platform remains highly available and can scale automatically to handle traffic spikes during peak seasons. Which Google Cloud networking service or feature should you integrate with your e-commerce platform to achieve these objectives effectively?

A) Google Cloud Armor with Google Cloud CDN
B) Traffic Director with Cloud Load Balancing
C) Google Cloud DNS with Cloud IAM
D) Cloud Interconnect with Cloud VPN
E) Google Cloud CDN with VPC peering

QUESTION 40

Your organization needs to ensure data redundancy and high availability for your cloud-based storage solution on Google Cloud. You are evaluating different storage options. Which combination of Google Cloud storage services or features should you choose to meet these requirements effectively?

A) Google Cloud Storage and Google Cloud Persistent Disk
B) Google Cloud Filestore and Google Cloud Storage Transfer Service
C) Google Cloud Storage Nearline and Google Cloud CDN
D) Google Cloud Spanner and Google Cloud KMS
E) Google Cloud Bigtable and Google Cloud Dataprep

QUESTION 41

Your organization operates a high-traffic online video streaming service. To enhance security, you've enlisted a DDoS protection service and need to limit your backend servers to accept connections solely from this DDoS mitigation provider. How should you proceed?

A) Create a VPC Service Controls Perimeter that blocks all traffic except for the DDoS protection service.
B) Create a Cloud Armor Security Policy that blocks all traffic except for the DDoS protection service.
C) Create a VPC Firewall rule that blocks all traffic except for the DDoS protection service.
D) Implement iptables firewall rules on your servers that block all traffic except for the DDoS protection service.
E) Create a VPC Peering connection with the DDoS protection service and use IAM roles to restrict access to your backend servers.

QUESTION 42

Your organization operates a high-traffic online video streaming service. Your servers are configured with private IP addresses, and users connect through a regional load balancer. To enhance security, you've enlisted a DDoS protection service and need to limit your backend servers to accept connections solely from this DDoS mitigation provider. How should you proceed?

A) Create a VPC Service Controls Perimeter that blocks all traffic except for the DDoS protection service.
B) Create a Cloud Armor Security Policy that blocks all traffic except for the DDoS protection service.
C) Create a VPC Firewall rule that blocks all traffic except for the DDoS protection service.
D) Implement iptables firewall rules on your servers that block all traffic except for the DDoS protection service.
E) Utilize a regional load balancer with no additional configurations.

QUESTION 43

Your company's Google Cloud-hosted, live telemetry analysis platform supports various vehicle types. The analytics team has requested guidance on how to differentiate routing for sensor data and location tracking information to distinct Google Cloud Bigtable instances. They would like to use URL maps to streamline management. Their current directory setup is as follows: [cars/sensors, trucks/sensors, bikes/sensors, /../sensors, cars/location, trucks/location, bikes/location, /../location. Which solution should you recommend?

A) Rearrange the directory structure, configure DNS CNAME records for sensors and location and leverage path matchers such as /sensors/ and /location/.
B) Rearrange the directory structure, create a URL map and leverage path matchers such as /sensors/ and /location/.
C) Maintain the directory structure as it stands, create a URL map and leverage a path rule such as /cars/sensors and /cars/location.
D) Keep the current directory structure, create a URL map and leverage a path rule such as /[a-zA-Z]+/sensors and /[a-zA-Z]+/location.
E) Rearrange the directory structure into separate subdomains for sensors and location, and use separate URL maps for each subdomain.

QUESTION 44

You are responsible for securing a Google Cloud project that includes multiple VPCs. Each VPC hosts sensitive data, and you need to implement strict access controls. Your organization uses Google Workspace for identity and access management. Which IAM best practices should you follow to enhance security?

A) Use Google Groups for managing permissions at the VPC level.
B) Implement VPC Service Controls for each VPC.
C) Create custom IAM roles for each VPC.
D) Leverage Google Workspace groups to manage access at the project level.
E) Use IAM conditions to restrict access based on IP ranges.

QUESTION 45

Your organization needs to ensure secure communication between on-premises data centers and Google Cloud. The on-premises network uses dynamic IP addresses. What is the recommended solution to establish a secure and reliable connection?

A) Implement a Cloud VPN with a static IP address on the on-premises side.
B) Set up a Dedicated Interconnect with a dynamic IP address on the on-premises side.
C) Use Cloud Interconnect to establish a direct, encrypted connection.

D) Deploy a Cloud Router to manage routing between on-premises and Google Cloud networks.
E) Create a hybrid VPC with Cloud VPN for secure communication.

QUESTION 46

Your organization plans to deploy a high-availability web application on Google Cloud. The application requires a global load balancer with SSL/TLS termination. You want to minimize the complexity and maintenance efforts of SSL/TLS certificate management. What is the most efficient way to configure SSL/TLS termination for your global load balancer?

A) Upload SSL/TLS certificates manually to the global load balancer.
B) Use Google-managed SSL certificates for the global load balancer.
C) Deploy a separate SSL/TLS termination proxy instance in each region.
D) Utilize a third-party SSL/TLS certificate management service.
E) Create custom SSL/TLS certificates for each region and associate them with the global load balancer.

QUESTION 47

For a GCP environment hosting a web application, you need to set up a network solution that dynamically scales to handle varying traffic loads and protects against DDoS attacks. The solution should also optimize the delivery of dynamic content to users worldwide. Which combination of GCP services and configurations is most appropriate?

A) Use Global HTTP(S) Load Balancer with Cloud Armor and Cloud CDN.
B) Implement regional Network Load Balancers with Cloud IDS for DDoS protection.
C) Configure TCP/SSL Proxy Load Balancers for each region and use Cloud Endpoints for content optimization.
D) Set up instance groups in each region with Internal Load Balancers and enable Cloud Armor for DDoS protection.
E) Establish Cloud Run instances globally with VPC Service Controls for traffic management and security.

QUESTION 48

You are tasked with designing a network architecture in GCP for a multi-tier web application. The application requires different network zones for the frontend, application logic, and database layers, each with specific communication needs. What is the most effective network setup for this application?

A) Use a single VPC with separate subnets for each layer and configure firewall rules for inter-layer communication.
B) Set up three different VPCs for each layer and use VPC Peering for communication between them.
C) Implement Shared VPC with dedicated subnets for each application layer.
D) Configure separate subnets within a Shared VPC and use Cloud VPN for inter-layer communication.
E) Establish individual VPCs for each layer and connect them with Cloud Interconnect for secure communication.

QUESTION 49

In a GCP deployment for a real-time data processing service, you need to configure a network that supports rapid scaling and efficient data transfer from various sources. The service involves streaming large volumes of data and requires instant processing and analysis. What network and service configuration optimizes performance for this real-time data analytics service?

A) Configure Cloud Pub/Sub for data ingestion, Cloud Dataflow for real-time processing, and BigQuery for analysis.
B) Use Cloud IoT Core for data ingestion, Compute Engine for processing, and Cloud Spanner for analysis.
C) Implement Cloud Storage for initial data ingestion, Cloud Functions for processing, and Cloud Bigtable for analysis.
D) Set up direct streaming to Compute Engine instances and use Cloud SQL for real-time data analysis.
E) Establish Cloud Endpoints for data ingestion, Kubernetes Engine for processing, and Cloud Firestore for analysis.

QUESTION 50

In a GCP deployment, you need to set up a network for a service that requires real-time data processing and analysis. The service involves streaming data from various sources and requires immediate processing. What network and service configuration optimizes performance for real-time data analytics?

A) Use Cloud Pub/Sub for data ingestion, Cloud Dataflow for real-time processing, and BigQuery for immediate analysis.
B) Set up Cloud IoT Core for data ingestion, Compute Engine for processing, and Cloud Spanner for real-time analysis.
C) Implement Cloud Storage for initial data ingestion, Cloud Functions for processing, and Cloud Bigtable for analysis.
D) Establish direct data streaming to Compute Engine instances and use Cloud SQL for real-time data analysis.
E) Configure Cloud Endpoints for data ingestion, Kubernetes Engine for processing, and Cloud Firestore for analysis.

PRACTICE TEST 10 - ANSWERS ONLY

QUESTION 1

Answer – C) Establish VPC Network Peering between offices

Option C - Establishing VPC Network Peering between offices allows secure communication while maintaining isolation.
Option A - Shared VPCs may not provide sufficient isolation between offices.
Option B - Creating separate projects can lead to administrative complexity.
Option D - Deploying VPNs for each office may not be the most efficient solution.
Option E - Google Cloud Interconnect is for dedicated connections, not internal communication between offices.

QUESTION 2

Answer – B) Google Cloud Dedicated Interconnect with a private VLAN.

Option B - Using Google Cloud Dedicated Interconnect with a private VLAN provides dedicated, high-speed, and low-latency connectivity between on-premises data centers and Google Cloud while ensuring private and secure communication.
Option A - VPNs may not provide the same level of performance and privacy as Dedicated Interconnect.
Option C - Direct Peering is for external connectivity, not private communication with on-premises data centers.
Option D - VPC Network Peering is for VPCs, not on-premises data centers.
Option E - Global Load Balancing is unrelated to dedicated connectivity.

QUESTION 3

Answer – B) Modify the VPC Network Peering connection used for Bnguery, and enable the import and export of routes.

Option B - Modifying the VPC Network Peering connection for Bigquery and enabling route import and export allows the finance team to access Bigquery datasets from the corporate network.
Option A - Changing the VPC routing mode may not address the issue related to Bigquery access.
Option C - Deploying an additional Cloud Router in a different region is unnecessary for this issue.
Option D - Changing the VPC routing mode may not resolve the specific problem with Bigquery access.

QUESTION 4

Answer – B) Use regional routing. Set the europe-north1 Cloud Router to a base priority of 800, and set the europe—west1 Cloud Router to a base priority of 10.

Option B - Using regional routing with MED values of 800 for europe-north1 and 10 for europe-west1 allows for automatic failover as required.
Option A - Setting europe-west1 to a lower priority may not prioritize it correctly.
Option C - Using global routing may not align with the desired regional failover.

Option D - The MED values should be reversed for the desired failover behavior.
Option E - Implementing a regional VPC does not address the dual connection requirement.

QUESTION 5

Answer - B) Implement VPC Network Peering connections between the VPCs.

Option B is the most appropriate solution for enabling secure, cross-regional communication between VPCs in different Google Cloud regions.
Option A with multiple VPNs may add complexity and may not provide the same level of reliability.
Option C, Dedicated Interconnect, may not be necessary for internal VPC communication.
Option D addresses DNS but doesn't provide the connectivity itself.
Option E introduces complexity and may not be cost-effective for this scenario.

QUESTION 6

Answer - A) Enable VPC Flow Logs for all VPCs and store them in a secure, compliant data store for auditing purposes.
Answer - B) Implement Google Cloud's Network Intelligence Center to monitor and report on network activities for compliance.

Options A and B are the appropriate approaches to ensure compliance with regulatory requirements regarding network activity monitoring.
Option A involves enabling VPC Flow Logs and securely storing them for auditing, while Option B utilizes Google Cloud's Network Intelligence Center for compliance monitoring and reporting.
Option C focuses on Monitoring metrics, which may not provide the same level of compliance details.
Option D discusses Traffic Director, which is more about access control than compliance monitoring.
Option E mentions Security Command Center, which is broader in scope and may not specifically address network compliance.

QUESTION 7

Answer – C) HA VPN with Cloud Router on GCP and dynamic BGP routing.

A) Incorrect. Matching ASN can cause routing conflicts.
B) Incorrect. Static routing lacks flexibility and can be error-prone.
C) Correct. Ensures high availability and dynamic routing adaptability.
D) Incorrect. Lacks redundancy and dynamic routing capabilities.
E) Incorrect. OSPF is not used in GCP Cloud VPN.

QUESTION 8

Answer - B) Cluster Autoscaler

Option B, Cluster Autoscaler, is the correct choice for automatically adjusting the size of a GKE cluster based on resource utilization, optimizing costs, and performance.
 Option A, Node Pools, allows you to manage groups of nodes within a cluster but does not provide automatic scaling based on resource utilization.
 Option C, Horizontal Pod Autoscaling, focuses on adjusting the number of pods based on resource usage

but does not control the cluster size.

Option D, GKE Autopilot, is a mode for managing clusters but does not specifically address automatic resizing based on resource utilization.

Option E, Google Kubernetes Engine Usage Metering, is related to monitoring and billing but does not handle automatic cluster resizing.

QUESTION 9

Answer - C) Set up VPC Network Peering to establish private connections between your VPCs and partner VPCs.

Answer - D) Implement Identity-Aware Proxy (IAP) to control and manage partner access to specific resources.

Option C is the recommended approach for establishing private connections between your VPCs and partner VPCs.

Option D provides additional control and management capabilities for partner access. Options A, B, and E do not directly address the requirement for secure and scalable access to specific resources across multiple VPCs.

QUESTION 10

Answer - B) Google Cloud Spanner for a globally distributed, strongly consistent database.

Option A is for managed relational databases but may not offer global distribution.

Option C is suitable for NoSQL storage but may not provide strong consistency.

Option D is for managed NoSQL databases but may not offer global distribution and strong consistency.

Option E is for in-memory data caching and doesn't cover data replication.

Option B is the correct choice as Google Cloud Spanner provides global data replication with strong consistency, ensuring high availability and low-latency access, making it suitable for complex global e-commerce platforms.

QUESTION 11

Answer - C) Google Cloud External IP Addresses with static assignment for persistent IP addresses.

Option A provides load balancing but may not specifically address IP address preservation.

Option B focuses on DNS and domain names but may not cover IP address preservation.

Option D offers VPN and secure communication but may not relate to IP address preservation.

Option E is for content delivery but doesn't address IP address preservation.

Option C is the correct choice as Google Cloud External IP Addresses with static assignment allows for persistent IP addresses, preserving the required static IP addresses during the migration, ensuring minimal disruption.

QUESTION 12

Answer – B) Use HA VPN with Cloud Router for each on-premises connection.

A) Incorrect. A single tunnel lacks redundancy.

B) Correct. HA VPN provides redundancy and high performance.

C) Incorrect. Static routing is less flexible and reliable than dynamic routing.
D) Incorrect. Overkill for legacy systems requiring only VPN-level throughput.
E) Incorrect. Partner Interconnect is not necessary for this scenario.

QUESTION 13

Answer - D) Google Cloud Shared VPC

D) Google Cloud Shared VPC - Shared VPC allows communication between instances in different VPCs while maintaining security boundaries, making it suitable for this scenario.
 A) Google Cloud VPN - Google Cloud VPN is used for secure remote access, not inter-VPC communication.
 B) Google Cloud Interconnect - Interconnect provides dedicated connections but is typically used for external connections.
 C) Google Cloud Network Peering - Network Peering is for communication within the same organization, not necessarily for different departments.
 E) Google Cloud VPC Peering - VPC Peering is used for communication between different VPCs, which may not align with departmental separation.

QUESTION 14

Answer – A) Allow ingress on port 22 (SSH) from the developers' IP addresses.

A) Correct. Provides secure and restricted access for development.
B) Incorrect. Too permissive and a security risk.
C) Incorrect. Allowing RDP from any source is not secure.
D) Incorrect. Egress on 443 is not necessarily required for development.
E) Incorrect. Egress should not be unrestricted, and ingress should be limited to known IPs.

QUESTION 15

Answer - C) Google Cloud Interconnect for dedicated high-speed connections.

C) Google Cloud Interconnect for dedicated high-speed connections - Interconnect provides the dedicated and high-speed connections required for high-throughput data transfer with minimal latency.
 A) Google Cloud Load Balancer for distributing traffic - Load Balancer focuses on traffic distribution, not necessarily on dedicated high-speed connections.
 B) Google Cloud CDN for content caching - CDN is for caching content, which may not address the high-throughput data transfer between VPCs.
 D) Google Cloud Network Peering for inter-VPC communication - Network Peering is for communication between VPCs but may not provide the same level of dedicated high-speed connections as Interconnect.
 E) Google Cloud VPN for secure communication - VPNs are for secure access but may not optimize network performance and throughput to the same extent as Interconnect.

QUESTION 16

Answer - C) Google Cloud Interconnect for dedicated high-speed connections.

C) Google Cloud Interconnect for dedicated high-speed connections - Interconnect provides the

dedicated high-speed connections required for high-performance computing workloads with maximum network bandwidth and low-latency communication.
 A) Google Cloud Load Balancer for distributing traffic - Load Balancer focuses on traffic distribution, not dedicated high-speed connections.
 B) Google Cloud VPN for secure communication - VPNs provide secure access but may not optimize network performance and bandwidth to the same extent as Interconnect.
 D) Google Cloud Network Peering for inter-VPC communication - Network Peering is for communication between VPCs, not necessarily for high-performance computing workloads.
 E) Google Cloud CDN for content delivery - CDN is for content caching and may not directly address the network requirements of high-performance computing.

QUESTION 17

Answer - B) Set up 1 VPC with 2 regional subnets. Position your services within these subnets and enable them to communicate via private RFC1918 IP addresses.

B) Set up 1 VPC with 2 regional subnets. Positioning services within these subnets and enabling communication via private RFC1918 IP addresses optimizes network performance and keeps costs low, meeting the requirements.
 A) Designing a single VPC with a global load balancer may not provide the low-latency communication needed for services concentrated in specific regions.
 C) Configuring 2 VPCs with VPN gateways introduces unnecessary complexity for inter-region communication.
 D) Leveraging public IP addresses for inter-regional connectivity may increase costs and expose services to the public internet unnecessarily.
 E) Creating 2 VPCs with VPC peering may not offer the same performance benefits as positioning services within the same VPC.

QUESTION 18

Answer – D) Configure a dedicated egress proxy or firewall appliance in the Shared VPC.

A) Incorrect. Cloud NAT in each project does not centralize inspection.
B) Incorrect. Cloud NAT does not provide inspection and control of traffic.
C) Incorrect. Egress-only firewall rules do not offer centralized traffic inspection.
D) Correct. A centralized egress solution enables compliance with inspection and control requirements.
E) Incorrect. VPC Peering is not used for centralized internet egress control.

QUESTION 19

Answer - B) Google Cloud Dedicated Interconnect.

B) Google Cloud Dedicated Interconnect provides high-performance, dedicated network connectivity between Google Cloud and on-premises data centers, making it suitable for large-scale data transfer requirements.
 A) Google Cloud VPN may not offer the same level of performance.
 C) Google Cloud Partner Interconnect may involve third-party vendors and may not provide dedicated high-performance connectivity.
 D) Google Cloud Interconnect with Carrier Peering is typically used for public internet access, not

dedicated connectivity.

E) Google Cloud Direct Peering is focused on public internet peering, not dedicated connectivity to on-premises data centers.

QUESTION 20

Answer - A) Design a single VPC with 2 regional subnets. Use a global load balancer to manage traffic between the services across the regions.

A) To optimize network performance and minimize costs for users in different regions, you can design a single VPC with 2 regional subnets and use a global load balancer to efficiently manage traffic between the services across the regions.

B) While setting up regional subnets is a good practice, it doesn't leverage the global load balancer for efficient traffic management.

C) Configuring 2 VPCs and connecting them via VPN gateways may introduce unnecessary complexity and latency.

D) Using public IP addresses for inter-regional connectivity may not be the most cost-effective and secure approach.

E) Deploying a hybrid architecture is not necessary to optimize network performance in this scenario.

QUESTION 21

Answer - C) Set up a managed instance group using one of the virtual machine images from your in-house rendering servers, and associate this managed instance group with a target pool that is connected to your network load balancer.

C) The appropriate method to transition your compute-heavy video rendering servers to Google Cloud while utilizing Google Cloud-native solutions is to set up a managed instance group (MIG) using one of the virtual machine images from your in-house rendering servers. This MIG can then be associated with a target pool that is connected to your network load balancer. This approach allows for scalability, load balancing, and management of the rendering instances in a Google Cloud-native manner.

A) Leveraging ECMP routing with static routes may not be the most suitable approach for this scenario.

B) Implementing a third-party front-end solution would introduce additional complexity and might not fully leverage Google Cloud's capabilities.

D) Establishing a target pool is part of the solution, but it alone does not cover the complete deployment strategy for the transition.

QUESTION 22

Answer - C) Set up a managed instance group using one of the virtual machine images from your in-house rendering servers, and associate this managed instance group with a target pool that is connected to your network load balancer.

C) To accomplish the deployment of compute-heavy video rendering servers from an on-site data center to Google Cloud while leveraging Google Cloud-native solutions, you should set up a managed instance group using one of the virtual machine images from your in-house rendering servers. Then, associate this managed instance group with a target pool that is connected to your network load balancer. This approach allows you to utilize Google Cloud's managed services and efficiently distribute incoming rendering requests to the rehosted servers.

A) Leveraging the Equal Cost Multipath (ECMP) routing feature with identical static routes may not provide the level of automation and load balancing capabilities offered by managed instance groups and target pools.
B) Implementing a third-party front-end solution introduces additional complexity and may not align with the goal of utilizing Google Cloud-native solutions.
D) Establishing a target pool is a step in the right direction, but it is recommended to use a managed instance group for better management and scaling of instances.

E) Deploying a dedicated Kubernetes cluster and using Google Kubernetes Engine (GKE) might be suitable for certain scenarios but may add complexity if not required for the straightforward rehosting of video rendering servers.

By setting up a managed instance group and connecting it to a target pool and network load balancer, you can efficiently manage the transition to Google Cloud while taking advantage of its native services for load balancing and scaling.

QUESTION 23

Answer - B) VPC firewall rules blocking egress traffic

Option A - Inconsistent service account permissions might lead to authentication issues but not necessarily access problems.
 Option C - Project quotas wouldn't directly affect Private Google Access.
 Option D - DNS settings may affect resolution but not access.
 Option E - Lack of OS packages would not necessarily block access to Google services.

QUESTION 24

Answer - C) Implement Google Cloud HTTP(S) Load Balancing with regional backend services.

Option A - While regional instance groups support autoscaling, they may not provide even distribution across zones.
Option B - Google Cloud CDN focuses on content delivery and caching, not load balancing and scaling.
Option D - An external HTTP(S) load balancer with a single instance group may lack redundancy and scalability.
Option E - Google Cloud Armor is primarily for security, not load balancing and scaling. Choice C (Implement Google Cloud HTTP(S) Load Balancing with regional backend services) - Google Cloud HTTP(S) Load Balancing with regional backend services automatically scales and evenly distributes traffic across multiple zones for high availability and scalability, meeting the requirements for the web application.

QUESTION 25

Answer - B) Utilize Google Cloud Filestore for NFS-based file storage.
C) Deploy Google Cloud CDN for content caching.

Option A - While Google Cloud Storage is suitable for file storage, it may not provide the low-latency access required for global distribution.
Option D - Google Cloud Memorystore is for in-memory caching and doesn't directly provide file storage.

Option E - Google Cloud Storage Coldline is for file archiving and may not provide low-latency access or high availability. Choice B - Google Cloud Filestore offers NFS-based file storage with low-latency access and can be deployed globally, ensuring high availability for serving files to users worldwide.
Choice C - Deploying Google Cloud CDN helps reduce latency by caching content at edge locations, enhancing the global user experience when accessing files.

QUESTION 26

Answer – A) Use Cloud Pub/Sub for data streaming, Dataflow for real-time processing, and BigQuery for analysis.

A) Correct. This setup provides an efficient pipeline for real-time data analytics.
B) Incorrect. Cloud IoT Core is specific to IoT data; Cloud SQL may not handle real-time analytics efficiently.
C) Incorrect. Cloud Storage is not optimal for real-time data streaming; Bigtable is more for high-throughput, low-latency workloads.
D) Incorrect. Data Fusion and Dataproc are not primarily for real-time processing; Cloud Spanner, while powerful, is overkill for this scenario.
E) Incorrect. Cloud Endpoints and Firestore are not suited for high-volume, real-time data analytics workflows.

QUESTION 27

Answer - C) Implement global load balancing with Google Cloud Load Balancers.

Option A - A single region with multiple availability zones provides redundancy within the same region, but may not cover multiple regions.
Option B - Deploying separate instances in each region with DNS failover can be complex to manage.
Option D - VPN connections are not designed for application redundancy and failover. Choice C - Implementing global load balancing with Google Cloud Load Balancers allows for high availability and failover across multiple regions, ensuring reliability for the application

QUESTION 28

Answer – B) Set up a dedicated VPC for Dataproc with restricted firewall rules and private access to BigQuery.

A) Incorrect. VPC Service Controls are for securing data within services but do not configure network traffic flow.
B) Correct. A dedicated VPC with strict firewall rules and private access ensures secure data handling and processing.
C) Incorrect. Cloud Interconnect is for on-premises connections; it's not necessary for internal GCP data handling.
D) Incorrect. VPN is for external connectivity, not optimal for internal GCP service communication.
E) Incorrect. Cloud Armor protects against external threats and is not used for internal data pipeline security.

QUESTION 29

Answer - C) Establish a new managed instance group and utilize it to canary test the updated template. Upon successful verification of the experimental algorithm within the canary group, apply the updated template to the initial managed instance group.

Option A - Directly applying patches manually does not involve the use of a new managed instance group for testing.
Option B - While it suggests a rolling update, it does not mention using a separate group for canary testing.
Option D - It describes a canary deployment but does not mention starting with a new managed instance group for testing. Choice C - Establishing a new managed instance group for canary testing and then applying the updated template to the initial group upon successful verification is a recommended approach to minimize potential issues when introducing a new template.

QUESTION 30

Answer – A) Configure multi-regional replication in Cloud Spanner.

A) Correct. Multi-regional replication in Cloud Spanner ensures data durability and availability, meeting the RPO requirement.
B) Incorrect. Automated exports to Cloud Storage might not guarantee the 15-minute RPO due to potential delays.
C) Incorrect. Custom scripts for backups are less reliable and harder to maintain than Cloud Spanner's built-in replication.
D) Incorrect. Read replicas are for scaling reads, not for disaster recovery.
E) Incorrect. Manually synchronizing a secondary instance every 15 minutes is less efficient and reliable than built-in replication.

QUESTION 31

Answer – B) Deploy read replicas of the Cloud SQL database in each region.

A) Incorrect. Cloud SQL does not offer a multi-regional option.
B) Correct. Read replicas in each region reduce latency for database access.
C) Incorrect. Cloud Spanner is an alternative but requires changing the database technology.
D) Incorrect. VPN tunnels are not optimal for this use case and do not reduce latency.
E) Incorrect. Global Load Balancing is not applicable for Cloud SQL instances.

QUESTION 32

Answer - B) Deploy Cloud Interconnect Dedicated to establish a dedicated, high-speed connection.

Option A - Creating a VPN tunnel may not provide the required high-speed connection.
Option C - Google Cloud Direct Peering is typically used for public internet traffic, not for connecting on-premises data centers.
Option D - Setting up an Interconnect connection using a Partner Interconnect provider may not guarantee the low latency and high availability needed. Choice B - Deploying Cloud Interconnect Dedicated ensures a dedicated, high-speed connection between your on-premises data center and Google Cloud's us-east1 region, meeting the requirements for high availability and low latency.

QUESTION 33

Answer - A) Global Load Balancer with Cloud CDN

A) Global Load Balancer with Cloud CDN - Explanation: This combination provides global load balancing and content delivery for low-latency access and high availability.

B) Anycast IP Routing with Global VPN - Explanation: Anycast IP routing can improve routing efficiency, but it doesn't provide load balancing or content delivery. Global VPN alone may not achieve the desired goal.

C) Transit Gateway with Private Google Access - Explanation: Transit Gateway is useful for connecting VPCs, but it may not directly address low-latency access and high availability. Private Google Access focuses on Google services access, not global network architecture.

D) Regional Load Balancer with Cloud Interconnect - Explanation: Regional Load Balancer operates within a region and may not provide global load balancing. Cloud Interconnect connects to Google Cloud, but it may not directly support global architecture.

E) Network Peering with Dedicated Interconnect - Explanation: Network Peering connects VPCs, and Dedicated Interconnect provides dedicated connections, but this combination may not provide global load balancing or content delivery.

QUESTION 34

Answer - D) Transit Gateway with Network Peering

A) Cloud VPN with VPC Peering - Explanation: Cloud VPN provides secure connections, but it may not provide the dedicated connectivity required for hybrid setups. VPC Peering is used for connecting VPCs within Google Cloud.

B) Cloud Interconnect with Cloud Router - Explanation: Cloud Interconnect connects to Google Cloud, but Cloud Router is used for dynamic BGP routing within VPCs, and this combination may not provide the dedicated connectivity needed for hybrid environments.

C) Dedicated Interconnect with VPN Gateway - Explanation: Dedicated Interconnect provides dedicated connectivity, and VPN Gateway is used for secure connections. However, this combination may not optimize the use of Google Cloud resources.

E) VPC Peering with Private Google Access - Explanation: VPC Peering connects VPCs within Google Cloud, and Private Google Access enables private access to Google services. This combination may not provide the dedicated connectivity required for hybrid setups.

D) Transit Gateway with Network Peering - Explanation: Transit Gateway can connect multiple VPCs and on-premises environments, and Network Peering is used for connecting networks. This combination provides a secure, reliable, and optimized connection between Google Cloud and on-premises resources, making it suitable for the hybrid cloud setup.

QUESTION 35

Answer - D) Create more specific custom routes than the default network routes, designating low-latency paths and data residency zones for routing, and assign network tags for secure communication, compliance, and precise traffic handling.

D) Create more specific custom routes than the default network routes, designating low-latency paths and data residency zones for routing, and assign network tags for secure communication, compliance, and precise traffic handling - Explanation: This approach combines low-latency routing, data residency compliance, security, and precise traffic control for a global e-commerce platform.

A) Set up custom routes with more precision than the default network routes - Explanation: While custom routes are useful, this option does not address data residency compliance comprehensively.

B) Replicate the entire e-commerce platform in each region - Explanation: This approach may introduce complexity and high operational overhead, and it may not be necessary for compliance.

C) Delete all default network routes and establish distinct custom routes - Explanation: Deleting default routes introduces complexity, and this option may not be necessary for achieving data residency compliance.

E) Implement Google Cloud's Global Load Balancing - Explanation: While Global Load Balancing addresses low-latency access, it may not directly cover data residency compliance requirements, which are crucial for this scenario.

QUESTION 36

Answer – A) Use VPC Service Controls to isolate Compute Engine and Cloud Storage, and enable Private Google Access for secure communication.

A) Correct. This setup provides isolation, ensures private communication, and encryption in transit.
B) Incorrect. VPN is not necessary for internal GCP communication.
C) Incorrect. Interconnect is for external connections, not for intra-GCP communication.
D) Incorrect. Private Service Connect is not typically used for Compute Engine to Cloud Storage communication.
E) Incorrect. While default encryption is standard, it does not address the requirement of not traversing the public internet.

QUESTION 37

Answer - A) Google Cloud CDN with Google Cloud Armor

A) Google Cloud CDN with Google Cloud Armor - Correct answer. This combination provides content delivery, DDoS protection, and traffic management capabilities for GKE clusters.
B) Traffic Director with Cloud Load Balancing - While these services provide advanced traffic management, they do not inherently offer DDoS protection.
C) Google Cloud DNS with Cloud IAM - DNS and IAM focus on access control and DNS resolution, not DDoS protection.
D) Cloud Interconnect with Cloud VPN - These services provide connectivity but not DDoS protection for GKE.
E) Google Cloud CDN with VPC peering - VPC peering is for connecting VPC networks and does not offer DDoS protection.

QUESTION 38

Answer - B) Cloud Interconnect with Google Cloud Router

A) Google Cloud VPN with VPC peering - VPN and VPC peering provide encrypted connectivity but may not offer the same low-latency dedicated connection as Interconnect.
B) Cloud Interconnect with Google Cloud Router - Correct answer. Interconnect provides dedicated, low-latency private connectivity between VPCs, and Router handles dynamic routing.
C) VPC peering with Cloud VPN - This combination focuses on connectivity but may not provide the same

low-latency, dedicated connection as Interconnect.
D) Google Cloud Load Balancing with VPC Service Controls - Load Balancing and Service Controls are for traffic distribution and access control, not low-latency connectivity.
E) Google Cloud CDN with VPC peering - CDN and VPC peering are used for content delivery and connectivity but do not inherently provide low-latency, dedicated connectivity between VPCs.

QUESTION 39

Answer - B) Traffic Director with Cloud Load Balancing

A) Google Cloud Armor with Google Cloud CDN - While this combination provides security and content delivery, Traffic Director with Load Balancing is more suitable for achieving high availability and automatic scaling for e-commerce platforms.
B) Correct answer. Traffic Director with Cloud Load Balancing offers advanced traffic management and automatic scaling capabilities to ensure high availability during traffic spikes.
C) Google Cloud DNS with Cloud IAM - DNS and IAM focus on DNS resolution and access control, not traffic management or automatic scaling.
D) Cloud Interconnect with Cloud VPN - Interconnect and VPN provide connectivity but do not inherently offer advanced traffic management or automatic scaling for e-commerce platforms.
E) Google Cloud CDN with VPC peering - CDN and VPC peering focus on content delivery and connectivity but may not provide the same level of traffic management and automatic scaling as Traffic Director.

QUESTION 40

Answer - B) Google Cloud Filestore and Google Cloud Storage Transfer Service

A) Google Cloud Storage and Google Cloud Persistent Disk offer storage but may not inherently provide data redundancy and high availability without additional configurations.
B) Correct answer. Google Cloud Filestore provides managed file storage with data redundancy and high availability, and Google Cloud Storage Transfer Service assists with data transfer, making them suitable for storage solutions requiring these features.
C) Google Cloud Storage Nearline is designed for archival storage, and Google Cloud CDN focuses on content delivery, but they may not provide the same level of data redundancy and high availability as Filestore.
D) Google Cloud Spanner is a database, and Google Cloud KMS is a key management service, but they may not be the primary solution for achieving data redundancy and high availability in storage.
E) Google Cloud Bigtable is a NoSQL database, and Google Cloud Dataprep is focused on data preparation; they are not primarily storage solutions.

QUESTION 41

Answer - C) Create a VPC Firewall rule that blocks all traffic except for the DDoS protection service.

A) VPC Service Controls Perimeter focuses on data security but may not be the primary solution for limiting access to backend servers.
B) Cloud Armor Security Policy is designed for web application security but may not be the best choice for restricting access to backend servers.
C) Correct answer. Creating a VPC Firewall rule allows you to explicitly control incoming traffic and limit it to the DDoS protection service, enhancing security for your backend servers.

D) Implementing iptables firewall rules on servers can provide a level of control but may not be as scalable and manageable as a VPC Firewall rule.

E) VPC Peering and IAM roles may not be the most suitable approach for restricting access to backend servers specifically for DDoS protection.

QUESTION 42

Answer - C) Create a VPC Firewall rule that blocks all traffic except for the DDoS protection service.

A) VPC Service Controls Perimeter is typically used for data protection and access control, not for allowing specific traffic like DDoS protection service.

B) Cloud Armor Security Policy is more focused on protecting against web threats and not suitable for restricting backend server access.

C) Correct answer. Creating a VPC Firewall rule allows you to specifically control traffic to the backend servers, ensuring that only the DDoS protection service is allowed.

D) Implementing iptables firewall rules on servers may not be as scalable or centrally managed as using GCP's network-level controls.

E) A regional load balancer alone doesn't provide the necessary security measures to limit backend server access to a specific service.

QUESTION 43

Answer - B) Rearrange the directory structure, create a URL map and leverage path matchers such as /sensors/ and /location/.

A) Configuring DNS CNAME records is not directly related to routing Bigtable instances, and using path matchers is a more appropriate approach.

B) Correct answer. Rearranging the directory structure and using URL maps with path matchers is a suitable solution for routing Bigtable instances based on directory paths.

C) Leverage path rules based on specific directory paths (/cars/sensors and /cars/location) can become cumbersome and inflexible as the directory structure grows.

D) Using /[a-zA-Z]+/sensors and /[a-zA-Z]+/location path rules could result in unintended behavior for routing.

E) Rearranging the directory structure into separate subdomains is not necessary for routing Bigtable instances based on directory paths and would complicate the setup.

QUESTION 44

Answer - C) Create custom IAM roles for each VPC.

A) Using Google Groups at the VPC level may not provide the necessary granularity for access control.

B) VPC Service Controls focus on data access rather than IAM roles.

D) Managing access at the project level may not be fine-grained enough for securing sensitive VPCs.

E) While IAM conditions can help, custom IAM roles tailored to each VPC offer the most precise control over access to sensitive data within the VPCs.

C) Creating custom IAM roles for each VPC allows you to define precise permissions and access controls specific to the security needs of each VPC.

QUESTION 45

Answer - C) Use Cloud Interconnect to establish a direct, encrypted connection.

A) Cloud VPN with a static IP address on the on-premises side might not work with dynamic IP addresses.
B) Dedicated Interconnect typically uses static IP addresses.
C) Cloud Interconnect provides a direct, encrypted connection suitable for dynamic IP addresses.
D) Cloud Router manages routing but is not the primary solution for secure communication.
E) A hybrid VPC with Cloud VPN is an option but not specifically designed for dynamic IP addresses.

QUESTION 46

Answer - B) Use Google-managed SSL certificates for the global load balancer.

A) Manually uploading SSL/TLS certificates can be cumbersome and is not the most efficient method.
B) Google-managed SSL certificates simplify certificate management for global load balancers.
C) Deploying separate SSL/TLS termination proxies in each region adds complexity and maintenance overhead.
D) Third-party certificate management services are not required when Google offers managed SSL certificates.
E) Creating custom certificates for each region can lead to increased complexity and maintenance.

QUESTION 47

Answer – A) Use Global HTTP(S) Load Balancer with Cloud Armor and Cloud CDN.

A) Correct. This configuration provides dynamic scaling, DDoS protection, and efficient content delivery.
B) Incorrect. Network Load Balancers are not ideal for dynamic content delivery and global traffic management.
C) Incorrect. TCP/SSL Proxy Load Balancers and Cloud Endpoints are not the best fit for this scenario.
D) Incorrect. Internal Load Balancers are for internal traffic management, not for global web traffic.
E) Incorrect. Cloud Run and VPC Service Controls do not provide the necessary load balancing and DDoS protection for a global web application.

QUESTION 48

Answer – A) Use a single VPC with separate subnets for each layer and configure firewall rules for inter-layer communication.

A) Correct. A single VPC with dedicated subnets for each layer and proper firewall rules provides efficient segmentation and controlled communication between layers.
B) Incorrect. Multiple VPCs add complexity and are not necessary for a single application.
C) Incorrect. Shared VPC is more suitable for multiple projects sharing common resources.
D) Incorrect. VPN within a shared VPC for a single application is not an optimal setup.
E) Incorrect. Cloud Interconnect is typically used for on-premises to cloud connections, not for internal application layering.

QUESTION 49

Answer – A) Configure Cloud Pub/Sub for data ingestion, Cloud Dataflow for real-time processing, and

BigQuery for analysis.

A) Correct. This configuration offers a scalable and efficient solution for real-time data ingestion, processing, and analysis.
B) Incorrect. Cloud IoT Core is specific for IoT data; Spanner, while powerful, may not be the best fit for real-time analytics.
C) Incorrect. Cloud Storage is not ideal for real-time data streaming; Bigtable is for high-throughput, low-latency workloads.
D) Incorrect. Direct streaming to Compute Engine is less scalable; Cloud SQL is not optimized for high-volume real-time analytics.
E) Incorrect. Cloud Endpoints and Firestore are not the best fit for high-volume, real-time data analytics workflows.

QUESTION 50

Answer – A) Use Cloud Pub/Sub for data ingestion, Cloud Dataflow for real-time processing, and BigQuery for immediate analysis.

A) Correct. This configuration provides a scalable and efficient solution for real-time data ingestion, processing, and analysis.
B) Incorrect. Cloud IoT Core is specific for IoT data; Spanner, while powerful, may not be the best fit for real-time analytics.
C) Incorrect. Cloud Storage is not ideal for real-time data streaming; Bigtable is for high-throughput, low-latency workloads.
D) Incorrect. Direct streaming to Compute Engine is less scalable; Cloud SQL is not optimized for high-volume real-time analytics.
E) Incorrect. Cloud Endpoints and Firestore are not the best fit for high-volume, real-time data analytics workflows.

ABOUT THE AUTHOR

Step into the world of Anand, and you're in for a journey beyond just tech and algorithms. While his accolades in the tech realm are numerous, including penning various tech-centric and personal improvement ebooks, there's so much more to this multi-faceted author.

At the heart of Anand lies an AI enthusiast and investor, always on the hunt for the next big thing in artificial intelligence. But turn the page, and you might find him engrossed in a gripping cricket match or passionately cheering for his favorite football team. His weekends? They might be spent experimenting with a new recipe in the kitchen, penning down his latest musings, or crafting a unique design that blends creativity with functionality.

While his professional journey as a Solution Architect and AI Consultant, boasting over a decade of AI/ML expertise, is impressive, it's the fusion of this expertise with his diverse hobbies that makes Anand's writings truly distinctive.

So, as you navigate through his works, expect more than just information. Prepare for stories interwoven with passion, experiences peppered with life's many spices, and wisdom that transcends beyond the tech realm. Dive in and discover Anand, the author, the enthusiast, the chef, the sports lover, and above all, the storyteller.